# STUDIES IN IMPERIALISM

general editor John M. MacKenzie

Established in the belief that imperialism as a cultural
phenomenon had as significant an effect on the dominant
as on the subordinate societies, Studies in Imperialism
seeks to develop the new socio-cultural approach which
has emerged through cross-disciplinary work on popular
culture, media studies, art history, the study of education
and religion, sports history and children's literature.
The cultural emphasis embraces studies of migration and
race, while the older political and constitutional,
economic and military concerns are never far away.
It incorporates comparative work on European and
American empire-building, with the chronological focus
primarily, though not exclusively, on the nineteenth and
twentieth centuries, when these cultural exchanges were
most powerfully at work.

# West Indian intellectuals in Britain

MANCHESTER
UNIVERSITY PRESS

## AVAILABLE IN THE SERIES

# West Indian intellectuals in Britain

edited by Bill Schwarz

MANCHESTER
UNIVERSITY PRESS
Manchester and New York

distributed exclusively in the USA by
PALGRAVE

Published by MANCHESTER UNIVERSITY PRESS
OXFORD ROAD, MANCHESTER M13 9NR, UK
and ROOM 400, 175 FIFTH AVENUE, NEW YORK, NY 10010, USA
www.manchesteruniversitypress.co.uk

Distributed exclusively in the USA by
PALGRAVE, 175 FIFTH AVENUE, NEW YORK, NY 10010, USA

Distributed exclusively in Canada by
UBC PRESS, UNIVERSITY OF BRITISH COLUMBIA,
2029 WEST MALL, VANCOUVER, BC, CANADA V6T 1Z2

British Library Cataloguing-in-Publication Data
A catalogue record for this book is available from the British Library

Library of Congress Cataloging-in-Publication Data applied for


ISBN  0 7190 6474 0 *hardback*
        0 7190 6475 9 *paperback*

First published 2003

11  10  09  08  07  06  05  04  03        10 9 8 7 6 5 4 3 2 1

Typeset in Trump Medieval
by Servis Filmsetting Ltd, Manchester
Printed in Great Britain
by CPI, Bath

# CONTENTS

# GENERAL EDITOR'S INTRODUCTION

In 1907, Sir Algernon Aspinall published his *Pocket Guide to the West Indies*. It is a classic case of 'imperial eyes' in print, of the rhetoric of colonial tourism. The section on 'population' occupies no more than three pages and is devoted almost entirely to slavery and labour. Thus the *Pocket Guide* concentrates on place rather than people, on alleged economic progress instead of cultural potential, on the imperial more than the local community. But this travel guide seems to have been as popular with its white audience as were so many others of the same genre. By the 1950s it had passed through ten editions and was still appearing in the 1960s, revised after Aspinall's death by Professor J. Sydney Dash. Astonishingly, the original text on 'population' was still being printed, almost unchanged, in the later version. There was also very little alteration to the suggestions for further reading. Trollope and Froude continued to feature prominently together with (for Jamaica), the hoary old texts Long, Bridges, and the more recent Cundall, who had published a handbook for settlers as recently as 1905. Not a single black Caribbean author figured at all.

The notion that the West Indies might produce an individual culture, with a lively literary, linguistic, musical and dance tradition, interrogating and interacting with Africa, the Americas and Europe, clearly never occurred to Aspinall, and probably not to Dash either. Nor would either have considered the possibility of a vibrant popular culture flowing out into an intellectual one. In some respects, the collection of essays in this book is about that mutual flow not only between a so-called low and high culture, but also within the eddies and backwashes of cultural phenomena on an inter-continental basis. It is about intellectuals in the broadest organic sense – enquirers, thinkers, activists, propagators – who centralise their supposed marginality through complex networks of cultural quests. They position themselves in respect of myths of empire, of origins, and of multiple radical streams flowing into the revolutionary impulses of the twentieth century. They become intellectual travellers, turning the imperial gaze and the rhetoric of tourism back upon itself, and discovering liberating ideas and ideologies, fresh literary conjunctions and print opportunities, enabling new and varied voices to be heard.

What is striking about all these West Indian intellectual voices is the extent to which their timbre was forged through radicalising moments – the first world war; the race riots of 1919; (above all) Mussolini's attack upon Abyssinia in 1935; the Jamaican riots of 1938. It is also striking that so many of them moved from concepts of imperial progress to notions of revolutionary progress. Partly this was based in nineteenth-century philosophies, partly in the crucibles of revolt of the twentieth century. But there were journeys to be made here too: from a largely masculine perspective to one that recognised the powerful insights and aspirations of the women who emerged among them; from illusions of hope to the disillusion of revolution betrayed; of colonialism giving way to neo-colonialism; of overt to covert racism.

Even in a supposedly mature historical and literary community, there are still those who regard empire as having had little or no effect upon British culture. There are also still those who give no credence to the instrumentality of nationalist thought and action. In 2003 a popular (and generally well-received) television series on the British empire, the good empire which laid low the evil empires of the fascists and the Japanese, suggested that nationalists did not win decolonisation, nor was it given by the British. It was forced, according to its author and presenter Niall Ferguson, upon all concerned by the new aspirant empire of the United States. The declining empire and the ambitious nationalists of Africa, Asia and the Caribbean were equally useless in the face of unstoppable global geo-political forces. By these lights, the individual voices and actions of the people in this book become hopelessly tossed torsos and limbs upon a historical raft of the Medusa.

It may well be that such a bleak assessment has no place in serious historical scholarship, however immediately appealing it may seem to some. This book offers a powerful contrary testimony. But there are interesting negative lessons here too. Intellectual and ideological group orthodoxies should never be permitted to become fundamentalist. The 'other' (of whatever sort) should never become the scapegoat for all historical ills, the excuse for present grievance and inaction. Those who experience and struggle against the oppression of race and marginality should never fail to spot, and rebel against, other modes of oppression, of gender, of different forms of ability, or of minority sexualities. Regime should never be justified solely by race, present oppression by a past record of overthrow. We should also be attentive to the possibility of new radicalising moments. Maybe 2003 offers the potential for just such a one. But as the cliché goes, only history will tell.

This volume offers many opportunities for pondering the significance of multiple diasporas, social and intellectual displacement and replacement, racism, definitions of culture, and the potential transformation of dominant societies by the cultures and ideas of the formerly subordinate. Above all, it reveals the complex routes by which individuals seek to secure the 'decolonisation of the mind'.

John M. MacKenzie

# LIST OF CONTRIBUTORS

**Helen Carr** is Pro-Warden Academic at Goldsmiths College. In 1996 she published two monographs: *Inventing the American Primitive, 1789–1936* and *Jean Rhys*. She is co-editor of *Women: a cultural review*.

**Mary Chamberlain** is Professor of Modern Social History at Oxford Brookes University and has written widely on Caribbean migration, Caribbean families, on oral history and on Caribbean culture, with a particular focus on Barbados. Her recent work includes *Narratives of Exile and Return* (1997); *Caribbean Migration, Globalised Identities* (editor, 1998); *Narrative and Genre* (co-editor with Paul Thompson, 1998); and *Caribbean Families in the Transatlantic World* (co-editor with Harry Goulbourne, 2001).

**Alison Donnell** is senior lecturer in postcolonial literatures at Nottingham Trent University. She has published widely on Caribbean's women's writing and is co-editor of the *Routledge Reader in Caribbean Literature* (1996) and editor of the *Companion to Contemporary Black British Culture* (2002). She is also joint editor of *Interventions: International Journal of Postcolonial Studies*.

**Glyne Griffith** is Associate Professor of English at Bucknell University, Lewisburg, Pennsylvania. He is the author of *Deconstruction, Imperialism and the West Indian Novel* (1996) and editor of *Caribbean Cultural Identities* (2001); he is also completing a book on the BBC's *Caribbean Voices*. He is an editorial board member of *Small Axe: A Caribbean Journal of Criticism*.

**Catherine Hall** is Professor of Modern British Social and Cultural History at University College, London. She is the co-author of *Family Fortunes* (1987; second edition 2002) and the author of *Civilising Subjects: metropole and colony in the English imagination, 1830–1867* (2002). She is an editor of *History Workshop Journal*.

**Stephen Howe** is tutor in politics at Ruskin College, Oxford. His books include *Anticolonialism in British Politics* (1993), *Afrocentrism* (1998), *Ireland and Empire* (2000) and *Empire: a very short introduction* (2002).

**Louis James** is Emeritus Professor at the University of Kent. He taught at the University of the West Indies, Jamaica, in the early 1960s and was later actively involved in the Caribbean Artists Movement. He has written widely on Caribbean literature, most recently in *Caribbean Literature in English* (1999).

**Winston James** is Associate Professor of History, Columbia University. He is the author of *A Fierce Hatred of Injustice: Claude McKay's Jamaica and his* *poetry of rebellion* (2000) and *Holding Aloft the Banner of Ethiopia: Caribbean radicalism in early twentieth-century America* (1998), which won the Gordon K. Lewis Memorial Award for Caribbean Scholarship of the Caribbean Studies Association. He is also the co-editor of *Inside Babylon: the Caribbean diaspora in Britain* (1993). He is currently at work on *Claude McKay: the making of a Black Bolshevik, 1889–1923*.

**David Killingray** was for several years a schoolteacher in Britain and Tanzania. In 1998 he was appointed Professor of Modern History at Goldsmiths College. His most recent books as editor or author are *The West Indies. British documents on the end of empire* (1999), *Guardians of Empire* (2000), *The Spanish Flu Pandemic of 1918–19: new perspectives* (2003). He was joint editor of *African Affairs* from 1990–2002. He is currently writing a study of Harold Moody and the League of Coloured Peoples.

**Bill Schwarz** teaches in the Department of Media and Communications at Goldsmiths College. He is an editor of *History Workshop Journal*.

**Sue Thomas** is the author of *The Worlding of Jean Rhys* (1999), co-author (with Ann Blake and Leela Gandhi) of *England Through Colonial Eyes in Twentieth-Century Fiction* (2001), and compiler of *Elizabeth Robins (1862–1952): a bibliography* (1994), and many other titles in the Victorian Fiction Research Guides Series. She has published extensively on nineteenth- and twentieth-century women's writing and decolonising literatures. She is Reader in English in the School of Communication, Arts and Critical Enquiry at La Trobe University, Melbourne.

# ACKNOWLEDGEMENTS

That this book proved a pleasure to produce is chiefly thanks to the energy, commitment and intellectual passions of the contributors. I've learned much from each of them, and I hope readers will too.

John MacKenzie has been a staunch supporter from beginning to end. Rob Nixon gave early encouragement. Our initial contributors included Delia Jarrett-Macauley, though sadly force of circumstances required her to withdraw. A decisive moment in organising the arguments of the volume occurred when the authors met together in London. We were particularly delighted that Sue Thomas was able to come from Melbourne and we would like to express our thanks to the Australian Academy of the Humanities who provided her with the Travelling Fellowship which made this possible. We were also joined by a group of friends and colleagues who, for no recompense, over two days worked hard on our behalf: Stuart Hall, Julian Henriques, Peter Hulme, David Scott, Richard Smith and Brett St Louis. Both Stuart Hall and Peter Hulme offered wise counsel during the longer duration of this project, while David Scott's dedication to bringing alive the intellectual traditions of the Caribbean served us beyond measure. We are deeply grateful to them all. Staff at Manchester University Press have been exemplary in every respect – and we should like to thank the anonymous reviewer whom the Press persuaded to comment on the original proposal.

I'm pleased to have the opportunity to record the influence on me (though not on me alone) of two fine Caribbean intellectuals, whose presence has touched the heart of this book: at some geographical distance for most of us, George Lamming; and closer to home, Stuart Hall.

Bill Schwarz

# INTRODUCTION

# Crossing the seas

## Bill Schwarz

There exists a moving photographic record of West Indian emigrants arriving in British cities in the 1950s, first by steamship and steam train, then later, by the end of the decade and into the 1960s, by plane. We still see, in our own times, these images of men and women who, for all their apprehensions, were stepping across the threshold into new lives, bringing with them a certain *presence*. These are images which evoke a sense of hardships in the past overcome and hardships just around the corner yet to confront. They give form to the dreams which had compelled a generation of migrants to pack up and cross the seas. And they capture too a sensibility founded on the conviction that these dreams were rightfully theirs: a dream, in other words, of colonials who believed that the privileges of empire were their due.[1]

These photographic images, and those of the flickering, monochrome newsreels which accompany them, have now come to compose a social archive. They serve to fix the collective memory of the momentous transformation of postwar migration.

At the same time, however, their very familiarity works to conceal other angles of vision. We become so habituated to the logic of the camera-eye that we are led to forget that the vision we are bequeathed is uncompromisingly one-way. The images which fix this history as social memory are images of the West Indians. The camera is drawn to them. The moment they enter the field of vision, the focal point adjusted, they become fixed as something new: as immigrants. The camera, in other words, organises the collective vision not of the West Indians but of the native Britons. There are in the public domain no reverse-shots, in which – from gangplank or from railway station platform – we see, through the eyes of the emigrant, the huddles of journalists and onlookers, police and social workers, white faces all. Without this perspective it is difficult to grasp that white Britons – ordinary people, doing the shopping or waiting for the bus – were, whether conscious of it or not, part of this drama of

[ 1 ]

migration. They too were actors in the larger history of empire from which the imperatives of migration to the mother country had arisen. To catch sight of the native population from the perspective of the disembarking migrant is to bring this deeper history into the light of day. Reverse-shots, or their historiographical equivalents, not only offer the virtues of an unfamiliar vantage; they may also provide a perspective which is more fully historical. After all, it was the migrants, especially, who carried with them the knowledge that: 'We have met before'.[2]

These contacts between migrant and native Briton, on the home ground of the metropolis, offer more than just another chapter in the progressive rise of 'multicultural Britain'. The emigrant experience cast a new way of seeing, in which consciousness both of the imperial past and of the inner forms of the imperial civilisation of the British assumed a new intensity. That this vision cohered is of the first importance, analytically, for the British themselves: it allowed the British to step outside themselves, or outside their own culture or habitus, and to see themselves afresh, through new eyes. What previously might have looked familiar, the natural way of doing things ordained by the peculiarly providential history of the old, ancestral nations, might, instead, come to look unfamiliar. From such dislocations new things might happen.

These analytical consequences of the encounter between West Indian and Briton form the conceptual core of our explorations in this volume. The figure who came closest to formulating our defining hypothesis was C. L. R. James.[3] James believed that it was through the encounter with the formerly colonial peoples of the Caribbean that native white Britons were first able to see themselves in their true historical light: what previously had happened elsewhere was now happening *here*. There were many occasions when he hinted at this. It is one of the themes running through *Beyond a Boundary*.[4] It is most explicitly stated in his eightieth birthday lectures, delivered in London in January 1981 on the eve of a momentous recasting of black life in Britain.[5] Here James offered a characteristically Hegelian rendition, elegantly turned inside out, in which he imagined the slave finally settling accounts with the master. But this was a settling of accounts in which the slave, forced by a profane, unforgiving history to do what the master himself cannot do, creates a future in which both slave and master discover new freedoms. In its local, specific setting, when former-colonisers confronted former-colonised in the conflagrations on the streets of metropolitan cities (in Brixton, Toxteth, Bristol), these were powerful and unusual words.

No one who has lived through the subsequent years in Britain, and who now witnesses the unfinished, continuing emergence of new lives specifically styled as 'black British', can fail to be moved by James's comments, for this process carries the promise of new possibilities for all: for former-colonisers and former-colonised alike. This is a project which still unfolds. There is today so much obeisance to the idea of multiculturalism that those domains in our lives which remain trenchantly untransformed, still subject to a racial or colonial logic, are too frequently forgotten, or lack the requisite vocabularies which make them speakable. In his own time James was not unaware of these tangled outcomes. One great virtue of his thought, however, is that it offers us historical depth of field. This, really, is critical. He reminds us (as did an entire generation of West Indians) that in these unfolding new lives, both black and white, the presence of the old empire is exactly that: a presence. He tells us that the history of empire is still of our time. Britain's colonial possessions, of course, are long gone. But inherited collective instincts may possess a longer life. End of empire runs along many different historical times, not all of which have reached their due, punctual point of termination. This is a difficult problem to discuss, for it asks us to ponder phenomena which are not easily observable to the naked eye. It requires us to unravel the-past-in-the-present, to see and listen to *those* pasts in *this* present. It requires us (all of us) to confront our own memories and mentalities. In a word, it demands that we think historically.

Implicit in James's thinking is the conviction that the West Indians of his generation played an active role not only in the decolonisation of their home territories in the Caribbean but also, through many displacements, in the rather less visible process of decolonising metropolitan Britain itself. This in turn (in James's thought) raised a further question: what memories of the historical past were required in order to think through the destruction of the old colonial order?

From long before the arrival of *Windrush* in 1948, West Indian emigrants came from societies well advanced in the prerequisites of breaking from colonialism. They arrived with long memories, recalling events which, in the collective imagination of the British, had slipped into forgetfulness.[6] The typewritten novels and poems in their suitcases, their mimeographed manifestos, their music: all were testament to the depth of emergent anti-colonial sensibilities. Formally or informally, explicitly or implicitly, the case for West Indian independence (and, indeed, for federation) registered in the public culture of the metropolis.[7] As they unpacked their bags, hawked their manuscripts around the little magazines of the capital, went on the stump agitating against injustices in far-off islands, they were improvising new lives for themselves, creating new possibilities for those whom they encountered, and decolonising the world about them.

[ 3 ]

Perhaps the prototype for such determinedly modern figures as these was John Jacob Thomas, who arrived in London from Trinidad in 1889, and who ensconced himself in rooms close by the British Museum in order that he could engage with the intellectual culture which had formed him.[8] His continuing renown derives from the fact that he took on the great imperial figure of J. A. Froude – disciple of Thomas Carlyle and regius professor of modern history at Oxford – and, with a relentless, lively irony, mashed him. In 1887 Froude had published *The English in the West Indies*. Thomas's riposte, appearing two years later, took the memorable title *Froudacity. West Indian fables by James Anthony Froude*. This spirited rebuttal was the formative text of black West Indian intellectual self-determination. Its influence was profound. James, especially, loved the fact that Thomas, a barefoot, backwoods schoolteacher from his native Trinidad bettered his distinguished metropolitan opponent. It was exactly the kind of guerrilla movement, in the field of ideas, which was guaranteed to delight him.[9] In 1968 it was a return to Thomas that prompted James's own essay on 'The West Indian intellectual'.

> This work of John Jacob Thomas, the Trinidad schoolmaster, without European or university education of any kind, shows that the impact which the West Indian writers, our writers of fiction and the politicians and political writers of the day, have made upon the consciousness and civilisation of Western Europe and the United States, is the result not of the work of certain brilliant individual men, but is due in reality to our historical past, the situation in which our historical past has placed us. This historical situation has produced a particular type of social and intellectual activity which we can definitely call West Indian.[10]

James's recourse to history is emphatic. Only by knowing themselves as historical individuals (he argued) could West Indians come to terms with their predicament; and, conversely, later generations can only appreciate the power of West Indian thought by appreciating the degree to which it embodied this deeper movement of history. The significance of Thomas is that he was the first (in James's eyes) to personify and express this history. This too carries James's Hegelian cast of mind.

> I have long believed that there is something in the West Indian past, something in the West Indian environment, something in the West Indian historical development, which compels the West Indian intellectual, when he gets involved with subjects of the kind, to deal with them from a fundamental point of view, *to place ourselves in history*.[11]

James's belief that West Indians 'are a people more than any other people constructed by history' may seem eccentric. But the premise on which it is based is not. Critically, for James, what made the Caribbean

distinctive was not colonialism, but the fact that since the inauguration of the slave plantation West Indians were, above all else, a modern
people. They lived in subjugation. But they experienced modernisation
– in the Middle Passage and on the plantation – at its most dynamic, at
its highest pitch and at its most brutal.[12] This, according to James,
instilled in Caribbean peoples a distinctive, immediate connection to
the historical past.[13]

To be conscious of history in this way was to confront memories of
slavery and the continuing imperatives of race. These were not matters
which in Britain, in the first half of the twentieth century, were easily
recognised or speakable in public. Even in the colonial Caribbean,
affiliation to the protocols of Britain made racial difference – despite
the ubiquity of its ritualised exclusions – awkward to articulate.
Nonetheless, the West Indian presence, after Thomas, created new possibilities within the metropolitan culture for these issues to be spoken.

James himself had arrived in Britain from Trinidad in 1932. We are
fortunate in that he has left a remarkable account of his first impressions, in which he contemplated the unanticipated strangeness of the
imperial centre.[14] In Trinidad he had already authored an attack on what
he perceived to be the moral and civic lapses of the colonial authorities,
as well as some short fiction.[15] He brought with him a manuscript
novel.[16] He had too some draft material on cricket and, more particularly, on Learie Constantine, who had been influential in persuading
James to make the journey to Britain.[17] In 1933 Leonard and Virginia
Woolf abridged some of his earlier writings on colonialism, republishing
them as *The Case for West Indian Self-Government*.[18] To hold together
these commitments to anti-colonial politics, to sport and to literature
was unusual. But as James himself later indicated, their common inspiration lay in an elevated aesthetic and moral sensibility whose origins
lay precisely in the codes of England in which he had been formed. As
he looked back on these early years he remembered his arriving in
England ready to 'enter the arena where I was to play the role for which
I had prepared myself. The British intellectual was going to Britain'.[19]
Even at this early stage, though, this was an idea of Britishness riven by
ambivalence, in which his critique of colonialism was animated by the
language of the colonial civilisation he was attacking. James never lost
his regard for the culture of those whom he always believed to be the
imperial oppressors. But over the next few years he gravitated to a firebrand variant of marxism, to Pan-Africanism, and to a much deeper
understanding of what was required to break the power of colonial
authority. In part, this shift in allegiance was abetted by his reacquain-
tance with his old childhood friend, George Padmore, who was instrumental in piecing together a new conception of anti-colonialism, in

which the historical resources of blackness – as an active agent in the making of the modern world – were to be given an insurrectionary twist.[20] And in part as well, larger events in the colonial world took effect, heightening the tempo of anti-colonial sentiment, both in colony and metropolis.

The invasion of Abyssinia by Italy in October 1935 had an immediate, cataclysmic effect on black peoples throughout the Americas, and worked to reinspire and unify disparate strands of anti-colonialism, especially in the Caribbean. London, in its unofficial capacities, served as a principal source of communication for those in the West Indies eager to know, day by day and week by week, what was happening across the ocean. From their London base, James, Padmore and other West Indians of marxisant sympathies were tireless both in the cause of Abyssinia, and in imagining a revivified Pan-Africanism. Yet anger at the abandonment of Abyssinia by the democratic nations was not just the prerogative of militant marxists, however heterodox. It was above all a colonial issue – perhaps *the* colonial issue – and it entered the souls of all those who had been touched by colonial politics. Thus from a very different stance from James or Padmore, Una Marson – feminist, inheritor of a humanitarian ethics, committed to the founding principles of the League of Nations – gave herself unswervingly to the cause of Abyssinia.[21] It 'took over her life', in the words of her biographer.[22]

Of yet greater significance were the riots and insurrections which swept through the Caribbean in 1937–38. In the recounting of the cumulative European catastrophe of these years, the devastation in the West Indies is sometimes accorded a footnote, or a sentence, in the established historiography. But this is to miss too much. The collapse of the Caribbean economies triggered an authentic imperial crisis. In the aftermath of the riots great volumes of official inquiry were produced. In page after page of steady prose the dead, wounded and indicted are calibrated; damage itemised (the number of shop-fronts smashed, of cars set ablaze in smart precincts, of potatoes pilfered from fields); and causes examined (Garveyism, gangster movies, Bolshevism, even chronic dispossession).[23] Yet none of this dispassionate prose conveys the deeper sense that the colonial Caribbean had changed forever. Indeed the juridical or actuarial remit of the various commissions worked to conceal the greater truth: that the real casualty was not the consequence of this or that violation, but the edifice of empire itself. In this extraordinary drama, West Indian exiles in London once more played a decisive role. Through Padmore and his coterie information was co-ordinated and news circulated. Lobbying of sympathisers in Britain was incessant. New (if shaky) alliances were struck between seasoned agitators in London and an emergent new generation of labour leaders in the Caribbean. What drew them together was the crisis itself, in the common realisation that for too long Britain had abdicated its responsibilities in its West Indian colonies. New voices could be heard in the Caribbean, declaring that allegiance to the tenets of British civilisation could be maintained by West Indians without the services of the British themselves. From the late 1930s, the forces pressing for independence became a powerful, immovable political reality.

From our own vantage in time if we look again at the old images of West Indians arriving in Britain we can see many things. But insofar as the camera-eye saw only an immigrant, so the complex, embodied memories of these Caribbean pasts came to be effaced. Immigrants, it seemed, had no past, coming into life only at that moment when they entered the line of the vision of the native, 'host' population. And yet the great majority of those West Indians who arrived in *Windrush* and after would have witnessed, as adult or child, the crises of the 1930s, and experienced the aftermath. Many, indeed, made a conscious choice to escape from the situation of continuing economic collapse which the insurrections had done little to forestall. Few were intellectuals in the conventional sense, and fewer still thought in terms like Padmore, intent on breaking the power of empires. But this does not mean memories of these events, and of the *longue durée* of the Caribbean itself, were absent. The history which binds the insurrections of the 1930s to the emigrants of the 1940s or 1950s is a discontinuous history, not least due to the agency of those determined that they depart from their homeland. Even so, those who made this journey were not without history, nor 'just' immigrants. In their speech, in their dedication to a certain styling of the self, in their music – let alone in the more formal artefacts of their literary culture – they brought their history with them.[24]

This was a history composed not only by Pan-Africanism and by Abyssinia, and by the attendant politics. It carried much further, across many contrary dimensions of lived experience. Of all Britain's non-white colonies, in terms of formal, official cultures the West Indian nations were closest to the mother country: in language, religion, schooling, literature, sport. Pride in these affinities to Britain ran deep, and affiliation to the British way of life, during the century from emancipation to the insurrections of the 1930s, was always of the first importance. But at every point these collective sentiments, for all their depth, vied with vernacular, blacker, more fluid cultures which constituted the traces – or more – of slavery, of other diasporas, and of a long history of racial mixing. (Or what Kamau Brathwaite, in Bakhtinian mode, designated '*belly centred* bawdy'.)[25] The irresolvable, continuing and dynamic conflict between these symbolic and lived polarities lay close to the heart of the West Indian intellectual life for the entire period we discuss. As

[ 7 ]

James remembered this: 'We lived in two worlds. Inside the classrooms the heterogeneous jumble of Trinidad was battered and jostled and shaken down into some sort of order'.[26] The force of these contradictions unsettled every aspect of 'the British way' in its Caribbean transplantations. The institutions of British culture, irredeemably syncretic, could never boast that taken-for-granted quality that they possessed on their home ground. Even when working to their fullest authority and effect, at any instant they could be experienced as second-hand or inauthentic. In one of his fictional voices, V. S. Naipaul gives this a practical, semiotic reading: 'I was used to living in a world where the signs were without meaning, or without the meaning intended by their makers'.[27] In the movement from metropolis to colony, these signs, and the ideas they represented, systematically acquired new and unpredictable meanings.

The complexities of this past made the reverse passage, from the Caribbean to Britain, a multi-layered phenomenon, which turned on the interplay between the familiar and the unfamiliar, the homely and the unhomely. The final reckoning between imperial Britain and its West Indian colonies can, in the field of culture, be properly understood as overdetermined. In part this was due to the fact that the last phase of the encounter between West Indian and Briton took place not only in the colonial territories but also in the metropolis itself. And in part it was due, precisely, to the proximity of the respective official cultures. For West Indians to 'become' postcolonial they were required to destroy the external authority of the British. But they also had to effect for themselves a separation from an interior culture constituted by the ideals of those whom they felt compelled to deem their enemies.

These instances of a decolonising impetus moving from the imperial margins to the imperial centre represent only the most concrete dimension of the passage of intellectual cultures which concerns us. Of equal significance, for our purpose, is the encounter itself. From the 1940s an accumulation of individual experiences was worked into a collective story of mythic properties, whose familiar forms and repetitions we can still hear today. This represented the moment when the emigrant came face to face with the lived realities of the civilisation in whose name he or she had been educated into adulthood, as distant subjects of the Crown. As the literature confirms, this transformation released a whole array of perplexed, painful musings on the unhomeliness of the imagined homeland. This is not a matter of 'ideas', narrowly understood. It is more an issue of the lived encounter between two conceptions of reality, each at odds with the other. Time and again we hear the home civilisation of the British described by West Indians as being 'unreal', the immediacy of the encounter redoubling the already existing, anxious sensation of strangeness characteristic of colonial life. To be an immigrant, in this context, was to live up against a discrepant reality, in which dislocation between expectation and experience was fierce. At the outset this was puzzling, thence – progressively – menacing.

Many aspects of this encounter proved difficult to comprehend. There was no language to hand in which this simultaneous sensation of homeliness and unhomeliness could be conveyed, or in which to articulate the experiences of a culture in which contrary perceptions of reality coexisted. This was not a metaphysical problem, dreamt up by the philosophers. It was a daily experience, at bus stops, in shops, at work. Much could not be spoken, or could only be perceived in terms of individual pathology. Race was particularly resistant in this respect. Unspeakability continued to shadow the life of the immigrant.[28]

And yet amongst the multitudes who made the journey to Britain there was a handful who had fled their home towns and villages with one driving purpose in mind: to become a writer. In the years after the second world war this seemingly personal, individual aspiration – to leave home and head for literary London – became a collective phenomenon. The emergence of the West Indian novel, as a form, coincides with the great migration of the 1940s and 1950s and, to a degree, was a consequence of it. The West Indian novel displayed a passionate concern for the West Indies – or more properly, perhaps, for the author's respective island nation. Worrying away at the puzzle of Britain was something of an incidental theme: necessary, but not where the writers' true energies lay. For our purposes, though, principally concerned as we are with Britain, this incidental theme offers a rich intellectual resource. The story of Caribbean peoples, as a modern people, has been one of movement. To narrate this story necessitates telling of many far-flung destinations. Britain, in the postwar world, proved to be one such destination. A generation of writers faced the challenge of devising a language which could make sense of the dislocations and make speakable the unspeakable. Samuel Selvon's *The Lonely Londoners* marks the comprehensive inauguration of this sub-genre of the West Indian novel, and in so doing, invented a new diasporic realism.[29]

'Poetry', according to George Lamming, 'is a way of listening.'[30] The West Indian emigrants who travelled to the metropole – familiar strangers, simultaneously located inside and outside the cultural field-force of the imperial civilisation – listened to Britain. We can see an early instance in Lamming's own novel, *The Emigrants*, published shortly after his arrival in 1954. He describes an imagined encounter between Collis, a Trinidadian student, and the Pearsons, a white, married, native couple, comfortably off, and inhabiting – one assumes – an anonymous pocket of the English suburbs. Collis is invited to lunch, and receives fastidious attention from his hosts. But from the outset two realities collide.

[9]

> The room seemed a persistent rebuke to the rudimentary shelter which Collis had found at the hostel. It was not only a habitation, remote and warm as the womb. It was an entire climate. The conveniences were natural elements by which the life of the Pearsons was nourished. Mr Pearson did not sit in the chair. He belonged to it. When he left it to serve sherry, it was not only unoccupied. It became incomplete.

In this habitus, communication between Collis and the Pearsons was perpetually on the verge of collapse, vulnerable (in Collis's mind) to invisible fluctuations in the atmosphere of the living room which he could barely sense. The hospitality of the hosts is measured out in unconscious rituals, which to the visitor appear merely bizarre. (He wants to watch television, which he had never seen; Pearson believes a tour of the garden more appropriate.) Intervention from outside disturbs these domestic rites. The phone rings. There has been 'trouble' at Pearson's factory, and the malefactors (it seems) are West Indians. The atmosphere turns chilly, though courtesies are maintained. Collis retreats to the lavatory, where he sits smoking, periodically flushing the toilet. On his return, although the polite rituals continue as before, an air of menace has descended. Pearson 'moved about you like the weather which you might avoid, but which would not be altered by the devices you had invented to protect yourself against it'. At the heart of this comfortable English domestic interior lies an unspoken sense of lives interrupted, of a culture which – inexplicably – is losing its authority and, ultimately, an apprehension that violence lies close by.[31]

This represents a single, momentary micro-encounter, imagined by a writer of fiction. Its value as historical evidence needs to be seen within these limits. Yet even so, it's clear that Lamming was attempting to find a way of putting these silences into words. Striking about these few pages is his reluctance to condemn outright the anxieties and prejudices of the English hosts. It's not their opinions which are at issue, for these are only be surmised. It is rather the enclosed, unconscious apparatus in which their lives are set – the hospitality, the sherry, the garden, the naturalised assumption of rightful possession of the world about them – which constructs a sense of reality from which the unspeakabilities of race and apprehensions of violence ensue. This was not the sort of racism which stalked mean streets in the dead of night. It was, Lamming suggested, something more pervasive than that, operating deep in the collective imagination of the English.

Lamming's reconstruction of this historic encounter between West Indian immigrant and indigenous whites was conducted in poetic vein. But it is plausible enough, and in its essentials can be confirmed by other kinds of contemporary testimony.[32] For all its poetry, it's also representative. If this is so, there are consequences which bear directly on the defining theme of our volume.

It's evident that Lamming's attention was drawn to politics in its broadest configurations. Committed to independence and to West Indian federation, he possessed as well an acute knowledge that independence demanded more than the transfer of political power from London to the respective island capitals. If West Indians were not merely to achieve self-government, but to create new societies free from the legacies of colonial mentalities, they needed to renovate the civilisation in which they themselves had been formed.

Given conventional views of the time, in which culture led an autonomous life free from the profane exigencies of political strife, thinking of this kind marked a significant shift. It's too simple, fifty years on, to suppose that such insights have always been with us. In the epoch of decolonisation a generation of West Indians found themselves wrestling with the 'deep' – symbolic and cognitive – systems of England. This comprised coming to terms with the formal curriculum of the metropolitan culture, internalised through the institutions of colonial schooling, and manifest in Britain in a powerful national literary imagination, in an ever-present written and remembered historical record, and in an array of prestigious institutions of learning and letters. At the same time it also meant coming to terms with the lived, everyday culture of the metropolis, in its many variations, at street corners and in shops, in schools and sports grounds, in churches, or when invited for a glass of sherry and a stroll around an Englishman's garden. It was as much in the social relations of this latter world (Lamming implies), even when at its most benign, that the silent authority of colonial mentalities continued to be reproduced.

The power of the Caribbean intellectuals of this generation lay in their collective capacities to connect these two domains: the arena of formal, or high, culture, and the unconscious practices of lived experience, on the ground. Evidence of this achievement can be found in two brilliant but representative volumes: Lamming's *Pleasures of Exile* (published in 1960) and James's *Beyond a Boundary* (1963).[33] These are complex texts, which do many things. Each is exemplary in conceiving the work of decolonisation in the most profound manner. But more than that, in ruminating on the intellectual requirements for decolonising the Caribbean, they also reveal a different prospect, inviting us to consider what the metropolis itself might look like if it too were decolonised.

*The Pleasures of Exile* and *Beyond a Boundary* represent the theorisation of the migrant view of England. Lamming eventually chose to return to Barbados, while James – though locating himself for many years in Brixton, in south London – still at this stage had before him political campaigns to conduct in his native Trinidad. The figure who subsequently did most to carry this critique into the heartlands of England itself was the Jamaican, Stuart Hall.[34] His early formation came precisely from the intellectual world of the migrant West Indians in Britain. His political commitments were to the cause of decolonisation, in the Caribbean, but in Africa too; the BBC's *Caribbean Voices* and the influential literary magazine based in Barbados, *Bim*, were his natural arenas of cultural involvement. His distinctive conceptual grasp of the relations between the systematised artefacts of high culture, on the one hand and, on the other, the experiential domains of lived, vernacular cultures can be seen to have derived (in part) from the characteristic concerns of this West Indian moment of exile in the 1950s. Simultaneously, though, Hall became a significant thinker in the domestic New Left, which worked quite separately from the intellectual groupings of the West Indians – and from which, later, there emerged the intellectual project of cultural studies. In Stuart Hall these conflicting inheritances fused. The long-term impact on British intellectual life has been dramatic, testament over many years to the continuing power of this early, decolonising moment of West Indian thought.[35]

James, Lamming, Hall, like all the emigrants from the Caribbean, found themselves in a paradoxical situation. They had made the choice to leave their native lands in order to seek new lives. Yet living in Britain they discovered themselves to be perpetually up against the civilisation of their old colonisers, on the front line – in effect – of the unofficial work of decolonisation. To live as an immigrant, on the home ground of the imperial nation, required many mental transformations, all of which depended on the capacities to interpret the signs and symbols of their new environment. It required that West Indians quickly learned the dispositions of the unspoken, invisible world about them – that they became, essentially, practical readers of the culture of the British. Despite the occasional plea from C. L. R. James, we should not be led into supposing that the forms of knowledge which resulted were unique to West Indians, a function only of their particular historical past and thus unavailable to colonials from other parts of the empire. We know that this was not so. But nor should we underestimate what was specific to the West Indian situation. In part, this raises the question of the unusually deep penetration of the institutions of Victorian civic life into the cultural organisation of the colonial Caribbean. And in part it indicates that we also need to take into account the collective experiences of early, mass emigration, from 1948 and through the following decade. The consequences of this experience of emigration were not confined to formally accredited intellectuals, to the poets and novelists alone. Decoding British culture came to be the necessary pastime of all who journeyed across the seas.

The extent of the great postwar migration represented a true diaspora of Caribbean peoples. By the middle of the 1960s the anglophone West Indian population in Britain was greater than in any single Caribbean territory, barring only Jamaica and Trinidad. Those who journeyed from the Caribbean recall that they became West Indian (as opposed, say, to Antiguan or Guyanese or St Lucian) in London or Birmingham: indeed for many of them this was part and parcel of *becoming black*.[36] In the 1950s, especially, West Indian was an identity in which the realities of the diasporic experience reverberated deeply – an identity, in fact, given special force by those who had departed their Caribbean homelands.[37] Cultural institutions in the Caribbean, consciously seeking to fashion a new collective West Indian identity free from the trammels of colonialism, called upon West Indian writers wherever they were to be found. The journal *Bim*, which effectively functioned as the resource for the BBC's *Caribbean Voices* from 1943 to 1958, drew its authors from metropolis or colony as the occasion demanded. Trinidad's organ of the People's National Movement, the *Nation*, under James's editorship from 1958, did likewise. (What other revolutionary, anti-colonial newspaper would republish articles from *The Times Literary Supplement*?)[38] The West Indian novel, the product of the Smolletts and the Fieldings (as Lamming liked to think it) of the new Caribbean nations, was for a time at least an expatriate form. What happened with the literary magazines, with political newspapers, with the novel, was repeated across the culture as a whole. Many fissures opened up as a result, especially between those who remained in the Caribbean and those who had left. There occurred, additionally, fierce contention about who could be deemed a true West Indian. However, the forces pressing for decolonisation operated not only in the territorial colonies of the West Indies but also inside the metropolis as well.

At every point throughout the last century Caribbean lives were shaped by the collective experience of migration and diaspora. Migrants coming to Britain after the war brought with them not only memories of the West Indies: they brought, too, other stories, of other places. Above all, they embodied (to varying degrees) the complex histories of what retrospectively has been termed the black Atlantic.[39] In the years which encompassed the decolonisation of the European empires, the civil rights and Black Power movements in the US, and the opening phase of popular mobilisation against the apartheid state in South Africa, the politics of the black Atlantic was at its most mobile.[40] This marked a new historical conjuncture in which many distinct, local historical times converged. The global, or Atlantic, dimensions of black politics pressed in at every turn. Independent Ghana, especially, provided a second (or third) home to an entire generation of West Indian migrants, more proximate in mental maps to Notting Hill and Brixton than many a London suburb.[41] As a consequence of the migration, native Britons were pulled into this field-force. Indeed, both in its British particulars and in the larger compass the role of West Indians in orchestrating the intellectual consequences of these evolving, transatlantic connections was striking.[42]

We can see, for example, something of this in the life of Claudia Jones, and something too of the impact on Britain. Claudia Jones was born in Port of Spain in 1915. Aged eight, she and her family travelled to New York, where they set up home in Harlem. As a young woman she became a tyro in the Young Communist League, and Harlem radicalism entered her being. Poor health and constant harassment from the authorities wore her down: she was repeatedly arraigned, suffered a stretch in prison, and faced the perpetual threat of deportation. In 1955 it was finally ruled that she be deported but, as the colonial government in Trinidad wanted nothing to do with her, she was shipped to Britain.

In December she was met off the boat-train in London by two West Indians active in socialist, anti-colonial politics, and who drove her off through the thick London fog on a motorbike barely capable of taking even one of them.[43] Though it seems the welcome was warm enough, it hardly matched the scale of her send-off from the United States. Despite the fact that she carried with her a remarkable reputation as a Communist militant it is evident that the British party was unnerved by her. Harlem, even Communist Harlem, was a world apart from the CPGB of the 1950s. Until her death in London in 1964, relations between her and the British party were both distant and strained. Even so, her years in Britain were dominated by tireless political activity in which she demonstrated a gift for bringing together people, organisations and ideas which customarily remained disconnected. Crucially, she determined to animate the specifically *West Indian* culture of the emigrant, on the home ground of Britain itself.

In March 1958 she launched the *West Indian Gazette* or, to give it its full title, the *West Indian Gazette and Afro-Asian Caribbean News*. Like many such ventures, this was the product of colossal human energy (hers mainly) and minimal material back-up. The paper functioned as an organiser for West Indians in the UK, but in addition addressed issues more strictly particular to the Caribbean. Into its orbit came almost the entire roster of West Indian intellectuals of the period: politicians in the Caribbean (Norman Manley, Cheddi Jagan and Phillys Allfrey);[44] expatriate political workers (David Pitt and John La Rose);[45] and the writers (Lamming, Selvon, Jan Carew and Andrew Salkey).[46] Harlem connections were maintained, most of all through Paul

Robeson and his wife, Eslanda, who were politically and personally close to Jones. Amy Ashwood Garvey, Marcus Garvey's first wife and a long-term friend of Claudia Jones's, was on the board of the *Gazette* and active across an entire spectrum of black politics in London.[47] Jomo Kenyatta (an old ally of James's and Padmore's in London twenty years earlier) was interviewed. Links were established with the principal British anti-colonial organisation, Fenner Brockway's Movement for Colonial Freedom. Through the auspices of the paper, Claudia Jones organised a hunger strike in solidarity with those indicted in the Rivonia trial in South Africa (amongst whom was Nelson Mandela), and a demonstration in London outside the US embassy to coincide with the historic march on Washington for civil rights in August 1963. She was active in attempting to counter the ferocious outbursts of race hatred, in Notting Hill in 1958 and again in Smethwick six years later. In sum, the *Gazette* and its public campaigning represented a new kind of politics in Britain, in which recognition of racial oppression was definitive – there simply was no comparable public voice at the time – and in which the diasporic or black Atlantic dimensions of being a West Indian registered as a critical resource from which Britain and its civil-isation might be understood. The *Gazette* represented a project pro-duced by West Indians, for West Indians. With the benefit of hindsight, however, we could also conclude that – had they chosen to read it – the paper would have offered metropolitan Britons the knowledge that decolonisation was not only something which happened 'over there', but operated closer to home. In a vernacular, journalistic and necessar-ily more impromptu voice it spoke from the same place, and to the same ends, as James and Lamming.

While Claudia Jones struggled to keep the *Gazette* alive she also poured her energies into a connected initiative – the recreation of carni-val, in Britain, as a lifeline for West Indian emigrants and, simply, as an assertion of the human worth of West Indian peoples. In August and September 1958 white riots erupted in Notting Hill, during which migrant residents in the neighbourhood were threatened with lynchings, and many were beaten. To read the national press of the time one can see that, although public opinion was initially confused, over the days which followed opinion shifted. By the end of the episode 'immigration' had come to signify 'too many', while 'the immigrant' increasingly appeared as an object for police intervention. Faced with this situation, in which neither integration nor everyday coexistence seemed possible, thousands of West Indians returned home. Those who stayed realised that in order to build a life in Britain they could rely only on their own resources. From this realisation the idea of carnival was resurrected. Claudia Jones was in the forefront of those who believed that carnival might prove to be a means for creating a community out of a situation of fear and hatred, as it had in the past. London's first carnival was held in the chilly, municipal environment of St Pancras Town Hall, in February 1959. (It was billed to coincide with carnival in the Caribbean, not with more appropriate climatic conditions in the UK.) From these inauspicious beginnings carnival and its allied occasions flourished. The BBC was persuaded to televise it. Mighty Sparrow travelled from Trinidad to sing.[48] The carnival queen contest marked an explicit attempt to instil popular pride in being black. West Indians involved in the performing arts were called upon: Pearl Connor, Pearl Prescod and Corinne Skinner-Carter.[49] Paul Robeson lent his talents and authority as (in differing contexts) did others amongst the Caribbean writers in London. White Britons were cajoled into participating, and little corners of British society found themselves to be undergoing incipient creolisation. (In 1962 the carnival queen judges included not only Earl Cameron, Althea McNish and Andrew Salkey, but the playwright John Osborne and theatre director Joan Littlewood.)[50] 'A pride in being West Indian', Jones wrote in the 1959 souvenir programme, 'is undoubtedly at the root of this unity: a pride that has its origin in the drama of nascent nationhood, and that pride encompasses not only the creativeness, uniqueness and originality of West Indian mime, song and dance – but is the genesis of the nation itself.'[51]

'The drama of nascent nationhood' was clearly active in Claudia Jones's imagination. But her commitments to the West Indies were mediated through an almost lifelong absence. She had left Trinidad as a young girl and never again returned either to Trinidad or to the Caribbean; thereafter, the realities of Harlem constituted her immediate mental world. Hers was a commitment to West Indian identity in which the experience of diaspora was uppermost. To be West Indian, in this sense, was a strategy to live with the dislocations imposed by migration.

The intellectual world which Claudia Jones's generation of West Indian emigrants brought to Britain was – for these reasons – much more extensive and multi-dimensional than the designation West Indian might at first imply. It provided one of the channels, for example, through which the innovatory jazz sounds of Greenwich Village and Harlem reached Britain. It offered an openness to the cultural forms of the United States which elsewhere in Britain in these years could barely be spotted, both in relation to the formal artefacts of high culture (the regard for Herman Melville, for example) or in the more complex arena of commodifed popular cultures.[52] Every aspect of black America was seized upon: the *West Indian Gazette*'s enthusiasm for James Baldwin was symptomatic. Through the 1960s, West Indians in

Britain were alive to the cultural developments in the newly independent countries of black Africa, and representatives of a new generation of black African novelists found in the Caribbean Artists Movement a welcoming home.[53]

Or in the more formal field of black politics the same was true. When Martin Luther King first travelled to London in March 1957, as an unknown representative of the southern black churches, it was C. L. R. James who acted as his unofficial host, introducing him to George Lamming and to David Pitt. On King's subsequent trip at the end of 1964, when he stopped over on his way to Stockholm to collect his Nobel peace prize, Claudia Jones arranged a private meeting at her home, to which David Pitt and Pearl Connor were also invited. Andrew Salkey, who managed to arrange three separate BBC interviews with King, remembers being 'galvanised' by this second visit.[54] Two months later Malcolm X returned to Britain, invited to speak on this occasion by the African Society of the London School of Economics. His guide and principal interlocutor turned out to be Jan Carew, who was so moved by the experience that many years later he wrote an entire book describing the meeting.[55] In July 1967 Stokley Carmichael came to London to address the Dialectics of Liberation conference at the Round House, at Chalk Farm in London.[56] He met with C. L. R. James for the first time; he spoke at public meetings in Brixton and Notting Hill; and John La Rose organised a smaller workshop discussion in Hackney. A short while after Brathwaite recalled the impact of Carmichael's arrival. According to Brathwaite, he

> enunciated a way of seeing the black West Indies that seemed to many to make sense of the entire history of slavery and colonial suppression, of the African diaspora in the New World ... He produced images of shared communal values. A black International was possible. West Indians, denied heroes by their imposed education, responded.[57]

Martin Luther King, Malcolm X, Stokley Carmichael: all, when they came to Britain, gravitated to the West Indians, who – in turn – 'responded'.

Or we can pause on one final image, whose juxtapositions are revealing. Thanks to the services of one of our present contributors, Louis James, the inaugural meeting of the Caribbean Artists Movement (CAM) took place in Canterbury, at the University of Kent in that same summer of 1967. For those unfamiliar with the imaginative landscape of England it can be said that Canterbury does not conventionally register as a redoubt of postcolonial passions. In opening the formal proceedings Brathwaite suggested that CAM would come to equal in significance the illustrious *Présence africaine* congresses of Paris

[ 17 ]

and Rome. Maybe there was a touch of hyperbole in this verdict. But the thought of the ghost of *Présence africaine* in Canterbury – that's something!

This, then, is the hypothesis: that generations of West Indian migrants coming to Britain in the twentieth century brought with them the gift of a particular vantage from which to comprehend the civilisation of the mother country. This was a gift which derived not from the social marginality of the migrant, but rather – as I've emphasised – from the consequences of a specific history and from the experience of crossing the seas. The work of the accredited intellectuals (calypso singers as much as novelists) was to transform this collective experience into a public language which, in turn, could become the medium through which new lives could be imagined, after colonialism.

Basically, this hypothesis is a distillation of one part of C. L. R. James's more general philosophy of history, although in its essentials it was an argument shared by many of his generation. The main modification attempted here has been to reposition these formulations in such a way that their specifically British concerns move from a secondary to a principal matter. This is an awkward and perhaps contentious manoeuvre, for it requires re-establishing (if only provisionally, or in new ways) the primacy of the relationship between metropolis and colony – which is, of course, exactly the predicament from which the West Indians were trying to free themselves. But the continuing incapacities in Britain to recall that these relations ever existed provide, we believe, appropriate justification.

The chapters which follow test this argument, empirically, in different domains and at different times. The contributors differ in their estimation of James. They differ too in their interpretation of the larger tradition of West Indian thought. How best to conceptualise the collective presence of West Indian intellectuals remains an open question. One purpose of our volume here is to heed (so far as we can) a plurality of voices: female as well as male; brown and white as well as black; religious as well as secular. This complicates the story, but it is a necessary complication. It requires a word.

It makes sense to establish a James, or a James-Lamming, or even a James-Lamming-Jones tradition of mid-century marxisant West Indian thought. But beyond that we have to be more circumspect. We can't elevate all the particular, contrary figures we discuss into a single undifferentiated West Indian *tradition*, of collective scriptural authority. Indeed, part of our argument is that for all James's insights it is the plurality and internal differentiation of this body of intellectual thought which best serve us, today.

In this, much turns on the notion of a tradition itself. In the abstract it can be put like this. Historians are now alert to the mystique which shadows the idea of traditions. They are taught to uncover the fact that traditions – even those to which they themselves are committed – don't fall from the sky, but are produced in particular historical circumstances, for particular purposes. Traditions are the result of painstaking cultural work, deployed for conscious or unconscious political ends, and the more effective they become the more powerfully they organise structures of inclusion and exclusion. Historians are trained to root out the mendacious, the bogus and the merely wishful dimensions of tradition. *And yet*: in our private and collective lives we need traditions (or something like them), for traditions are a means for connecting the past to the present, and for enabling us to imagine the future. This, then, leaves us in a double-bind, both suspicious of tradition and yet requiring what it delivers.

This can be argued more concretely. James came to write about the West Indian intellectual, as a specific object of study, in 1968, at a time when insurrectionary politics took hold of public life across the globe and when, in the Caribbean, Black Power emerged as a new political force. It was in this context that James and those around him found it necessary to recover John Jacob Thomas and to inaugurate a tradition of West Indian intellectuals, so named. The making of the tradition was explicit. James identifies the four principal 'descendants' of Thomas, and names them: Marcus Garvey, Aimé Césaire, George Padmore and Frantz Fanon. We shouldn't be surprised that James fashioned Thomas in his own image, emphasising his dispossession, rather than his social standing, in Trinidad. Nor that James turned him into something of a lone manful hero, in a characteristically Victorian manner (borrowing more than he cared to notice from Thomas Carlyle). Nor indeed that James should declare: 'Today Thomas would be quite at home with the concept of Black Power'.[58] Indebted though we are to James for his recuperation of Thomas, we can also appreciate that the historical circumstances in which this recovery took place imposed certain silences. It's impossible to tell from James's account, for example, the degree to which both Froude and Thomas (and thus James himself) shared certain defining assumptions about civilised values – a point to which Wilson Harris (from his own location) has drawn our attention.[59] We can't, in other words, take James's tradition on trust.

James wasn't unaware of the conceptual complexities of the task he was engaged in. With his usual sense of history he realised that, in this moment as much as in any other, he was responding to 'the situation in which our historical past has placed us'.[60] In *that* situation, in 1968, *that* tradition (Thomas, Garvey, Césaire, Padmore, Fanon) appeared the most urgent to hold to. But we, a generation after, have been placed by history in a different situation, and need to act accordingly. This doesn't imply we jettison the Jamesian pantheon; but it calls for its rethinking and *relocation*.

A number of questions follow.

The starkness with which James (at this point in his life) imagined the tradition of his predecessors reveals too the force of its exclusions. Most striking of all, from a contemporary view, is the masculine imperative. It is still difficult to get *past* James, and past those formed in his image, to grasp the plurality of those who have contributed to the full complex of Caribbean thought. James's figure of the West Indian intellectual was silently but powerfully male, reflecting his own subjective trajectory: his smart school, modelled on the lines of the English public school (Queen's Royal College in Port of Spain), cricket, and his vocation to be a writer. To be a man of letters was to engineer an escape from the confines of colonial life; to aim to be a woman of letters, improvising on the way, was a more perilous – indeed, often unimaginable – option. Through much of the last century, conventional sexual divisions were reproduced in the various radical coteries of Caribbean intellectual life, with the women assisting, editing, organising – which, although activities of the intellect, were rarely accredited as such. Una Marson knew Padmore and James in London in the 1930s, and her views of them are recorded. But what of their views of her?

These social realities, and the inequalities they represented, are familiar – but no less important for that. These suppressed, submerged, fragmentary histories need to be revealed. But this will only take us so far. We also need to explore how specifically feminine perspectives reconstituted the given intellectual ground of the intellectuals, and the consequences of this on the British scene.

First, we might think about the persona of the intellectual, *per se*. There is an important literature on the role of boys' schooling in the making of the intellectual culture of the colonial Caribbean.[61] The profound consequence of this system of education cannot be overestimated. The elite institutions of this system were designed to produce intellectuals of a very traditional sort, modelled on the English pattern, with the masculine enclaves of the private schools and Oxford and Cambridge in command. How far this worked is a matter for debate. But something of the resultant social disconnection can be seen in the writings of the migrant intellectuals of the 1950s and 1960s – especially, for example, in the internal debates of the Caribbean Artists Movement.[62]

Second, we could consider the connection between a certain kind of feminist consciousness and broader conceptions of popular life. Claudia Jones, for example, arrived in Britain with an unparalleled understanding of the specific forms of exploitation of black working women.[63] In terms of political practicalities this gave her an unusually sure sense of how to intervene in migrant popular life. The reasoning which led her to launch carnival is instructive, for it highlights the degree to which she could translate the popular aspirations of the intellectuals into the lived realities of daily experience. Even her championing of carnival queen competitions and her insistence that the *West Indian Gazette* carry beauty tips – although not exactly conforming to the desiderata of contemporary feminism – indicate her determination to win a specifically female audience to the goals of black self-realisation. Or we could recall again Una Marson who – like many West Indians of her and later generations – discovered herself as black in London, by imagining her own historical links to Africa. In so doing, she positioned herself in new and significant ways, as a West Indian. However, we can also detect in her thinking a subtle critique not only of colonialism overseas, but of proximate social authority closer to the mother country: forms of social authority more deeply implicated in the idea of *England*. This, in some respects, makes her a more contemporary and a more interesting figure than some of her male peers.

Third, we need to reflect on the particular forms of knowledge which were produced. Here, as an example, we can turn to Jean Rhys.[64] Rhys does not sit comfortably in any given political tradition nor – given the fact that she was white – is she easily accommodated into any larger Caribbean collective. The degree to which her work can claim any West Indian identity has been, and perhaps continues to be, a matter of sharp controversy. Brathwaite has expressed his impatience with the attention given to Rhys's *Wide Sargasso Sea*, claiming that it interferes with a proper appreciation of the dynamics of racial exploitation. From a contrary position, Kenneth Ramchand believes her early novel, *Voyage in the Dark*, while only tangentially West Indian in content, represents the Caribbean's 'first Negritude novel'.[65] Tactically, however (for our purposes), it may be possible to sidestep these disputes about race and ethnicity and to consider how her fiction works.

Rhys wrote in a recognisably modernist manner, in which the inner subjective life of her protagonists never seems to be reconciled with the diktats of the given social world. Much of her inventiveness as a writer derives from her capacities to craft a narrative which in itself dramatises and makes evident the workings of these discrepant realities – social and subjective – in all their textured, phenomenological everydayness. Generally this is organised in her fiction in terms of her female protagonists encountering the norms of a patriarchal world, in which the inner lives of her characters cumulatively assume a disturbing *unreality*. This is a narrative, in other words, which takes as its principal object the coexistence of discrepant realities. It's not possible to divine the extent to which this derived from her memories of her West Indian childhood; but it is at least a parallel or homologous problem to that experienced by the non-white West Indians encountering the white norms of the metropolis, as I suggested earlier when I introduced the passage from Lamming's *The Emigrants*. The knowledge her narratives produced can, minimally, function as a wider resource for understanding the characteristic experience of those who had crossed the seas, allowing us to reach the unreality not only of the new world they had encountered, but also of their own subjective sense of being.

These points are summarily stated. They suggest, only, that different conceptual or political starting points produce different sorts of tradition – or call into question those traditions which are bequeathed to us. The more different lived identities are respected, the harder it is to think in terms of a unitary tradition.

One final question, though, remains in the air. In a variety of ways most of those discussed here, with differing degrees of passion, would have thought of themselves as West Indians, and committed themselves in some way to a West Indian future. This is not true, though, of V. S. Naipaul. Of those we discuss, he remains the joker in the pack. What of him?

With perhaps no exceptions, Naipaul would regard the political philosophies of those represented in the chapters which follow as demonstrable vanities, harmful not only to their practitioners but to the world at large. He has neither sympathy nor interest in their preoccupations. The questions which prompted this book he would, we can be sure, deem irrelevant, signifying (in his mind) only a toxic combination of vulgarity and hubris. Locating Naipaul himself as a West Indian, emphasising the commonality of his history with those others we discuss, would be an undoubted source of vexation. But if for a moment we ignore the postures, we can see that – *in formation* – he is, as an intellectual, a kind of paradigmatic West Indian of his generation. Partly because of the calculated sourness of his public pronouncements, and partly because of the palpably autobiographical nature of much of his fiction, a deal of the comment on his writing dwells on his well-paraded psychological quirks and flaws. But to locate him in a larger body of West Indian writing offers a different viewpoint. As he relates on numerous occasions and in numerous forms, in 1938 he moved from his grandmother's Hindu house in rural Trinidad, which was still close to the rituals and social ways of village life in India, to the urban, black world of Port of Spain; twelve years later, he made the journey to Britain and to Oxford University. This double migration haunts his memories so intensely that he repeatedly returns to it in his fiction, rewriting these journeys time and again, introducing different motifs but acting out in his imagination the same repetitions. We know from his stories that the psychic shocks of these journeys went as deep into his inner life as it did for others of his generation. As he understands well enough, this is a past which refuses to disappear – however much he wishes that it would. His hatreds of the indignities of colonial life are on record, as are his deep disappointments with England once he came to know it, including its normalised racial bigotry. The 'schizophrenia' which he identifies underpinning his own life represents only another way of describing the more familiar condition of living as a colonial, and migrating to the metropolis. While others expended much energy in working through these issues, recognising their collective properties, Naipaul chose to reconcile the dislocations he experienced by inventing his 'other' self, in breathtakingly traditional manner, as *the writer*, with all appropriate affectations properly in place.

Despite indications of an early regard, Naipaul's contempt for C. L. R. James runs deep. The fact that – in the new century – he still feels moved to speak this contempt may itself be revealing, for James appears to represent (for Naipaul) a phantom of an unappeased West Indian past. If in their respective formations there are certain formal similarities, in the manner they chose to live out their histories they are each other's contrary.

Naipaul remains in England. Nothing could possibly induce him to return to Trinidad. Many of those West Indians who felt obliged to come to Britain moved on – returning to the Caribbean when independence offered some space, or creating a location in North America, or living with the interruptions of a more peripatetic transatlantic life. We are now in a different historical situation, when sons and daughters, or grandsons and granddaughters, of those who made the crossing, but who themselves are British-born, carry these generational memories and use them to intervene in their own political times, as truly immigrated citizens of the British polity.[66] This past is still with them – and, through the displacements which we hope this book reveals, also with those of us who have only heard the stories.

When the authors met to discuss their contributions it became increasingly apparent that our selection of individual intellectuals, and our selection of the wider spectrum of intellectual organisations which represented Caribbean thinking, was so partial it could be deemed idiosyncratic. Discussion impressed upon us the fact that it represented only a tiny sample from a rich and complex intellectual presence. The more we talked the more we realised there was to do. Furthermore it may seem strange that James – whose arguments first triggered the idea of producing such a volume – receives just a single chapter.[67] But we were persuaded that other voices needed to be heard. We were also persuaded that to do justice to this collective presence would require more volumes than we could possibly contemplate.[68]

# Notes

1 See especially Stuart Hall, 'Reconstruction work', *Ten:8*,16 (1984).

2 George Lamming, *The Pleasures of Exile* (London: Allison and Busby, 1984; first published 1960), p. 12.

3 C. L. R. James, born in Trinidad 1901. Came to Britain in 1932, and thereafter lived and worked in Britain, the USA and Trinidad, with brief sojourns in Ghana. The foremost anglophone intellectual of the Caribbean in the twentieth century. Died in Brixton, London, 1989, buried in Tunapuna, Trinidad.

4 C. L. R. James, *Beyond a Boundary* (London: Hutchinson, 1986; first published 1963). In the Preface he states: 'If the ideas originated in the West Indies it was only in England and in English life and history that I was able to track them down and test them.'

5 C. L. R. James, 'Immigrants to Britain: formerly colonial peoples', in his *80th Birthday Lectures* (London: Race Today, 1984). See too, from the same period, his 'Africans and Afro-Caribbeans: a personal view', *Ten:8*,16 (1984).

6 Donald Hinds interviewed a Jamaican, Devon, who after a series of frustrated attempts to get a job (including in the police force), migrated to Britain. He brought with him his grandmother's stories, the most vivid of which concerned the terror which followed the Morant Bay uprising. 'The war in distant Korea and Indo-China and especially the Mau-Mau forced a dialogue between me and me. It was seditious. It forced me to search around for some more material on the Morant Bay Rebellion of 1865. My grandmother's grandmother lived through the hell of it.' Donald Hinds, *Journey to an Illusion: the West Indian in Britain* (London: Heinemann, 1966), p. 24.

7 C. L. R. James argued that the West Indies arrived at a 'national' consciousness, in part, through cricket. But as his comments on the 1963 test between the West Indies and England indicate, more problematically he suggested that West Indians needed to be recognised in the metropolis before they could recognise themselves: *Cricket* (London: Allison and Busby, 1986), pp. 116–65.

8 John Jacob Thomas, born in Trinidad 1840, the son of freed slaves. Author in 1869 of the pioneering *The Theory and Practice of Creole Grammar*. Died in London in 1889, shortly after his arrival in Britain.

9 J. A. Froude, *The English in the West Indies: or, The Bow of Ulysses* (London: Longman Green, 1909); and J. J. Thomas, *Froudacity: West Indian fables by James Anthony Froude* (London and Port of Spain: New Beacon Books, 1969). It is important to grasp how long-lasting has been the shadow of Froude on English-speaking Caribbean intellectuals.

10 C. L. R. James, 'The West Indian intellectual', which serves as the introduction to the New Beacon edition of Thomas, *Froudacity*, p. 27.

11 James, 'The West Indian intellectual', pp. 47 and 45.

12 James, 'The West Indian intellectual', p. 46.

13 It is indeed the case that twentieth-century Caribbean fiction does carry a profound consciousness of historical time. For an overview, see Nana Wilson-Tagoe, *Historical Thought and Literary Representation in West Indian Literature* (Gainesville: University of Florida Press, 1998), and more specifically, Supriya Nair, *Caliban's Curse: George Lamming and the reconfiguring of history* (Ann Arbor:

University of Michigan Press, 1996). It is also significant that both Lamming and Wilson Harris make the case for including C. L. R. James's *The Black Jacobins: Toussaint L'Ouverture and the San Domingo Revolution* (London: Allison and Busby, 1980; first published 1938) as part of a specifically West Indian narrative tradition of realism: Lamming, *Pleasures of Exile*, and A. J. M. Bundy (ed.), *Selected Essays of Wilson Harris: the unfinished genesis of the imagination* (London: Routledge, 1999), pp. 148–50; more generally, in a rather less satisfactorily located context, Edward Said, *Culture and Imperialism* (London: Chatto and Windus, 1993), pp. 295–313.

14 See his various reports published in the *Port of Spain Gazette*, July and August 1932.

15 C. L. R. James, *The Life of Captain Cipriani* (Nelson, Lancashire: Coulton and Co., 1932); two of the short stories appear in Anna Grimshaw (ed.), *The C. L. R. James Reader* (Oxford: Blackwell, 1992).

16 C. L. R. James, *Minty Alley* (London: Secker and Warburg, 1936).

17 Learie Constantine, a childhood friend of James's, born in Trinidad in 1902. Star cricketer of the 1920s and 1930s, playing for Lancashire between 1929 and 1937. Employed by the Ministry of Labour during the second world war as a welfare worker for West Indians employed in Liverpool. Trained as a barrister. Returned to Trinidad in 1954 to chair Eric Williams's People's National Movement. Trinidad's High Commissioner in London, 1962–64. Remained in London when his term of office finished. Governor of the BBC and a member of the Race Relations Board. Peerage, 1969 – the first black man to sit in the House of Lords. Died, 1971.

18 C. L. R. James, *The Case for West Indian Self-Government* (London: Leonard and Virginia Woolf, 1933). It appears that James dealt primarily with Leonard. It is left for us to wonder what would have been generated in an intellectual rendezvous between James and Virginia Woolf.

19 James, *Beyond a Boundary*, p. 114.

20 George Padmore, another childhood friend of James's from Trinidad, born in 1902. Studied at Howard University in the USA, where he became a Communist. High in the firmament of the Communist International and Soviet system until he was expelled from the Communist movement in 1934. Thereafter devoted himself to Pan-Africanism and, in particular, to the cause of Kwame Nkrumah and of independence for the Gold Coast. Died in London in 1959, two years after he had witnessed the birth of independent Ghana, his ashes interred in Accra.

21 Una Marson, born in Jamaica 1905. Travelled to Britain in 1932, where she lodged with Harold Moody in Peckham and became active in his League of Coloured Peoples. Poet and writer. Launched *Calling the West Indies* on BBC radio in 1941, the precursor to the influential *Caribbean Voices*. Lived in Britain between 1932–36 and 1938–46. Died in Jamaica, 1965.

22 Delia Jarrett-Macauley, *The Life of Una Marson, 1905–65* (Manchester: Manchester University Press, 1998), p. 100.

23 Garveyism – the movement inspired by Marcus Garvey. Born into a Methodist family in Jamaica in 1887. Travelled throughout Central America and, in 1912, to Britain, where he attended lectures at Birkbeck College, and found employment around the docks of London, Cardiff and Liverpool. Returning to Jamaica in 1914 he founded the Universal Negro Improvement Association (UNIA) which was to be, in the 1920s and 1930s, the single most important organiser of black popular politics in the Atlantic world. Died in London, 1940; after independence his remains were transferred to Jamaica.

24 This is the argument, wonderfully marshalled, of Dick Hebdige, *Subculture: the meaning of style* (London: Methuen, 1979). An exuberant sample of the music can be heard in the terrific compilation *London is the Place For Me: Trinidadian calypso in London, 1950–1956* (London: Honest Jons Records, HJRCD2, 2002).

25 Edward (Kamau) Brathwaite, 'Jazz and the West Indian novel II', *Bim*, 12:45 (1967), p. 40. Brathwaite here is appropriating a term which was originally used to denigrate local popular forms. Kamau (Edward) Brathwaite, born 1930 in Barbados, and travelled to Britain in 1950 to study history at Cambridge University, arriving (as he now

claims) as 'a citizen of the world' and expecting to be greeted at the quayside 'by William Shakespeare'. Followed by eight years in the Gold Coast (during its transition to independence and to its new identity as Ghana). Taught history in St Lucia and Jamaica before returning to the UK to study at Sussex University. A founding spirit of the Caribbean Artists Movement. Returned to Jamaica in 1968. Historian, poet, cultural activist.

26  James, *Beyond a Boundary*, p. 34.

27  V. S. Naipaul, *The Enigma of Arrival* (Harmondsworth: Penguin, 1987), p. 120. V. S. Naipaul, born in Trinidad in 1932. Arrived in Britain in 1950 to attend Oxford University. Presenter and editor of *Caribbean Voices*, 1954–56. Novelist, essayist and travel writer. Nobel prize for literature in 2001. Hostile to the aesthetics and realities of Caribbean life, Islam, democratic cultures, actually existing England, C. L. R. James, and much else.

28  Mary Chamberlain appropriates the term 'cognitive dissonance' to describe this collective experience: *Narratives of Exile and Return* (London: Macmillan, 1997), pp. 74–5.

29  Sam Selvon, *The Lonely Londoners* (London: Longman, 1985; first published 1956). Sam Selvon, born in Trinidad 1923. Journalist on the *Trinidad Guardian* before coming to Britain (on the same boat as George Lamming) in 1950. Novelist and writer, involved from early on with *Caribbean Voices*. Left Britain for Canada in 1978. Died 1994.

30  Lamming, *Pleasures of Exile*, p. 14. George Lamming, born in Barbados 1927. Moved to Trinidad and thence, in 1950 with Selvon, made the journey to Britain. His first novel (*In The Castle of My Skin*) was written in Chiswick and published in 1953. Novelist of renown, writer, political activist. Returned to Barbados in the 1960s, establishing himself as a powerful Pan-Caribbean public voice.

31  George Lamming, *The Emigrants* (Ann Arbor: University of Michigan Press, 1994), pp. 138–48.

32  There are many instances. But particular mention should be made of Philip Donnellan's fine television documentary, shown on BBC television in June 1964, *The Colony*. This was an unusual account of black immigrant life in Britain, for the protagonists represented themselves, either talking direct to camera or (with a bit more artifice) by means of internal monologue.

33  For a rare discussion which sees the import of exploring these volumes within a single historical and conceptual frame, see Simon Gikandi, *Writing in Limbo: modernism and Caribbean literature* (Ithaca: Cornell University Press, 1992).

34  Stuart Hall, born Kingston 1932; travelled to Britain to study at Oxford University in 1951. A foremost activist of the New Left in Britain in the late 1950s and early 1960s. Director of the Centre for Contemporary Cultural Studies at Birmingham University, and subsequently Professor of Sociology at the Open University. A leading public intellectual in Britain: active in many arenas of cultural and political life, with a special commitment to the world of black visual arts.

35  See especially Stuart Hall, 'Lamming, Selvon and some trends in the W. I. novel', *Bim*, 23 (1955). How these themes crossed over to work as a resource for addressing the question of England can be charted in Stuart Hall, 'The deep sleep of England', *Universities and Left Review*, 3 (1958). It is remarkable how long it took British commentators to *notice* this West Indian formation in Hall's work. Indeed, it wasn't really until he pointed them out himself that they gained some currency: Stuart Hall, 'The formation of a diasporic intellectual', in David Morley and Kuan-Hsing Chen (eds), *Stuart Hall: critical dialogues* (London: Routledge, 1996).

36  Evidence can be found in Sam Selvon, 'Finding West Indian identity in London', *Kunapipi*, 9:3 (1987); in Stuart Hall, 'Postscript', *Soundings ('Windrush' special issue)*, 10 (1998); and in Horace Ové's film, *Baldwin's Nigger* (1968).

37  See especially the closing argument of Hinds, *Journey to an Illusion*.

38  On 20 December 1958, under James's editorship, the *Nation* reproduced an article from the *TLS* in which Naipaul had condemned Trinidad for being a philistine nation. James was angered, and called upon the readership to respond.

39    Contemporary use of the term derives from Paul Gilroy, *The Black Atlantic: modernity and double consciousness* (London: Verso, 1993).
40    The comparative work needed is yet in its infancy. A significant anticipation can be found in Penny Von Eschen, *Race Against Empire: black Americans and anticolonialism, 1937–1957* (Ithaca: Cornell University Press, 1997).
41    For representative documentation, see the chapter 'The African presence', in Lamming, *Pleasures of Exile*. In addition to Lamming – Padmore, James, Makonnen, Brathwaite, Carew, Arthur Lewis, Amy Ashwood Garvey, David Pitt and Neville Dawes were in Ghana during these first years of independence. When the Irish BBC producer Henry Swanzy was relieved of his job on *Caribbean Voices* in 1954 he chose to be posted to the Gold Coast. The West Indian connections are powerfully visible in Kevin Gaines, 'Revisiting Richard Wright in Ghana: black radicalism and the dialectics of diaspora', *Social Text*, 67 (2001).
42    This is also the implicit argument, for the francophone arena of the Caribbean, of David Macey's *Frantz Fanon: a biography* (London: Granta, 2000).
43    These were Trevor Carter, who had arrived from Trinidad the year before, and who was a member of the Communist Party of Great Britain. And Billy Strachan (1921–98), a Jamaican who had served in the RAF during the war, and returned to the UK shortly after, though it's not clear whether at this time he was still a CP member. Communism forms a significant strand in the larger story of West Indians in Britain in these years. Early in the decade there existed a West Indian branch of the CP in London, composed of some fifty members. Both Carter and Strachan were also active in the London branch of the Caribbean Labour Congress which, although proscribed by the Labour Party as a Communist front, appears to have acted independently from the CP. See Trevor Carter, with Jean Coussins, *Shattering Illusions: West Indians in British Politics* (London: Lawrence and Wishart, 1986).
44    Norman Manley, Jamaican, 1893–1969. Oxford University trained lawyer. Founded Jamaica's People's National Party in 1938. Prime minister, 1959–62. Cheddi Jagan, born the son of labourers on a sugar plantation in British Guiana in 1918; died in independent Guyana in 1997. Studied dentistry at Howard University, where he gravitated to marxism. Founder of the People's Progressive Party in 1950, the first modern mass party in British Guiana, which won the elections in 1953. Jagan was deposed by British troops 133 days later, and jailed. Phillys Allfrey, a white Dominican born in 1908, novelist, poet and politician. Travelled between the USA and Britain. In 1936 worked for the BBC and involved herself in literary, left-wing London, meeting too Paul Robeson and James. Returned to Dominica in 1957 to participate in the election, on behalf of the Dominica Labour Party which she had founded two years earlier. Died in 1986.
45    David Pitt, born in Grenada in 1913; studied medicine at Edinburgh University. Returned to St Vincent and Trinidad. Back in Britain, his surgery in Gower Street, London, was a focus for expatriate West Indians. Stood for Labour in the 1959 and 1970 general elections. Chair of the Greater London Council, 1974–75; President of the British Medical Association in 1985; followed Constantine into the Lords as only the second black peer. Died 1994. John La Rose, born in Trinidad in 1927; active in trade union and radical politics. Worked as a teacher in Venezuela from 1958. Arrived in Britain in 1961. Founder member of the Caribbean Artists Movement, and leading spirit in the New Beacon publishing and bookselling venture, both of which were founded in 1966.
46    Jan Carew, born in British Guiana in 1920. Served in the army during the war. A customs officer in Georgetown, 1943–44. Worked in Trinidad, and studied at Howard in the USA and at university in Prague. In Britain between 1952 and 1962, and again from 1963–65. Director of Culture in Cheddi Jagan's government in Guyana, 1962. In Ghana, 1965–66. In Canada, 1966–69, thence to the US. Writer, painter, actor and distinguished US academic. Andrew Salkey, Panamanian-born Jamaican, writer, anthropologist and political activist. Born in 1928. Arrived in Britain in 1952 to study at London University. One of the founders of the Caribbean Artists Movement. Left London to teach in the US in 1976, where he died in 1995.

47  Amy Ashwood Garvey: met Marcus Garvey in Kingston the month before the UNIA launched, of which they were the first two members. Itinerant political life between the USA, the Caribbean, Britain and West Africa. Chair of the Pan-African Conference in Manchester in 1945. In Ghana in 1957 for independence. Possibly a social worker in London and Birmingham in the 1950s. Lived in Notting Hill during the white riots of 1958, her house serving as a centre for black resistance.

48  Mighty Sparrow (Francisco Slinger), Grenadian-born who transformed himself into the great Trinidadian calypso singer. Of him James said: 'He is living proof that there is a West Indian nation'.

49  Pearl Connor, born in Trinidad, where she was involved in theatre and anti-colonial politics. Travelled to Britain in 1948 to study law, though continued to be active in the theatre; in 1963 established the Negro Theatre Workshop, and thereafter an influential theatrical agency for non-white actors. First met Claudia Jones in London shortly after the latter had arrived, of whom she remarked: 'She made you fearless'. Pearl Prescod, Tobagan singer, with commitments to a wide range of political and cultural issues; resident in the 1950s in Notting Hill. Corinne Skinner-Connor, Trinidadian dancer, who came to Britain in 1959. A long subsequent career in British TV soaps.

50  Earl Cameron, the foremost black actor in the British cinema during the 1950s. Born Bermuda 1917; merchant seaman; arrived in Britain from Harlem in 1939. Althea McNish, a Trinidadian artist, whose work was shown by the Caribbean Artists Movement.

51  Marika Sherwood, with Donald Hinds and Colin Prescod, *Claudia Jones: a life in exile* (London: Lawrence and Wishart, 1999), p. 157. I have relied on this for my information on Claudia Jones, in conjunction with Buzz Johnson, *'I Think of My Mother.' Notes on the life and times of Claudia Jones* (London: Karia Press, 1985).

52  Astonishing in this respect is C. L. R. James, *American Civilization* (Oxford: Blackwell, 1993); although not published until much later, this was first drafted in 1949–50.

53  James Ngugi (Ngugi wa Thiong'o), working on a Masters on Lamming at Leeds University, was one of these to involve himself in CAM. John Hearne was a visiting fellow at Leeds at this time.

54  Anne Walmsley, *The Caribbean Artists Movement, 1966–1972* (London: New Beacon Books, 1992), p. 45.

55  Jan Carew, *Ghosts in our Blood: with Malcolm X in Africa, England and the Caribbean* (Chicago: Lawrence Hill, 1994). Carew emphasises both the strong Garveyite roots of Malcolm X's parents (who first met at a UNIA rally in Montreal in 1918), and his Caribbean connections, by virtue of his Grenadian mother. Indeed, he comes close to establishing Malcolm X *as* a Caribbean radical. A week after his conversations with Carew he was dead.

56  Stokley Carmichael, born in Trinidad. Migrated to the USA. Attended Howard University. An influential figure in the Student Non-violent Coordinating Committee, before becoming the leading theoretician of Black Power. After his speech at the Round House he was deported back to the US.

57  Walmsley, *Caribbean Artists Movement*, p. 93.

58  James, 'The West Indian intellectual', pp. 44–5. New Beacon Books, based in both Trinidad and Britain, chose to republish at the same time John Jacob Thomas, *The Theory and Practice of Creole Grammar* (London and Port of Spain: New Beacon Books, 1969). An invaluable account of New Beacon and of the immediate intellectual background is given in Brian Alleyne, *Radicals Against Race: black activism and cultural politics* (Oxford: Berg, 2002). I am grateful to Brian Alleyne for allowing me to read this in proof. This should be read in conjunction with Roxy Harris and Sarah White (eds), *Foundations of a Movement: a tribute to John La Rose* (London: John La Rose Tribute Committee, 1991).

59  Wilson Harris, *History, Fable and Myth in the Caribbean and the Guianas* (Ithaca: Calaloux Publications, 1995), pp. 16–18. See too Faith Smith, 'A man who knows his roots: J. J. Thomas and current discourses of black nationalism', *Small Axe*, 5 (1999).

Wilson Harris, born British Guiana 1921. Government surveyor. Came to Britain in 1959. Inspired writer.

**60**  James, 'The West Indian intellectual', p. 27.

**61**  A recent discussion, relevant to our argument here, is Simon Gikandi, 'The embarrassment of Victorianism: colonial subjects and the lure of Englishness', in John Kucich and Diane Sardoff (eds), *The Post-Victorian Frame of Mind* (Minneapolis: University of Minnesota Press, 1999), which focuses on James. And of great importance, George Lamming, 'Western education and the Caribbean intellectual', in his *Coming, Coming Home: conversations II* (Philipsburg, St Martin: House of Nehesi, 2000).

**62**  It may be worth pondering, in this context, the electrifying effect of Elsa Goveia's lecture to the Caribbean Artists Movement in the summer of 1967, in which just this issue was raised: 'The social framework', *Savacou*, 1:2 (1970). Or to put this another way: one wonders whether James's insistence on the historicity of the Caribbean can't be understood without taking into account the customarily matriarchal conventions of family story-telling. For rich clues, see footnote 5, above, and more fully Chamberlain, *Narratives of Exile and Return*.

**63**  See especially Claudia Jones, *An End to the Neglect of the Problems of Negro Women* (New York: CPUSA, 1949).

**64**  Jean Rhys, born in Dominica in 1890. Came to Britain in 1907 to complete her schooling and to study at the Royal Academy of Dramatic Art, only returning once – some thirty years later – to the Caribbean. Worked as a chorus girl and, during the war, in a soldiers' canteen. In 1919 travelled and lived in continental Europe. Started writing fiction in Paris in the 1920s. Disappeared from the public eye in the postwar decades, until the publication in 1966 of *Wide Sargasso Sea*, which she wrote whilst living in Bromley. Died in 1979, in Exeter.

**65**  These difficulties were dramatised in the following exchange: Peter Hulme, 'The place of *Wide Sargasso Sea*', *Wasafiri*, 20 (1994); Kamau Brathwaite, 'A post-cautionary tale of the Helen of our wars', *Wasafiri*, 22 (1995); and Peter Hulme, 'A response to Kamau Brathwaite', *Wasafiri*, 23 (1996). Kenneth Ramchand, 'Introduction', in Selvon, *Lonely Londoners*, p. 3; Jean Rhys, *Voyage in the Dark* (Harmondsworth: Penguin, 1985; first published 1934) and Jean Rhys, *Wide Sargasso Sea* (Harmondsworth: Penguin, 1976; first published 1966). There is a significant genealogy linking *Voyage in the Dark*, via *Lonely Londoners*, to Zadie Smith's *White Teeth* (Harmondsworth: Penguin, 2001; first published 2000). Kenneth Ramchand: left Trinidad for Edinburgh University. Professor of West Indian Literature at the University of the West Indies; energetic member of Caribbean Artists Movement.

**66**  I follow here the argument of Stuart Hall's prescient lecture to the second Caribbean Artists Movement conference at Canterbury in 1968: see Walmsley, *Caribbean Artists Movement*, p. 162.

**67**  When ten years ago Alistair Hennessy published his ground-breaking collection on anglophone intellectuals in the Caribbean, three of the ten chapters were about James, while no other individual merited even a single chapter. Hennessy conceded the fact that readers might find this imbalance to be 'wilful', but defended it on the grounds that it represented 'a small tribute to pay to one of the giants': Alistair Hennessy (ed.), *Intellectuals in the Twentieth-Century Caribbean. Vol. I. Spectre of the New Class: the Commonwealth Caribbean* (London: Macmillan, 1992), p. xiii.

**68**  Most relevant to our concerns here are Paget Henry and Paul Buhle (eds), *C. L. R. James's Caribbean* (Durham: Duke University Press, 1992); Selwyn Cudjoe and William Cain (eds), *C. L. R. James: his intellectual legacies* (Amherst: University of Massachusetts Press, 1995); and Selwyn Cudjoe, 'C. L. R. James and the Trinidad and Tobago intellectual tradition, or, not learning Shakespeare under a mango tree', *New Left Review*, 223 (1997). More specifically: Paget Henry, *Caliban's Reason: introducing Afro-Caribbean philosophy* (New York: Routledge, 2000); and Lloyd Braithwaite, *Colonial West Indian Students in Britain* (Moha: University of West Indies Press, 2001). There is much illuminating material in Ivar Oxaal, *Black Intellectuals Come to Power: the rise of creole nationalism in Trinidad and Tobago*

(Cambridge, Mass.: Schenkman, 1968). The past twenty years have seen develop a sophisticated discussion of Caribbean intellectuals as Caribbeans. See Gordon K. Lewis, *Main Currents in Caribbean Thought: the historical evolution of Caribbean society in its ideological aspects, 1492–1900* (Baltimore: Johns Hopkins University Press, 1983). Note should also be made of the extraordinary energy of a new journal of Caribbean criticism, *Small Axe*, edited by David Scott. Of great importance is *Small Axe*, 4 (1998), devoted to 'Aspects of Caribbean intellectual tradition', as well as Scott's illuminating interviews with: Stuart Hall (issue 1, 1997); Lloyd Best (issue 1, 1997); Anthony B (issue 2, 1997); Richard Hart (issue 3, 1998); Ken Post (issue 4, 1998); Robert Hill (issue 5, 1999); Sylvia Wynter (issue 8, 2000); Rupert Lewis (issue 10, 2001); and George Lamming (issue 12, 2002).

# CHAPTER ONE

# What is a West Indian?

## Catherine Hall

For C. L. R. James West Indian identity was something to be cele-brated, associated as it was for him, with the whole of the Caribbean, from Cuba and Haiti to Martinique, Trinidad and Jamaica.[1] Its distinc-tive character he saw as intimately linked to its particularly modern history, with the plantation at the centre of a global capitalist system linking slavery with finance, industry and European domestic con-sumption. The intellectual tradition which came out of this history was associated for him with 'the struggle for human emancipation and advancement'. West Indian writers and social actors were 'a particular social product' producing a 'particular type of social activity which we can definitely call West Indian'. The carriers of this tradition were men such as Toussaint L'Ouverture, hero of the San Domingue revo-lution, J. J. Thomas, the Trinidadian schoolmaster who took on the celebrated Oxford professor James Froude, Marcus Garvey, the black nationalist born in Jamaica, Aimé Césaire, the Martiniquan poet and theorist of *négritude*, Frantz Fanon, also from Martinique, who became a critical anti-colonial voice, and Fidel Castro. They shared 'an ocean of thought and feeling' which provided the roots of what it was to be West Indian.[2]

James wrote his history of the revolution in San Domingue, *The Black Jacobins*, in 1938, after leaving Trinidad to live in the metropole, the place where journalists and writers from the colonies could hope to make a name for themselves. James was steeped in Victorian English culture, and perhaps was expressing in this book a confidence about the future which was characteristic of much Victorian thought.[3] Such a desire for progress was also a tenet of the marxism which, from this period, he began to espouse. The book was about a revolution which, he imagined, would happen in Africa, and told the story of the one which had happened in Haiti. Reflecting on the writing of *The Black Jacobins* in 1971, James noted that his aim had been to demonstrate that we had a history and in that history there were men who were fully able to stand comparison with great men of that period ... I was trying to make clear that black people had a certain historical past ... by the historical record I tried to show that black people were able to make historical progress, they were able to show how a revolution was made, they were able to produce the men who could lead a revolution, and write new pages in the book of history ...[4]

James's identification with the struggles of black people and the futures which were possible for him and them was central to his thinking. The capacities of black people and the part they had played in their own histories had been denied by the colonisers. His intellectual magic would allow others to see that heroic and tragic story and celebrate the distinctive West Indian virtues. His was a historical vision and consciousness. As Anthony Bogues argues, '*The Black Jacobins* is a rare text because it serves as marker for history, the practice of politics and a partial answer to the question of who and what is a Caribbean person'.[5]

The creation of intellectual traditions always involves inclusions and exclusions, remembering some and forgetting others. Roots 'are not hallowed artefacts shrouded in mystery, but rather we seem continually to dig them up according to our needs at particular points in time'.[6] While James sought a tradition of struggle for freedom as characteristically West Indian, his fellow Trinidadian, V. S. Naipaul, had a much more deeply pessimistic view. Naipaul came to England in 1950 to study English literature at Oxford. Thirty years younger than James, he also sought to make his name as a writer. In 1961 he wrote *Middle Passage*, his account of a return journey to the West Indies. He took as his epitaph Froude's judgement on the islands in 1887. 'There are no people here in the true sense of the word', Froude had written, 'with a character and purpose of their own.' Naipaul shared this conviction. 'Nothing was created in the British West Indies', he wrote, 'no civilization as in Spanish America, no great revolution as in Haiti or the American colonies. There were only plantations, prosperity, decline, neglect: the size of the islands called for nothing else.' Or, 'how can the history of West Indian futility be written? What tone shall the historian adopt? The history of the islands can never be satisfactorily told. Brutality is not the only difficulty. History is built around achievement and creation; and nothing was created in the West Indies.'[7] This was a harsh legacy with which to live, the mirror-image, perhaps, of James's high-tragic conception of history.

These two contrasting visions have provided my starting point for exploring the legacy of being West Indian from which Caribbean intellectuals have developed their own sense of West Indianness and, intimately connected with this, their sense of history. They inform my inquiry into the different meanings of West Indian – meanings which different generations have had to learn, confront and fashion anew. Like all the chapters in this book my investigation focuses on the metropole: what picture of the West Indian was generated in the metropole and for what purposes? When, how and where did a West Indian identity emerge? Who, at any one time, was included and who excluded? Like all cultural identities that of the West Indian is historically specific. But what kind of term was it? Did it refer to location, ethnicity, parentage, or culture? Did it refer to different groupings at different times? Is it perhaps an identity like 'European', a regional identity which transcended national borders? Was it ever conceived as a national identity? Could the West Indian islands be a nation? Who claimed it and when? I want to ask what a genealogy of the term would look like. Being a West Indian was neither fixed nor essential. My focus here is on the metropolitan lens: this is, of course, only a part of the story.[8]

The term West Indies is complicated in itself. Is it the West Indies of the colonial period, when the islands were named by their European 'discoverers'? Is it the British West Indies, or the French or the Spanish or the Dutch? C. L. R. James's West Indian consciousness crossed the whole of the Caribbean. My concern in this chapter, as with the other chapters in the book, is the islands, and parts of the mainland, which were colonised by the British from the early seventeenth century and named as the British West Indies. This process was in itself a long and complicated history of conquest, associated with the great European wars of the seventeenth, eighteenth and nineteenth centuries. By 1958, when the postwar migration of West Indians to Britain was well under way, and when a West Indian Federation came briefly into being, the participating territories comprised Jamaica in the western Caribbean, and Trinidad and Tobago, Barbados, Grenada, St Vincent, St Lucia, Dominica, Antigua, St Kitts, Nevis, Anguilla and Montserrat in the eastern Caribbean. Neither of the two mainland colonies, British Guiana (Guyana) and British Honduras (Belize) was included. These British West Indian colonies formed a link between North and South America and were strategically vital to the European powers, particularly in the era of the sailing ship. They shared a history, of colonisation, displacement, slavery, emancipation, indenture, nationalism and anti-colonialism: a history out of which a particular kind of West Indian identity has emerged, that of the anglophone Caribbean.

According to the *Oxford English Dictionary* the first recorded use of the term West Indian, in 1597, serves both to describe the indigenous inhabitants of the islands, and to condemn the acts of another colonising power: thus, 'those cruelties that were practised by the Spanish nation upon the West Indians'. By 1661, only a few years after Cromwell's forces had taken Jamaica, the term had come to mean 'an inhabitant or native of the West Indies, of European origin or descent'. In a dramatic, if largely unacknowledged transformation, the West Indian had been whitened: he, and it is mainly he, is one of the settlers from England, Scotland or Ireland, fortune-seekers in the Wild West of the seventeenth century. This meaning held for many decades. As late as George Eliot's *Daniel Deronda* in 1876, the *OED* notes, the West Indian was a byword for fabled wealth brought back to the metropole. By the 1960s, however, (according to the abbreviated genealogy the *OED* gives us) the West Indian had become black. So, *The Times* records in February 1957 that, '26,000 West Indians migrated to Britain in 1956'. Finally, the *OED* notes an inclusive use of the term West Indian in 1961: all inhabitants of the Federation, of European, African, American Indian, East Indian, Chinese, Portuguese or Jewish descent are named as West Indian. 'In his message to West Indians on Christmas day Sir Grantley Adams, the Prime Minister of the Federation, spoke of West Indian unity.' 'Out of many one people', as the newly independent nation of Jamaica claimed in its national motto in 1962.

According to the *OED*, then, West Indian was initially associated with the indigenous inhabitants of the islands, then became a white identity and not until the 1950s, with the migration of African-Caribbean men and women to the metropole, did it register as black. As the Trinidadian John La Rose pointed out, 'When the term West Indian originated it was the Anglo West-Indian who claimed the honour of the description'. Yet it was to become 'an uncertain amalgamation'.[9] It is the postwar generation of migrants who tell of their discovery of becoming West Indian in the metropole: their meeting for the first time with those from other islands of the Caribbean, and recognising a common identity in the face of shared histories and the shared need to confront the racial realities of their new lives in Britain. Sam Selvon, one of those who found a language in order to tell this story, put it this way:

> When I left Trinidad in 1950 and went to England, one of my first experiences was living in a hostel with people from Africa and India and all over the Caribbean. It is strange to think I had to cross the Atlantic and be thousands of miles away, in a different culture and environment, for it to come about that, for the first time in my life, I was living among Barbadians and Jamaicans and others from my part of the world.

And he continues, 'As far as the English were concerned, we were all in one kettle of fish and classified as Jamaicans'.[10] Islanders came to think of themselves as West Indian, while the English called them all Jamaican. Jamaica, the largest of the British West Indian colonies and source of great wealth in the eighteenth century, had always been the island best known in England and continued to dominate the English imagination.

If we then turn to the *OED* for the meaning of Negro, we find it a term firmly tied to black skin. A Negro signified 'an individual belonging to the African race of mankind, which is distinguished by a black skin, black tightly-curled hair, and a nose flatter and lips thicker and more protruding than is common amongst white Europeans'. While the West Indian could be white or black, the Negro stayed Negro locked in his or her skin and hair.[11]

Identities are brought into being through discursive or symbolic work, demarcating the self from the other. Identity is formed by 'the outside': by the interconnections of the positive presence of the self, and the negative and excluded dimensions distinguished as the other. Being English or being West Indian meant being some things and not others. This distinction between self and other, between included and excluded, carried with it a desire to mark the boundaries of social authority. That which is external to an identity, the 'outside', marks the absence or lack which is constitutive of presence. The African's 'excitability', for example, in nineteenth-century metropolitan discourse, was counterposed to the Englishman's rationality; 'excitability' signalled an incapacity for both self-restraint or self-government. Or, the African's 'indolence' was contrasted to the Englishman's capacity for hard work. Englishness and West Indianness have always existed in relation to each other: they have been mutually constitutive over a long connected history. But the colonial relation has been one of power: the British were the colonisers – English, Scots and Welsh – while the majority inhabitants of the islands – Africans, and then, following emancipation, Indians brought in as indentured labour – were the colonised. Complicating that binary division of coloniser and colonised was the ambivalent status of the white settlers, the creolised natives of the islands, who became West Indians and claimed rights of self-government from the mother country. They were both colonisers and colonised, for at critical moments their power to govern themselves was overruled by the imperial parliament, critically in the case of emancipation which the planters opposed to the end. At such times the white West Indian creoles debated the virtues of separating from the mother country and aligning themselves to those who had thrown off colonial rule in the United States.

From the moment of its 'discovery' the West Indies has always been one kind of inside/outside to Britain. In the seventeenth century it was imagined in the metropole as a frontier, a place of danger and adventure, where fortunes could be made and few questions asked.[12] Initially the

[ 35 ]

destination of buccaneers and pirates, it became transformed into the sugar-bowl of Europe, part of the great plantation settlement which stretched from the southern regions of colonial America to Brazil. By the late seventeenth century the sugar regime, dependent on the labour of enslaved Africans, was established in Barbados and Jamaica, and the West Indies became renowned as the site of slavery, where fabulous wealth could be accumulated but where no white person – let alone a white woman – would care to live. It was an unEnglish kind of place. By the eighteenth century, the historian Kathleen Wilson argues, the Caribbean was associated with 'ineffable otherness'. The wealthy planters represented forms of vulgarity, backwardness and degeneracy that inverted the standards of English civility and culture. The Caribbean became 'the secret underground self', she suggests, of English society and eighteenth-century representations of its rapacious and menacing characteristics circulated widely. Teresia Phillips, courtesan, memoirist, sexual predator and possible murderer, known in Jamaica as 'the Black Widow' and memorably invoked by Wilson, is only the most dramatic of these figures.[13]

The degeneracy of the West Indies in the English imagination is powerfully evoked in Jane Austen's *Mansfield Park*, written in the years after the slave trade had at last been abolished in 1807. Sir Thomas Bertram is the complacent patriarch who rules Mansfield Park, the comfortable gentry home in the south of England where the main part of the novel is set. But that home relies for its comforts on plantations in Antigua and when troubles erupt on the island the absentee landlord has to go himself to reassert his authority, presumably over managers and the enslaved alike. But while he is away from home the young people at Mansfield Park, no longer restrained by his patriarchal presence, abandon the decencies of respectable society and break loose with theatricals. Their performance of illicit feelings mirrors the troubles in Antigua, where slavery threatens the destruction of civility, and more generally of English ways of life. Only the return of Sir Thomas, the husband and father, secures a reordering of domestic life.[14]

White inhabitants of the West Indies, however, were determined to counter the injurious views of them propagated in the metropolis and redeem their reputations. They wrote for both West Indian and British audiences, assuming a readership across metropole and colony. These were the organic intellectuals of the white West Indies, writers who articulated a distinctive creole identity and hoped to explode metropolitan prejudices. In 1774 Edward Long, an English planter who lived in Jamaica for twelve years but whose family had long connections with the island, published his influential *History of Jamaica*. A committed Whig, Long was strongly critical of the imperial government and creole in his sympathies. He was concerned to reconcile the political liberties of the planters, Britons who had carried their natural rights as free men with them to the colonies, with the institution of slavery. Africa was imagined as a place of barbarism and terror, the West Indies a paradise in comparison.[15] Long's chosen form was history, for like all those who followed him he had to establish the West Indies as a place with its own history, rather than an extension of the mother country. He combined this with encyclopaedic information on the island. This was a book which was to be endlessly cited, its harsh deployment of fixed racial difference providing an authority apparently rooted in empirical observation. It was drawn on by successive generations of those claiming white racial supremacy. Long distinguished between creoles or natives of the island, who could be white, black or Indian. Creole, in other words, simply meant born on the island. Creolised whites had particular characteristics which distinguished them from Englishmen. The men were 'tall and well-shaped', the sockets of their eyes tended to be deeper than those of the English, for this guarded them from the glare of the sun. The effects of climate produced varieties of feature amongst Europeans, Long argued, but could not explain the distinction between black and white. Creole men were remarkable for their excellent character, as were the women, apart from a regrettable lack of education and tendency to indolence. Both men and women generally had skins 'of a fainter white' than in England, and a 'suffusion of red' from the sun which gave them a healthy complexion. The mistaken notion that they tended to swarthiness, Long opined, was because the English could not recognise the mixed parentage of those illegitimate children of the rich who were sent to expensive schools in the metropole, and passed for white. 'The genuine English breed', he insisted, 'untainted with these heterogeneous mixtures, is observed to be equally pure and delicate in Jamaica as the mother country'.[16]

By the time that Bryan Edwards, an Englishman who was a long-term resident of the island, was writing his history of Jamaica twenty years later, the accusations of metropolitan abolitionists of the immorality – especially of the sexual immorality – of the planters were in the forefront of his mind. He was determined to enlist British sympathy for the good work which the colonists believed themselves to be promoting in their rescue of Africans from barbarism. Edwards was a powerful advocate of the colonists' claims for the rights of freeborn Englishmen: these were men who had carried their natural rights with them to new settlements, outposts of the mother country. Once there, however, they developed characteristics and commitments particular to the West Indies and appropriate for the maintenance of colonial rule: their virtues were racially specific. 'There is something of a marked and predominant character common to all the white residents', he argued, the 'leading feature' of which was 'an independent spirit and a display of conscious equality throughout all ranks and conditions'.[17] The critical distinction on the island was that between freeman and enslaved, between white and black.

Lady Nugent, wife of the Governor of Jamaica in the early nineteenth century, was less kind about West Indians. She recorded her impressions of the island, and was shocked by the effects of climate, as she saw it, on the habits of the Europeans. 'In the upper ranks', she remarked, 'they become indolent and inactive, regardless of everything but eating, drinking and indulging themselves, and are almost entirely under the dominion of their mulatto favourites'. In 'the lower orders', they were even worse, for 'conceit and tyranny' were added to their vices, alongside their treatment of 'Negroes as creatures formed merely to administer to their ease, and to be subject to their caprice'.[18]

By the late 1820s the Rev. George Bridges, Rector of St Ann's Bay in Jamaica, again an Englishman who had settled in the West Indies, adopted a much shriller tone than that of the apparently moderate Bryan Edwards. Bridges too set out to defend the planters against the imprecations of what was now a powerful abolition movement. The anti-slavery activists in the metropole had set their sights on being rid of the system of slavery itself, while at the same time the enslaved were increasingly vocal in defence of their right to freedom. Bridges wanted to rally the defenders of slavery, both in the islands and at home, against the gathering threats to their interests. He aimed to justify racial inequalities, and argued that for the foreseeable future Africans needed the civilising hand of Europeans. Bridges sought to strengthen the spirit of the white population, whose exertions he saw as paralysed by the climate. 'An Englishman', he argued, 'born beneath a sky of varying temperature, is continually sensible of new impressions, which keep his senses awake. He is vigilant, active and inconstant as the air he breathes.' 'The West Indian', he continued, 'who is constantly exposed to the same intolerant temperature, to the same oppressed sensations, is listless, languid, and dejected.'[19] Such were the contrasting varieties of whiteness.

But a further complication arises from the fact that West Indian and English could also be seen as one and the same. Those in Britain who had interests or properties on the islands were also known as West Indians. From the late seventeenth century West Indians – in this sense of the term – had taken to meeting in London to defend their common cause. In 1781, as part of the reaction to the American Revolution, the Society of West India Planters and Merchants had been formed.[20] As B. W. Higman has shown, the West India interest included those 'at home' as well as in the colonies. It included 'almost every person who is connected with the colonies, either in respect of West Indian property, or as a West India merchant'. Its personnel were constituted by an inner ring of those born in the islands, who had been members of the colonial assemblies or who had held office there. There were, too, absentee planters and merchants who had never visited the colonies. Finally there were the colonial agents, relatives and friends, naval and military men who had served in the islands. The task of the West India interest was, especially as the anti-slavery movement became increasingly active, to lobby the government and counter the abolitionists. They established regular meetings, set up an active committee, raised funds to vindicate themselves when misrepresented in the press, paid an agent whose job it was to organise their interests on every front, and employed lecturers to tour the country making the case for slavery. In the unreformed House of Commons the West India interest was able to summon up considerable numbers of votes. By the early 1830s this had shrunk as the economic and political problems of the plantations discouraged investment. Eighteen peers sitting in the House of Lords were compensated after abolition, indicating that some of the British aristocracy were still substantial West Indian property owners.[21]

By 1831, when the tide was turning on the question of abolition and when its inevitability seemed increasingly certain, the House of Lords, mindful of its members' interests in the Caribbean and hoping to delay emancipation, inaugurated a Select Committee on slavery. Some of the Committee members were themselves West India proprietors. The witnesses were planters, merchants, medical and military men, judges, attorneys, colonial officials, Anglican clergy and dissenting missionaries – all those who could claim West Indian experience. One ostensible subject of investigation was the character of 'the African': what kind of a man was he, what kind of a woman was she?[22] But another preoccupation concerned white West Indians: a number of the witnesses were keen to mark off their characteristics from those of the Englishman. Every night at the West India Club the members discussed what was going on in the Committee. It was impossible, reported the planter John Baillie, for 'a West Indian to carry on a conversation when so mighty a Question is before this Committee'. Everything came back to the deliberations in the House of Lords. This was the first time that the evidence of the plantocracy, as to what life was like on the plantations, had been seriously challenged. And now it was challenged by dissenting missionaries, by men who had seen the effects of slavery with their own eyes. Those still supporting slavery told stories of contented Negroes, suffering from no coercion or severity: 'my sleek well-fed Negroes', reported the attorney William Shand, 'would form an extraordinary contrast with the wretched half-starved weavers in Angus and Kincardineshire'. The moral tone of Kingston, insisted William Burge, the paid agent of the Jamaican planters, was no lower than that of England. Indeed, it could be favourably contrasted to London. The accusations of rape and depravity on the plantations had no basis in truth. But the missionaries had other stories to tell: of the sound of the whip across the islands, of the licentiousness and cruelty, of the scale of concubinage, of the profoundly unEnglish behaviour of the West Indians. As Admiral Sir William Lawrence Halsted, who had served as a naval commander in the Caribbean, was constrained to put it, 'Of course, as an Englishman I cannot possibly advocate anything like Slavery in England'.[23] England was one thing, the West Indies another. By the 1830s it was clear that in the public mind slavery and the ideals of England could no longer coexist. West Indians, it followed, could not be English.

If there recurred a recurrent *lack* of identity between West Indian and English, so too doubts could arise about the West Indian creoles as white – the formal colouration of their skin notwithstanding. For even early in the nineteenth century, the idea of the West Indian could also signify inhabitants of the islands who were not white. In the first years of the wars with France in the 1790s, the Commander-in-Chief of the British forces in the West Indies had written to the Home Secretary. He proposed a corps of one thousand 'blacks and Mulattoes' who, he opined, would make better soldiers than the regular troops since they were accustomed to the climate. The enemy had shown the way, he pointed out: enslaved black men had been armed by the French during rebellions in San Domingue and Martinique, and had been found to be good fighters. White West Indians were appalled by such a proposal and successfully used the West India Committee to lobby against what was, to their mind, a dangerous plan. They were fearful both of British involvement in island affairs, for they greatly valued their independence, and of the spectre of armed black men. Following a Carib rising in St Vincent and Grenada, however, new regiments of black troops were authorised from London. Finding that the supplies of available men were limited the British army began to buy enslaved men, and it is estimated that at least 13,000 were bought before the abolition of the slave trade. 'The British Army became the biggest single purchaser of slaves anywhere in the Westindies [sic].'[24]

These men formed the new West India Regiments, two of which were to survive until 1926. From the beginning it was envisaged that the officers would be white and the soldiers black or coloured. Since few free men, either black or coloured, enlisted, the majority of the troops were subject to the slave code until 1807, when the British government imposed its will on the colonial assemblies and freed all serving men. From then on, free black men, stationed in the Caribbean, were central to the survival of white West Indians. The island authorities strongly objected to having these troops on their territories. Jamaica would not even countenance free men of colour for 'they would entertain notions of equality, and acquire habits pernicious to the welfare of the country'.[25] As a traveller to Jamaica wrote in 1823, 'The embodying and employing of such a corps in the West Indies is considered by the inhabitants, and doubtless with much reason, as an impolitic step. The more perfect these troops may become in their discipline, the more dangerous and formidable they would be in case of defection ...'.[26] But nor did the settlers wish to be responsible for their own defence, and so they were forced to accept the West India regiments, who throughout the nineteenth century provided military protection for the colonies and were used against black resistance and rebellions.

The naming of black regiments as West Indian fractured the prevailing image of West Indian as signifying an exclusively white identity. Similarly the militia in Jamaica, which was essential to the maintenance of white authority, included free men who were black, coloured, or Jewish (for there had been Jewish settlement on the island), though again all officers were white. As Kamau Brathwaite has pointed out, this was a creole institution from its inception in 1681, for there were too few white men to be able to have an exclusively white militia.[27] The position of free men of colour imposed another complicating factor. From the early 1790s, in the wake of the revolution in San Domingue, the so-called free coloureds in Jamaica, originally the offspring of white masters and enslaved women, who suffered from restricted economic, political and legal rights, began to make claims for equality. In 1823 a campaign began: a petition was organised across the island, the leadership made contact with the anti-slavery movement and sought British government support. In 1830, the Jamaican House of Assembly, fearful that coloured people would unite with the enslaved, granted them the same economic, legal and political rights as enjoyed by the white community. In the wake of the great rebellion of 1831 and the passing of emancipation, some coloured men formed an opposition in the House of Assembly. They argued that they represented the interests of the island more effectively than the white population, many of whom were still absentee proprietors and who believed England to be home.[28] These men were some of the first to identify themselves as distinctively Jamaican. Their home was not England but the island on which they were born, lived and died. This entrenchment of a coloured creole mentality disrupted the division between black and white and highlighted other layers of West Indian identity.

Emancipation marked a critical break in ideas about the West Indian. From 1838, the time of full emancipation, the possibility of black self-government was always present, even if envisaged to be far in the future. West Indian could no longer be conceived of as a predominantly white identity. The islands had majority black populations and the numbers of mixed-race men and women were fast increasing. These people were all there to stay. The 1820s had seen the revival of anti-slavery feeling, once it had become clear that the ending of the slave trade was not going to result in the ending of the system of slavery. The combination of a popular campaign on a massive scale, the declining fortunes of the plantations and a major revolt of the enslaved in Jamaica in 1831 led to the abolition of slavery in 1834, and of apprenticeship (a form of fixed-term labour introduced to appease the planters) in 1838. There was great enthusiasm amongst the British public for the 'great experiment' of emancipation. The abolitionist conviction that black men and women could, with education and guidance, become like white, industrious workers and domesticated wives and mothers, was widely shared. The Colonial Office expected the plantation economy to continue but believed that black men would increasingly become small property owners, acquire the franchise and eventually have significant power in island affairs. But such opinion was relatively short-lived. By the late 1840s contrary perceptions emerged in Britain as the plantation economies of the islands went from bad to worse and as the plantocracy blamed the endemic laziness of 'the Negro'.[29] Yet at the same time West Indian whites were still regarded with considerable suspicion in the metropole, as not quite white. Indeed the West Indies was increasingly seen as a troublesome place in every respect, with planters who made constant claims on the British and expected to give nothing in return, and a black population who were deemed to be lazy, thus bringing the 'gift' of emancipation into question.

It was in this moment that William Thackeray wrote *Vanity Fair*, a historical novel and one of C. L. R. James's favourites.[30] Thackeray's novel of 1847–48 offers an extraordinary imperial panorama, set at the time of Waterloo. The novel is permeated with empire – from Sambo, the Sedleys' grinning black footman who appears on the very first page, to Jos Sedley who has made his fortune in India, the Irish Colonel O'Dowd and his vulgar wife Peggy, to the hypocritical Pitt Crawley, friend of Wilberforce, with his love for Negro emancipation, the Chickasaw Indians and the Ashantee mission. And there is Miss Swartz, the West Indian heiress. From her first appearance she reminds us of racial mixing, the prevalence of which threatens all attempts to define West Indian as white. She is described as 'the rich woolly haired mulatto from St. Kitts'. She is impetuous, generous and affectionate. Her 'jet black hair' is 'as curly as Sambo's', 'her diamonds as big as pigeon eggs are set off by her mahogany complexion'. She has 'no one knows how many plantations in the West Indies, a mansion in Surrey, a house in Portland Place, a deal of money in the funds and three stars to her name in the East India stockholders list'. Her father is supposedly a German Jew, 'a slaveholder in the Cannibal Islands'. 'I'm not going to marry a Hottentot Venus', declares the insufferable George Osborne to his domineering father who wants him to marry for money.[31] The West Indian heiress carries the instability of West Indian identity inscribed on her body, and in her lack of 'polish', her ignorance, her failure to learn how to be a lady at Miss Pinkerton's Academy. She is patently not an Englishwoman, marked as she is with the polluting taint of the African. It is this threatened mixing of blood which works, decisively, to distinguish West Indians from the English.

At the same time, in 1847, Charlotte Brontë published *Jane Eyre*, with its well-known representation of West Indian degeneracy portrayed in the figure of Bertha Mason, Rochester's first wife, the mad woman in the attic, the crazed, violent, bestialised, creole figure who haunts Thornfield Hall. But Bertha is not the only West Indian in the novel. As Sue Thomas has noted, her brother Richard, who arrives from Jamaica, also carries the signs of degeneracy in his face, features and body. As Jane Eyre herself described him, he was a fine looking man at first sight, but 'his features were regular but too relaxed: his eye was large and well cut but the life looking out of it was a tame, vacant life'. He was handsome but repulsive, 'there was no power in that smooth-skinned face of a full oval shape; no firmness in that aquiline nose and small cherry mouth; there was no thought on the low, even forehead: no command in that blank, brown eye'. The contrast with the rugged, powerful, physically energetic and thinking Rochester could not be more striking.[32] Here was West Indian man and Englishman, two irreconcilable kinds of whiteness. The late 1840s saw an increasing preoccupation with racial thinking: whether in relation to the differences between one kind of whiteness and another, between Anglo-Saxons and Negroes or between Anglo-Saxons and Celts, a matter of serious concern given the growing presence of the Irish in Britain.[33]

Two years later Thomas Carlyle published his 'Occasional discourse on the Negro question', an essay which was to mark a watershed in metropolitan thinking about race. Refusing the abolitionist orthodoxy on the potential of black men and women to be civilised, Carlyle argued that white people were born to be lords and black people to be mastered. This was the lesson that should be learned from emancipation: equality between the races was neither desirable nor practical. It was also unnatural. Black men could not civilise themselves, would not work without compulsion, could not possibly govern themselves. Englishmen should face their responsibilities as empire-builders and reassert their control in the West Indies.[34]

The three most influential metropolitan books on the West Indies to be published in the second half of the nineteenth century were all written in the wake of Carlyle and indebted to him: Anthony Trollope's *The West Indies and the Spanish Main* (1859); Charles Kingsley's *At Last: a Christmas in the West Indies* (1872) and James Anthony Froude's *The English in the West Indies or The Bow of Ulysses* (1887).[35] Those of Kingsley and Froude were also written in the aftermath of the rebellion at Morant Bay in Jamaica of 1865, after which majority opinion in England had concluded that black people were certainly not yet fit for self-government.[36] All three texts were to have a long life, evident not least in the fact that they were to be much quoted by Naipaul in his gloomy assessment of Caribbean civilisation.

Trollope was in the very early days of his success as a writer when he was sent by his employer, the Post Office, to investigate postal services in the West Indies, and decided to write a travel book recording his impressions. The book was an immediate success, the first of his series of traveller's tales.[37] By the time he arrived in the Caribbean, freedom had been enjoyed for over twenty years, and in Guiana and Trinidad substantial immigration, in the form of indentured Indian labour had altered the balance of the races. It also added new complexities as to forms of belonging in the Caribbean, for when did the East Indian become West Indian? Trollope aimed to describe the peoples of the West Indies, white, black, brown and coloured, all of whom he saw as necessarily having a future in the islands. 'The Negro population is of course the most striking feature of the West Indies', he wrote, for to a white man the sight of a majority black society was indeed astonishing. The West Indian Negro knew nothing of Africa and saw himself as immeasurably superior to Africans. Yet creolised Africans were, he observed, 'a servile people in a foreign land', 'they have no country of their own, yet they have not hitherto any country of their adoption'. Inevitably, however, that creolised African had, in Trollope's mind, to be a West Indian. He was clear that slavery could never be restored for it was 'a system abhorrent to the feelings of a Christian Englishman'. Yet black men were created by God as 'an inferior race' and if left to themselves would become savage again. They had no desire to work, and labour for Trollope, as for Carlyle, was a great civiliser. They needed the guidance of those more educated and advanced and intelligent than themselves. Yet Trollope thought that the days of the Anglo-Saxons might well be over in the Caribbean, particularly in Jamaica. The white men on the island were 'hospitable, affable and generous', but they abhorred hard work and thought of England as home. They dreamed of the mother country rather than improving the island. It was the coloured men that he saw as capable of inheriting the future, though he was sharply critical of the character of coloured women, with their traditions of illicit sexuality and illegitimacy. 'Providence has sent white men and black men to these regions in order that from them may spring a race fitted by intellect for civilization; and fitted also for physical organisation for tropical labour'. Unlike many of his contemporaries, particularly the 'racial scientist' Robert Knox, Trollope favoured miscegenation and saw West Indian as a hybrid category. The coloured population, alongside the Indians and Chinese who had come to the Caribbean, represented the future. Africa could mix with Asia and the West Indies would survive without Anglo-Saxons: for they had left their mark and done their work. Like many mid-Victorians, Trollope was not convinced that dependencies (those colonies with majority non-white populations) were critical to England's future: Britain should be content to let these tropical colonies go their own way.[38]

Charles Kingsley's perspective was somewhat different. Clergyman, writer and social activist, Kingsley had been sympathetic to radicalism in the 1840s. By 1872, however, when he went to the West Indies, he had abandoned his earlier views on the potential of black men and women to become equal and was convinced that races were born into inequality. Yet for him, as for Trollope, there was no gainsaying the mixed population of the islands. Bred on the tales of his West Indian forefathers (his grandfather was a well-to-do Barbadian planter and judge, his mother born in the family home there) he had long felt a connection with the West Indies and longed to see the islands.[39] Kingsley believed that 'the gallant race of planters and merchants' was recovering its prosperity and that if only more young English men and women would emigrate they would be able to be 'a little centre of civilization for the Negro, the Coolie'. While Negroes were still savages, 'Coolies' came from a decayed and idolatrous civilisation. But if Negroes left much to be desired then the British bore responsibility for this: 'we brought him here, and we have no right to complain of our own work. If, like Frankenstein, we have tried to make a man, and made him badly; we must, like Frankenstein, pay the penalty'. Like Trollope, Kingsley saw hope in coloured people, who claimed to be, and indeed were, 'our kinsfolk', partially white, and 'a race who ought, if they will be wise and virtuous, to have before them a great future'.[40] They should be encouraged to become landholders and producers in a small way, while white people should continue to rule the islands.

By the 1880s, when Froude travelled to the West Indies, a growing body of influential English intellectuals were convinced that the destiny of the nation needed to be harnessed to the larger empire over-seas and that enthusiasm for empire needed to be revived. Froude, inti-mate friend and biographer of Carlyle, was a passionate advocate for empire, but deeply sceptical of the propriety of extending any form of self-government to dependencies where there existed a black majority population. While he believed that colonists of the white settlements were 'part of ourselves', an extension of the great Anglo-Saxon race, India, or the West Indies, or indeed Ireland, were a different matter entirely. At the time of his visit to the Caribbean there was an expec-tation in the Colonial Office that a West Indian federation would be formed, and that eventually this would be self-governing. This was the context for Froude's diatribe against black people, which turned on his conviction of the immovability of black inferiority and on his appeal to white Britons to take seriously their responsibilities in the region and recover the heroic traditions of their forefathers. He was convinced that his own generation of Englishmen could rise to the challenge and restore white influence. 'The sections of men on this globe are unequally gifted', he believed: some were strong and could govern themselves, others needed to be governed. 'It will be an ill day for mankind', he wrote, echoing Carlyle, 'if no one is to be compelled any more to obey those who are wiser than himself'. He saw no evidence of improvement amongst black men and women, 'they have shown no capacity to rise above the condition of their ancestors except under European laws'. They were servants to be ruled with impartiality. For Froude the only true West Indian was a white West Indian, an Anglo-West Indian, one who could demonstrate his connectedness with the English. 'Those beautiful West Indian islands were intended to be homes for the overflowing numbers of our own race, and the few that have gone there have been crowded out by the blacks.' It was essential that England should support those white men whom they put on those islands, for they were like 'one of our limbs'. England must once again regard 'the West Indies as essentially one with herself'.[41]

Froude's return to an insistence on white West Indians as 'part of our-selves', as the key to a Caribbean future, provides an endpoint to this preliminary charting of the shifting meanings of West Indian. For it was Froude's book which provoked J. J. Thomas, the Trinidadian school-master and educationalist, to speak back to the metropole. *Froudacity: West Indian fables explained*, first published in London in 1889, pro-vides one of the symbolic starting points for a new kind of West Indian identity – one in which brown and black men, and it was mostly men, could claim collective rights as islanders, as diasporic Africans, as West Indians, and as Britons, citizens of the empire. The history of anti-colonialism and nationalism, of the failed attempt to establish a West Indian Federation, and of the winning of independence in the British Caribbean is not my story here. Suffice it to say that what was clear from the West Indian response to Froude, in articles and letters in the press as well as in Thomas's text, was that it was no longer possible to maintain the fiction that the West Indian was white.

Thomas took it upon himself to take apart the arguments of the esteemed Oxford scholar and Victorian man of letters and to demonstrate, in their place, the capacities of black men. He deployed an inclusive notion of West Indianness, making reference to 'my fellow-West Indians, men of various races'. He insisted on the racially mixed nature of the population, and argued that this was a long established feature of the islands. But he also focused on the achievements of 'us West Indian Blacks', meaning all those of African descent.[42] As Faith Smith argues:

> To a travelogue asserting colonial incompetence, black pathology and primitivism, Caribbean backwardness, and England's continuing need to govern, Thomas systematically challenged these metropolitan assertions, offering the accomplishments of black people throughout the African diaspora as proof of the imagination and creativity that would rehabilitate African people, and stressing the ability of British Caribbean residents generally to chart their own destinies.[43]

Arguments such as this were to be replayed throughout the rest of the nineteenth and the first half of the twentieth century, as brown, black and indeed white creolised West Indians claimed their rights to citizenship, self-government and nationhood. Island nationalists had been active in the islands for some time, G. W. Gordon in Jamaica in 1865, or Theophilus Scholes or Robert Love in the 1880s and 1890s, claiming rights as Jamaicans. It was the colonial relation, the power of the metropole in defining the British territories in the Caribbean as connected, which drove nationalists towards a West Indian, alongside an island, identity.[44] For all West Indians the deep, shared experience of colonialism was a powerful bond. Yet at the same time the British had kept the islands 'unnaturally apart', in G. K. Lewis's phrase, for three centuries, for 'colonialism decreed that the avenues of communication should be between each individual West Indian fief and London rather than the territories themselves'.[45] While colonial officials from the 1860s onwards periodically proposed the idea of a West Indian federation as an administrative solution for the region, the British could barely comprehend what was required in order to foster a sense of West Indian nationhood. In the event, it was anti-colonialism which bound the island nationalists together.

It is with J. J. Thomas, as we have seen, that C. L. R. James began his construction of a tradition of distinctively West Indian intellectuals, the tradition which the chapters in this book explore. West Indian is a term which has now fallen, for the most part, into disuse. It survives as a trace of a once bolder, more visible, more heroic history. For a time West Indian was also used to describe the independent intellectual traditions which we describe in this book, and the peoples who migrated to Britain after 1945. But these traditions have now been reconstituted, as Caribbean, or African-Caribbean, or as black – raising new questions about the inclusion of Indians or Chinese or creole whites. West Indian is part of an older tradition of both colonial and anti-colonial thought. Yet even if it is a category which has been superseded, it needs to be interrogated and understood, for it illuminates not only the formation of the historical realities of the Caribbean, but of the metropole too.

The question 'What is a West Indian?' was never finally settled, as perhaps by now we might expect. In part at least such issues, turning on the dynamics of identity, remain forever open. But the chapters which follow pose further questions, which may be equally difficult to resolve. How do the many varieties of Caribbean thought, formed deep in the histories of colonialism, speak to our own historical present? And how can they illuminate the contemporary mentalities of the old metropolis?

## Notes

1   Thanks to Stuart Hall, Bill Schwarz, Gail Lewis, all the participants at the two-day symposium on this collection of essays and those who discussed a version of my paper at the Caribbean seminar, Institute of Commonwealth Studies, November 2001.
2   C. L. R. James, 'The West Indian intellectual', introduction to the New Beacon edition of J. J. Thomas's *Froudacity: West Indian fables explained* (London and Port of Spain: New Beacon, 1969), pp. 27 and 45.
3   See Simon Gikandi, 'The embarrassment of Victorianism: colonial subjects and the lure of Englishness', in John Kucich and Diane Sardoff (eds), *The Post-Victorian Frame of Mind* (Minneapolis: University of Minnesota Press, 1999).
4   C. L. R. James, 'Lectures on *The Black Jacobins'*, *Small Axe*, 8 (2000).
5   Anthony Bogues, 'Afterword', *Small Axe*, 8 (2000), p. 114.
6   Faith Smith, 'A man who knows his roots: J. J. Thomas and current discourses of black nationalism', *Small Axe*, 5 (1999).
7   V. S. Naipaul, *The Middle Passage* (London: André Deutsch, 1962), pp. 27–9.
8   It should also be noted that since my own historical work has focused on Jamaica my knowledge of the West Indies is heavily skewed in that direction. Furthermore, as a historian of the nineteenth century, my inquiry is centred on that period.
9   John La Rose, 'All are consumed', in Bhikhu Parekh (ed.), *Colour, Culture and Consciousness: immigrant intellectuals in Britain* (London: Allen and Unwin, 1974), p. 120. I am grateful to Anna Snaith for this reference.
10  Sam Selvon, 'Three into one can't go', in David Dabydeen and Brinsley Samaroo (eds), *India in the Caribbean* (London: Hansib, 1987), pp. 16–17.
11  I am not dealing here with the shifts in terminology associated with blackness. See, for example, Stuart Hall, 'New ethnicities', in David Morley and Kuan-Hsing Chen (eds), *Stuart Hall: critical dialogues in cultural studies* (London: Routledge, 1996).

12  Richard S. Dunn, *The Rise of the Planter Class in the English West Indies 1624–1713* (London: Cape, 1973).

13  Kathleen Wilson, *The Island Race: Englishness, empire and gender in the eighteenth century* (London: Routledge, 2003).

14  Jane Austen, *Mansfield Park* (Harmondsworth: Penguin, 1966; first published 1814). For a particularly interesting reading of this see Moira Ferguson, 'Mansfield Park: plantocratic paradigms', in her *Colonialism and Gender Relations from Mary Wollstonecraft to Jamaica Kincaid: East Caribbean connections* (New York: Columbia University Press, 1993).

15  Elsa V. Goveia, *A Study on the Historiography of the British West Indies to the End of the Nineteenth Century* (Mexico City: Instituto Panamericano de Geografía e Historia, 1956).

16  Edward Long, *The History of Jamaica*, 3 vols (London: Frank Cass, 1970; first published 1774). See especially Book II, pp. 261–85.

17  Bryan Edwards, *The History, Civil and Commercial, of the British Colonies in the West Indies*, 4 vols (Philadelphia: James Humphreys, 1806), vol. 2, p. 202.

18  Lady Maria Nugent, *Lady Nugent's Journal: Jamaica one hundred years ago*, ed. Frank Cundall (London: West India Committee for the Institute of Jamaica, 1934), p. 131.

19  George Wilson Bridges, *The Annals of Jamaica*, 2 vols (London: Frank Cass, 1968; first published 1828), vol. 2, pp. 10–11.

20  Edward Brathwaite, *The Development of Creole Society in Jamaica* (Oxford: Clarendon, 1971), p. 111.

21  B. W. Higman, 'The West Indian "interest" in parliament 1807–33', *Historical Studies*, 13:49 (1967), pp. 1–19.

22  For a longer discussion of this see Catherine Hall, *Civilising Subjects: metropole and colony in the English imagination 1830–1867* (Cambridge: Polity, 2002), especially pp. 107–15.

23  *Parliamentary Papers* 1831–32 (127) CCCVI, vols 11 and 12, Select Committee of the House of Lords on the state of the West India Colonies: vol. 11, pp. 93, 239 and 299.

24  Brian Dyde, *The Empty Sleeve: the story of the West India Regiments of the British Army* (St John's, Antigua: Hansib Caribbean, 1997), pp. 15 and 23.

25  Dyde, *The Empty Sleeve*, p. 25.

26  J. Stewart, *A View of the Past and Present State of the Island of Jamaica*, quoted in Dyde, *The Empty Sleeve*, p. 61.

27  Brathwaite, *The Development of Creole Society*, p. 26.

28  On this history see Gad J. Heuman, *Between Black and White: race, politics and the free coloreds in Jamaica 1792–1865* (Westport, Conn.: Greenwood, 1987).

29  For a longer discussion of this see Hall, *Civilising Subjects*.

30  C. L. R. James, *Beyond a Boundary* (London: Hutchinson, 1963).

31  William M. Thackeray, *Vanity Fair* (Harmondsworth: Penguin, 1968; first published 1848–49) pp. 42, 244–5 and 256.

32  Charlotte Brontë, *Jane Eyre* (Harmondsworth: Penguin, 1966; first published 1847), p. 219; Sue Thomas, 'The tropical extravagance of Bertha Mason', *Victorian Literature and Culture*, 27:1 (1999), pp. 1–17.

33  Nancy Leys Stepan, *The Idea of Race in Science: Great Britain 1800–1960* (London: Macmillan, 1982); Christine Bolt, *Victorian Attitudes to Race* (London: Routledge and Kegan Paul, 1971).

34  Thomas Carlyle, 'Occasional discourse on the Negro question', *Fraser's Magazine*, 40 (Dec. 1849), pp. 670–9.

35  These three texts have all been extensively discussed by various authors. For a most illuminating reading see Simon Gikandi, *Maps of Englishness: writing identity in the culture of colonialism* (New York: Columbia University Press, 1996), especially chapter 3. My emphasis here is exclusively on the relevance of their writing to the question as to what is a West Indian.

36  Bernard Semmel, *The Governor Eyre Controversy* (London: McGibbon and Kee, 1962).

37   For a longer discussion see Hall, *Civilising Subjects*, pp. 209–29.

38   Anthony Trollope, *The West Indies and the Spanish Main* (London: Chapman and Hall, 1859), pp. 55–6, 61–3, 75, 81, 84, 98 and 226.

39   Charles Kingsley, *His Letters and Memories of his Life*, edited by his wife. 4 vols (London: Macmillan, 1901); Susan Chitty, *The Beast and the Monk: a life of Charles Kingsley* (London: Hodder and Stoughton, 1974).

40   Charles Kingsley, *At Last: a Christmas in the West Indies* (London: Macmillan, 1872), pp. 7, 90, 130 and 297–8.

41   James Anthony Froude, *The English in the West Indies, or The Bow of Ulysses* (London: Longmans, Green and Co., 1909; first published 1887), pp. 4–5, 182–4, 207–8, 252, 306 and 318–20.

42   Thomas, *Froudacity*, pp. 60 and 123.

43   Smith, 'A man who knows his roots', p. 2.

44   Patrick Bryan, *The Jamaican People 1880–1902* (Basingstoke: Macmillan with the University of Warwick, 1991). Thanks to Gad Heuman for drawing my attention to Robert Love.

45   Gordon K. Lewis, *The Growth of the Modern West Indies: perspectives on a new nation* (Westport, Conn.: Greenwood, 1961), p. 18.

# CHAPTER TWO

# 'To do something for the race': Harold Moody and the League of Coloured Peoples

David Killingray

In the century following 1850 the West Indies produced a steady flow of West Indian intellectuals, predominantly men, who either spent short spells of time in Europe and North America or who lived outside the Caribbean for a good part of their lives. A significant early figure was Edward W. Blyden;[1] in the twentieth century there were Marcus Garvey, George Padmore, C. L. R. James, Eric Williams and the Nobel prizewinner, W. Arthur Lewis.[2] But there are many more less well-known figures who contributed to the intellectual life of the Caribbean consistently to challenge prevailing views of race and empire: J. J. Thomas whose brief book *Froudacity* criticised the prejudices of the eminent English historian James Froude; Samuel Jules Celestine Edwards from Dominica, dead at an early age while editing *Lux*, the London journal of the Christian Evidence Society;[3] that sharp critic of politics and imperial racism, the Jamaican doctor Theophilus Scholes; Henry Sylvester Williams who organised the first Pan-African Congress in London in 1900; and the medical doctors John Alcindor, James Jackson Brown and Harold Moody, all of whom had practices in London in the early part of the twentieth century.

Harold Moody is in many ways an underrated figure.[4] Recently published accounts of Pan-Africanism and black political activity in Britain pay some attention to Moody and the League of Coloured Peoples which he founded in 1931, but the tendency is to give pride of place to radicals such as Padmore and James.[5] Moody's Christian, calculated and cautious agenda in combating what was known in the first half of the twentieth century as the colour bar, was often seen by black radical activists to have been Fabian and too conservative. Indeed, the Communist paper, *The Negro Worker*, in 1933 attacked Moody with that misused label, an 'Uncle Tom'.[6] However, distaste for Moody and his methods did not prevent some radicals from seeking the company, charity, comfort, cash and contacts which his home and the League afforded them. Moody was also prepared on occasions to work with them 'for the sake of the race'. While leftist radicals in the 1930s talked in terms of kicking down the doors of authority, Moody's policy was to knock politely, wait to be admitted, and then to argue for wrongs to be righted. As a result Moody was invited in to government and private offices, listened to by people in positions of influence and, although they might often disparage his activities, his persistence in lobbying did yield some results as he challenged the prevailing policies and practices of racial discrimination in Britain and the colonial empire.

## Moody's formative years

Harold Moody was born in Kingston, Jamaica, in 1882, the son of a pharmacist, although the most enduring influence on his development as a young man was clearly his mother who had little formal education but was a very forceful presence. Moody's childhood home was loving and secure; he was encouraged to study and as a serious-minded boy he did well at school, although not quite well enough (and here colour may have been a factor in that race-conscious colony) to secure a prized 'island scholarship'. Nevertheless, in 1904 he sailed for Britain to study medicine at King's College London.

After completing his studies, Moody married in 1913 a white English woman, Olive Tranter, a nurse whom he met while working on the wards of the Royal Eye Hospital in London. Rejected for a hospital post at King's College Hospital because of his colour, he set up a medical practice in Peckham, south London, where he remained for the rest of his life. He returned to Jamaica on only three occasions, in 1912, 1919 and 1946–47. He made his life in London, convinced that this was the place where he should be, initially to help one of his younger brothers through university,[7] but also in order to combat racial prejudice. Increasingly in demand as a preacher Moody used the pulpit to pro-claim to predominantly white congregations the Christian message of a colour-blind society, which he believed essential if the British empire were to survive. By the late 1920s Moody realised that the ingrained racial prejudice that he continued to experience in Britain needed to be opposed by more systematic action and better directed pressure. In 1931, with the support of Quakers, he founded the League of Coloured Peoples (LCP), a multi-racial lobby which began to campaign for full civil rights for black people in Britain, and which came increasingly to condemn white racial superiority in the empire overseas. As preacher, lobbyist and campaigner Moody drove himself hard. In the spring of 1947 he returned home from a strenuous tour of the West Indies and died twelve days later at the age of sixty-four.

Harold Moody certainly thought of himself as an intellectual. In the context of his considerable achievements, coming from an island with a high level of non-literacy and low level of formal education, that was an easy assumption for a man with advanced medical qualifications – he gained an MD in 1919 – who read widely and intelligently on theology, history, contemporary politics and economics, and who also spoke and wrote words that were widely promoted and reported. Moody's intellectual capacities enabled him to set the racial problems that he encountered in their historical context; but he was also practically minded in actively seeking strategies to deal with racial prejudice. He firmly believed that intellect was God-given; that the mind had to be used to its full extent and particularly for human good; and, as a black Jamaican, that included striving for the 'good of the race'. But there was probably another element. Moody came from the 'brown middle class' in a colonial society that was highly conscious of race, and that undoubtedly drove him to prove his intellectual worth before white people. Jamaicans who had received a higher education, Moody believed, had clear responsibilities. Writing in 1932 he argued that Jamaicans should not seek to emulate the 'manner(s), behaviour and bearing' of white people and to be 'ashamed of his own colour and his own heritage'. 'Herein, to my mind', he wrote, 'lies the main reason why so few intellectual Jamaicans do anything actively to help on their own race. We are not proud of it. We do not belong to it. We want to pass into the ranks of our white rulers.' Moody included himself within this educated class and urged that we 'identify ourselves with the masses and make their inaudible cry our own', and not to abandon Jamaica in order 'to find a better livelihood either in America, Canada or Britain'.[8]

Moody published relatively little: a few pamphlets, regular contributions to the LCP journal *The Keys* and to its wartime successor *News Letter,* as well as several manuscripts including an unpublished book entitled *Race Problems*.[9] At the same time there were his many sermons and addresses delivered to congregations and audiences up and down the country and often reported, sometimes verbatim, in provincial newspapers and in the Christian press and magazines. Much of what he said and wrote had a similar message. Occasionally Moody's talks were broadcast by the BBC, including wartime talks to the West Indies. In addition there are his numerous campaigning letters to government departments and individuals. In his surviving papers there exists the interleaved Bible, which he received as a prize at King's College, his many annotations providing further insight into his intellectual development, particularly into his theological and political ideas.[10]

[ 53 ]

In this chapter I will examine two matters: first, the influences that shaped Harold Moody's thinking and behaviour; and second, how those beliefs were applied throughout his active life in countering racial prejudice and promoting the interests of black peoples.

Moody's formative years and early education in late nineteenth-century colonial Jamaica exposed him to the pernicious influences of a social order based on colour discrimination, and gave shape to his later ideas and perceptions of a colour-blind society based solely on merit. Jamaica's social structure was largely determined by a hierarchy of colour, a pigmentocracy; people with lighter coloured skins – brown Jamaicans – headed the social and economic order while those with darker skins were mainly at the bottom. Moody was black although his father was brown and his paternal grandfather white. As a child Moody's mother, although dark in complexion, urged her son to find companions amongst those who were lighter in colour, believing this to be the way for his social advance.

The educational system in Jamaica encouraged all Jamaicans, regardless of social origin or complexion, to think of themselves as British. The curriculum in the primary schools, and particularly so in the few secondary schools, was anglocentric, functioning as a principal means by which the ideals of the British way were projected into the colony. At Wolmer's Free School, a mixed-race secondary school in Kingston, Jamaica, Moody's mind was shaped by ideas from British books and white teachers, a fare very similar to that offered to schoolboys thousands of miles away in Kingston, England. In his early years in London as a medical student Moody recalled that he 'sought to become as much English as I could and to discard everything Jamaican'. This was associated with a deep antipathy to any idea of an African origin, as he recollected towards the end of his life:

> I had been educated away from my heritage and towards the country which I had learnt to call 'home'. My desire then was to have as little as possible to do with my own people and upon Africans I looked down as a species too low in the rank of human development for me in any way to associate with. I was black indeed but I was not African, nor was I in any way related to Africa. To what family of man I belonged I really did not know. At heart I really believed I was English.[11]

Moody only began to take pride in his Jamaican and African heritage after many years' experience of encountering racial antipathy in Britain. It was a gradual realisation that black people, whether from the Caribbean or from Africa, had a common identity and experience shaped by slavery and colonial subjugation. In 1927, addressing a missionary meeting on Africa at the City Temple, in London, Moody spoke firmly of his 'pride as I contemplate the pit from which I was dug, and feel overwhelmed with satisfaction to belong to a race which has its whole future yet to achieve'.[12] Twenty years later, on his last visit to Jamaica, he declared: 'I have never been more a Jamaican than I am today. I believe in Jamaica ... As a son of the soil, I want to do, what I believe is the desire of every true Jamaican, everything in my power to further the very best interests of the land of my birth.'[13] Moody's path to recognising his black and African-descended identity was a slow one, but it was firmly forged by his struggle in confronting British racism.

## Moody's Christian faith

The most decisive influence in Moody's life was his conversion to Christianity as a teenager in the late 1890s. Thereafter reading the Bible, prayer and the practice of a Christian life underpinned his life. He did little that was not accompanied by lengthy prayer and this often gave him a conviction that he was about God's purposes, arising out of his belief in a God who was holy, righteous and active in a world corrupted by sin.[14] Moody's faith was the mainspring of his life. If C. L. R. James's values stemmed from the ethos of the public school and the manners of the cricket field, then Moody certainly could recognise the influence of the former. However, much more enduring for him was the moral and spiritual teaching of his home and that which he received from the North Street Congregational Church and the Christian Endeavour branch in Kingston.[15]

Congregationalism combined a thoughtful, critical Biblicalism with a social agenda which appealed to the serious and scholarly-minded Moody. Many Congregationalists, including Moody, had a high view of the Bible but not one that shunned critical hermeneutics. Before he left Jamaica he had read Ernest Renan's de-deifying *Life of Jesus*. He was also familiar with Darwinian evolutionary ideas, confiding in his Bible that the critical question was not 'how' creation happened but that God's hand was behind it. As a young medical student he seems to have thought of offering himself as a medical missionary in Africa, and thereafter he retained a deep and active involvement in the work of the London Missionary Society, becoming chairman in 1943. When he arrived in London, Moody immediately attached himself to a Congregational church, and from then on he was active in the Congregational Union, both locally and nationally, as a Sunday school teacher, deacon and lay preacher. In the mid 1940s his name was on the list of those under consideration as a future chairman of the Congregational Union. He continued to be associated with Christian Endeavour, becoming London, and then national, president of the Union in the 1930s. Another movement with which he was always

pleased to be associated was the Christian Brotherhood, a largely noncon-
formist organisation that flourished during the Edwardian years offering
working men the Gospel and social improvement.[16]

Christian doctrine underwrote Moody's ideas of humanity and race.
In a pamphlet addressed to young members of Christian Endeavour, he
said:

> Christ came to help me to realise that in spite of all my failings I was
> worth dying for; as one of His followers, I must impact to each man, no
> matter how degraded he may be at the moment, a consciousness of the
> fact that he was created in the image of God, and that it is possible for
> him to rise into that likeness, and recognise that 'I too am a man'.[17]

A text much used by Moody in his sermons was the Apostle Paul's revolutionary statement to the Judaeo-Greek Christian church in Galatia:
'There is neither Jew nor Greek, there is neither bond nor free, there is
neither male nor female: for ye are all one in Christ Jesus'.[18] In calcu-
latedly preaching from such texts, Moody challenged his mainly white
congregations to practise their Christian lives in a way that ran directly
counter to the endemic racial prejudice in British society, and from
which active Christians were not exempt. All people were equal in
God's sight and the colour bar, whether practised in Britain or in the
empire, was contrary 'to the principles and teaching of our Lord Jesus
Christ, who used every possible opportunity to put the so-called
despised and outcast in the best possible light', the Samaritan, the
Roman, the Greek and Syrophoenician, gentiles, white and black,
Christ had died for all without exception.[19] In the1930s, at a time when
fascism and Communism appealed to corporate identity, Moody
stressed Christianity's emphasis on individual worth, arguing that
Jesus Christ had said 'the very hairs on your head are numbered', and
more pointedly, Moody claimed, that 'Every one is a child for whom
Christ died'.[20]

Christian redemption was for all without exception. But this was
personal salvation by which individual lives were transformed by
Christ's saving grace. Integral to the spiritual challenge was the conviction that people of different races and cultures should genuinely love
and accept one another without distinction. Moody did not think that
collective social attitudes could be changed or engineered in the short
term. His social and political agenda was evolutionary not revolutionary. Faced with widespread British ignorance and race prejudice which
extended from the Cabinet table to the slum bar, Moody knew that to
counter this would take generations. The process of educating white
British people, of changing social and cultural attitudes would require,
he concluded, the force of legislative intervention. On the other hand,

in the short term it might be possible to bring about change in official attitudes and policies by direct pressure on Whitehall. In this dual process of persuasion and pressure, Moody enlisted the help of white people of influence. At the same time he firmly believed that black people had an important role to play: they had to demonstrate their worth and to combine with progressive interests, including white people, to advance the interests of black civil rights. Thus Moody had a high regard for Booker T. Washington's achievements in the United States although he was not uncritical of his policies.[21] In Moody's assessment Christian piety, hard work, merit and commitment to the cause were qualities he prized most highly.

Moody was a great publicist, seeking opportunities wherever he could to speak against the colour bar, using the pulpits and platforms offered by his own Congregational Union and those of other noncon-formists, the Brotherhood Movement and the Quakers, Anglican churches and cathedrals, and secular organisations such as the Colonial Institute, and Save the Children Fund. He was probably most comfort-able in a pulpit where preachers were above contradiction. There is no evidence that he spoke on the stump or out of doors, though he had prob-ably done so as a teenager in Jamaica and while a student at King's College during a rural mission in Bedfordshire. He liked to have his life ordered; he was no tub-thumper or populist although no doubt he would have coped well if Speakers' Corner had been the only platform avail-able. In any case, he was a busy man with a large medical practice and a growing family of six children. Although his income was considerable, in excess of £3,000 in 1938, so was his expenditure, not least on the private schooling and university fees for his children, while he gave gen-erously to finance the League of Coloured Peoples.

He preached most Sundays throughout his life, sometimes several times a weekend, invariably proclaiming a Christian message of salva-tion but also social inclusiveness and racial harmony. As a physically large man he had a forceful presence on a platform; his sermons and speeches, usually Biblically based, were presented in an authoritative voice; they were well structured, spiced with vivid illustrations and contemporary evidence. Political comment was not ignored. He was a popular and much sought after speaker; being black may indeed have lent weight to that appeal, but Moody rarely allowed condescension to keep him from a chance to speak out. Racial prejudice he commonly referred to as 'a mental and spiritual disease which has taken a heavy toll of human happiness'.[22] More forcefully he denounced it as a product of fear, a sin of pride. In so doing he did not exempt black people from the charge, stating that it was 'a common sin of all peoples throughout history'.[23]

He frequently drew on his scientific knowledge to discount popular ideas of racial hierarchies: 'Scientifically all men are equal', he often proclaimed, drawing support from another favourite text from a Pauline sermon that 'God hath made of one blood all nations of men'.[24] Speaking in Wolverhampton in October 1929 he declared that Africa was the cradle of humanity and that 'examined scientifically, anatomically, or physiologically, there is nothing in the organic make-up of coloured people that implies inferiority'.[25] He also employed medical metaphors to illustrate the effects of racial prejudice, which he frequently described as 'an infection in the blood stream' or a virus infecting society.

Temperance, the welfare of children and pacifism were other causes that Moody embraced. He eschewed alcohol and tobacco, devoted some of his energies to the Save the Children Fund, and spoke out against war and armaments. The Great War convinced him that war was immoral and un-Christian, but those convictions may have been in his mind before 1914.[26] Nevertheless, for the rest of his life he was a pacifist. However, the outbreak of war in 1939 – the LCP had long denounced the racial policies of Nazi Germany – taxed his convictions. Before the outbreak of the war, Moody and the LCP lent weight to the campaign to amend King's Regulations which stated that commissions could only be granted to those of 'pure European parentage'. In 1941 Moody's son, Arundel, received an army commission as did several of his other children during the war years. The lucrative business of munitions manufacturers, 'those terrible Pharaohs', earned Moody's ire as did the compromise and passivity of the churches with their 'desultory prayers' as they embraced nationalism and denied 'Christ the Prince of Peace'. War was slavery, Moody argued as he praised the Oxford students in the spring of 1933 for 'refusing to fight "for King and Country"', and appealed 'for an anti-war pact by the churches'.[27]

## Racial prejudice in Britain

From the moment that Harold Moody landed in Avonmouth in the autumn of 1904 he ran into racial prejudice expressed both overtly and in various subtle forms. The black population of Britain then may have numbered 10,000, mainly concentrated in port cities, with a small number of black people, some occupying professional positions, scattered throughout the country.[28] As a black student seeking lodgings in London Moody was rebuffed on several occasions. Black people were often stared at by people in the street; rude and curious street children shouted catcalls. Non-Europeans, especially Africans, were displayed on the stage or in 'tribal villages' at international exhibitions. Few Britons were well informed enough to distinguish between people from Africa and those who came from the Caribbean. Moody's spoken English was frequently marvelled at by those who patronisingly invited him to tea; even in later life provincial newspaper reports complimented him on his fluency in the language.[29] Even some of his friends within the Christian Union at King's College proved to be jealous of his achievements and sought to slight him because of his colour. When he complained of racial prejudice he was told that he had a 'chip on his shoulder'.

One aspect of race prejudice that Moody lived with, and which he often argued against, was over what were called 'mixed marriages' and the children produced from those relationships. Moody was himself the product of parents and grandparents of different colours. When he planned to marry Olive Tranter in 1912 her family objected, but so did his parents in Jamaica: 'the only painful letter which I had from my beloved Mother, was the one in reply to the information I gave her of my proposed marriage'.[30] A friend of the couple told Olive that by marrying a black man she was letting down the white race; acquaintances, and even strangers, openly told them that children from such a marriage would result in social degeneracy. It is hardly surprising that Moody spoke and wrote often on the question of inter-racial marriage and that he took a pride in the educational progress of his children, most of whom entered the professions. As a new, well-qualified doctor, he was denied a hospital post at King's because a matron would not have a black man on her wards. Several years later, when his medical practice was well established in south London, the Camberwell Guardians rejected Moody's application to serve as a poor law doctor on the grounds that the poor 'would not have a nigger to attend them'.[31]

His expanding medical practice, his growing number of preaching engagements, and the respectable position that he occupied, meant that during and after the first world war a stream of black nurses and students came to his Peckham door in search of his support after they had been refused positions promised at hospitals. Other men who came to his house during the war were graduates and professionals refused military commissions, some even being rejected at recruiting stations as they sought to enlist in the ranks. Critics of the LCP condemned Moody for being only concerned with the interests and welfare of middle-class people. It is true that in the early years he had much more to do with black professionals. However, the LCP campaigned for the rights of black British seamen who were put on the aliens' register, and took up the cause of working-class black people who fell foul of racial abuse. A glance through the pages of Moody's visitors' book for the 1940s shows a steady stream of black people of all social backgrounds visiting and staying at 164 Queen's Road in

Peckham.[32] Moody welcomed them as he did elite figures, because he was doing 'something for the race'.

## The Lobbyist

Racial prejudice was if anything more pronounced in the two decades following the first world war. There were more black people in Britain than before and the earlier curiosity and submerged spirit of tolerance had been slowly overtaken by a harsher perception of non-Europeans. For all his efforts preaching and speaking against the colour bar – and Moody probably addressed many more white people on this issue than did any one else from the 1920s until his death in 1947 – it was a Sisyphean struggle. Perhaps most hurtful to Moody was the lack of sympathetic understanding of his cause from his close associates in the London Missionary Society on whose councils he sat. Middle-class whites knew nothing of the slights and rebuffs that their confident black colleague and fellow Christian had experienced. Even less could they envisage what it was like to be a black person in a sea of white hostility and indifference: a black skin meant for many that employment was refused, doors to accommodation slammed shut, entry to hotels, restaurants and public houses denied, and those who married across the colour line ran the risk of obloquy. When the distinguished actor Paul Robeson was refused service at the Savoy Grill in London in autumn 1929, the insult was reported in the press as a scandal.[33] Many black people suffered similar and worse rebuffs on a daily basis and yet their injuries went unheard and unreported.

Moody did not think that the pulpit and the sermon had to be abandoned but by the late 1920s he did come to recognise that a parallel strategy was needed. This would still have a Christian focus but would go outside the churches in order to cultivate secular forces that could help apply added pressure in combating racial prejudice. Moody appears not to have joined any of the small and often short-lived black pressure groups that had been created in Britain, mainly by students and professionals, in the period after 1918. He does not figure in the meetings of bodies such as the African Progress Union and the Society of Peoples of African Origin. He cannot have been unaware of their existence and indeed he must have known of the Committee for the Welfare of Africans in Europe, established in 1919, which had close links with the Student Christian Movement and with which the Rev. John Harris was closely involved.[34] That kind of organisation was one to which Moody would have been sympathetically inclined. His non-involvement was probably due to his heavy commitments as doctor, family man and preacher. At the same time he had his own agenda and circuit. However,

[ 60 ]

in December 1927 Moody did speak at the London service of the Union of Students of African Descent (USAD), a group which had grown out of the London-based and apolitical West African and West Indian Christian Union. His address contained references to African nationalism and self-determination for Africa and, inevitably, to the race situation in Britain, concluding with the critical prayer that 'the British people will do their utmost to repair the past – oh, God, give us grace'.[35]

By the mid 1920s the USAD was acting as a political pressure group on questions of racial discrimination, stimulated by the Nigerian law student Lapido Solanke who, in 1925, was a founder member of the West African Students Union (WASU).[36] Moody knew Solanke, for later the LCP was to clash with the WASU over the question of control of Aggrey House, a student hostel in London. By the late 1920s Moody was in his mid-forties, far removed from student politics and the world in which those affairs were conducted. He was also a West Indian whereas most of the leading lights in these black organisations and political groups were from West Africa. Geographical origins made for personal and territorial disputes, while some West Indians were not averse to looking down on Africans.

## The League of Coloured Peoples

By late 1929 an increased number of reports in the national press of instances of the 'colour bar occurring ... in certain hotels' stimulated a group of Quakers, led by John Fletcher and members of various missionary bodies, along with representatives of the Labour and Liberal parties, to convene a series of meetings at Friends House in order to discuss how to combat the colour bar. Moody was among those who attended along with James Marley, Labour MP for North St Pancras, the feminist novelist Winifred Holtby and C. P. Scott, editor of the *Manchester Guardian*. The result was the creation in January 1931 of the Joint Council to promote Understanding between White and Coloured People in Great Britain, which had as its principal aim 'to overcome colour prejudice in this country'.[37] Sir Francis Younghusband was the chairman, Moody the vice-chairman; other members included Vera Brittain, Professor C. G. Seligman and Lancelot Hogben.[38]

The day before the Joint Council was inaugurated, Moody had attended a meeting of the Missionary Council which had set up a Sub-Committee on Africans in England. The sub-committee reported in March 1931 and suggested the need for 'one union' of all coloured people to deal with problems of the colour bar and to help black people adjust to life in Britain.[39] Moody had eyes on leading that 'one union' and in this idea he appears to have been encouraged by Dr Charles Wesley, an

African-American professor of history at Howard University, active in the National Association for the Advancement of Colored Peoples (NAACP), who was visiting Britain as a Guggenheim Fellow. A preliminary meeting, 'attended principally by coloured students from the Colonies', was held in the Central London YMCA in March 1931.[40] Moody clearly had in mind a body on the lines of the NAACP, an organisation big enough 'which would capture the imagination of the black and white peoples'.[41] In June of that year, at a meeting called by Moody in the Memorial Hall, Farringdon Street, London, attended by a mixed race audience including Paul Robeson and Ellen Wilkinson MP, the League of Coloured Peoples was inaugurated.[42]

Although the LCP was a multi-racial body, Moody's intention was that it should be led solely by black people. Race was clearly a central motif of the League and from the outset Moody proclaimed his Pan-African credentials. According to his biographer Moody decided to found another organisation because:

> The Christian Church had many tasks and could not leave all the others to concentrate on this one. Missionary Societies were intimately concerned with this question and it had a real bearing on their work, but it was not the reason for their existence. The same was true of all other sympathetic organisations and societies.[43]

Besides promoting the interests of its members, the other major objects of the LCP were 'to interest members in the welfare of coloured peoples in all parts of the world' and 'to improve relations between the races'. The LCP was the first black-led organisation to give effective voice to West Indians and West Africans living in Britain. It was dominated by Moody, with key positions at times occupied by members of his family, and largely sustained by subscriptions which he solicited from supportive church groups supplemented by his own money. The paid-up membership of the League never rose above a few hundred and *The Keys*, its journal, had a similarly small circulation; expenditure invariably outstripped income. The LCP executive was mainly West Indian with some Africans and an occasional Asian member. Prominent roles were played by the cricketer Learie Constantine, W. Arthur Lewis, and later Hugh Springer. Paul Robeson lent his support to early LCP activities, although as the 1930s progressed his sympathies increasingly lay with the more radical James–Padmore grouping. Over the next fifteen years, until Moody's death, the League lobbied, campaigned and protested to change the domestic scene of race relations; its remit also extended to colonial issues, and to any other matter, such as that of the Scottsboro Boys, where race was a central issue. However, on the latter cause Moody was characteristically careful in his selection of his allies.[44]

[ 62 ]

Moody regarded the LCP as a Christian organisation. This is clear from the regular church services held in the name of the LCP, the Christian language in the early issues of the League's journal, *The Keys*, and the prayers written in Moody's Bible in which he sought the Almighty's help in conducting League affairs. The League's multi-racial focus was indicated by the title given to its journal which Moody took from Aggrey's aphorism that musical harmony was only possible when the black and white keys of the piano were played together.[45] Nevertheless, *The Keys*, first published in spring 1933, constantly stressed black achievement. In its early years the LCP acted more as a social welfare society, holding meetings, arranging sporting activities, and helping to arrange summer outings in the country for poor black children from the capital. Many West Indian and West African students were active members of the LCP – W. Arthur Lewis, for example, the future Nobel prizewinner – but its racial embrace also included C. L. R. James who spoke at an early conference and contributed to *The Keys*.[46] Moody successfully recruited white elite support for the League: Margery Perham, Professor Malinowski, and Lord Lugard were all associated,[47] while colonial governors and academics were invited to address League meetings. This helped promote the LCP's image of reasoned seriousness while also identifying, even if only by name, influential people whose support could be claimed in the cause of race relations.

The League was energetic in confronting the colour bar. Much of the energy came from Moody himself. Racist language was challenged whether it was on the BBC, in parliament or in the press; letters were written to departments of state, and on major issues delegations lobbied the Colonial Office; and on less exalted matters – securing positions for black nurses, for example – the League was active. Common humanity was stressed by Moody although he often proclaimed the significant role of Africa in the history of the world and the names of 'really great Africans and persons of African descent', invariably men with whom he thought he could most easily identify such as the late nineteenth-century Tswana leader, Khama, Booker T. Washington and Aggrey. Moody once stated: 'I am proud of my British citizenship, but I am still more proud of my colour, and I do not want to feel that my colour is going to rob me of any of the privileges to which I am entitled as a British citizen'.[48] But inevitably this meant that black people had to prove themselves to white people, to demonstrate that they were worthy of respect which invariably required a polite passivity.

Moody was delighted the LCP secured the support of prominent, especially titled, women. Titles, after all, helped open doors. League administration relied heavily on women. This included Olive Moody, although probably she often resented the intrusions into family life

[ 63 ]

of League activities, and Moody's elder daughter Christine, who for several years served as LCP secretary. Another active female member was Una Marson, the Jamaican poet and broadcaster, who on her arrival in Britain lodged with the Moodys in Peckham, as Alison Donnell describes in her chapter. The LCP offered a more sympathetic home for many black women than did the male-dominated WASU or the marxist bodies, with their often cold radical rigour.

Racial prejudice, Moody believed firmly, was partly cultivated by the use of pejorative language and by stereotypical images of black people in schools, books, the press and films. The LCP challenged both the media and schools. In 1944 it set up a committee to inquire into how questions of race were handled in English schools. The result was a pamphlet entitled *Race Relations and the School*, produced by a committee of six educationalists, including Kenneth Little, with a foreword provided by the historian G. P. Gooch.[49] This critically examined school textbooks, and went on to advocate radical changes in the elementary and secondary school curriculum, including the adoption of courses of world history and the study of Africa and Asia. Although well received by several academics the report made little impact on the educational world or the school curriculum.

There is not space here to detail the many busy activities of the LCP in the late 1930s and throughout the war years of 1939–45. The Italian invasion of Ethiopia in 1935–36 radicalised and gave a new political direction to black groups around the world. The League was similarly affected. It adopted a more robust vocabulary in condemning the racialism that pervaded the British empire. The labour unrest in the West Indies in the late 1930s gave new purpose to the LCP, particularly as it competed for the leadership of black opinion against the radical demands of the small militant black organisations led by George Padmore and Ras Makonnen. Probably the position of the LCP, astride the moderate middle ground, was never under serious threat. When war came in September 1939 the League found many new causes which helped to increase support: commissions in the armed forces for black people; the discriminatory policies of the US military and the position of black GIs; the working conditions of black immigrant labour; continued discrimination in housing and the workplace; and the future of illegitimate children of mixed race. The membership of the League grew to some 500 paid-up members and by 1943 the organisation was probably at the height of its influence. There was an active travelling secretary and organiser in John Carter, branches in London and Liverpool, a short-lived group in Freetown and one also in Georgetown, British Guiana.[50]

Before the invasion of Ethiopia, colonial affairs had occupied part of the League's time. Afterwards the interest heightened. In wartime it increased considerably and the term 'Herrenvolk' began to appear in Moody's writings when he referred to British colonial labour and land policies, especially in Kenya, central Africa and South Africa. In the late 1920s Moody had talked of empire as based on greed and exploitation.[51] Imperial rule, he argued, should be based on trusteeship; indirect rule needed to be extended; African education expanded with the use of vernacular languages; economic investment and development were vital; and there needed to be a colour-blind empire with Africans promoted to positions of authority and trust. For the West Indies, the LCP urged federation, self-government, a university, and insisted that generations of economic neglect be drastically reversed by a programme of social development. Despite his often pessimistic language about colonial rule, Moody did not oppose the empire, even in the late 1930s; indeed, he thought that it could be a great force for good, but only if it were rapidly reformed. Failure to do that, he believed, would lead to its collapse. However, the slowness of colonial change modified Moody's thinking, and by the middle of the war he was arguing that 'the whole idea [of empire] is now out of date and in some senses immoral. There is no moral difference between one man possessing another and one nation possessing another.'[52]

The more radical tone of the LCP was given voice in 1943 when 'A Charter for Colonial Freedom' was discussed at the annual conference held in Liverpool and attended by over 500 people.[53] A year later, the eighth annual conference of the League adopted a 'Charter for Coloured Peoples', urging on 'the Governments of the United Nations' legislative measures to end racial discrimination and proposing 'that the indigenous peoples of all dependent territories shall have immediately a majority on all law-making bodies, and shall be granted full self-government at the earliest possible opportunity'.[54] By the autumn of 1944 Moody was in touch with W. E. B. DuBois of the NAACP, Amy Jacques Garvey and others, to plan a fifth Pan-African Congress. Moody had suggested such a congress in 1938 although he thought it should take place in Africa. What he now sought was to realise 'the force of a united front and with the help of God to remove the present world outlook whereby we all have been treated as pawns in the European game'. Moody told DuBois that he looked forward to a 'United Africa … to achieve the full emancipation of our peoples'.[55]

Any ambitions that Moody and the LCP had for a Pan-African congress was lost to the newly formed Pan-African Federation, led by Padmore and Makonnen. Their initiative and energies led to the Pan-African Congress meeting in Manchester in October 1945. Moody did not attend and there was only a token LCP presence. This was probably because he had grown increasingly suspicious of what he called 'Labour Groups', and, as he told DuBois, 'I do not want to tie ourselves to any one group either politically or in any other way'.[56] It is not unreasonable to assume that Moody saw the proposed Congress in Manchester as just another talking shop where black radicals would revisit the ideas that the LCP had adopted in Liverpool in 1943 and 1944. So it was not a gathering in which Moody invested overmuch importance.

Though pressure of work during the war had forced Moody to surrender much of the day-to-day running of League business, he nevertheless jealously guarded the body that was largely his creation and over which he had presided for nearly fifteen years. Anxiety about the left also became more prominent in his thinking. He was worried that if racial discrimination were not urgently challenged in the colonies, then anti-colonial passions would become enlisted by a militant, atheistic Communism. In addition to this need to guard the integrity of the LCP, there was another possible reason for Moody's absence from the Manchester Congress. By the middle of 1945 he had ambitions to build a Cultural Centre in London, which would also serve as the League's headquarters. The Centre would, he hoped, provide a place where black students and visitors to London could meet each other and also with white people, thus improving race relations. In late 1946 Moody and his wife set sail to the United States and the West Indies to raise money for the Centre. Moody saw this as a spiritual, not a political, cause. In a 'Prayer Call' to supporters in the churches he said: 'I go at the bidding of the King of Kings and to carry out his work'. Within a few days of his return from the West Indies Moody died. The Cultural Centre was never realised.

## An assessment

Moody's formative years were in the late nineteenth century. He was influenced by a godly mother and one or two European clergymen whose lives and behaviour provided models, not least in that they seemed not to show to him any sense of race distinction. Moody's Christian conversion was an enduring experience and one that was definitive in guiding his career, his marriage, his decision to remain in Britain, and eventually to form the LCP in 1931 and to lead it until his death. Energy, commitment and integrity, but also paternalism, marked the course which he plotted with a sharp intellect and pertinacity of purpose as he sought to 'do something for the Race'.

Moody was undoubtedly a visionary, to use Sam Morris's term.[57] The vision that he had was for a racially integrated and tolerant Britain where women and men, whatever their colour or creed, would be accepted and judged solely on merit. In turn a moral and righteous Britain would continue to possess a colonial empire but one marked by the forms of free association that existed between the white dominions. The old face of a race-ruled colonial empire would be transformed by representative institutions; trusteeship would be marked by impartial equity. This daydream, despite the language of democracy and representation, was elitist and little different from the discourse of many politicians in the African colonies. Moody, after all, was in the tradition of that hard-working, self-improving, Christian ethos which characterised the lives of men such as Booker T. Washington and James Aggrey. The LCP under his direction never lost what Drake has called its 'liberal-humanitarian' focus. Nevertheless, the LCP was carried forward on that surge of anti-colonial reaction following the Italian invasion of Ethiopia, and by the early 1940s it had adopted a more outspokenly radical programme for Britain's future race relations as well as for the colonial empire. But Moody's innate caution and conservatism meant that the LCP was left behind by the rapid pace of political change which led to the Manchester Congress.

What contribution did Moody and the LCP make to the West Indies and, more importantly to its major concern, that of improving race relations in Britain? The first question is the easiest to answer. The LCP was active in demanding a Royal Commission to inquire into social and welfare reforms in the West Indian islands, and from the late 1930s it served as a watchdog for Caribbean colonial interests at the heart of empire. The second question is more difficult to answer. From the late 1930s Moody argued for legislation to prevent racial discrimination. This was a radical idea rejected then and later by government as impractical. In those demands Moody was a generation or more ahead of his time. The LCP, along with other organisations, kept the question of race relations prominently before British politicians. Moody was an efficient lobbyist although less effective than he thought and sometimes claimed. Despite all the lobbying, by the time of his death race relations were little different from the situation which had prevailed ten or twenty years before.

The LCP had already lost its way by the time Moody, tired and worn out, died in 1947. The vision was still there but the will and the energy far less apparent. By 1945 the LCP had been outflanked by other groups, more radical in their demands. Although the LCP continued to function for a few years after Moody's death, led first by Learie Constantine, it became bogged down in internal disputes, slowly faltered and then folded. This was a tragedy for race relations in Britain: at a time when an increased number of West Indians were entering the country, the new immigrants were without a visionary leadership or politically acute black-led organisation to speak for their interests and to protest against escalating discrimination. Perhaps a figure such as Moody would not have been able to do this, but it was unfortunate that someone equal in his vision and stature was not then prominent.

## Notes

1  Edward Wilmot Blyden, 1832–1912, born Danish West Indies; studied theology in the United States, emigrated to Liberia 1850 where he was active in politics; Liberian ambassador to London. He advocated the return of Black people to Africa and political unity and modernisation in West Africa. His best-known work is *Christianity, Islam and the Negro Race* (1887).

2  W. Arthur Lewis, 1913–91, born St Lucia; studied London School of Economics; editor of League of Coloured Peoples journal, *The Keys* 1935–36; taught at LSE 1938–47; author of *Labour in the West Indies* (1939); wartime civil servant in Board of Trade and Colonial Office; Stanley Jevons professor of political economy, University of Manchester 1948–58; consultant to Caribbean Commission 1949; economic adviser to prime minister of Ghana 1962–63; principal and then vice-chancellor, University of West Indies 1959–63; professor of public and international affairs, Princeton University 1963–68; author of many reports and books on economic development and politics; knighted 1963.

3  Celestine Edwards, 1865–94, born St Lucia; studied theology at King's College London; evangelical and temperance lecturer in Britain; editor of *Fraternity*, the monthly journal of the Society for the Recognition of the Brotherhood of Man.

4  There is a brief and uncritical biography by Moody's friend and pastor: David Vaughan, *Negro Victory: the life story of Dr Harold Moody* (London: Independent Press, 1950). An early study, which drew on the files of the then extant LCP files, was by the African-American sociologist St Clair Drake, 'Value system, social structure and race relations in the British Isles', unpublished PhD thesis, University of Chicago, 1954. Recent articles include two by Roderick J. Macdonald, 'Dr. Harold Arundel Moody and the League of Coloured Peoples, 1931–1947: a retrospective view', *Race*, 14:3 (1974); and the 'Introductory essay' to the reprint of *The Keys: the official organ of The League of Colored* [sic] *Peoples* (Millwood, NY: Kraus-Thomson, 1976). David Killingray, 'Race, faith and politics: Harold Moody and The League of Coloured Peoples', inaugural lecture, Goldsmiths College, University of London, 23 March 1999.

5  See Immanuel Geiss, *The Pan-African Movement* (London: Methuen, 1974); P. Olisanwuche Esedebe, *Pan-Africanism: the idea and the movement 1776–1963* (Washington DC.: Howard University Press, 1982); and also Peter Fryer, *Staying Power: the history of black people in Britain* (London: Pluto, 1984).

6  *The Negro Worker*, August–September 1933, p. 17.

7  Ludlow Moody, 1892–1987, studied at King's College Hospital, London (1913–18), and returned to Jamaica to become the government bacteriologist; his first wife was Vera, the sister of Norman Manley. Ronald Moody, 1900–84, Harold's third brother, studied dentistry at King's College London, practised for a few years, and then became a professional sculptor. He had exhibitions in Paris and became an influential figure in the Caribbean Arts Movement.

8  Certain personal papers (hereafter Moody papers) have been entrusted to me by Moody's five surviving children while I write his biography. Moody papers. Unpublished ms., 'Race Problem', chapter on 'Culture', c. mid 1932. The manuscript was rejected by Hodder and Stoughton.

9  Moody papers. This ms. was also entitled 'Some dangers of governing in the colonies', and developed from various of Moody's speeches and sermons in 1931–32, e.g. 'Some of the dangers besetting our colonial governments', address to the Threefold Movement tea conference, 14 December 1931.

10   The interleaved Authorised Version of the Bible is in the possession of Garth Moody, Harold's youngest son.

11   Moody papers. 'The story of my life', ms. dd. early 1940s.

12   *Daily Gleaner* (Kingston), 12 November 1929, reporting address at LMS meeting, 22 October 1927.

13   Moody papers. Notes on visit to Jamaica, 1946–47.

14   Most of the studies that deal with Moody also mention his profound Christian belief, but they fail to develop this further. Vaughan, *Negro Victory*, predictably stresses Moody's Christian faith; see also David Killingray, 'Harold Moody and The League of Coloured Peoples: the Christian dimension', *Christianity and History Newsletter*, 11 (1993); and Killingray,'Race, faith and politics'.

15   The Christian Endeavour Society, formed in 1881, had Congregational origins but was a non-denominational organisation to promote the spiritual life of young people. It became an international Union in 1895, and by 1908 it had many societies around the world and an estimated membership of 3.5 million.

16   The Brotherhood Movement developed from the weekly meetings known as the 'Pleasant Sunday Afternoon'. Brotherhood members included a number of early labour leaders, and also several black Britons and African visitors to Britain. See A. E. H. Gregory, *Romance and Revolution: the story of the Brotherhood Movement* (Sevenoaks: Hodder and Stoughton, 1975).

17   Harold Moody, *Youth and Race* (London: Young Christian Booklets No. 5, Christian Endeavour Union, c. 1938–39), pp. 20–1.

18   Galatians 3: 28.

19   Harold Moody, *The Colour Bar* (London: St Luke's College, Mildmay Centre, 1944; second edition, 1945), pp. 19–20.

20   Moody, *Youth and Race*, p. 13.

21   Booker T. Washington, 1856–1915; born a slave, he advocated African-American progress and pioneered vocational schools, establishing the Tuskegee Industrial Institute in Alabama. He worked to improve race relations and also secretly financed legal challenges to the racially discriminatory Jim Crow laws.

22   Harold Moody, *Christianity and Race Relations* (London: League of Coloured Peoples and Fellowship of Reconciliation, n.d. c.1943), p. 16.

23   Moody, *The Colour Bar*, pp. 5–6.

24   Moody frequently used this text and the passage from Acts 17: 24–8 in sermons. See also his pamphlet *Race and Youth*, p. 5.

25   *Express & Star* (Wolverhampton), 14 October 1929.

26   Looking backwards and forwards in mid 1935, Moody combined pacifism and Pan-Africanism when he wrote: 'I would therefore call upon Africans throughout the world to decide that if Europe chooses to fight, we will on no account take up arms. United response to this call will mean that the 200,000,000 Africans in the world will save Europe, the world and humanity from the bloodiest disaster ever known', *The Keys*, 2:4 (April–June 1935), p. 67.

27   Sermon to Essex Congregational Union, Brightlingsea, reported in *Evening Star* (Ipswich), and the *East Anglian Daily Times*, 28 April 1933; *Essex County Standard*, 29 April 1933.

28   See Jeffrey Green, *Black Edwardians: black people in Britain 1901–1914* (London: Frank Cass, 1998).

29   For example, in a report headed, 'African Native Startles Assembly', it was stated that 'Speaking faultless English, Dr. Moody told the Assembly ...', *Bulletin* (Glasgow), 5 May 1933.

30   Moody papers. Notes on 'Intermarriage', n.d. c.1934.

31   This is mentioned in a number of books and articles referring to Moody but so far I have not been able to find an original source.

32   Arundel Moody kindly photocopied the Visitor's Book for me. Unfortunately the volume covering the 1920s-1930s has not been found.

33   Martin Bauml Duberman, *Paul Robeson: a biography* (New York: Ballantine Books, 1989), pp. 123–4.

34  John Harris (1874–1940), former missionary in the Belgian Congo, who became secretary of the Anti-Slavery and Aborigines Protection Society.

35  Reported in *West Africa*, 17 December 1927.

36  Hakim Adi, *West Africans in Britain 1900–1960: nationalism, Pan-Africanism and communism* (London: Lawrence and Wishart, 1998), pp. 23–39.

37  Friends House Archives, Euston Road, London. L051.7. See also *The Friend*, 6 December 1929, 10 January 1930, 1 May 1931, and *West Africa*, 2 May 1931.

38  Sir Francis Younghusband (1863–1942), formerly of the Indian Political Department; Vera Brittain (1896–1970), feminist author and pacifist; C. G. Seligman (1873–1940), the anthropologist; and Lancelot Hogben (1895–1975), the biologist and academic.

39  Drake, 'Value systems', p. 82, fn. 1. In the early 1950s, when Drake was carrying out research for his thesis, he was able to use the files of the LCP. Unfortunately the files cannot be located; they appear to have been destroyed or dispersed.

40  *The Times*, 16 March 1931.

41  Vaughan, *Negro Victory*, p. 54.

42  See *The West India Committee Circular*, 25 June 1931; *The Times*, 16 March 1931.

43  Vaughan, *Negro Victory*, p. 53.

44  The Scottsboro Boys were several young African-American men sentenced to death for supposedly raping a white woman in Alabama in 1931. In supporting the Scottsboro Boys defence campaign, Moody made it clear that he was backing the efforts of the NAACP and not supporting the Communist-led International Labor Defense organisation. Drake, 'Value systems', p. 98.

45  James Emman Kwegyir Aggrey (1875–1927), pioneer educationalist from the Gold Coast and vice-principal of Achimota College. See Edwin W. Smith, 'Aggrey of Africa', *The Keys*, 2:3 (January–March 1935), pp. 48–9.

46  James spoke at the League's first weekend conference, High Leigh, 24–26 March 1933, on the 'West Indian'; see *The Keys*, 1:1 (July 1933), p. 5. See James, 'West Indies self-government', *The Keys*, 1:4 (April–June 1934), pp. 73 and 84.

47  Lord Lugard (1858–1945), colonial pro-consul and major adviser to British government on colonial policy from 1921 until his death; Bronislaw Malinowski (1884–1942), the distinguished anthropologist; Margery Perham (1896–1982), the major student of British colonial administration.

48  Moody speaking to the Baptist Union, Glasgow, May 1933; see *Bulletin*, 5 May 1933.

49  The League of Coloured Peoples, *Race Relations and the Schools: a survey of the colour question in some aspects of English education with a number of proposals* (London: League of Coloured Peoples, n.d. c.1944).

50  Dr Hastings Banda, future dictator of Malawi, was the secretary of the Liverpool branch. Branches were claimed in other colonies, but Georgetown, British Guiana, was the only successful one, and by the late 1940s that had become a racist political organisation.

51  For example, at a meeting of the League of Nations Union, Kingswood, Bristol, 3 October 1928, as reported in *The Western Press*, 4 October 1928.

52  Moody, *The Colour Bar*, p. 23.

53  LCP *News Letter*, 43 (April 1943), pp. 4, 16–17. The *News Letter* was the wartime successor to *The Keys*.

54  LCP *News Letter*, 59 (August 1944), pp. 73, 86–8.

55  LCP *News Letter*, 59 (August 1944), p. 88.

56  Herbert Aptheker (ed.), *The Correspondence of W. E. B. DuBois: vol. II. Selections 1934–1944* (Amherst: University of Massachusetts Press, 1976), pp. 66–7.

57  Sam Morris, 'Moody – the forgotten visionary', *New Community*, 1:3 (Spring 1972), pp. 193–6.

# CHAPTER THREE

# A race outcast from an outcast class: Claude McKay's experience and analysis of Britain

## Winston James

*I am ... a social leper, a race outcast from an outcast class.* (Claude McKay, 1921)

### The road to London

I've a longin' in me dept's of heart dat I can conquer not,
'Tis a wish dat I've have been havin' from since I could form a t'o't,
'Tis to sail athwart the ocean an' to hear de billows roar,
When dem ride aroun' de steamer, when dem beat on England's shore.

Just to view de homeland England, in de streets of London walk,
An' to see de famous sights dem 'bouten which dere's so much talk,
An' to watch de fact'ry chimneys pourin' smoke up to de sky,
An' to see de matches-children, dat I hear 'bout, passin' by.[1]

These stanzas from McKay's poem – 'Old England' – express the conventional, British Caribbean and colonial view of the mother country. It was published in 1912. His opinions, however, were to change radically, especially after he visited the metropolis seven years later. He ended his days hating England and the civilisation it represented.

Unlike the other Caribbean intellectuals represented in this volume (barring only Padmore) McKay's journey to England was indirect: he journeyed not from the Caribbean, but from New York after an absence of more than seven years from his native Jamaica. For most of the time in the US he was part of America's black proletariat, earning his living, as his friend Max Eastman put it, 'in every one of the ways that northern Negroes do, from "pot-wrestling" in a boarding-house kitchen to dining-car service on the New York and Philadelphia Express'. McKay regarded himself as 'not only a Negro but also a worker', and we might add for greater precision, a *manual* worker, one of Afro-America's menials.[2]

By the time he arrived in London, he was no 'black Briton' except in the most formal, judicial sense of that term. He certainly was from the British Caribbean but his self-identification had expanded through experience, travel and conscious decision He was a Pan-Africanist and a socialist – a race man and a class man, not merely a West Indian.[3]

His reflections on Britain and the British (especially the English) mark a historic departure. They break with the adulatory, often cloying celebration of Britain characteristic of most previous black writings, anticipating a sensibility that was to become more pronounced in the writings of the 1950s and 1960s. McKay's distinguished Caribbean predecessors, such as Henry Sylvester Williams and Theophilus Scholes, insofar as they were critical of Britain, by and large focused on imperial issues. McKay was the first Caribbean intellectual to describe what it meant to be black in Britain.[4] He wrote with anger and bitterness – feelings that intensified the older he got.

In this respect McKay stands in striking contrast to C. L. R. James. In McKay there is no anglophilia, no celebration of 'Western Civilisation'.[5] To McKay, England was, as he put it in one of his poems, the 'arch conspirator' in the oppression of black people. And when it came to 'Western Civilisation', he was on the side of Gandhi, who when asked what he thought of modern civilisation said it would be a good idea: in his novel, *Banjo*, McKay spoke through the character Ray when he remarked that 'there is no such animal as a civilized nation', and castigated 'Civilization'. Ray 'hated civilization'. 'Civilization is rotten', he declared. 'And the more he travelled and knew of it, the more he felt the truth of that bitter outburst.' Nor was it only in fictional form that he denounced civilisation. 'I loathe it', McKay wrote in a Harlem journal, 'and desire its disintegration and the birth of a proletarian order'.[6]

## The man who went to London

McKay was born in Jamaica into a prosperous peasant family in 1889. He was educated by his eldest brother, Uriah Theodore. U. Theo, as he was known to all, had been a prize student at Mico College and became one of the island's outstanding schoolmasters; he trained Claude in the virtues of socialism, feminism and militant rationalism. After a brief stint in the constabulary, which radicalised him further, McKay emigrated to the United States in 1912 to study agriculture at Tuskegee Institute. Hating the 'semi-military, machinelike existence' of Booker T. Washington's school, he transferred to Kansas State College.[7] But in 1914 he gave that up, too, for New York. Before leaving Jamaica, he had had a reputation as a poet and had published two volumes of verse to critical acclaim. To make a living in New York he laboured at the tasks described by Eastman, stealing time on the job to work at the craft of poetry. His first American poems appeared in 1917; by 1919 he had become famous (and notorious) throughout America, mainly because of his militant sonnet, 'If we must die'.[8]

American racism shocked and appalled him. 'I had heard of prejudice in America but never dreamed of it being so intensely bitter', he wrote in 1918.[9] He was attracted by Garvey's Universal Negro Improvement Association, wrote for its newspaper, the *Negro World*, but never joined the organisation. However, while working in a Manhattan factory, McKay did join the Industrial Workers of the World (IWW), the most radical and inclusive working-class organisation in the US. The IWW embraced skilled and unskilled workers, men and women and – going against the American grain – white and black.

Before he left the USA, two events had crucially affected McKay and contributed to his deepening radicalisation. The first was the mass carnage wrought by the first world war. This 'great catastrophe', as he called it, had proved the 'real hollowness of nationhood, patriotism, racial pride and most of the things which one was taught to respect and reverence'. The war epitomised the 'blind brute forces of tigerish tribalism which remain at the core of civilized society'.[10]

But out of that catastrophe came the second event that fired McKay. This was the Russian Revolution. 'Holy' Russia, as he dubbed Soviet Russia in 1920, had returned to McKay his 'golden hope'.[11] He became an ardent enthusiast. Before the second anniversary of the Revolution he was debating the subject with the black nationalist Garveyites. He vigorously promoted the significance of the Revolution to the struggles of black people the world over. 'Every Negro', he wrote in a letter to the *Negro World*,

> who lays claim to leadership should make a study of Bolshevism and explain its meaning to the colored masses. It is the greatest and most scientific idea afloat in the world today that can be easily put into practice by the proletariat to better its material and spiritual life. Bolshevism ... has made Russia safe for the Jew. It has liberated the Slav peasant from priest and bureaucrat who can no longer egg him on to murder Jews to bolster up their rotten institutions. It might make these United States safe for the Negro.[12]

McKay was not alone in advocating black liberation through Bolshevism. But he was one of the first black persons in the US to do so, vigorously and openly.[13]

The pogroms against black people in the United States, the so-called 'race riots' of 1919, also touched McKay profoundly. White mobs, led mainly by ex-soldiers, went on a rampage of unparalleled breadth and savagery. Twenty-six riots – north and south, east and west – with their blood and fire, death and destruction, consumed urban America. These events of 1919 were dubbed the 'Red Summer' by James Weldon Johnson, black poet and executive secretary of the National Association for the Advancement of Colored People.[14] The Red Summer had a catalytic effect upon McKay. He was transformed into a revolutionary. It was his open, militant and courageous response that first brought him into the limelight. And it was for his reaction to 1919, 'If we must die', that he is most widely remembered.

## England, their England

But McKay wanted to get away from the horror of 1919; he wanted to get away, too, from both his fame and notoriety. An admirer gave him the money for a passage to England in the autumn of 1919. American friends provided him with contacts in London and letters of introduction. Frank Harris, editor of *Pearson's Magazine* and a staunch supporter of McKay's, wrote letters to George Bernard Shaw (whom McKay was to meet shortly after his arrival) and the publisher Grant Richards. Harris asked Richards to introduce McKay to Siegfried Sassoon. 'See that he gets a good welcome[,] will you', Harris wrote, in a tone at once beseeching and commanding.[15] Max Eastman and his sister Crystal Eastman, editors of the *Liberator* to which McKay had contributed, knew Sylvia Pankhurst and, though less formal in smoothing the way for McKay, would have encouraged him to drop in on their revolutionary friend. The associate editor of the *World Tomorrow*, Walter Fuller, the English husband of Crystal, was a close friend of Charles Ogden, editor of the *Cambridge Magazine*. 'I am asking my friend, Mr. Claude McKay', he wrote to Ogden, 'the bearer of this letter, to call on you during his visit to London because I feel sure that you will be glad to know one another.' Fuller also wrote to the publishers Allen and Unwin on McKay's behalf.[16]

These introductions to the representatives of the literary world suggest certain privileges. They did nothing, however, to mitigate the profane realities of racism. McKay soon became acquainted with the English version. He was denied long-term lodgings – and all the while in England he rented from foreign landladies, who, in at least one instance, were taunted by their English neighbours for doing so. He was refused service in pubs. He was insulted while accompanying white women in the streets, on more than one occasion physically attacked, and was 'nearly mauled in Limehouse'. It is little surprise that McKay was forced to conclude of England: 'One must always be on one's guard'.[17] At the time he had lodgings with a German family at Provence

Street in Islington. Despite its alluring name, Provence Street was a 'hideous little gutter street near the Angel'.[18] In February 1920 he claimed that he did not mind living there; a few months later, however, he was more ambivalent, making sure that he got home before it was too late at night. By then he was hoping to move further to the west of London, where it was 'a little safer' and '[t]he grown-ups are more sensible & the children are not so disgustingly provocative & bad-mannered'.[19] In London McKay often felt like a man under siege.

## The Workers' Socialist Federation and the Workers' Dreadnought

Soon after his arrival, McKay made contact with Sylvia Pankhurst and before the end of 1919 began to work with her party, the Workers' Socialist Federation (WSF), and on the newspaper she edited, the *Workers' Dreadnought*. The following summer he attended the historic Communist Unity Convention in London, which laid the foundations for the formation of the Communist Party of Great Britain (CPGB).

McKay's job at the *Dreadnought* entailed covering the volatile labour situation on the London docks, getting news from 'coloured' and white seamen. He was also assigned the task of reading the foreign press, with an eye for items about the empire. He wrote book reviews on topics ranging from the shop stewards' movement to Gorky on Tolstoy; and he published a large number of poems, including some of his most revolutionary. Pankhurst entrusted him with great responsibility and he privately complained of being overworked. 'I should have written before', he told Ogden,

> but I have been kept so frightfully busy by Sylvia Pankhurst since she came back [from abroad]. She has been experiencing all sorts of domestic and business difficulties, due to her own erratic nature, & all the routine work of getting out the paper falls upon me in consequence.[20]

As a disciplined revolutionary McKay attended WSF meetings. He was responsible for selling his quota of *Dreadnoughts* on the streets. He recalled selling the paper along with Pankhurst's pamphlet, *Rebel Ireland*, and Herman Gorter's *Ireland: the Achilles heel of England* at a big Sinn Fein rally in Trafalgar Square in the summer of 1920.[21] McKay's involvement with the *Dreadnought* group clearly involved far more than 'a little practical journalism' that he later claimed. British intelligence exaggerated when they later alleged that McKay had entertained ambitions of taking over the leadership of the WSF from Pankhurst. But McKay's deep involvement with the British far left is incontrovertible.[22]

The WSF was one of the most radical political formations in Britain. 'Left-wing communists', Lenin called them as he chided Pankhurst and her followers for boycotting parliamentary elections and rejecting affiliation to the Labour Party. Of all the currents on the British left, 'the WSF came out by far the most strongly in support of the Irish Easter Uprisings'.[23] It was quickest in supporting the Bolsheviks. Resolutely anti-imperialist, it explicitly called for self-determination for India and Ireland.[24]

Under the leadership of Sylvia Pankhurst, the *Dreadnought* was the most principled anti-racist organ on the left. At the height of the madness in June 1919, when attacks on black communities in Britain flared up, Pankhurst produced a bold editorial in the *Dreadnought*. In 'Stabbing Negroes in the London dock area', she submitted 'a few questions for the consideration of those who have been negro hunting':

> Do you think that the British should rule the world or do you want to live on peaceable terms with all peoples?
> Do you wish to exclude all blacks from England?
> If so, do you not think that blacks might justly ask that the British should at the same time keep out of the black peoples' countries?
> Do you not know that capitalists, and especially British capitalists, have seized, by force of arms, the countries inhabited by black people and are ruling those countries and the black inhabitants for their own profit? ...
> Are you afraid that a white woman would prefer a blackman to you if you met her on equal terms with him?
> Do you not think you would be better employed in getting conditions made right for yourself and your fellow workers than in stabbing a black-man ...?[25]

Uncommonly courageous and decent, Pankhurst sought to lead, not follow – to break the prejudices among her own constituents in the East End rather than remain silent. To her eternal honour, wherever imperialism 'got drunk and went wild among native peoples, the Pankhurst paper would be on the job'.[26] Small wonder that the WSF proved the most congenial political home for McKay.

His membership of the WSF provided McKay with important insights into the politics of the metropolis. He found himself in 'the nest of extreme radicalism in London'. He got to know the politics and personalities of Britain's far-left groups. He also became acquainted with different sections of the trade union movement – especially with the shop stewards, which appealed to his syndicalist predilections. And he became deeply familiar with London proletarian life. Pankhurst and the WSF had their base in Old Ford Road in Bow, in London's East End, where he lived for a time. His view of Britain was dominated by this perspective.

## The International Socialist Club

The International Socialist Club (ISC) was McKay's primary redoubt in London. Crystal Eastman almost certainly told him about the club before he left the US. Eastman was in Britain in the summer of 1919 and she knew the radical scene there well. McKay joined the club soon after arriving and quickly became a familiar presence. It was at the ISC that he established some of his most enduring friendships across the Atlantic, and it was there, he said, that he made his most interesting contacts in Britain.[27] At the ISC he heard some of Britain's most distinguished left-wing orators of the day, including J. T. Walton Newbold, Britain's first Communist MP; Indian-born Shapurji Saklatvala, who in 1922 was elected an independent MP for Battersea and soon thereafter switched to the CP; A. J. Cook of the Miners' Federation of which he later became leader; Jack Tanner, a leader of the shop stewards' movement; Guy Aldred, the editor of the anarchist organ, the *Spur*; Arthur MacManus and William Gallacher, labour agitators from the Clyde; George Lansbury, editor of the *Daily Herald*; and Sylvia Pankhurst herself.[28]

McKay paints a vivid portrait of life at the ISC. It was 'full of excitement with its dogmatists and doctrinaires of radical left ideas: Socialists, Communists, anarchists, syndicalists, one-big-unionists and trade unionists, soap-boxers, poetasters, scribblers, editors of little radical sheets which flourish in London'.[29] He noted that foreigners formed the majority of the membership, among which predominated Jews. He was the only 'African' when he joined and he introduced others, including the remarkable radical black seaman, Reuben Gilmore.[30]

The club had a two-fold impact upon McKay, one political, the other intellectual. As he recalled later, it was the first time that he had found himself in an atmosphere in which people 'devoted themselves entirely to the discussion and analysis of social events from a radical and Marxian point of view'. He sought his reading ticket from the British Museum largely in order to keep up with the comrades at the club. 'I felt intellectually inadequate', he confessed, 'and decided to educate myself.' He read Marx systematically for the first time at the British Museum.[31]

## C. K. Ogden and the 1917 Club

Outside the radical circles around Pankhurst and the ISC, C. K. Ogden was the only British writer with whom McKay had sustained relations. As a student at Cambridge University in 1909 Ogden became the co-founder of the Heretics Society, which aspired to lift the smothering hand of religious orthodoxy from British intellectual and political life. Before graduation he was recognised as an outstanding intellect and he was offered the opportunity to edit a journal of his own, *The Cambridge Magazine*, in 1912. A gifted linguist, and anti-racist and cosmopolitan in outlook, Ogden carried news from all over the world through the translation and republication of articles from the foreign press, including anti-war writings from Germany. Because of his outspoken pacifism, Ogden earned ferocious opposition from jingoists who wrecked his offices on Armistice Day. He is best remembered as a polymath, talented in the fields of linguistics, aesthetics and psychology. He was the first to translate the then-obscure Austrian engineer and mathematician, Ludwig Wittgenstein, bringing to the English-reading world the *Tractatus Logico-Philosophicus* in 1922. With his close friend and collaborator, I. A. Richards, he published *Foundations of Aesthetics* (1921) and *The Meaning of Meaning* (1922).

Politically Ogden had much in common with McKay. He was an agnostic, a supporter of birth control, an outspoken advocate of women's suffrage and, like McKay, he deplored the futility and devastation of the war. McKay first made contact with Ogden in February 1920. His primary reason for going to London was, McKay claimed, to publish his poetry. He turned to Ogden, sending him Fuller's letter of introduction and some of his poems. McKay explained that he hesitated in contacting Ogden because 'I don't think it right to bother with business matters persons to whom one is practically a stranger'.[32] He need not have worried. Ogden responded enthusiastically, they met and became good friends. Ogden offered to help get McKay's poetry published. 'Thanks very much for devoting so much time and being so naturally nice to me', McKay told him.[33]

By May 1920 arrangements were well under way for the publication of the book. Ogden allocated a generous spread in the *Cambridge Magazine* for twenty-three of the poems, providing McKay a splendid introduction to the British reading public in a prestigious publication.[34] By September 1920 Grant Richards had brought out *Spring in New Hampshire*, McKay's first book since *Constab Ballads*, which came out the year he left Jamaica.[35] Ogden not only helped to choose the poems, but he edited the volume as a whole, and persuaded his friend, I. A. Richards, to write a preface.

But McKay had substantial disagreements with Ogden over *Spring in New Hampshire*. Though intellectually adventurous and politically courageous, Ogden had difficulty accepting McKay's more revolutionary poems. He regarded them as 'propagandistic' and thought them best excluded. Ogden rejected a number of poems on these grounds, including the most famous of all, 'If we must die'. In agreeing to this, for the sake of getting the volume published, McKay made what he always regarded as a grievous error, which he continued to regret. (He also conceded over the title: McKay had originally planned it be called *Songs of Struggle*.) Though it does contain some fine lyrics, including some of his finest pastoral and nostalgic verses, *Spring in New Hampshire* is a tarnished book, and unrepresentative of McKay's poetry at the time. It is more Ogden's book than McKay's.

After his offices were ransacked, Ogden began spending more time in London. His primary locale was the 1917 Club, where he frequently met McKay.[36] Located in Soho's Gerrard Street, the 1917 Club was founded by Leonard Woolf and friends in December 1917. In contrast to the Athenaeum – the 'nadir of respectability', Woolf called it – the 1917 Club was the 'zenith of disreputability'. Woolf recalled that Gerrard Street in those days was 'the rather melancholy haunt of prostitutes daily from 2:30 p.m. onwards'.[37] The membership of the club, he said, was a 'curious mixture': 'mainly political and the politicals were mainly Labour Party, from Ramsay [MacDonald] downwards. But there was also an element of unadulterated culture, particularly at tea time, so that if one dropped in about 4 o'clock and looked round its rooms, one would hardly have guessed that it was political'. Virginia Woolf and the Stracheys, including Lytton and his 'retinue of young women and young men', were frequently there.[38] In short, the 1917 Club was the primary haunt of Fabians and the Bloomsbury set.

But to McKay the 1917 was hardly different from the Athenaeum: it was posh – 'nice society', he called it – very different from the ISC.[39] With the help of Ogden, he did, however, manage to get a small exhibition mounted there of the work of his anarchist-artist friend, Henry Bernard.[40] Even here, though, he came up against abuse, on this occasion from an '"extreme left" fellow'. He was sanguine: 'I am always coming up against his type and worse – in America & also here, so I'm used to it. My colour alone makes me so conspicuous; I must reconcile myself to such things.'[41]

## The Drury Lane Club

In addition to the ISC and the 1917, McKay for a short time frequented a small club on Drury Lane specially established for non-white colonial and Afro-American soldiers. Organised by the YMCA, it was run by a patronising English woman – she called the men her 'coloured boys' – who, after reading McKay's critical article on the place in the *Negro World*, banned him from the place. McKay, however, had had enough time to get to know the black soldiers and hear of their terrible experience of racism in the British army during the war and on the streets of London after the armistice. McKay was himself a witness to one of these nasty moments in London. After one of the men from the club defeated an English rival in a boxing match, a cockney admirer came through the knot of black friends to congratulate the boxer. But when the boxer introduced his English wife to his white fan, the man called the boxer a 'damned nigger'. McKay was shocked and angered by the men's racist ordeal during the war but was glad that in the hearts of black men the 'grievances against things British' were 'rapidly growing greater instead of disappearing'. He gave the men radical literature and invited the most 'forwarding-thinking' among them to the ISC. His encounters with these men had a profound impact upon McKay.[42] Regarding them as too conservative, and too given to petitioning rather than fighting, McKay kept clear of the members of London's small, but important, black middle class. He preferred the company of the black soldiers and boxers, and comrades at the ISC.

## Grievances against things British

In April 1920 French troops, retaliating against German violation of the Versailles treaty, extended their control of the Rhineland by occupying the major cities on the east bank of the Rhine. Only 25,000 of the quarter of a million French troops in the Rhineland were non-Europeans (mainly north Africans), of which only 5,000 were black west Africans – a mere 2 per cent of the French forces.[43] But the presence of *black* troops occupying part of a European nation created a storm of controversy. In Britain, the principal figure who orchestrated this reaction was E. D. Morel – a man of pacifist and anti-imperialist inclinations, who had done much to alert the British public to the atrocities committed in King Leopold's Congo.

After a clash between French troops and German civilians in Frankfurt in the spring of 1920, the *Daily Herald*, the British labour movement's newspaper, reported the incident in racial terms. 'Frankfurt Runs With Blood / French Black Troops Use Machine Guns on Civilians', it announced on the front page. George Lansbury, the *Herald*'s editor, was a close friend of Morel's and the headline was probably inspired by Morel himself, who fed his material to Lansbury. The following day, Morel spoke in his own voice, again on the front page. He was not interested in the rights and wrongs of shootings in Frankfurt. Morel was preoccupied with the matter of sex: more specifically, with relations between black soldiers and white women in occupied Germany. 'Black Scourge in Europe / Sexual Horror Let Loose by France on the Rhine', the headline declared.[44] 'My information is not yet as complete as I should wish', Morel confessed, but he could not wait: '[T]he news in to-day's papers, to the effect that France is thrusting her black savages still further into the heart of Germany, is such that I do not propose to hold my hand any longer'. As his article made clear, there were no reliable reports, let alone substantiated charges, of rapes by African troops. But this was beside the point. 'The abundance or otherwise of specific reports is immaterial.' The mere presence of Africans, occupying a portion of Europe, was cause enough for alarm. 'The African race is the most developed sexually of any. These levies are recruited from tribes in a primitive state of development ... Sexually they are unrestrained and unrestrainable. *That is perfectly well known.*'[45] The very *presence* of the black troops, 'unrestrained and unrestrainable', was tantamount to their having committed rape. Morel was not bothered to ask what French troops were doing in the Rhine, but only what the black troops *might do*. He condemned the 'French militarists', but only for their use of 'black savages' in Europe, thus their responsibility for 'perpetrating an abominable outrage upon womanhood, upon the white race, and upon civilisation'. The black troops, 'primitive African barbarians', 'have become a terror and a horror unimaginable to the countryside, raping women and girls'. He explained the dangers arising from the racial dimension: 'for well-known physiological reasons, the raping of a white woman by a negro is nearly always accompanied by serious injury and not infrequently has fatal results'.

Morel ended with an appeal to the British working class. For the use of these 'negro mercenaries ... from the heart of Africa, to fight the battles and execute the lusts of capitalist Governments in the heart of Europe is ... a terrific portent'. The workers of Britain, France and Italy would be 'ill-advised if they allow it to pass in silence because to-day the victims happen to be German'. He appealed to white women whose 'decent instincts', he believed, needed to be mobilised.

Lansbury, in an editorial note accompanying Morel's article, declared that the *Herald* was not in the business of encouraging colour prejudice. On the editorial page itself, he returned to the subject. Under the heading 'A New Horror', he stated:

> We are not amongst those who consider that because a man's skin is black he should be considered as an inferior human being to a white man; but nature has given us all qualities of temperament suitable to the conditions and climate in which we are born.
>
> It is an odious outrage to bring thousands of children of the forests from Africa to Europe *without their womenfolk*, and settle them down as enemies amongst the women and children of Germany ...
>
> For organised Labour there is another question, too. If the manhood of these races, not so advanced in the forms of civilisation as ourselves, are to be used against Germans, *why not against the workers here or elsewhere?*[46]

Thus, by his ostensibly anti-racist words, Lansbury revealed his racist self.

McKay picked up the *Herald* and was appalled. The following day, after consulting friends, he dispatched a letter to the editor. Lansbury refused to publish it, apparently never even replying to McKay.[47] Sylvia Pankhurst, once again, came to the rescue and published the letter in the *Workers' Dreadnought*.

Under the heading, 'A black man replies', McKay revealed that he first wrote to the *Herald*, 'but apparently the *Herald* refuses a hearing to the other side, which is quite inarticulate'. He told Lansbury that the 'odiousness' of Morel's article was not mitigated by his editorial denying encouragement of race prejudice and asserting his championing of native rights in Africa. 'If you are really consistent in thinking that you can do something to help the white and black peoples to a better understanding of each other', McKay wrote, 'there is much that you might learn from Liberal and Conservative organs like the *Nation*, the *New Statesman* and the *Edinburgh Review*, which have treated the problem ... in a decent and dignified manner'. McKay confessed ignorance of the 'well-known physiological reasons that make the raping of a white woman by a negro resultful of serious and fatal injury'. Any violent rape, he said, 'whether by white, yellow or black, civilised or savage man, must entail injury, serious or fatal, especially if the victim be a virgin'. In short, 'Why all this obscene, maniacal outburst about the sex vitality of black men in a proletarian paper?' He concluded:

> I do not protest because I happen to be a negro (I am disgusted when I read in your columns that white dockers would prohibit their employers using Chinese and Indian labour), I write because I feel that the ultimate result of your propaganda will be further strife and blood-spilling between the whites and the many members of my race, boycotted economically and socially ... I have been told in Limehouse by white men, who ought to know, that this summer will see a recrudescence of the outbreaks that occurred last year. The negro-baiting Bourbons of the United States will thank you, and the proletarian underworld of London will certainly gloat over the scoop of the Christian-Socialist-pacifist *Daily Herald*.[48]

What disheartened McKay most was the fact that such blatantly racist propaganda could so easily penetrate the workers' movement. At the annual meeting of the Trades Union Congress in September 1920, covered by McKay for the *Dreadnought*, the Standing Orders Committee gave permission to the Union of Democratic Control, Morel's publishers, to present each delegate with a copy of his pamphlet, *The Horror on the Rhine*. According to one of Morel's friends, the item was enthusiastically received and 'produced a profound impression ... I was astonished at the number who came and expressed their views about it'. It left the trade unionists with 'a feeling of physical and spiritual revulsion' that such things could happen on European soil.[49] Even

[ 82 ]

a man such as Robert Smillie, president of the Miners' Federation, whom McKay admired and praised on the front page of the *Dreadnought* – ascetic, incorruptible, a cross between Gandhi and Big Bill Haywood of the IWW – even he was caught up in the sordid business, lending his name to Morel's campaign.[50] As he reported to Leon Trotsky, McKay noted with disgust and horror that in 1922, even the *Communist*, the paper of the newly-formed CPGB, had joined the racists.[51]

Looking back at the furore, McKay admitted that maybe he was not 'civilized enough to understand why the sex of the black race should be put on exhibition to persuade the English people to decide which white gang should control the coal and iron of the Ruhr'.[52] The ease with which the labour movement fell prey to such a primitive racism shocked McKay beyond all measure, and went deep into his imagination, influencing for the rest of his days his bitter distrust of the English.

The *Spectator*'s review of *Spring in New Hampshire* only confirmed his worst views of the English. Declaring the book 'extrinsically as well as intrinsically interesting', it drew readers' attention to the fact that the book was written by 'a full-blooded negro'. The *Spectator* continued:

> Perhaps the ordinary reader's first impulse in realizing that the book is by an American negro is to inquire into its good taste. Not until we are satisfied that his work does not overstep the barriers which a not quite explicable but deep instinct in us is ever alive to maintain can we judge it with genuine fairness. Mr. Claude McKay never offends our sensibilities. His love poetry is clear of the hint which would put our racial instincts against him whether we would or no.[53]

In *A Long Way From Home* McKay discloses his verdict:

> My experience of the English convinced me that prejudice against Negroes had become almost congenital among them. I think the Anglo-Saxon mind becomes morbid when it turns on the sex life of colored people. Perhaps a psychologist might be able to explain why.[54]

George Bernard Shaw, his childhood hero, asked him why he did not pursue pugilism instead of poetry. Despite the 'beastly modern white savagery' of the first world war, H. G. Wells had the nerve, McKay noted, to wonder 'whether the Negro is capable of becoming a civilized citizen of a world republic'. The depth to which racism saturated the British social fabric is perhaps best illustrated by the case of J. T. Walton Newbold, the country's first Communist MP. In 1922 at a congress in Moscow, a Chinese delegate pleased to meet the comrade from Britain greeted him, 'Hello Comrade Newbold'. 'Hello Chink', Comrade Newbold replied. To their eternal credit, the leading Bolsheviks gave Comrade Newbold a good going over. Less than two years later

Newbold wrote to the CP leadership: 'I am, perhaps, too English in outlook and in thought too grounded in insularity and tradition to be a good Communist. Therefore, I am saying, farewell.'[55]

McKay described his time in London as 'that most miserable of years'; an 'ordeal'. Even the 'suffocating' fog of London – which 'not only wrapped you around but entered your throat like a strangling nightmare' – seemed to McKay more welcoming than the Londoners themselves: 'The feeling of London was so harshly unfriendly to me that sometimes I was happy in the embrace of the unfolding fog'. 'Oh blessed was the fog that veiled me blind!', he rejoiced in a poem on the city. To him, the English as whole were 'a strangely unsympathetic people, as coldly chilling as their English fog'.[56]

McKay's disappointment with England stems not only from his experience but also from his expectations. Just as the stark reality of US racism shocked him despite having prior information about the situation there, so was he taken aback by British racism despite an abstract knowledge of its existence before arriving in London. But in the end, he felt more cheated – conned, even – than disappointed. In retrospect he felt angry that his teacher in Jamaica paraded him and his schoolmates, singing 'Rule Britannia', in the breathless celebration of Queen Victoria's Diamond Jubilee in the Clarendon hills in 1897.[57] He felt angry because the colonial Jamaican notion that England was the mother country was so distant from the facts of life as a black Jamaican on the ground in London, where he had to dodge cockney mobs who saw him as nothing more than a nigger, at best a darky, paradigmatically foreign, not British at all.

Given this hostile environment, it is not surprising that it was in London that he wrote his most powerful poetry of nostalgia – 'The Spanish needle', 'Flame-heart', 'Home thoughts', 'I shall return', even 'The tropics in New York' – reliving in his imagination the distant pleasures of his homeland. These sorrow songs issued not only from the necessary distance, perspective and loss that exile brings but also from a new discovery: the discovery of his un-Britishness and the simultaneous discovery of a more thoroughly Caribbean, Jamaican and black identity. They are the fruits of a reverie of reminiscences, triggered by the search for oases of solace. It was also in London, not Marseilles, as is commonly believed, that McKay first developed a powerful identification with Africa. It was there that he first expressed a desire to visit his ancestral homeland. His befriending of west African soldiers at the Drury Lane Club combined with British racism probably contributed to the yearning. Almost a decade before the publication of *Banjo*, McKay confided to Ogden his intention of going to Africa before returning to the US and his wanting to 'keep my poor people awake and discontented'.[58]

London, McKay wrote, 'was not wholly Hell, for it was possible for me to compose poetry some of the time. No place can be altogether a God-forsaken Sahara or swamp in which a man is able to discipline and compose his emotions into self-expression'.[59] That may be true as far as it goes. But why would he repeatedly take refuge in an idealised Jamaican past if London were not a 'God-forsaken Sahara or swamp'? Why the emotional retreat? Why did he write not even one poem about London or Britain during his stay? 'I had to realize', he subsequently wrote, 'that London is a cold white city where English culture is great and formidable like an iceberg. It is a city created for English needs, and admirable, no doubt, for the English people. It was not built to accommodate Negroes. I was very happy when I could get out of it to go back to the Negro pale of America', where life was more robust and less hypocritical.[60]

Yet despite his hurt and professed hatred of the English, McKay engaged in working-class revolutionary activity in Britain. It is an apparent contradiction – how could he collaborate with those he deemed 'congenitally' racist? – but not a real one. In December 1919 McKay sent a remarkable letter to Marcus Garvey, enclosing a report and editorial from the *Herald* sharply critical of British policy in India. 'I think it is a splendid thing to have the representative organ of British Labour denouncing so strongly Imperial abomination and endorsing the self-determination of Britain's subject peoples', he told Garvey. He continued:

> As I have said before in your paper, radical Negroes should be more interested in the white radical movements. They are supporting our cause, at least in principle. To me they are the great destructive forces *within*, while the subject races are fighting without. I don't mean that we should accept them unreservedly and put our cause into their hands. No: they are fighting their own battle & so are we; but at present we meet on common ground against the common enemy. We have a great wall to batter down and while we are working on one side we should hail those who are working on the other. We need have no fear if, as a race, we have ability to safeguard our own peculiar rights.
>
> It is amusing, but very pathetic, to see Negroes under British rule wasting valuable money sending deputations & petitions to the Imperial capitalists in Downing Street. For, after all, what are we but poor black devils whom our exploiters put a little lower down in the scale of human life than their poor white devils. And if, in spite of the fact that they have robbed us for centuries, they have been unable to make existence for their masses worth-while, can we reasonably expect improvement of our conditions at their hands?

He signed off: 'Yours for an awakened Negro race'.[61] For McKay, the critical insight was the need to defeat what he called here 'the common enemy', even if it meant working with those who regarded him as a social leper.

McKay's meditation on Britain did not end with departure from London. The fact that the British, in connivance with the French authorities, harried him, especially during his time in Morocco, caused him much anguish. For example, after he informed British consulate officials in Morocco in 1928 of his wish to travel to Liberia and Sierra Leone, 'to visit the land of his ancestors', the Foreign Office duly banned him from all British colonies *except* his native Jamaica. The decision reached McKay in garbled form: he was informed in writing that he had been banned from *all* British colonies. Angered, McKay privately referred to his British tormentors as 'dogs', and 'those dirty British bastards working respectably in the dark'. The abusive language, though never exchanged between the parties, was not one-sided. The British vice-consul at Fez, who went through McKay's luggage, read some of his poems and saw the radical literature, called him a 'nasty dangerous fellow'. When McKay's French *carte d'identité* and his British passport were stolen from his house near Tangiers in 1932, he suspected the British.[62]

McKay's grievances remained with him. Rather than heal, his wounds festered. He grew more bitterly anti-British, his animus almost pathological in intensity by the end.[63] He never ceased watching the British ruling class, noting its misdeeds at home and abroad.

His claim that he had 'looked upon the face of the British nation, fulfilling [his] boyhood wish' is, however, questionable. He had never secured lodgings in a British, let alone English, home. He spent much of his time with black soldiers at the Drury Lane Club and elsewhere, and the remainder at the International Socialist Club. Because of this involvement, each 'overwhelmingly foreign', McKay felt that he was 'living on foreign instead of English soil'.[64] His friends were mainly foreigners or, in one way or another, outsiders. Among his 'little group that stuck together' at the ISC, Frank Budgen was the only white Englishman among them – a man of unusually cosmopolitan temperament. '[A]lthough I could say I lived in London', he told Nancy Cunard, 'it was altogether in a foreign milieu – chiefly Russian-Jewish – except for the little time I worked with a Miss [Nora] Smyth on Sylvia Pankhurst's *Workers' Dreadnought*. And that was very uncongenial.'[65]

In short, McKay can hardly be said to have known the British at large, for the British would not let him. This has been the general pattern with non-European immigrants, including Caribbean intellectuals. They occupied the outhouses of the great British mansion. The few allowed into the main edifice were locked out of so many rooms, especially the more salubrious ones, that they barely knew the place. Marginalisation and isolation set these Londoners apart, not their loneliness. McKay never complained of loneliness; he complained of hostility.

He had arrived in London at a particular dark moment, a time of racist upsurge, during the riots of 1919 and 1920. The East End, McKay's primary site of work and recreation, was particularly hostile to black people and non-Europeans in general. The dockers were notoriously racist. Unemployment among them had increased dramatically with the end of the war; retail prices in 1920 were 176 per cent higher than they had been in 1914. The cost of food had almost tripled, that of clothing more than quadrupled over the same period. Rent had also increased, though not as steeply.[66] For the wageless, including the large number of ex-servicemen, this was no consolation – and black men became a convenient scapegoat. The East End was probably the worst place in the country for a black man to be. Considerations of time and place, then, must temper McKay's more far-reaching extrapolations. One can only speculate as to what his reaction would have been had he arrived at a more favourable moment and had stayed in a less inhospitable part of Britain.

This is not to diminish what McKay had to say about Britain: his experiences were his experiences and he had every right to relate them as he saw fit. It is a codicil to his more sweeping generalisations, for their foundations are narrow and unsteady. He spent just over a year in Britain (December 1919 to January 1921); except for passing through for a week on his way to Russia in 1922, he never returned. His view was necessarily partial. Even so, McKay's keen powers of observation come through all his work. One is repeatedly struck by the fine nuances of British society that he picked up. In *Banjo*, a Briton is overcharged in a Marseilles bar and complains vehemently. He explains to Ray that he 'didn't care about the few sous, but it was the principle of the thing'. 'You English certainly love to play with that word "principle"', was Ray's only comment.[67]

There is certainly bitterness in McKay's reflections. But who can blame him? As he noted in another context, 'if the Negro is a little bitter, the white man should be the last person in the world to accuse him of bitterness'. He averred that what matters is not so much the bitterness, but rather 'how one has developed out of it'.[68] Despite his outbursts, he remained profoundly human. Indeed, his bitterness arose from his humanitarian impulses and uncommonly fine sensibilities. Intensely alive, McKay loved music, he loved to dance and to swim. His love poems are as passionate as those of revolt. Friends recall his gift of laughter and mischievous sense of humour. It is precisely because of all this that he hated a civilisation that exploited, excluded and humiliated. His anger reached boiling point when this basic right to what the

Spirituals call 'the tree of life' – 'ain't we got a right to the tree of life?' – was denied people because of the colour of their skin; racism, he said, was the worst superstition in the world.

In personal relations he transcended the narrow boundaries of nationality and race. Like Ray, he

> would have considered the white world an utterly contemptible thing from its attitude toward the black if it were not for his principle of stressing the exception above the average ... He often pondered if an intellectual life could have been possible for him without that principle to support it.[69]

He explicitly addressed this problem. 'In ordinary propaganda language', he wrote to a friend in 1924,

> we say white vs. black but we know that it is more than that. The Irish and Indian peoples hate the English nation because they visualize it as the Power oppressing them. It is only from that point of view that their nationalist movement is at all tenable because when we look at facts we find many members of the English nation working for Irish and Indian Independence. And it is thus also with Negroes – the whites *en masse* represent a system that oppresses Negroes, but it is a system that a great body of thinking whites were accidentally born into and would like to change ... But it isn't an easy matter and in the common fight we use the ordinary phrases – black vs. white and working class vs. bourgeoisie – that are not at all correct. For life isn't narrow and definite like that.

He bemoaned the fact that 'the really fine people in this world are so few and *so powerless* that sometimes one is seized with a fit of despair in contemplating life'.[70]

In the same year McKay wrote a poem which stands in marked contrast to the one he had entitled 'Old England'. His experience of living in England divides the two. It has never been published before. It is simply called 'England'.

> How like a fixed and fortressed rock she stands,
> Cliff-featured arrogance against the world
> Of change the striving human spirit demands!
> Lofty Reaction! When shall she be hurled
> From her pedestal proud, whence she sways power
> Over the millions raped of strength and will,
> And trained before her armored pride to cower,
> Yet whose low murmurings she cannot still.
>
> How like a rock against the tides of change
> She rises up from out the Northern sea,
> The universe a lottery in her range;
> The waters billow round her angrily,

The castled lord entrench behind their walls,
But the mean multitude about her base,
Where rage the violent storms, the thunder falls,
Upon that rock can find no sheltered place.

The angry tempest will not lash in vain,
Against thy granite, arch conspirator,
Scheming to shackle men with the ancient chain.
Afar the slaves revolt, the distant roar
Tocsins thy plundered native multitude,
That reach out hungry for thine ancient crown,
Thine ancient titles, with strong hands and rude,
From thy high eminence to dash thee down.[71]

## Notes

I wish to thank Mark Shipway for sharing with me his knowledge of the Pankhurst group and other anti-parliamentary communists; Ken Weller, for alerting me to the existence and importance of Reuben Gilmore, his patience with my questioning, enthusiasm for the project and sharing files with me; Fabian Tomsett, for giving me an informative tour of Poplar and Docklands, and sharing his extraordinary knowledge of British anarchism; and Bill Schwarz for comments on an earlier draft, and his diligence and forbearance as editor.

1  Claude McKay, *Songs of Jamaica* (Kingston: Aston W. Gardner, 1912), p. 63.
2  Max Eastman, 'Introduction' to Claude McKay, *Harlem Shadows: the poems of Claude McKay* (New York: Harcourt, Brace, 1922), pp. xvi–xvii. McKay to Max Eastman, 23 March, 1939; McKay Manuscripts, Manuscripts Department, Lilly Library, University of Indiana, Bloomington, Indiana. The McKay/Eastman correspondence cited in this chapter is from this collection.
3  These facts escape Wayne Cooper and Robert Reinders, who in their article on McKay's visit to England, frame their argument around the notion of a black Briton coming home only to be disillusioned. It is as if McKay had not changed between 1911, when he wrote 'Old England', and December 1919, when he arrived in London. Wayne Cooper and Robert C. Reinders, 'A Black Briton comes "home": Claude McKay in England, 1920', *Race*, 9:1 (1967), pp. 67–83.
4  In 1909 a Sierra Leonean, A. B. C. Merriman-Labor, published *Britons Through Negro Spectacles or A Negro on Britons* (London: Imperial and Foreign Company, n.d. [1909]). Though it carries interesting anecdotes it lacks analysis.
5  I dealt with this problem in the work of C. L. R. James elsewhere: 'C. L. R. James and the spell of "western civilisation"': paper presented at the conference, 'C. L. R. James: his intellectual legacies', Wellesley College, April 1991. I never claimed, contrary to Paget Henry's caricature of my argument, that James's celebration of Western civilisation 'has its roots in Eurocentric tendencies that James inherited from Marxism': Paget Henry, *Caliban's Reason: introducing Afro-Caribbean philosophy* (New York: Routledge, 2000), p. 48. I know better than that and made it clear in my paper.
6  Claude McKay, *Banjo: a story without a plot* (New York: Harper, 1929), pp. 163, 274; McKay, 'English journalists investigate Bolshevism', *Crusader*, June 1921.
7  McKay, 'Claude McKay describes his own life', *Pearson's Magazine*, 39:5 (1918).
8  McKay, 'If we must die', *Liberator*, July 1919.
9  McKay, 'McKay describes his life'.
10  McKay, 'McKay describes his life'; McKay, *A Long Way From Home* (New York: Lee Furman, 1937), p. 55.
11  McKay, 'To "Holy" Russia', *Workers' Dreadnought*, 28 February 1920.

12  *Negro World*, 20 September 1919; quoted in A. Mitchell Palmer, *Letter From the Attorney General Transmitting In Response to a Senate Resolution October 17, 1919: a report on the activities of the Bureau of Investigation of the Department of Justice against persons advising anarchy, sedition, and the forcible overthrow of the Government* (Washington, DC: Government Printing Office, 1919), pp. 163–4.

13  Theodore Kornweibel, *No Crystal Stair: black life and the* Messenger, *1917–1928* (Westport: Greenwood, 1975); Winston James, *Holding Aloft the Banner of Ethiopia: Caribbean radicalism in early twentieth-century America* (London: Verso, 1998), and idem, 'Being red and black in Jim Crow America: on the ideology and travails of Afro-America's socialist pioneers, 1877–1930', in Charles Payne and Adam Green (eds), *Time Longer than Rope: a century of African American activism* (New York: New York University Press, 2003).

14  See James Weldon Johnson, *Black Manhattan* (New York: Knopf, 1930), p. 246; and his *Along This Way: the autobiography of James Weldon Johnson* (New York: Viking Press 1933), p. 341.

15  Frank Harris to Grant Richards, 8 November 1919, Frank Harris Papers, Albert H. Small Collections Library, University of Virginia; McKay to Grant Richards, 31 August 1920, C. K. Ogden Fonds, William Ready Divisions of Archives and Research Collections, Mills Memorial Library, McMaster University. All the McKay correspondence with Ogden cited here is from this collection.

16  Fuller to Ogden, 11 November 1919; McKay to Ogden, 17 August 1920; both in the Ogden Fonds.

17  McKay, 'Up to date' [1934] (Fragment of an unpublished sketch of his time in Britain); Nancy Cunard Collection, Harry Ransom Humanities Research Center, University of Texas at Austin. McKay to Ogden, 2 April 1920.

18  McKay to Ogden, 25 February 1920.

19  McKay to Ogden, 2 April 1920.

20  McKay to Ogden, 9 October 1920.

21  McKay to Max Eastman, 18 May 1923; McKay, 'How black sees green and red', *Liberator*, June 1921.

22  A detailed examination of these matters is to be found in my forthcoming study, *Claude McKay: the making of a black Bolshevik, 1889–1923*.

23  V. I. Lenin, *'Left-Wing Communism': an infantile disorder* (Moscow: Progress Publishers, 1970; first published 1920), pp. 60–73; Raymond Challinor, *The Origins of British Bolshevism* (London: Croom Helm, 1977), p. 168. Mark Shipway, *Anti-Parliamentary Communism in Britain: the movement for workers' councils in Britain, 1917–45* (London: Macmillan, 1988), provides the most detailed analysis of the disagreement between Lenin and Pankhurst.

24  *Workers' Dreadnought*, 1 June 1918.

25  *Workers' Dreadnought*, 7 June 1919. For a comprehensive analysis of the riots see Jacqueline Jenkinson, 'The1919 race riots in Britain: their backgrounds and consequences' (PhD thesis, University of Edinburgh, 1987).

26  McKay, *Long Way*, pp. 76–7.

27  McKay, 'Up to date', p. 4.

28  McKay, *Long Way*, pp. 69–70.

29  McKay, *Long Way*, p. 68.

30  McKay, *Long Way*, p. 70; idem, 'Up to date', p. 4; for more on Gilmore see Ken Weller, 'Direct action and the unemployed', *Solidarity*, July 1964; and idem, *'Don't be a soldier!' The radical anti-war movement in North London, 1914–1918* (London: Journeyman Press, 1985), and James, *McKay: the making of a black Bolshevik*.

31  McKay, *Long Way*, pp. 68–9.

32  McKay to Ogden, 18 February 1920.

33  McKay to Ogden, 7 March 1920.

34  *Cambridge Magazine*, 10:1 (1920).

35  Claude McKay, *Spring in New Hampshire and Other Poems* (London: Grant Richards, 1920).

36  McKay to Ogden, 25 February 1920. For Ogden's relation to the 1917 Club, see P.

Sargant Florence, 'Cambridge 1909–1919 and its aftermath', in Florence and J. R. L. Anderson (eds), *C. K. Ogden: a collective memoir* (London: Elek Pemberton, 1977).

37  Leonard Woolf, *Beginning Again: an autobiography of the years 1911 to 1918* (New York: Harcourt Brace Jovanovich, 1975), p. 216.

38  Woolf, *Beginning Again*, p. 217.

39  McKay to Ogden, 26 March 1920.

40  McKay to Ogden, 26 March and 14 April 1920.

41  McKay to Ogden, 26 March and 2 April 1920.

42  McKay, *Long Way*, pp. 67–8; McKay, 'Our London letter', *Negro World*, 13 March 1920. Although McKay's letter, which is in fact a long article on the club, was published in March 1920, it is datelined, 'London, Jan. 14, 1920'; 'Pismo Mek-Kaia Tovarishu Trotskomu' ['Letter from McKay to Comrade Trotsky'], *Pravda*, 1 April 1923.

43  Sally Marks, 'Black Watch on the Rhine: a study in propaganda, prejudice and prurience', *European Studies Review*, 13:3 (1983), p. 299.

44  *Daily Herald*, 9 and 10 April 1920.

45  *Daily Herald*, 10 April 1920. All emphases in these articles are from the original.

46  *Daily Herald*, 10 April 1920. Note the seamless shift from 'children of the forests' to 'manhood of these races'.

47  Privately, Lansbury claimed that the letter was too long and that McKay refused to shorten it. Cutting of letter by A. W. Simpson to unidentified newspaper. Cuttings Album (F15/3/4), E. D. Morel Papers, British Library of Political and Economic Science, London School of Economics and Political Science, University of London.

48  Claude McKay, 'A black man replies', *Workers' Dreadnought*, 24 April 1920.

49  Quoted in Robert Reinders, 'Racialism on the left: E. D. Morel and the "Black horror on the Rhine"', *International Review of Social History*, 13 (1968), p. 6.

50  C. E. Edwards [McKay], 'Robert Smillie', *Workers' Dreadnought*, 14 August 1920; McKay, *Long Way*, pp. 80–1; Woolf, *Beginning Again*, pp. 219–21; Reinders, 'Racialism on the left', p. 8.

51  'Pismo Mek-Kaia Tovarishu Trotskomu' ['Letter from McKay to Comrade Trotsky'], *Pravda*, 1 April 1923; *Communist*, 8 April 1922.

52  McKay, *Long Way*, p. 75.

53  [Unsigned], 'Poets and poetry', *Spectator*, 23 October 1922, p. 539.

54  McKay, *Long Way*, p. 76.

55  See James, *McKay: the making of a black Bolshevik*.

56  McKay, *Long Way*, pp. 63–7, 123, 303; McKay, 'London', in his manuscript, 'Cities'; McKay Papers, Beinecke Rare Book and Manuscript Library, Yale University.

57  See McKay's untitled review of Lytton Strachey's book, *Queen Victoria*, in *Liberator*, September 1921; and Winston James, *A Fierce Hatred of Injustice: Claude McKay's Jamaica and his poetry of rebellion* (London: Verso, 2000), pp. 93–8.

58  McKay to Ogden, 25 February 1920.

59  McKay, *Long Way*, p. 73.

60  McKay, *Long Way*, p. 304.

61  McKay to Marcus Garvey, 17 December 1919; copy in Hubert Harrison Papers. My thanks to Jeffrey Perry, the custodian of the Harrison Papers, for giving me a copy of this letter.

62  McKay touches upon his Moroccan troubles in *Long Way*, pp. 300–4. The South African authorities, on hearing rumours that McKay might slip into the country, had banned the 'notorious negro and Communist' as early as March 1924. See Winston James, *Claude McKay: from Bolshevism to black nationalism, 1923–1948* (forthcoming).

63  See letter from Mary Keating to Wayne Cooper, 4 March 1964; quoted in Cooper and Reinders, 'Black Briton comes "home"', p. 83.

64  McKay, 'Up to date', p. 4; McKay, *Long Way*, p. 67.

65  McKay to Cunard, 30 April 1932. Cunard Collection.

66  Gordon Phillips, 'The social impact', in Stephen Constantine, Maurice W. Kirby and

Mary B. Rose (eds), *The First World War in British History* (London: Edward Arnold, 1995), pp. 106–40.

67 McKay, *Banjo*, pp. 142–3.

68 McKay, 'A Negro writer to his critics', *New York Herald Tribune Books*, 6 March 1932.

69 McKay, *Banjo*, pp. 275–6.

70 McKay to Josephine Herbst, 18 August [1924], emphasis in original; Josephine Herbst Papers, Beinecke Rare Book and Manuscript Library, Yale University.

71 McKay, 'England' [1924], in 'Cities'. Quoted with permission of the estate of Claude McKay.

# CHAPTER FOUR

# Jean Rhys:
# West Indian intellectual

## Helen Carr

Samuel Beckett, it is said, when asked in Paris on one occasion if he were English, replied unequivocally, *'au contraire'*. Jean Rhys might have said much the same. If she was sure about her identity in any way, it was in her certainty that she was not English – 'pseudo-English' at the most, as she puts in her memoir, *Smile Please*.[1] But what was she? In what sense could she be called a West Indian? Rhys herself was uncertain at times, and some of her critics have hotly debated the question. There is no doubt of her love for the disturbing beauty of her native Dominica, a recurrent if occasional theme from her earliest stories onwards, evoked most powerfully in her final novel, *Wide Sargasso Sea*. Yet in all her writing about the island there is the sense, sometimes sad, sometimes envious, sometimes resentful, that it belongs more to the black majority than to the white creoles: they were, she wrote, 'more a part of the place than we were'.[2] On the one hand, she could say, like Anna in *Voyage in the Dark*, 'I'm a real West Indian ... I'm the fifth generation on my mother's side'.[3] Yet on the other, like Antoinette in *Wide Sargasso Sea*, a white cockroach to the ex-slaves and a white nigger to the English, she could also say – and during the time she was writing that novel increasingly felt – 'between you I often wonder who I am and where is my country and where do I belong and why was I ever born at all'.[4]

As the white descendant of slave-owners, coming to England in 1907 at the age of seventeen, and during the course of her long life returning only once for a visit to her birthplace, should she be considered a West Indian writer at all? After all, three of her first four novels, and many of her short stories, are placed in Europe, and have heroines with no apparent knowledge of the Caribbean. Yet her situation has in fact some striking similarities to that of her fellow colonial, Beckett, also born a member of an affluent, ethnically distinct, Protestant minority, in a part of the British empire where the majority were poor Catholics, leaving that country as a young adult, and spending a long life else-where. He similarly often produced works whose setting was by no means overtly that of his native land. The Irish, however, have had no problem claiming Beckett an Irish writer, even though he went even further than Rhys in his denial of an English heritage by starting to write in French. More direct comparisons with other West Indian writers have been made by Evelyn O'Callaghan. Jamaica Kincaid, V. S. Naipaul and Caryl Phillips, she points out, are all emigrant writers, Phillips 'arriv[ing] in England "at the portable age" of one'.[5] They too have written fiction that does not have a Caribbean setting. Yet their right to be called West Indian writers is not questioned. It is Rhys's race that calls her status in doubt, for herself as much as for others.

The fiercest battle over her place in West Indian literature was fought out in the 1970s, though it was revived again in the pages of *Wasafiri* in the 1990s. Until the publication of *Wide Sargasso Sea*, few of her critics or readers – and there were not in any case a large number of them – thought of her as Caribbean. An exception was Ford Madox Ford, who first published her in his journal, the *transatlantic review*, and who wrote the introduction to her first collection of short stories, *The Left Bank* (1927). With his usual insight, he made clear the importance of her origins for her writing: 'Coming from the Antilles', he wrote, 'with a terrifying insight, and a terrific – an almost lurid! – passion for stating the case of the underdog, she has let her pen loose on the Left Banks of the Old World – on its gaols, its studios, its salons, its cafés, its crimi-nals, its midinettes – with a bias of admiration for its midinettes and of sympathy for its law-breakers'.[6] One might note that it was of course easier for Ford than reviewers of, say *Quartet*, *After Leaving Mr Mackenzie*, and *Good Morning, Midnight* to recognise her Caribbean roots. For one thing, in three of the stories in *The Left Bank* the narra-tor identifies herself as West Indian; in addition, Ford knew Rhys per-sonally, and during the course of their love affair her alien origins were for him both a source of fascination and of eventual alarm. Alec Waugh was another exception. He had met Rhys in England, and mentioned her in passing in an article he wrote on Dominica in 1948. He makes it clear he does not expect many of his readers to have heard of her: 'Her novels have not reached a large public', he writes apologetically, 'but they have a personal flavour'. But he then goes on to say: 'Re-reading *After Leaving Mr. Mackenzie*, I could see how many flashbacks to Dominica – imperceptible to the unacquainted reader – occurred in it. I could see how Dominica had coloured her temperament and outlook.'[7] Such a view would not be put forward again for many years.

When *Wide Sargasso Sea* first appeared in 1966, most British and American critics continued to ignore the question of Rhys's origins,

Paul Theroux in 1972 going so far as to ask if it was her 'placelessness' which had caused her to be neglected for so long.[8] With those from the Caribbean itself it was another story. The idea that there could be something called West Indian literature was just emerging, and both Wally Look Lai in 1968 and Kenneth Ramchand in 1970 wanted to claim the novel as specifically West Indian.[9] However, Kamau Brathwaite in a fierce denunciation famously propagated the contrary view: 'White creoles in the English and French West Indies have separated themselves by too wide a gulf, and have contributed too little culturally, as a group, to give credence to the notion that they can, given the present structure, meaningfully identify or be identified with the spiritual world on this side of the Sargasso Sea'.[10] Revisiting these comments twenty years later, Brathwaite tempered his argument, if not his tone. On this occasion he was replying to an article by Peter Hulme, on the location of *Wide Sargasso Sea*, in which Hulme had criticised Brathwaite for exploiting as part of his argument the non-African derivation of Rhys's supporters, Ramchand being of East Indian origin, and Look Lai of Chinese.[11] In his stormy but illuminating response, Brathwaite made clear that his earlier comments had to be read in the historical context of African-Caribbean writers' determination to establish their work as central to West Indian writing, and in the wider framework of black nationalism in the West Indies in a period, 'not so long after', as Elaine Savory puts it, when 'virtual apartheid' prevailed in Brathwaite's native Barbados.[12] His anger in 1974, Brathwaite explained, had been directed against those whom he saw as using *Wide Sargasso Sea* as a weapon to attack 'African barbarism & darkness' in writers like himself.[13] In his 1995 reading, Brathwaite explicitly refers to *Wide Sargasso Sea* as a 'great Caribbean novel', and in fact is hostile to other kinds of identification that can be given it, most vehemently rejecting the appellation 'postcolonial'.[14] He points out that 'When WSS first appeared … it was we West Indians who paid it mind. It was "ours" as it shd be. But since in the 60s we were so race-consciously fragmented, some of us at least fought over the importance / value / significance of its … ENIGMA. CO [his 1974 book, *Contradictory Omens*] in fact, from that point of view, is part of those uncivil civil wars in Caribb culture & I can't tell you how we get beyond that yet.'[15] His point had been, he stresses, that 'in talking about Caribb culture … who you are inc yr ETHNICITY determines how you SEE Caribb (or any?) culture'.[16] Jean Rhys at least would have concurred with that last comment, once saying: 'What you see depends on what you are'.[17]

The Caribbean's violent imperial history has as its legacy a population which is heterogeneous and hybrid; its inhabitants include African Caribbeans, East Indian Caribbeans, Far Eastern Caribbeans, white

Caribbeans of various European extractions, people of a mixture of races and a small number of indigenous Caribs. As Brathwaite indicates, there have been historical tensions and hostilities between them all, and, as he says, 'those uncivil civil wars in Caribb culture' are by no means over. The position of the white European Caribbeans is, of course, different in kind from any of the others; they were the historical oppressors, responsible, in the pursuit of their own wealth, for the presence in the region of all the others except the Caribs – in their case being responsible for their scarcity – and thus ultimately responsible as well for giving rise to all of those 'uncivil civil wars'. Yet their lives have been shaped by that brutal history as much as have the other groups; they are part of the material social reality of the West Indies, even if their right to be part of its 'spiritual world' has been challenged. Even Brathwaite, who in the 1970s wanted to see the white Creole as an alien outsider – something Jean Rhys makes clear she at times felt herself to be – by the 1990s accepts her as a part of that dark history; but he still wants to suggest that though 'Rhys was honest in her sense of GUILT', she self-defensively makes a 'beautiful figment' of Antoinette's relationship with Tia and Christophine, of white with black.[18]

How any of the inhabitants of the Caribbean, including the white creoles, '**SEE** Caribb (or any?) culture', does, as Brathwaite argues, depend on their ethnicity, historical experience and cultural memories of the Caribbean. It will also depend on which island or part of the mainland they come from. One further way in which Jean Rhys only ambiguously belongs to the West Indies is that the term – West Indies – is traditionally used only of the British Caribbean. Her island, Dominica, was owned by the French for many years, sandwiched between the French islands of Martinique and Guadeloupe, and only finally secured for good by the British in 1805, though even then remaining predominantly French in sympathy as J. A. Froude observed with disapproval in the 1880s. There was in Rhys's childhood only a tiny English Protestant elite; the island was overwhelmingly Catholic, and the African-Caribbean majority, as now, spoke a French patois. Rhys went to a Catholic convent school, where whites were in the minority, so it was only at home that she learned to absorb British culture, inculcated in the British Caribbean through the school system. As a white creole from Dominica she was 'West Indian' in a different way from the other figures examined in this book, but the importance of her Caribbean childhood and its legacy have been increasingly recognised.[19] Paradoxically, her lifelong sense of homelessness begins there. Rejected as she felt herself to be by her mother, and ignored for the most part by her father, she longed to be black, one of those who were 'part of the place', but she repeatedly discovered she was alien, suspect, even hated. Even though she loved the beauty of the island, the place itself, she felt, rejected her: 'I wanted to identify myself with it, to lose myself in it. (But it turned its head away, indifferent, and that broke my heart.)'[20] When she arrived in England from the West Indies, Rhys would find herself alien again, and that experience would, as it did for many of her fellow West Indians, play a crucial part in forming her understanding of the world. From her disturbing Dominican childhood and that painful entry into the metropolis came the beginnings of her insights into the workings of the hierarchical English social system, insights that grew with her struggles against prejudice and poverty in the metropolitan world.

Yet though Jean Rhys's sense of homelessness, even in her native island, is undoubtedly stronger than for some of her fellow Caribbeans, perhaps even that is something that is more common in the West Indies rather than is customarily acknowledged. Bill Schwarz raises in his introduction the question of what is specific to the West Indian expatriate situation, asking if, as well as similarities, there are differences between West Indian and other colonial immigrants. Perhaps one difference lies here. Almost everyone in the West Indies has come, or their ancestors have come, from elsewhere. No one is wholly at home. Even the indigenous Caribs, on their poverty-stricken reservations, have been encircled and displaced, their home made unhomely. In the West Indies there was nothing comparable to the insistent ideological construction of nationhood that formed the United States, and turned its immigrants into a nation. As colonies, the West Indies related to Britain; historically their identity was unequivocally dependent. C. L. R. James describes himself in his youth as 'A British intellectual long before I was ten, already an alien in my own environment, even my own family'.[21] The West Indian spiritual world that Brathwaite evokes is significantly an African one: the West Indies is only in a partial sense, a hyphenated sense, the African-Caribbean's home. 'The Caribbean', George Lamming suggests, 'may be defined as the continuum of a journey in space and consciousness.'[22] Or as Stuart Hall has pointed out, 'The Caribbean is already the diaspora of Africa, Europe, China, Asia, India, and this diaspora re-diasporized itself [in Britain]'.[23] And as he reflects on his own migration: 'I am not entirely of either place. And that's exactly the diasporic experience, far enough to experience the sense of exile and loss, close enough to understand the enigma of an always-postponed "arrival"'.[24] Jean Rhys is another diasporic intellectual, with the migrant's consciousness of the shifting complexity of identities and the impossibility of an assured 'arrival'. But that is not to say her diasporic experience is not very specifically shaped by the culture that she has come from and that which she meets.

   The other term in the title of this book, 'intellectual', has been as contentious a term to apply to Jean Rhys as West Indian. When, late in life she achieved fame and critical attention in the wake of the publication of *Wide Sargasso Sea*, one reason for the breakthrough was the changed cultural climate; her attacks on the established order, on snobbishness, on conventional English sexual mores, on racism, were now in tune with the times. It was a very different period from the years of postwar Cold War conformity, when she had been unable to persuade Constable to publish a book of her short stories. Her long publishing silence from 1939 was not the result of her ceasing to write; what she had to say proved unacceptable. Even in the 1920s and 1930s Rhys's books had frequently been described as 'sordid', but in the 1960s she had become up-to-date. Yet the circumstances that made her late success possible also adversely affected the way in which she came to be defined as a writer. Each novel, it was averred, told the story of the 'Rhys woman', as her heroines were dubbed, avatars always of herself. They were the transcription of experience, very sensitive, very fine, but they had no message beyond the delineation of her individual life. In addition, for all the liberalisation of sexual attitudes, 1966 predated the feminist reaction against the 1960s' simultaneous hyper-sexualisation and infantilisation of women. Rhys's own reliance as a young woman on her sexual attractiveness – in this she was undoubtedly like her heroines – as chorus girl, artist's model, mannequin and mistress necessarily meant she could not be considered as a thinker. It was still difficult to think of a woman as both sexual and intellectual, or indeed as intellectual at all. Ironically, it's a complaint some of Rhys's heroines make themselves. Frances, in Rhys's early short story, 'Vienne', bemoans how she's been damaged by men 'always disdaining my mind and concentrating on my body'.[25] When Sasha in *Good Morning, Midnight* says to the gigolo René that she is a '*cérébrale*', he rejects the idea out of hand saying: 'I should have thought you were rather stupid ... Don't be vexed. I don't mean stupid. I mean that you feel better than you think.'[26] That stereotype of the feeling rather than thinking woman was firmly attached to Rhys, even by some of her most admiring critics. When Al Alvarez sealed her reputation in 1974 by claiming in the *New York Times* that she was 'the best living novelist', he insisted that although she 'has a marvellous artistic intelligence – no detail is superfluous and her poise never falters as she walks her wicked emotional way – yet [she] is absolutely non-intellectual: no axes to grind, no ideas to tout'.[27] For him this is wholly admirable. But it meant the powerful social critique that emerges from Rhys's fiction could not be seen

   The myth of the naïve, ignorant yet instinctive writer has been particularly emphasised by those who have written about Rhys biograph-

ically who, ignoring the ample evidence of her wide reading, have portrayed her working unaware of other writers and in isolation from the
intellectual currents of her day. David Plante, in his grimly unsympathetic and luridly sensation-seeking account of her old age, produced a
list of writers he claims that she said she had not read, most of whom
are mentioned in her novels and letters and whose work she clearly
knew.[28] At much the same time, however, Judith Kegan Gardiner,
wrote a ground-breaking essay in which she argued against the prevailing trend, demonstrating that Rhys was a literary, self-conscious and
modernist writer, who in *Good Morning, Midnight* alone alluded to
Emily Dickinson, Joyce, Keats, Rimbaud, Wilde, Anatole France, Woolf
and Colette.[29] Already in the 1980s more attentive readings of Rhys's
fiction and letters made it more difficult to ignore her extensive knowledge of literature, particularly English and French nineteenth- and
twentieth-century literature, to say nothing of the visual arts and
history. Yet in 1990, Carole Angier, in her 700–page biography of Rhys,
was still writing: 'This is one of the most intriguing of all the paradoxes
about Jean Rhys, that she knew so little, and wrote only about herself,
and yet she managed to write novels which were completely modern,
full of feeling, ideas, even literary terms that were absolutely of her
time'.[30] Angier has done extensive work in tracing acquaintances and
lovers, but she makes no attempt at intellectual biography. She is hor-
rified by Rhys's bad behaviour, her drunkenness, her conflicts with the
law, her rows at dinner parties, and in the end sees a split between the
genius and the anarchic woman. Ironically, given her uncompromisingly biographical approach to Rhys's fiction, she is unable to reconcile
Rhys's refusal to accept the status quo in her life with the same refusal
in her work.

Angier is aware that Rhys condemns the metropolitan world that she
met when she came to England, but she ascribes those criticisms to
Rhys's desire to vindicate her own failures rather than to any insight.
Even Diana Athill, her editor at Deutsch who gave Rhys much support
as a writer and friend in her later years, and who gives a less morally
reproving account of Rhys in her memoir, makes Rhys's condemnation
simply the response of a frightened, ignorant colonial from the outback,
coming from a world so limited that it could not even be considered
parochial.[31] She suggests that Rhys, who, she points out, could not even
recognise a train when she first reached England, remained incapable of
learning to understand this new world, escaping into impotent rage
whenever baffled or defeated. Yet though Rhys had not learned in
Dominica that landladies were mean with hot water, or that young
ladies must not walk out by themselves, she had learned other things.
She knew about injustice, she knew about racial hatred, she knew

'there is always another side'.[32] She knew whites had money and that blacks did not. She knew the colonialists in the past had behaved with unspeakable cruelty; she knew they still assumed their right to oppress economically and to maintain a legal system in their own interests. She knew about fear. She saw in stark and extreme form all the inequalities and prejudices that she would meet in England; there was no danger that she would not recognise their more subtle formations when she reached 'home'. Jean Rhys was never an intellectual in the sense that she published discursive essays or theoretical books. The language of her fiction and memoirs – and here she has much in common with other West Indian writers – is always the vernacular, and though it is often a different vernacular from, say, Selvon's, like him she writes in the voice of the disempowered. Rather than use, she mocks and exposes the authoritative language of power.

Like other West Indians, Rhys met immediate prejudice when she reached England. When she arrived in 1907 she was not marked out as different by skin-colour as the majority of her fellow Caribbeans would be but, as soon as she spoke, her strong Caribbean accent identified her as alien. Accents were all important in assigning places in the English class system, and were only just beginning to lose their defining role when Rhys died in the late 1970s. In *Voyage in the Dark*, Anna's step-mother Hester, Anna tells us, had 'an English lady's voice with a sharp cutting edge' which said to her interlocutor: 'Now I've spoken you can hear that I'm a lady. I have spoken and I suppose you now realise that I'm an English gentlewoman. I have my doubts about you. Speak up and I will place you at once.'[33] As with the inquisitive Mrs Wilson in Rhys's short story 'Outside the machine', the silent question would be asked: 'An English person? English, what sort of English? To which of the seven divisions, sixty-nine subdivisions, and thousand-and-three sub-subdivisions do you belong?'[34] Rhys was forced to give up her desire to be an actress because her drama school could not rid her of her West Indian voice, and for years afterwards she would only talk in a whisper. In *Voyage in the Dark* Anna is accused by Hester of having an 'awful sing-song voice … Exactly like a nigger you talked – and still do'.[35] Probably the same comments were made to Rhys; they were certainly made of her. In Dominica, Rhys, the daughter of a government doctor and landowner was undoubtedly respectable, undoubtedly a lady. In England her status was immediately in question.

As Catherine Hall argues in her chapter, both white and black West Indians were stigmatised in Britain in the nineteenth century. The image of plantocracy culture that grew up in the days of slavery was a deeply insalubrious one, partly perhaps an evasion of metropolitan guilt over the wealth garnered through slavery by the projection of all blame on to the depraved colonial executors. In spite of efforts to dispel it, the white creole reputation for degeneracy was still circulating in the early twentieth century. (The image of white West Indian creoles contrasts with that of Anglo-Indian colonials, who lived in India in social isolation from the native population, and were regarded as respectable, noble upholders of empire.) White creoles were reputed to be, as Kenneth Ramchand points out, 'indolent' and 'licentious', qualities also ascribed to black Caribbeans, the planter class having undoubtedly gone native in terms of moral character, and very likely having interbred as well.[36] They could no longer be regarded as wholly white, and certainly not as truly English. White creole women were reputed to be even more corrupt than the men. As Rochester had said of Bertha in *Jane Eyre*, in the words Jean Rhys would echo many years later in *Wide Sargasso Sea*, they were seen as 'intemperate and unchaste', those harsh condemnatory Victorian words that drop like dead weights, cold and inhuman, in the fluid and poetic language of Antoinette's thoughts.[37] The qualities associated with the 'coloured' or 'mulatto' women, 'highly sexed and sensuous', as Ramchand puts it, are ascribed to white creole women, but in addition, like Bertha, they are deeply dangerous.[38]

Whilst Jean Rhys most powerfully writes back to this set of stereotypes in *Wide Sargasso Sea*, she presents the viewpoint of the 'intemperate and unchaste' woman in all her novels. Jean D'Costa has suggested that *Wide Sargasso Sea* 'predates conceptually all other Rhys texts', and certainly that is true here; looking back from *Wide Sargasso Sea*, one can see she is arguing the case for the despised creole woman all along.[39] Even when her heroines are not explicitly Caribbean, they are regarded with suspicion; they fail to pass, as Sacha realises in *Good Morning, Midnight*, as *'femmes convenables'*.[40] As Ford had gone on to make clear, the reason that Rhys's Caribbean origins gave her a 'passion for stating the case of the underdog' was that those origins in themselves labelled her as unacceptable; they link her by association with the prostitutes and lawbreakers who engage her sympathy. That note of sympathy, he had gone on to say, is one 'of which we do not have too much in Occidental literature with its perennial bias towards satisfaction with things as they are. But it is a note that needs sounding, that badly needs sounding, since the real activities of the world are seldom moved forward by the accepted, or even by the Hautes Bourgeoisies'.[41] Rhys's fiction is always engaged in giving the viewpoint of those like herself who are not accepted, those who are despised by the *hautes bourgeoisies*. Unacceptably white in Dominica, she was still racially unacceptable in Europe; if she did not have the experience of other West Indians arriving in England that Bill Schwarz refers to as 'becoming black', she certainly became something besmirched, muddied. Had she

[ 101 ]

been more adept at acquiring the required accent, she could of course, unlike most of her fellow West Indians, have learnt to 'pass'. But, as Ford was aware, she had rapidly fallen foul of the English rules of respectability in ways other than her colonial origins. Becoming a chorus girl symbolised a downward step, a move into one of those professions, like acting or dancing, which at that period were always suspected of sexual laxity. Chorus girls were largely working class, and could perhaps be acceptable as such. As Mrs Wilson, the suspicious interrogator in 'Outside the machine', says of a working-class chorus girl: 'Yes, this is permissible; it has its uses. Pretty English chorus girl – north country – with a happy, independent disposition and bright teasing eyes. Placed! All correct'.[42] A chorus girl who had been brought up to be a lady, however, was indubitably incorrect. Elaine Savory comments that Jean Lenglet, Rhys's first husband, had in 1939 'argued that her clarity of vision resulted in part from her experience of leaving behind an idyllic Caribbean childhood for the brutal realities of London's disappointed and marginalised: he understood Rhys's change of class status as critical in her writing'.[43] Her childhood was not always idyllic (though it is surely significant that she had given Lenglet the impression it was), but by and large Lenglet is right about the importance of that cultural shock. Savory herself suggests that Rhys became 'effectively working class' in taking on the job of a chorus girl, but that is to misunderstand the workings of the British class system.[44] People do not become working class by changing occupations. In *Voyage in the Dark* Anna's use of language is quite different in class terms from that of the other chorus girls. After all it's Anna who is actually reading *Nana* with, incidentally a picture on the cover of a 'stout, dark woman brandishing a wine glass' – unchaste *and* intemperate – and dark into the bargain. It's the working-class Maudie, however, who forthrightly pronounces: 'That's a dirty book, isn't it? … I know; it's about a tart. I think it's disgusting. I bet you a man writing about a tart tells a lot of lies one way and another. Besides, all books are like that – just someone stuffing you up.'[45] Maudie comments that Anna 'always look[s] lady-like', but Anna, by becoming a chorus girl, can no longer be considered to *be* ladylike. As a West Indian, her position is already ambiguous: her fellow chorus girls call her the 'Hottentot', drawing from a vernacular rooted in nineteenth-century racial theory, implying that she exists on the lowest rung of the human evolutionary ladder, and also that she is highly sexed.[46] Through her dubious occupation, she has slipped further out of the respectable middle classes, into the interstices of the English class system, neither one thing not the other; an anomaly; unlike the pretty north-country chorus girl, she is out of place, liable always to rejection or insult. Walter asks her if her stepmother thinks 'she disgraced the family or something', and Anna shrinks, thinking 'Oh God, he's the sneering sort. I wish I hadn't come.'[47]

Becoming a kept woman was Jean Rhys's next step down the social ladder, a signifier both of her sexual fall and of her poverty. 'Intact, or not intact, that's the first question. An income or not an income, that's the second', as Marya imagines Heidler putting it in *Quartet*.[48] In the English system class and money were not the same thing, but they were closely entwined. Just as in the West Indies, Rhys suggests, it was hard to be truly 'white' without money, in England it is difficult to remain a 'lady' without an income. In *After Leaving Mr Mackenzie*, Julia's sister Norah strives to do so against the odds. She is appalled that Julia 'doesn't even look like a lady now', and wonders, 'What can she have been doing with herself?' She herself is

> labelled for all to see ... 'Middleclass, no money.' Hardly enough to keep herself in clean linen. And yet scrupulously, fiercely clean, but with all the daintiness and prettiness perforce cut out. Everything about her betrayed the woman who had been brought up to certain tastes, then left without the money to gratify them; trained to certain opinions which forbad her even the relief of rebellion against her lot; yet holding desperately to both her tastes and her opinions.[49]

As Julia thinks as she walks round the West End later, 'This place tells you all the time, "Get money, get money, get money, or be for ever damned"'.[50] Julia is damned in one way, Norah in another.

Throughout Rhys's fiction, she not only gives the viewpoint of 'underdogs' like herself (one reviewer described *Voyage in the Dark* as being 'like a Salvation Army tract rewritten from the inside'); she contests the way the society that she met judges those like her.[51] That is not to say her heroines always successfully contest the social order – they are more often defeated – but Rhys's imaginative vision exposes the injustices that keep, in Ford's words, 'things as they are'. The women in her stories are often silenced by their oppressors, male or female, but they argue with them in their thoughts. Nancy Harrison has pointed out how much 'talking back' Rhys's heroines do in their heads, so the fiction itself presents their defiance, even though it may be telling the story of their apparent defeat.[52] Julia thinks of Neil James, when she goes to him to appeal for money: 'Because he has money he's a kind of god. Because I have none I'm a kind of worm. A worm because I've failed and I have no money.' But her very statement of those terms of social power presents their immorality, though all she says aloud is: 'I got fed up. I felt I needed a rest. I thought perhaps you'd help me to have a rest.'[53]

Writing back to *Jane Eyre* and giving the first Mrs Rochester a chance to give her point of view was perhaps the culmination of this technique. But although Rhys is conscious of the way women are the losers in the patriarchal metropolitan and colonial world, she is also aware that women can oppress and men be oppressed. Downtrodden men are shown as much sympathy as exploited women: in 'Vienne', Frances says silently to the deceived, diminutive André, 'Hail, brother Doormat, in a world of Boots'.[54] Even in *Wide Sargasso Sea* part of the skilful shaping of the plot is achieved by the way in which, when we first meet the Rochester figure, we realise he as second son is himself the unhappy victim of a patriarchal system; as the novel goes on and he finds wealth and power, Rhys depicts the process whereby through fear, jealousy and fierce suppression he takes on the role of cruel patriarch, a mercenary and possessive oppressor himself. In Rhys's analysis, metropolitan society operates, as she says in 'Vienne', as a 'huge machine of law, order, respectability' that destroys or maims those who do not fit in, whether they are misfits for reasons of race, class, nation, sexual mores or poverty.[55] She is most scathing about what she sees as the English bourgeois desire for conformity. Mr Mackenzie – one of the most mocked of all her creations – had 'a certain code of morals and manners, from which he seldom departed ... His code was perfectly adapted to the social system, and in any argument he could have defended it against any attack whatsoever. However, he never argued about it, because that was part of the code. You didn't argue about these things. Simply under certain circumstances you did this, and under certain circumstances you did that.'[56] Her stories do not deal with the really wealthy and powerful – even the rich lovers are generally working in the City, and would have been sniffed at in the best circles. Power for Rhys takes many different forms at different levels of society; it operates in stepmother Hester's voice, and through Mrs Wilson's inquisitorial gaze. It is found in the bullying landlord in a Paris hotel, who looks like a fish 'lording it in his own particular tank, staring at the world outside with a glassy and unbelieving eye'.[57] It is found repeatedly in the dealings of well-to-do men and their impoverished mistresses. It is possessed by the black policeman in *'Temps perdi'*, well supplied with bayoneted rifles with which to control the Carib reservation in Dominica. When asked if there had been anyone hurt in a riot, the policeman replies: 'Oh, no, only two or three Caribs ... two-three Caribs were killed'; the narrator comments – 'It could have been an Englishman speaking'.[58]

Yet in Rhys's writing while prejudice, cruelty and hypocrisy can be found in both men and women, and in people of any race, the primary focus of her attack is on English patriarchy. Rhys's attitudes are never simple, and she says at one point that her hatred of England was really 'disappointed love'.[59] As a colonial child, her reading was of English books, and her view of England, she says, was taken from them. She had grown up thinking England was glamorous, magnificent. When she arrived she found it cold, grey, unwelcoming, xenophobic, snobbish and endemically misogynist. Yet at times Rhys suggests that her critical stance towards the English was already developing in Dominica. She wrote much later that the reason she hated the English was that as a child she had realised 'the white people have everything and the black people have nothing, in money'.[60] Economics again, something unavoidable in a childhood in the Caribbean, where as Lamming insists, the Europeans carried out 'their first experiment in capitalism overseas'.[61] In 'The day they burned the books', the young creole protagonist is told by visiting English children that she is not really English, just a 'horrid colonial', and she reacts by retorting she doesn't want to be English: she'd rather be French or Spanish – very much Rhys's own view. There are other elements in her upbringing perhaps that prevented her from succumbing to the norms of English hierarchy. It was because her father was a 'liberal' in Dominican terms, prepared to meet socially with the non-whites, even though vociferously opposed to the coloured middle classes in Dominican politics, that she was allowed to attend the mixed-race Catholic convent. Her fellow Dominican novelist, Phyllis Shand Allfrey, by contrast had an English-born father who did not hold with 'mixing', and who was thus educated at home. (Allfrey's grandfather, a doctor like Rhys's father, would always examine his black patients with gloves on.)[62] Rhys had met more non-whites than other white creoles might have done, and even if, as her account of her convent education shows, that taught her as much about racial tensions as racial tolerance, it gave her insights she might not otherwise have had. Significantly, in addition, the convent had introduced her to the French language and to French poetry, to which she was deeply drawn and which she felt had far more affinities with the black Dominicans than English did. It was in Paris that she began to write, and French writers were her models. In 1959 she wrote to Francis Wyndham, 'When I say write for love I mean that there are two places for me. Paris (or what it was to me) and Dominica, a most lovely and melancholy place ... Both these places or the thought of them make me want to write.'[63]

One other element in her estrangement from Englishness might also have been her identification with her Celtic origins. Her father, whom she often idealised, in spite, or perhaps because, of his comparative neglect of her, was Welsh – Jean Rhys's name was originally Ella Gwendoline Rees Williams. She had an Irish grandmother who sent her fairy-tales and books of legends, and her mother's ancestry was

Scottish. Sue Thomas notes that Rhys felt her family, though middle class, was regarded as below 'the solidly English middle classes' in the island.[64] This is confirmed by an incident recounted in Phyllis Shand Allfrey's biography: Allfrey met Rhys in England in the 1930s, and when on one occasion she was asked, 'How were the white people now in Dominica?' replied they were now 'of the common variety, the Smiths and the Browns'.[65] Rhys was enraged, saying she had been one of the Smiths, and refused to speak to Allfrey for the rest of the evening. It is unlikely her family's tone was lowered by her mother – the Lockharts were a well-respected family among the whites. So it must have been her Welsh father, and while it may not have been to do with his Welshness, Rhys may well have felt it was. She remained proud of the fact that she only had one-sixteenth English blood. Her enemy was emphatically only the English. As a writer she believed her work was only possible because she had 'escaped from an exclusively Anglo-Saxon influence and … never returned to it'.[66]

Rhys, Savory suggests, can be seen as deeply Caribbean in her consciousness of her colour.[67] As George Lamming writes of Caribbean society, 'Race is the persistent legacy … No one born and nurtured in this soil has escaped its scars, and … everyone – whatever their ancestral origin – is endowed with an acute racial consciousness.'[68] Some critics, most notably Veronica Marie Gregg, have argued that Jean Rhys is racist; Savory concludes she is both racist and anti-racist. Rhys certainly does not escape the racial generalisations of her time. That could be said of her depiction of the English as much as of the black Caribbeans (though as far as I know the only critic to protest on behalf of the English is Robert Young). For her day she was remarkably opposed to racism, endeavouring to resist or complicate conventional essentialising definitions.[69] Rhys's characters can be situated within the archive of colonial stereotypes with which we are now so familiar, but they most often break out of them. Gregg appears to interpret her awareness that the whites are regarded with hostility or hatred by some of the black or coloured Dominicans as racist; it might be thought more, in the early twentieth century and possibly even more in 1936, when Rhys had her one return visit, a painfully honest realisation of the facts.[70] Rhys says that as a child she felt the black Caribbeans were 'more alive' than the white, that she longed 'so fiercely to be black and to dance', but she also records the fear and shock that those glimpses of hostility aroused in her.[71] Her nurse Meta who 'always seemed to be brooding over some terrible, unforgettable, wrong' was the 'terror of [her] life'; as if to punish the white child for the cruelties of colonialism she terrorises her with tales of soucriants, loups-garoux and zombies, introducing her to 'a world of fear and distrust', the 'terrified consciousness' which Ramchand identifies as central to the colonial subjectivity.[72] Rhys describes another black servant, Francine, who also introduces her to African traditions, but whose 'stories were quite different, full of jokes and laughter'.[73] To Gregg, Rhys is simply setting up the stereotypically good versus bad native, but as Savory points out, she 'marks both women as fundamentally influential in her cultural development: she was often engaged with both elements in a binary split'.[74] What is significant is that Meta's hostility, like that of the blacks who burn Coulibri in *Wide Sargasso Sea*, is not presented as a product of a savage nature, but of a colonial history. It is the English Mr Mason who deals in essentialising racist assumptions: the blacks are 'children' and 'too damn lazy to be dangerous'. He pays no attention when Annette says to him: 'You don't like, or even recognise, the good in them ... and you won't believe in the other side ... They are more alive than you are, lazy or not, and they can be dangerous and cruel for reasons you wouldn't understand.'[75]

Rhys's fiction imagines Englishness as the apotheosis of whiteness, in contrast to Caribbean blackness. This is another area in which her use of racial tropes has been questioned. In *Voyage in the Dark*, she writes, 'Being black is warm and gay, being white is cold and sad'.[76] The Caribbean is a place of scents and colours; England a place of grey streets and dark houses. English culture is figured as machine-like, unfeeling, driven by money, repressed. The Caribbean is sensuous, passionate, vibrant, spontaneous. England, Teresa O'Connor has argued, is for Rhys male-dominated; the Caribbean is largely identified with women. Anglo-Saxon men, Rhys complains, despise women writers. In her version of the Caribbean, women are always singing songs, telling stories. Ramchand famously called *Voyage in the Dark* 'our first negritude novel', and certainly there is much in common with *négritude*'s celebration of black warmth and creativity.[77] Rhys deeply admired many European writers. Yet she does, intriguingly, in one unpublished essay, talk of 'us black people', and she sees the West Indies as a source of creativity that she weaves into her multivoiced, heteroglossial texts.[78] She wrote in 1962: 'I am very sold on the poems of a man called Derek Walcott (I think) from Lucia coloured I believe or a Negro. Read some & was delighted ... Do you know I believe the West Indies may produce artists and poets – the climate, atmosphere and the mixture of races all exactly what is wanted'.[79]

Sue Thomas has quite rightly pointed out the close links between Rhys's portrayal of the Caribbean and other forms of modernist primitivism current at the time, of which *négritude* is one.[80] *Négritude* inverted many of the conventional colonial assumptions about race, and many conceptual and political difficulties followed. But its historical importance should not be underestimated. Modernist primitivism took many forms, and one suspects Rhys's version, which places so much emphasis on song and dance, as well as growing out of her childhood experiences, was influenced by the fascination with blackness, and in particular with black music and dance, in Paris in the 1920s, where she lived for most of the decade. She was later to tell her friend Peggy Kirkcaldy, 'Adore Negro music … It's life according to my gospel'.[81] Its popularity in Paris at the time must be one more reason for her sense of being more at home there than in Britain. *Négritude* took root in Paris. Like the *négritude* writers, Rhys's inversion of the usual assumptions of white superiority marked a significant political statement. European modernist primitivism is often most importantly a sign of the loss of confidence in Western civilisation, an unsettling, even if not a routing, of nineteenth-century racial hierarchies. But as far as Rhys is concerned one can make another point. Simon Gikandi has argued that one of the characteristics of modernist primitivism is what he calls its 'regressive temporality', in which the primitive is relegated to some former time or to timelessness itself.[82] *Voyage in the Dark,* the story of a young white Caribbean woman, still in her teens, facing the emotional as well as metrological chill of England, does indeed present the modernist trope of the loss of a warmer, vital past in a devitalised, mechanised modern world, as in many ways the novel is shaped by the contrast between metropolitan bleakness and Anna's vivid memories of her Caribbean childhood. But there is no comforting 'regressive temporality': the fact of a shared and disturbing history which black and white cohabit breaks through the nostalgia. Anna's memories of the warm, laughing Francine are jolted by the thought of the day she saw Francine looking at her with hatred because of her whiteness. Her Uncle Bo, who first figures in her recollections in opposition to the supercilious Hester, easy-going, affec-tionate, jovial, with his numerous illegitimate offspring 'all colours of the rainbow', as Hester accusingly says, suddenly leaps into her mind as a figure of terror, when she recalls the day she saw his false teeth slip, looking 'like long yellow tusks like fangs'.[83] The memory comes as she reads a letter telling her that her lover wants to break with her, and the image of the fangs links the exploitative and sexually predatory patri-archies of the metropolitan and colonial worlds. That cruelty, hatred and oppression were part of the Caribbean history is made clear. In her delirium at the end of the novel she remembers carnival, still full of colour, movement and music, but menacing, an opportunity to express the resentment the colonials have earned.

George Lamming has said, as Mary Chamberlain reminds us, that 'every Caribbean carries with him the weight of history'. The pressure of that history pervades Rhys's writing, nowhere more overtly than in *Wide Sargasso Sea*, a novel whose awareness of the painful guilt and intractability of the legacy of colonial infamy is perhaps only paralleled by J. M. Coetzee's *Disgrace*. As Gayatri Spivak has written, in the novel Rhys shows how 'so intimate and personal thing as human identity might be determined by the politics of imperialism'.[84] Spivak's famous essay has provoked much debate: whilst she praised Rhys for her resistance to Charlotte Brontë's deep individualism, like Brathwaite she raises questions about the role of Christophine, declaring that she 'cannot be contained by a novel which rewrites a canonical English text within the European novelistic tradition in the interest of the white Creole rather than the native'.[85] One knows what she means by 'native' of course, but as Peter Hulme has pointed out, Christophine is scarcely one in the strict sense – a woman of African descent born in Martinique and now in the British West Indies.[86] While Rhys is undoubtedly contesting the English stereotype of the white creole, she does not make Antoinette representative of creole whiteness; on the contrary she is an outsider even to them, though she shares their inheritance of guilt.[87] Christophine's nativeness is one thing; Antoinette's whiteness another. As the book begins we are told: 'They say when trouble come close ranks, and so the white people did. But we were not in their ranks.'[88] They are poor; Antoinette's mother is French; they are despised. Because of their poverty they live more closely with black people, share more with them; but because of their whiteness and their position as former slave-owners they can never be accepted by them either. Christophine emerges as the moral authority in the text; the Rochester figure finds her 'judge's voice' echoing accusingly in his head, the French black woman denouncing the English man, a classic Rhys binary.[89] As Benita Parry has argued, Christophine is an 'articulate antagonist of patriarchal, settler and imperialist law'.[90] She exposes the injustice that masquerades as legality in the colonial world: 'No more slavery! She had to laugh! Those new ones have Letter of the Law. Same thing. They got magistrates. They got fine. They got jail house and chain gang. They got tread machine to mash up people's feet. New ones worse than old ones.'[91] Sue Thomas has made clear the historical truth of Christophine's accusations in the immediate aftermath of slavery, but her words also resonate more widely as a condemnation of the hypocrisy of the imperial civilising mission. Christophine has to leave, because the Rochester figure can evoke that immoral but powerful letter of the law, but her words deliver the judgement with which the text concurs.[92]

*Wide Sargasso Sea* is Rhys's most Caribbean novel, linguistically as well as in subject matter. Rhys blends the different voices, Caribbean

English, French patois, white creole, English into a polyphonic text that draws together the composite strands of Caribbean life. In 1959 Rhys had written sadly to Francis Wyndham that she had 'no country really now', but possibly she began to feel – late in her life – that in completing the novel she had, in her own imagination, re-established her connections to the Caribbean.[93] David Plante informs us that she wondered if her Spanish great-grandmother might have been partly black. Yet she was aware that in Dominica she would always be white. She told Allfrey she couldn't go back because of her fear of cockroaches; perhaps it was more fear of being seen as a 'white cockroach'.[94] Yet if it had not been for her stigmatisation as the always racially-dubious West Indian when she reached England, her insight into the injustices of metropolitan and colonial society might never have been so acute.

## Notes

1   Jean Rhys, *Smile Please: an unfinished autobiography* (Harmondsworth: Penguin, 1981; first published 1979), p. 135.
2   Rhys, *Smile Please*, p. 50.
3   Jean Rhys, *Voyage in the Dark* (Harmondsworth: Penguin, 1969; first published 1934), p. 47.
4   Jean Rhys, *Wide Sargasso Sea* (Harmondsworth: Penguin, 1968), p. 85.
5   Evelyn O'Callaghan, 'Jumping into the big ups' quarrels', *Wasafiri*, 28 (1998), p. 35.
6   Jean Rhys, *The Left Bank and Other Stories* (New York: Books for Libraries, 1970; first published 1927), p. 24.
7   Alec Waugh, 'Typical Dominica', in his *The Sugar Islands: a Caribbean travelogue* (London: Cassell, 1958), pp. 284–5.
8   Quoted in Elgin W. Mellown, *Jean Rhys: a descriptive and annotated bibliography of works and criticism* (New York: Garland, 1984), p. 31.
9   Wally Look Lai, 'The road to Thornfield Hall: an analysis of *Wide Sargasso Sea*', *New Beacon Reviews*, 1 (1968); Kenneth Ramchand, *The West Indian Novel and its Background* (London: Heinemann, 1970).
10  Edward Kamau Brathwaite, *Contradictory Omens: cultural diversity and integration in the Caribbean* (Mona: Savacou Publishing, 1974), p. 38.
11  Peter Hulme, 'The place of *Wide Sargasso Sea*', *Wasafiri*, 20 (1994), pp. 5–11.
12  Elaine Savory, 'Jean Rhys, race and Caribbean/English/criticism', *Wasafiri*, 28 (1998), p. 33.
13  Edward Kamau Brathwaite, 'A post-cautionary tale of the Helen of our wars', *Wasafiri*, 22 (1995), p. 70.
14  Braithwaite, 'Post-cautionary tale', pp. 69 and 78.
15  Braithwaite, 'Post-cautionary tale', p. 75.
16  Braithwaite, 'Post-cautionary tale', p. 70.
17  Quoted in Elaine Savory, *Jean Rhys* (Cambridge: Cambridge University Press, 1998), p. 23.
18  Braithwaite, 'Post-cautionary tale', p. 74.
19  Louis James, who wrote the first book on Rhys, *Jean Rhys* (London: Longman, 1979) was one of the first British critics to recognise this. Teresa O'Connor examined the overtly West Indian texts in her book, *Jean Rhys: the West Indian novels* (New York and London: New York University Press, 1986). Since the 1990s most critics have stressed the necessity of reading Rhys's work in the context of her Caribbean roots.
20  Rhys, *Smile Please*, p. 81. Sasha in *Good Morning, Midnight*, is not identified as West Indian, but when she hears Martiniquan music she thinks of lying in a

hammock, thinking 'The hills look like clouds and the clouds like fantastic hills': Rhys, *Good Morning, Midnight* (Harmondsworth: Penguin, 1969; first published 1939), p. 77.

21  C. L. R. James, *Beyond a Boundary* (London: Hutchinson, 1986), p. 28.

22  George Lamming, 'Western education and the Caribbean intellectual', in his *Coming, Coming Home. Conversations II* (St Martin: House of Nehesi, 2000), p. 24.

23  Stuart Hall, 'The formation of a diasporic intellectual', in David Morley and Kuan-Hsing Chen (eds), *Stuart Hall: critical dialogues in cultural studies* (London: Routledge, 1996), p. 501.

24  Hall, 'Diasporic intellectual', p. 490.

25  Rhys, *The Left Bank*, p. 231.

26  Rhys, *Good Morning, Midnight*, p. 135.

27  Al Alvarez, 'The best living novelist', *New York Times Review of Books*, 17 March 1974.

28  David Plante, *Difficult Women: a memoir of three* (London: Gollancz, 1983), p. 45.

29  Judith Kegan Gardiner, 'Good morning midnight; good night, modernism', *Boundary*, 2:11 (1982–83).

30  Carole Angier, *Jean Rhys* (London: Deutsch, 1990), p. 218.

31  Diana Athill, *Stet: an editor's life* (London: Granta, 2001), pp. 158–61.

32  Rhys, *Wide Sargasso Sea*, p. 106.

33  Rhys, *Voyage in the Dark*, p. 50.

34  Jean Rhys, *Tigers are Better-Looking* (Harmondsworth: Penguin, 1972; first published 1968), p. 81.

35  Rhys, *Voyage in the Dark*, p. 56.

36  Ramchand, *West Indian Novel*, p. 33.

37  Charlotte Brontë, *Jane Eyre* (London: Penguin, 1996; first published 1847), p. 345; Rhys, *Wide Sargasso Sea*, p. 152.

38  Ramchand, *West Indian Novel*, p. 41. 'Coloured', in the West Indian creole sense that Rhys also uses, here means of mixed race. For a powerful sense of the continuing significance of these conventional projections of white Caribbean creoles in the twentieth century, see the important novel by the white Jamaican, Herbert G. de Lisser, *The White Witch of Rosehall* (London: Ernest Benn, 1929).

39  Jean D'Costa, quoted in Veronica Marie Gregg, *Jean Rhys's Historical Imagination: reading and writing the creole* (Chapel Hill: University of North Carolina Press, 1995), p. 80.

40  For example, Rhys, *Good Morning, Midnight*, p. 88.

41  Rhys, *Left Bank*, p. 24.

42  Rhys, *Tigers are Better-Looking*, p. 84.

43  Savory, *Rhys*, p. 200.

44  Savory, *Rhys*, p. 203.

45  Rhys, *Voyage in the Dark*, p. 9.

46  See the frequently cited essay by Sander Gilman on the Hottentot and the prostitute, 'Black bodies, white bodies: towards an iconography of female sexuality in late nineteenth-century art, medicine and literature', *Critical Inquiry*, 12:1 (1985), pp. 204–42. Both Savory and Gregg discuss Gilman's work in relation to Rhys.

47  Marya in *Quartet*, who has been a chorus girl in the past, is also conscious of her 'limbo' position: 'She learned, after a long and painstaking effort, to talk like a chorus girl, to dress like a chorus girl and to think like a chorus girl – up to a point. Beyond that point she remained apart, lonely frightened of her loneliness, resenting it passionately.' Jean Rhys, *Quartet* (Harmondsworth: Penguin, 1973; first published 1928), p. 16.

48  Rhys, *Quartet*, p. 125.

49  Jean Rhys, *After Leaving Mr Mackenzie* (Harmondsworth: Penguin, 1971; first published 1930), p. 53.

50  Rhys, *After Leaving*, p. 65. Nothing shocked early reviewers more than Rhys's unblinking account of the economics of sex.

51  Mellown, *Jean Rhys*, p. 43.

52   Nancy Harrison, *Jean Rhys and the Novel as Women's Text* (Chapel Hill: University of North Carolina Press, 1988).
53   Rhys, *After Leaving*, p. 81.
54   Rhys, *Left Bank*, p. 201.
55   Rhys, *Left Bank*, p. 241.
56   Rhys, *After Leaving*, p. 18.
57   Rhys, *Good Morning, Midnight*, p. 13.
58   Jean Rhys, *Tales of the Wide Caribbean* (London: Heinemann, 1985; 'Temps perdi' first published 1969), p. 159.
59   Rhys, *Smile Please*, p. 165.
60   Quoted Savory, *Rhys*, p. 27.
61   Lamming, 'Western education', p. 23.
62   See Lizabeth Paravisini-Gebert, *Phyllis Shand Allfrey: a Caribbean life* (New Brunswick: Rutgers University Press, 1996), p. 13.
63   Jean Rhys, *Letters, 1931–1966*, ed. Francis Wyndham and Diana Melly (London: Deutsch, 1984), p. 171.
64   Sue Thomas, *The Worlding of Jean Rhys* (Westport: Greenwood, 1999), p. 32.
65   Paravisini-Gebert, *Allfrey*, p. 48.
66   Rhys, *Letters*, p. 281. See Sue Thomas's discussion of Rhys's attitude to the English in Ann Blake, Leela Gandhi and Sue Thomas, *England Through Colonial Eyes in Twentieth-Century Fiction* (Basingstoke: Palgrave, 2001) and in 'Jean Rhys, "human ants" and the production of expatriate creole identities', in Andrew Benjamin, Tony Davies and Robbie Goh (eds), *Postcolonial Cultures and Literatures: modernity and the (Un)Commonwealth* (New York: Peter Lang, 2002). My warm thanks to Sue Thomas for sharing her work with me.
67   Savory, *Rhys*, p. 32.
68   George Lamming, 'Coming, coming, coming home', in his *Coming, Coming Home*, p. 39.
69   Robert J. C. Young, *Colonial Desire: hybridity in theory, culture and race* (London: Routledge, 1995), pp. 2–3.
70   See the chapter on 'The return of the native: Jean Rhys and the Caribs, 1936', in Peter Hulme, *Remnants of Conquest: the island Caribs and their visitors, 1877–1998* (Oxford: Oxford University Press, 2000) for a discussion of the situation in Dominica at the time of Rhys's 1936 visit.
71   Rhys, *Smile Please*, pp. 50 and 53.
72   Rhys, *Smile Please*, p. 29; Ramchand, *West Indian Novel*, p. 225.
73   Rhys, *Smile Please*, p. 31.
74   Savory, *Rhys*, p. 30.
75   Rhys, *Wide Sargasso Sea*, p. 28.
76   Rhys, *Voyage in the Dark*, p. 27.
77   Introduction to Sam Selvon, *The Lonely Londoners* (Harlow: Longman, 1985), p. 3.
78   Quoted in Gregg, *Rhys's Historical Imagination*, p. 44.
79   Savory, *Rhys*, p. 23.
80   See chapter 5 of Thomas, *Worlding of Rhys*.
81   Rhys, *Letters*, p. 45.
82   Simon Gikandi, 'Race and the modernist aesthetic', in Tim Youngs (ed.), *Writing and Race* (London: Longman, 1997), p. 155.
83   Rhys, *Voyage in the Dark*, pp. 54 and 79.
84   Gayatri Spivak, 'Three women's texts and a critique of colonialism', *Critical Inquiry*, 12:1 (1985), p. 250.
85   Spivak, 'Women's texts', p. 253.
86   Peter Hulme, 'The locked heart: the creole family romance of *Wide Sargasso Sea*', in Francis Barker *et al.* (eds), *Colonial Discourse/Postcolonial Theory* (Manchester: Manchester University Press, 1994), p. 75.
87   Hulme makes a similar point in 'The place of *Wide Sargasso Sea*'.
88   Rhys, *Wide Sargasso Sea*, p. 15.
89   Rhys, *Wide Sargasso Sea*, p. 126.

90  Benita Parry, 'Problems in current theories of colonial discourse', *Oxford Literary Review*, 9 (1987), p. 38.
91  Rhys, *Wide Sargasso Sea*, pp. 22–3.
92  See Thomas, *Worlding of Rhys*, pp. 167–71.
93  Rhys, *Letters*, p. 172.
94  Paravisini-Gebert, *Allfrey*, p. 244.

# CHAPTER FIVE

# Una Marson: feminism, anti-colonialism and a forgotten fight for freedom

## Alison Donnell

When we think about the factors that have contributed to the begin-nings of a West Indian British intellectual tradition, we would com-monly bring to mind the towering figure of C. L. R. James and his comrades of the pre-*Windrush* generation, such as George Padmore. It would also be important to acknowledge the generation of nationalist writers and thinkers based in the Caribbean itself, such as Roger Mais and Victor Stafford Reid. We might also think of the BBC's *Caribbean Voices* which provided a much needed outlet, as well as a valuable source of income, for new writers and writings, and also, of course, of the talented community of male writers and intellectuals, such as George Lamming, Sam Selvon and V. S. Naipaul, who had come to London in the 1950s. Yet what is so commonly neglected in accounts of West Indian and black British literary and intellectual histories of the first half of the twentieth century is mention of Una Marson, a black Jamaican woman whose experiences and achievements provided a link to all these major movements and figures.

It is perhaps not surprising that Marson's identity as an intellectual is not straightforward. As an educated, middle-class daughter of a Baptist minister, Marson's intellectual development took place within the context of a religious home where the activities of playing music and reading poetry were prized, and the conservative and colonial Hampton High School where she received an 'English public-school education'.[1] However, as one of a small number of black scholarship girls, Marson was apprenticed in the operations of racism by the time she left school. As a woman, Marson's education was directed towards ideas of service rather than intellectual grandeur, and even the pupils of this prestigious school were encouraged towards teaching, nursing, helping their fathers in business and homemaking. When Marson left in 1922, her father had already died and she felt that she needed to support her mother. She had directed her studies towards commerce and secretarial work, and chose to take work with the Salvation Army and the YMCA, indicating that her understanding of service was already framed by ideas of social justice, ideas that would take her outside of the traditional spaces of middle-class women's work.

It is also clear that Marson's intellectual energy was never abstracted from her reading of a world in need of change, and it is easy to trace her determination to see her ideas translated into action. She did not pursue the conventional avenues to personal recognition but consistently sought to initiate and participate in collective action. However, this is not to say that Marson was able to translate all her ideas into a better social reality. As a woman she felt a responsibility to draw attention to both the problems and the possibilities facing other black women of her time, but her particular focus on issues of gender and women's liberation, alongside those of racial equality and cultural nationalism, meant that she was challenging structures of inequality that were commonly regarded as less urgent and less central in the intellectual and political agendas of her time.

This chapter will offer a reading of Marson's intellectual positions as articulated in her journalism and speeches, and seek to explore to what extent she was able to use her travelling between London and Kingston to reconfigure her political understanding and cultural projects in each location through an understanding of the other. Work to date has tended to examine Marson's creative works, four volumes of poetry and three plays, but there has been almost no scholarship that examines the politics of her journalism and public works.[2] It is clearly no accident of history that Marson speaks more than she is spoken of, and therefore it is difficult to quantify her ability to bring about change in Britain and almost impossible to gauge how the British may have seen themselves anew through her work, especially as most of her articles were produced for a Jamaican audience. This chapter will position Marson's work as influential and radical in both a British and a West Indian context, and pay particular attention to the ways in which her life in Britain impacted upon her ideas relating to gender politics, cultural identity, nationalism and political organisation.

## London, Kingston and the world

The people of England are gradually waking up. They have been uneducated about the coloured people for a long time but they are now beginning to wake up and learn about us.[3]

Life in Jamaica is dull and monotonous. Intellectual life does not find expression in any form of art, custom or even recreation. Anything that does not bear the hallmark of British is looked upon with suspicion ... I lay the blame at both doors, that of Great Britain and that of ourselves.[4]

Although Marson's arrival in London in 1932 coincided historically with that of C. L. R. James, the ideas and beliefs she brought with her set her apart from both the young – male – intellectuals of Trinidad in the 1930s and the later generation of emigrants in important ways. She had left Jamaica in the very year in which her first play, *At What A Price*, was staged in Kingston, to public acclaim. She had also, by the age of twenty-seven, established her journalistic credentials, founding in 1928 the monthly journal *The Cosmopolitan: a monthly magazine for the business youth of Jamaica and the official organ of the Stenographers Association*. Both her creative and her journalistic works already articulated her strong commitment to women's rights. Moreover, unlike the male writers who came to England, Marson did not seem to need, as Lamming so succinctly stated, to 'get out'.[5] For her, the journeys to Britain were prompted more by an awareness of the need to see Jamaica as part of the larger colonial, Caribbean, and later African, picture. Indeed, despite the fact that her works register that she was often restless, frustrated and impatient with Jamaicans, she maintained a strong investment in Jamaica and in the establishment of a national cultural identity. In the first issue of *The Cosmopolitan*, published in May 1928, Marson stated that 'Our chief aim is to develop literary and other artistic talents in our Island (sic) home ... to encourage talented young people to express themselves freely'.

Indeed, London was not initially an open stage of opportunity for Marson and, as a black woman and a novice traveller, she was daunted by the hostility and the loneliness of the metropolis. Moreover, arriving in 1932, she came to Britain twenty years before mass immigration, before the flourishing of West Indian literary voices and before the recognised presence of a difference had 'creolised the metropole'. Her story cannot invoke the familiar images and narratives of shared crossings, of boats, railway stations and landladies. Rather its telling demands that we extend our history of this creolisation backwards, to account for the smaller but significant places of exchange and encounter between West Indians, Africans and Indians in Britain, such as the Florence Mills café in Oxford Street, London, run by Amy Ashwood Garvey from the early 1930s or the Ethiopian Teashop in Oxford Road, Manchester, run by Ras Makonnen from 1939, or, indeed, the home of Dr Harold Moody in Peckham, a fellow Jamaican, with whose family Marson lodged.[6]

Through Moody, Marson became involved with the League of Coloured Peoples, an organisation he had founded in 1931 to address the issues of racial division and prejudice and, through her work for the League and their journal, *The Keys*, she found both companionship and purpose. Throughout her life, it was an opportunity to advance her own learning and her deeply felt causes that carried Marson from place to place, and soon London was providing her with opportunities in both these directions. In her work for the League, Marson had met many African students, a smaller number of professionals and Nana Ofori Atta, a paramount chief from the Gold Coast, and around this time her awareness of Africa as offering a potentially unifying identity for black people in all continents emerges in her work. Her editorial in *The Keys*, which appeared in the first quarter of 1935, offers a general message of unity and collective gain for people of African descent and calls for collaboration and reciprocal education for the betterment of the race.

> The Negro world must come together ... And who is going to do these things for us? We have got to do it ourselves – if we can co-operate ... if every educated Negro will feel the burden of his brother is too great for him and help him to carry it – then things will be done. Then, and only then will the Negro race be a race contributing richly to the world.[7]

At this same time, Marson was taking a public platform on the issue of women's rights. In 1934 she gave a speech at the Women's International League Conference in London. In 1935 she was the first Jamaican invited to speak at the International Alliance of Women for Suffrage and Equal Citizenship Conference in Istanbul. On this occasion, as others, Marson used her platform at women's organisations to argue for black liberation. Indeed, if she had travelled to London to claim her equal citizenship as a woman – as her early journalism in Jamaica may suggest, 'This is our age – we have won the freedom we have been fighting for, let us use it to the full advantage' – then Britain, with its blatant racism, demanded a more complicated and plural understanding of fights for freedom.[8] It was in this context, compelled by her growing awareness of Pan-African movements and the political urgency of contesting racial hierarchies, that Marson initiated the discourse on mutual liberation that is arguably her most significant intellectual contribution: 'Negroes are suffering under enormous difficulties in most countries of the world. We must count upon all countries where there are Negroes – for women always possess a better developed sense of justice – to obtain for them a life more pleasant and less severe.'[9]

Later that year, Marson was the first black woman invited to attend the League of Nations at Geneva and her meeting there with the Abyssinian delegation made a great impact on her. Marson was outraged by Mussolini's invasion of Abyssinia in 1935, and moved to action:

> I was anxious to do something for Abyssinia but people said it was unwise to go out to Ethiopia and they suggested that I go and assist in the Legation in London.
>
> I went straight back to London and went to the Legation where I met Dr. Martin, the Ethiopian Minister, and they had a colossal amount of work as they did not have a regular typist to handle their correspondence. I said that I was anxious to help but they said they had not much money and I said that I did not mind and I worked there right through the war. I studied the country and lectured on behalf of Ethiopia in England.[10]

She went on to work as personal secretary to Haile Selassie, with whom she travelled to Geneva. However, by September of 1936 she was severely depressed and unable to continue. In an interview with *The Gleaner* on her arrival back in Jamaica, Marson admitted 'The position of Ethiopia is very heart-breaking and the tribulations of the Ethiopians have cracked me up'.[11] Although by now the idea of transnational black alliance was integral to Marson's intellectual convictions, the emotional consequences of her empathetic link with others' suffering, which she claimed gave women a privileged access to an understanding of injustice, had exerted a negative effect on her health.

Although her time spent in Britain had enabled Marson to develop her ideas on African unity and women's rights, her work also discloses her difficulty and unease in challenging the authority of the metropole or European culture at close quarters. Indeed, her writings which reflect on her time spent in England offer us both a condemnation of racism and a testimony to its effects. In an article for the *News Chronicle* in 1934 she speaks of racism as a form of disarticulation: 'In America they tell you frankly where you are not wanted by means of big signs, and they don't try to hide their feelings. But in England, though the people will never say what they feel about us, you come up against incidents which hurt so much that you cannot talk about them.'[12] This inability to articulate her political convictions with force in a British context, here the League of Nations Conference, is made very clear in 'Traitors all!', where she describes her sense of injustice and outrage at the lack of a protective quota for the colonies and Jamaica.

> I felt like getting up in the conference and screaming out that such was the loyalty with which some Jamaicans had chewed and digested the Union Jack that Jamaica had not been able to enter at all into their system. Instead, I crept up to the platform after the Session like a worm and had a talk with Mr Beresford, who told me he had not fully realised that there was any Colony anxious for such a Quota.[13]

Marson's honesty in registering her own reticence and sense of powerlessness in Britain helps us to appreciate the kinds of subtle as well as direct oppression that racism generates.[14]

[ 118 ]

Nevertheless, being back home was no respite from tribulation. Marson had returned to Jamaica, which had been hit even harder than other West Indian islands by the economic depression of the 1930s, at a time of intense social and political unrest. However, the climate of political ferment and the promise of change appear to have restored her voice and her commitment to politics, as by 1937 she had a regular column in *Public Opinion*. This weekly paper, started in 1937 and affiliated to Norman Manley's People's National Movement, foregrounded issues of cultural politics, was soon staffed by many of the island's culturally active women: Edna Manley was editor, Una Marson and Amy Bailey were board members and Gloria Escoffery, 'artist and poet', was the editor of the literature page.[15] Marson's journalism of this period reveals a voice that is strident, polemical and radical, and this two-year period spent in Jamaica is arguably the high point of her intellectual career, when she was writing regularly on issues that really mattered to her, with energy and clarity. A combination of factors – being back in Jamaica; being part of a majority; and being witness to the unrest of her people at home – meant that from 1937 her work was overtly, loudly political.

It was at this point that Marson's work most emphatically fulfilled James's call for West Indians 'to place ourselves in history'.[16] For Marson, Jamaicans could only come to know themselves as historical subjects by disconnecting themselves from false notions of white ancestry and reconnecting to their African past. Although she herself had an Irish great-grandfather, she chose not to play to this heritage and admonished others who did.

> The point I want to make is that educated Jamaicans spend their whole lives thinking they are not coloured, and it is an insult to call them 'Negro' because one or two generations back they had some white ancestor of the male sex. Now we can never be free from inhibitions, complexes, indecision and lack of confidence until we accept ourselves for what we are.[17]

At a time when eurocentric ideals of beauty, morality and culture were championed in middle-class Jamaica, Marson sought to position a new politics of identity through the connection to Africa. In the face of 'Many Jamaicans [who] would like to rewrite the social history of Jamaica to prove that they have no Negro blood in their veins', Marson herself mapped a new history for an emergent nation, a history that denounced racism, which she identified as a West Indian predicament.[18] In '"But my own"', her most polemical piece for *Public Opinion*, Marson connected the denial of Africa to the estrangements and limitations of colonial dependence.

[ 119 ]

Is Jamaica to be allowed to remain in the morass of indifference to cultural matters and true education? ... Are we the younger generation to remain resigned to the sham and shallowness of the artificial life into which we have been cast? Are we to remain strangers in our own land, eaters of the crumbs that fall from the tables of others when we have it in our power to sit at a table well garnished by our own hands?[19]

Although Marson's immediate goal was the cultural and political transformation of Jamaica, her connection with Africa, especially Ethiopia and the Gold Coast, via England, had clearly provided a new lens through which to refine her ideas of cultural identity. Indeed, what was so significant about Marson's experience in Britain was that it had given her a wider frame through which to view the issue of national self-representation, as well as the links between colonial and national politics.

By the time the social conditions in Jamaica became critical and protests became violent, Marson was reporting for the *Jamaican Standard*. Although engrossed by the drama of the labour rebellions and by their challenge to colonial power, she remained concerned about welfare issues and once again turned to a more direct mode of service, raising money for a Jamaica Save the Children Association.[20] Seeking not only to argue for change, but to work for it as well, she returned to London in order to report on and to the Moyne Commission, to raise money for Jamsave and generally to stimulate awareness about the situation in Jamaica. Although she had been keen to point out the responsibilities that Jamaicans had to claim their rights and freedoms within a Jamaican context, in London she took on the role of advocate. At a meeting of the League of Coloured Peoples, 'Miss Marson further emphasised the need for help and appealed to her audience to let people outside know what the poor people were suffering in Jamaica owing to neglect'.[21]

After the declaration of war in 1939, Marson witnessed changes in the black community in Britain: fewer students came and many of those based in London now moved north. In an undated article written during wartime, she paid special attention to the predicament of the 'coloured woman'. Drawing on her own situated knowledge and that of others, she pointed to the effects of racism, but the voice of her Jamaican polemics is somewhat subdued.

The young coloured woman has to face many problems. More often than not she is poorly educated and she finds the problem of finding work a serious one ... In London, most avenues of work except that of entertaining in the dance or Music halls, are closed to coloured people ... I know of their difficulties and I myself have experienced difficulty in finding work when I urgently needed it. Once I tried to register for work as a stenographer. One agent told me she didn't register black women because they would have to work in offices with white women. Another agent tried to find me a position and he told me that though my references were excellent firms did not want to employ a black stenographer.[22]

Marson's own fortunes improved when she took freelance work with the BBC and in 1941 was appointed full-time programme assistant for the BBC's *Calling the West Indies* which evolved into the now famous *Caribbean Voices*. Here again, Marson was able to establish avenues through which peoples and cultures could speak to each other and realise the ideal of collaborative effort and mutual education that underpins many of her projects. Although accounts commonly suggest that Henry Swanzy had the main hand in nurturing and directing West Indian writing, in fact, by the time Marson returned to Jamaica in 1945, she had already established an important forum for literary expression that drew on her local knowledge of the literary culture, which she had gained through her contacts with the Jamaican Poetry League and *Focus*, the successor to *Public Opinion*. She was, at the time, suffering from another severe episode of depression and was eager to return to the West Indies and come to know the islands and people with whom she had become familiar across the airways. Marson was not present at the 1945 Manchester Pan-African Congress, but she did meet Eric Williams, among other prominent West Indians, in New York, where she made a stop on her journey home.[23]

The fact that on Marson's return to Jamaica in 1945, 'everywhere she went, huge crowds gathered as though she were royalty', and that a lunch in her honour organised by the Poetry League of Jamaica was attended by Edna Manley and Roger Mais, amongst others, speaks of the high profile and recognition that she was accorded within her life-time.[24] After a brief return to London, and thence a prolonged recuperation from ill-health and depression, in 1949 Marson became organising secretary for the Pioneer Press, the book-publishing department of the *Gleaner*. The Pioneer Press was the first serious Jamaican publishing house and redressed the great absence of publishing facilities within the West Indies that so many writers subsequently bemoaned when explaining their reasons for migration to the metropolis. This focus on local, committed publishing was another crucial step in the development of West Indian literature that Marson had helped to advance, this time on home soil. Its programme outlined a new emphasis upon the recognition and promotion of local literary talent: 'The Pioneer Press seeks to serve the literary ambitions of the people of Jamaica in an organised way by publishing the meritorious work of local authors'.[25]

For Marson, this project represented the links between literary expression and cultural development that she had identified as being a significant absence in Jamaica back in 1937. In 'Wanted: writers and publishers', in *Public Opinion*, Marson had called for local publishing ventures that could foster links between nationalism and writing, the sharing of local knowledge and the need for self-scrutiny:

> We are passing through the birth pains of bringing forth a new Jamaica. In this new era literature must take its place. Indeed, the writing and production of books by us about ourselves and our problems is essential ... Now in Jamaica we have no publisher. I have known of two books written by Jamaicans who tried to get them published in England ... I am sure that if we had a publishing house in Jamaica books that would do us credit would be published annually. Can we get anything done about this?[26]

There is a note of irony in the fact that by the time Marson was able to help establish a Jamaican publisher the fortunes of West Indian writers in the metropolis had changed somewhat, partly due to her own efforts in establishing *Caribbean Voices*. For Marson, bringing 'authentic' and local voices into print was high on the agenda of cultural nationalism and the fact that Pioneer Press were the first to publish work by the 'nation-language' writer Louise Bennett in 1949, decades before she would receive widespread critical acceptance, is testimony to Marson's radical understanding of cultural value at this time.

Although Marson did not return to London until 1964, just one year before her death and two years before the formation of the Caribbean Artists Movement, there is a sense in which Britain, as the colonial motherland, had been the catalyst for her many journeys, providing both the political and intellectual impetus behind the internationalism and transnationalism that was so crucial to the freedom movements of this time. Being in London during the 1930s and 1940s had enabled Marson to realise the Pan-African dimension of her thinking and had brought her into contact with a network of liberation movements congregated in Britain at this time. For Marson, as for other West Indians living through this period in Britain, there was a strong sense that history necessitated their movements, the journeying that colonialism had set in motion was now being replayed in a climate of highly-charged political restlessness and mobility that was to change profoundly the national identities and cultures of both Britain and its West Indian colonies. In her later years Marson continued to travel, spending 1952 to 1960 in the US. By the time she returned to London in 1964 she was able to appreciate that a very different cultural and literary scene had emerged but she remained cautious about the freedoms and opportunities open to West Indians in the metropolis.

Although recorded history has left us little evidence by which to judge how other West Indian intellectuals in Britain thought of Marson or reacted to her ideas, the close network of personalities, organisations and places through which those who were black and in Britain moved during the 1930s and 1940s also leaves little doubt that Marson must have met and engaged with many of the intellectuals of her time. As assistant secretary to the League of Coloured Peoples, she not only had close contact with its president, Harold Moody, but must have encountered C. L. R. James, whom *The Keys* described as a 'brilliant young man' in the editorial to their first issue, and whose 'eloquent address was followed by a lively discussion', at their first conference in March 1933. By a similar token, she is likely also to have known and talked with Padmore, who was a friend of Moody (as well as of James) and who visited the Moody family home where Una first lodged. It is regrettable that we know nothing in detail of how Marson and the young radicals James and Padmore viewed each other, especially since she seems to have made a strong impact on those who did know, or know of, her.

Her fellow Jamaican, Marcus Garvey, was aware of Marson and her experience of Britain by 1933, when she had only been in the metropolis for a year. Indeed, Garvey uses Marson's own disillusionment with Britain in order to exemplify his theory that black people had not anticipated the racism of the metropolitan motherland.

> Our countrywoman Miss Una Marson went to England some time ago to be disillusioned. She thought she was going to a country where she would be accepted on equal terms with those who built it, and made its civilization possible. Like most of our race, she thought we have nothing else to do than to project ourselves into the civilization of other people and to claim all its rights. When she found a contrary attitude, she rebelled and wrote some very nasty things about the English.[27]

It is possible that Garvey was referring to Marson's poem 'Nigger' which was published in the first issue of the *Keys* in 1933 and remained her strongest critique of English racism. Garvey's observation of Marson is interesting in its claims for her optimistic attitude towards metropolitan life as, although already 'race conscious', Marson had written mainly about gender inequality before coming to England. Her early writings in Britain did register her shock and distress at encountering racial abuse and prejudice, reactions that would soon inform her renegotiated ideas of freedom struggles and collective campaigning as she shifted towards a more deeply anti-racist and nationalist politics.

As more research is conducted on women intellectuals and nationalists during this period, their links to each other will become clearer and that two-way conversation with history will begin to emerge more clearly. One such link, between Maida Springer, an activist in

American and African labour movements, and Una Marson, has come to light recently.[28] Springer first met Marson on the *Caribbean Voices* programme and their encounter, in the early 1940s, was important to Springer who was soon to meet Padmore and form a close political association with him, and, through Padmore, gain an introduction to Ras Makonnen and Jomo Kenyatta. In Marson, Springer met a woman of her own generation (she was born 1910) who was determined in her political convictions and committed to women's emancipation. Moving mainly within the male-dominated circles of international labour movements and Pan-Africanist organisations, Springer, who was herself very concerned to address women's inequalities and acknowledge their nationalist activities, was impressed by Marson. Springer recalled a night spent in Marson's flat in the company of African and Caribbean soldiers:

> They had no illusions about what they were doing and for the most part – because I think Una was very selective about the people she invited – these were men who had a vision of the future and they were looking to the day when they were going to have a country, not a colonial dependency. So it was very good to talk at night. Very explosive talk! Had they been heard, they would all have been court-martialled.[29]

Although the prospect of court-martialling may seem dramatic, it is important to remember that Roger Mais was imprisoned in Jamaica on charges of sedition in 1944.[30] Springer's recollection reminds us of the depth of Marson's anti-colonialism during this period.

Positioned at either end of Marson's time spent in England, these two reports of her activities and associations – by Garvey and by Springer – suggest that it was her unequivocal condemnation of the domestic culture of the imperial nation-state that made an impact on others. While these convictions remained strong, a close examination of her journalistic and creative writing from the 1930s, through wartime and beyond, foregrounds Marson's persistent effort to bring issues of gender inequality into political agendas and movements for social change.

## Woman and intellectual

> Men in the past have never been over partial to intellectual women but today mental development is essential.[31]

> A man is never a career man … But the woman is called career woman because her 'career' in modern society demands she place herself in a subordinate position or even renounce normal life. The social dice are loaded against her; and even the plain fact of the matter is that they are loaded not only in the economic opportunities, but in the minds of men.[32]

Throughout her life Marson sought out forums for the exchange and collectivity of ideas – in her journalism, lectures and organisational work, she was opening her ways of seeing to others in the hope that they might respond in kind. At the beginning of her career she was specifically concerned that women begin to view themselves as political beings with social responsibilities and rights. Although her editorials for the *Cosmopolitan* were directed at professional (middle-class) women, she consistently encouraged them to think and act beyond the assumed protocols and routines of their lives. In her 1929 article, 'Jamaica's victory', she seeks to answer newspaper criticism of the modern Jamaican woman for wearing make-up and short skirts by arguing that women should take their freedoms seriously and use them responsibly. Already, at the age of twenty-four, she had a strong sense of what could be achieved by liberated women who took up their place in history:

> Is it not possible for the women of Jamaica to realise what a gift is theirs to be living in an age where there can be no limit to what they may achieve? ... It is a privilege to be living in an age such as this. History is bound to repeat itself. With the wonderful progress of civilisation all our problems have not been solved – there is great work ahead for the good of humanity, and women are to play a great part in that work. No more must we be regarded as toys – but women of foresight, strength and skill. Women who can forget self in the work that lies ahead for the good of humanity.[33]

Marson also insisted that action, as well as conviction, was the pathway for women to achieve change: 'A big rally of women workers would be the best thing to sweep the cobwebs from certain brains and dust out the eyes so they can see better'.[34]

Indeed Marson's own priorities for a feminist agenda (awareness of inequality, responsibility to others, collaboration and public action) were already in place before her first visit to London in 1932. It is also significant that back in Jamaica in 1937, she reported favourably on the collaborative success of women in Britain and described her own participation as part of a larger collective project. Feminism was not a politics that she first encountered or adopted in England – although she was eager to promote the positive experience of women's organisations, using her first interview after returning to declare that:

> England is a wonderful country for its women's organisations ... I got in touch with the British Commonwealth League, the Women's Freedom League, The Women's Peace Crusade, the Women's International League, the International Alliance for Suffrage and all these women's associations get together ... I was invited to go to Turkey to the great Congress of the International Alliance of Women for suffrage and citizenship which is

[ 125 ]

held every three years. There were three hundred women present, representatives of thirty countries ... We all came together as though we were
one big family and it was wonderful to see how everyone was eager to
learn something of other countries.[35]

In order to understand her emphasis here it is important to recognise
that in the Jamaica that Marson had left in 1932, women's organisations had a quite different political currency. The Social Purity
Association of Jamaica, formed in 1917, and the 1918 Women's Social
Service Club did not work to liberate women in any meaningful way,
but rather served to reinforce their position within a male-dominated
society and to establish codes of behaviour which corresponded to traditionally eurocentric concepts of femininity. Even the first black
women's society, the Jamaica Women's Liberal Club, formed during the
period when Marson was writing for *Public Opinion*, was governed by
a profound social conformity. In this context, then, Marson's ideas of
what might be achieved by women's organisations in Jamaica was
informed by her experience of Britain, but also calibrated against her
experience of home.

In terms of understanding the reciprocal routes of intellectual
exchange between the West Indies and Britain, I would contest Delia
Jarrett-Macauley's conclusion that 'Una's proposals for Jamaican feminist activism as propounded in *Public Opinion* consisted largely of a
reworking of initiatives she had witnessed and admired in England'.[36]
Marson did bring ideas and inspirations back to Jamaica and – having
described the public debates pressed by five British women (Eleanor
Rathbone, Erina Reiss, Mrs Oliver Strachey, Alison Neilans and Mary
Agnes Hamilton) – she did commend Jamaican women to 'take a leaf
out of their book'.[37] Nevertheless, she did more than transport these
ideas and strategies from one locale to another; she was actually trans-
forming her ideas on women's liberation in the light of her growing
understanding of racial antagonism, the politics of anti-colonial movements and the potentially unifying connection to Africa, all of which
she developed as a result of living in Britain.

The opposing ideologies of racism and Pan-Africanism that Marson
had encountered in Britain led her to work through a new politics of
identity and agenda for social justice. Both her creative and her journalistic work testify to her capacity to synthesise the politics of feminism
and the politics of anti-colonialism, translating each into the other. In
most of her articles that address women's rights, Marson refers to the
issue of racial hierarchies and to the importance of self-determination:

There is a crying need for a few feminists, wide awake to the needs of the
corporate area, to sit on the City Council ... the need for women in our

Legislative Council is even greater. Our women should be there, our women must be there in the near future ... Why is it that the social work that is being done in Kingston ... *remains in the hands of a few members of the older set, who are for the most part English people or women from Jamaica's white social circle?'*[38]

We cannot expect people from abroad to be more interested in us than we are in ourselves ... WE do not need an expert from abroad to tell us that we can collect money and appoint women in every part of the island to work among children.[39]

However, as Jarrett-Macauley points out, Marson's intellectual interventions on women's rights were not necessarily appreciated and her insistence led to her being seen as out of step with the 'positive ideas' of the day by those who could have been her political allies. Although her voice was now strong on these issues there was no community, intellectual or political, receptive to her ideas:

She was the one always pushing the woman question but who never had any constructive ideas other than the assertion that women must speak up ... I used to think her speeches a bit empty of content, I don't think she was very much in tune with the positive ideas that were coming up, the idea that we should rule our own country and that sort of thing, the idea of promotion of culture.[40]

Marson was a committed cultural nationalist and had a wealth of positive ideas. What Richard Hart's estimation reflects is how irrelevant, distracting and even unwelcome her insistence on the 'woman question' was seen to be in Jamaica of the late 1930s. Seeking to expand and refine the narrow nationalist agendas of this time, Marson was perceived only to be missing the point.

The fact that Jamaica was not ready to listen to her calls was evident in other ways too. The wider field of state power after 1938 still functioned as a powerful agency of patriarchal power. Married women were not allowed to pursue careers as civil servants, the school curriculum was revised to promote female education as matrimonial training in 1939, and the 1941 Committee on Concubinage and Illegitimacy recommended that working-class women be directed into domestic duties.

In Britain of the 1930s and 1940s, Marson's interest in the woman question was less exceptional and she found many audiences and like minds in the organisations she joined and in those she addressed. Nevertheless, her ability to open out debates about inequality and injustice to the politics of colonial rule and the operations of racism should not be underestimated. This is not to argue that Marson initiated a

[ 127 ]

tradition of black British feminist thought. Indeed, it is difficult to construct a continuous genealogy of black British feminist thought when, as Mirza points out, 'concerted black feminist activity in Britain reaches back only over the last 50 years'.[41] It is to suggest, though, that Marson was well placed to comprehend British society in ways that James and the other male figures were not, and that her observations and interventions, particularly those which focused on the liberation of women, were both distinctive and combative. Indeed, given that the demands for British feminism to account for race are conventionally traced back to Hazel Carby's 1982 essay 'White woman listen! Black feminism and the boundaries of sisterhood', Marson's insistence upon gender and race as mutually affective identity categories was both innovative and intellectually challenging.[42]

The absence of Marson from most literary and cultural histories is lamentable. She was a woman of extraordinary creativity and ambition, qualities that she directed towards the great causes of her time: the advancement of women's rights; the struggle against colonialism; and the strengthening of cultural and literary nationalism. However, if Marson is now becoming an acknowledged figure, what about other 'critical women' from the Caribbean who are still waiting for history to write the narratives into which they can be accommodated?[43] Although Marson was clearly an exceptional woman, she was not unique. A consideration of other West Indian women intellectuals in Britain proves that there was a small number who were passionately involved in the burning political and cultural issues of the day, and who – in so doing – created new modes of thought. While more research is emerging on women's histories, there remains an unspoken tension in many accounts around the issue of gender politics and the naturalised tendency towards centring male activity and thought.

A striking example of just this can be found in Simon Gikandi's representation of Amy Ashwood Garvey.

> In the late 1930s and 1940s, so the story goes, a group of colonised black intellectuals, whom I have come to call the Afro-Victorians, used to meet regularly at a restaurant owned by Mrs Amy Garvey on Oxford Street in London … The men and women who met in Mrs Garvey's restaurant were working under the shadow of colonialism, its technologies of domination and its polity, but their desires were informed by a fundamental belief that they were the vanguard of a movement towards a decolonised future.[44]

Despite the inclusive description of 'men and women', the only women Gikandi mentions by name are Queen Victoria, Elspeth Huxley and Mrs Amy Garvey. The article goes on to list George Padmore, C. L. R.

James, Ben Nnamdi Azikiwe, Francis Kwame Nkrumah and Johnston Jomo Kenyatta as the key players in discussions on Pan-Africanism. Gikandi does not even make it clear which Mrs Amy Garvey he is discussing here, Amy Ashwood Garvey, Garvey's first wife, or Amy Jaques Garvey, his second. Moreover, there are no footnotes to the story about Mrs Garvey, her politics, or even her restaurant. She is just the backdrop, her restaurant the venue for the real story that is to be told, the story of meetings of men and men's minds.

The way in which Amy Ashwood Garvey functions as a narrative opener, literally positioned at the margin of this piece, is less forgivable given that this 'Mrs Garvey' was among the close network of West Indian and African intellectuals who were working together for the International African Friends of Abyssinia.[45] Her speech to the 1945 Pan-African Congress in Manchester conveys both her specific and direct interest in the gender politics of political movements and – ironically – predicts her own historical fate: 'Very much has been written and spoken of the Negro, but for some reason very little has been said about the black woman. She has been shunted into the social background to be a child-bearer.'[46] Half a century later, the history of women's contribution to a West Indian intellectual tradition is still not fully represented.

Now emerging from the background, Marson merits serious attention as a political intellectual and as an imaginative writer. Her substantial contribution stems from her awareness of the collocation of African subjects and women within the political matrix of British colonialism. Although many of Marson's ideas were based on the ethical obligations and possibilities for mutual empowerment that bonded Africans and women to each other, what was most daring about her contribution was her willingness to break the masculine consensus of the West Indian intellectual community. In so doing, she could see colonial authority from a quite new perspective, and grasp too the deep complexities of the colonial civilisation of the British. Although in retrospect this insight can be judged as of inestimable value, being out of step with the prevailing politics of her day has, to date, cost Marson a place in most histories of political and intellectual change.

## Notes

1  Delia Jarrett-Macauley, *The Life of Una Marson, 1905–65* (Manchester: Manchester University Press, 1998), p. 19.
2  See Alison Donnell, 'Sentimental subversions: the poetics and politics of devotion in the poetry of Una Marson', in Vicki Bertram (ed.), *Kicking Daffodils: essays on twentieth-century women's poetry* (Edinburgh: Edinburgh University Press, 1997), pp. 113–24; Alison Donnell, 'Contradictory (w)omens? Gender consciousness in the poetry of Una Marson', *Kunapipi*, XVII (1995), pp. 43–58.

3   'Racial prejudice in London not improving says Miss Marson', *Daily Gleaner* (28 September 1936), p. 5.
4   Una Marson, '"But my own"', *Public Opinion* (19 June 1937), pp. 3 and 15.
5   George Lamming, *The Pleasures of Exile* (London: Michael Joseph, 1960), p. 41.
6   See John McLeod, 'A night at "The Cosmopolitan": axes of transnational encounter in the 1930s and 1940s', *Interventions: International Journal of Postcolonial Studies*, 4:1 (2002), pp. 53–67.
7   Una Marson, *The Keys*, 2:3 (January–March 1935), pp. 45–6.
8   Una Marson, 'The age of woman', *Cosmopolitan*, 1:11 (March 1929), p. 65, in Linette Vassall (ed.), *Voices of Women in Jamaica, 1898–1939* (Kingston: University of the West Indies Press, 1993), pp. 24–6.
9   Jarrett-Macauley, *Life of Una Marson*, p. 90.
10  'Jamaican girl who was personal secretary to Haile Selassie', *Daily Gleaner* (25 September 1936), p. 17.
11  'Jamaican girl', p. 17.
12  *News Chronicle* (15 June 1934), in *The Keys*, 2:1 (July–September 1934), p. 54.
13  Una Marson, 'Traitors all!', *Public Opinion* (18 September 1937), p. 5.
14  See also Una Marson, 'A call to Downing Street', *Public Opinion* (11 September 1937), p. 5.
15  Cedric Lindo, private letter to Alison Donnell (22 December 1990).
16  C. L. R. James, 'The West Indian intellectual', introduction to J. J. Thomas, *Froudacity: West Indian fables by James Anthony Froude* (London and Port of Spain: New Beacon Books, 1969), pp. 47 and 45.
17  Una Marson, 'Racial feelings?', *Public Opinion* (17 July 1937), p. 3.
18  Una Marson, 'I can tell you what's wrong with Jamaica says Una Marson', *Daily Gleaner* (17 February 1951), p. 9.
19  Marson, '"But my own"', p. 15.
20  Jarrett-Macauley, *Life of Una Marson*, p. 139.
21  'BWI affairs topic of talk at League meeting in England', *Daily Gleaner* (1 October 1938), p. 10.
22  'Problems of coloured people in Britain', no date, Una Marson Papers box 1944C, p. 1.
23  'Una Marson on visit home', *Daily Gleaner* (18 August 1945), p. 15.
24  Jarrett-Macauley, *Life of Una Marson*, p. 169.
25  *14 Jamaican Short Stories* (Kingston: Pioneer Press, 1950).
26  Una Marson, 'Wanted: writers and publishers', *Public Opinion* (12 June 1937), p. 6.
27  Marcus Garvey, *New Jamaican* (20 February 1933), in Rupert Lewis and Patrick Bryan (eds), *Garvey: his work and impact* (Mona, Jamaica: ISER, University of the West Indies, 1988), p. 232.
28  Yvette Richards, 'Race, gender, and anticommunism in the international labor movement: the Pan-African connections of Maida Springer, *Journal of Women's History*, 11:2 (1999), pp. 53–67.
29  Richards, 'Race, gender and anticommunism', pp. 45–6.
30  Mais's article, 'Now we know', *Public Opinion* (1 July 1944), was considered capable of inciting disaffection during wartime.
31  Una Marson, 'Feminism', *Public Opinion* (10 April 1937), p. 10.
32  C. L. R. James and Anna Grimshaw, *The C.L.R. James Reader* (Oxford: Blackwell, 1992), p. 144, quoted in Ato Quayson, *Postcolonialism: theory, practice or process?* (Cambridge: Polity Press, 2000).
33  Una Marson, 'Jamaica's victory', *Cosmopolitan*, 2:2 (June 1929), pp. 66–7.
34  Marson, 'Jamaica's victory', pp. 66–7.
35  Marson, 'Racial prejudice in London', p. 5.
36  Jarrett-Macauley, *Life of Una Marson*, p. 114.
37  Una Marson, 'Some things women politicians can do?', *Public Opinion* (27 February 1937), p. 10.
38  Una Marson, 'Should our women enter politics?', *Public Opinion* (20 February 1937), p. 10, emphasis added.
39  Una Marson, 'We must save the children', *Public Opinion* (13 March 1937), p. 10.

**40** Richard Hart, quoted in Jarrett-Macauley, *Life of Una Marson*, p. 115.

**41** Heidi Safia Mirza (ed.), *Black British Feminism: a reader* (London: Routledge, 1997), p. 6.

**42** Hazel Carby, 'White woman listen! Black feminism and the boundaries of sisterhood', in Centre for Contemporary Cultural Studies, *The Empire Strikes Back: race and racism in 70s Britain* (London: Routledge, 1982).

**43** In particular, the Jamaican, Amy Bailey, and Dominican, Phyllis Shand Allfrey, who both spent time in London.

**44** Simon Gikandi, 'Pan-Africanism and cosmopolitanism: the case of Jomo Kenyatta', *English Studies*, 43:1 (2000), p. 3.

**45** See Peter Fryer, *Staying Power: the history of black people in Britain* (London: Pluto Press: 1984), p. 345.

**46** Fryer, *Staying Power*, p. 350.

# CHAPTER SIX

# George Padmore

Bill Schwarz

After a prolonged courtship, on 10 September 1924 in Port of Spain, Trinidad, Malcolm Nurse married Julia Semper. It was a respectable social occasion. The groom was twenty-two (or thereabouts: there is some doubt about his date of birth), the son of a well-regarded elementary teacher, while his wife-to-be was the daughter of the highest-ranking black man in the service of the island's constabulary. The ceremony took place in an Anglican church, the bride in a lengthy train, the groom in tails. The reception was held in the police barracks on the edge of Port of Spain's Savannah. A few days later Nurse left Trinidad, and his pregnant wife, to travel to Fisk University in Nashville, Tennessee, where he intended to study medicine. Two years on his wife (though not his baby daughter, whom he insisted be christened Blyden) joined him in the US. Gradually, Nurse was drawn into the Communist Party. He acquired a new identity which was to remain with him for the rest of his life: George Padmore. In late 1929 the party gave him two one-way tickets to Moscow. These were stolen, but Padmore scraped together enough cash to cover the cost of a single passage, and he set sail. So far as we can tell he never saw his wife again; was never to see his daughter; and he never returned to the Caribbean.

This represents a particular variant on the theme of emigration which underwrites the story of twentieth-century Caribbean intellectuals. From 1929 to 1933 Padmore energetically devoted himself to the ideals of Soviet Communism, rising high in the firmament of the Communist administration; thereafter, until his death in 1959, his political passions were mobilised in the cause of Pan-Africanism. He was an intellectual formed deep in the vortex of the age of extremes, and for most of his life he espoused positions which others perceived to be both extreme and fanatical. His politics forced an abrupt separation from the modes of life which an aspiring colonial professional would have anticipated: his future experience of police barracks was to be more conventional. As much as his boyhood friend, C. L. R. James, Padmore fashioned himself as a universal intellectual, driven by the constraints imposed by colonial locality to imagine a larger world.

For good reason, James is regarded as the magisterial, world-historical intellectual of the twentieth-century anglophone Caribbean. But James's life moved in tandem with Padmore's. They grew up together, both the sons of elementary teachers. They both arrived in London for the first time in 1932: James to begin his career as a writer, Padmore from Moscow, on an official assignment for the Red International of Labour Unions (RILU). James recounts his surprise, turning up to a political meeting in Gray's Inn Road, to find that the speaker, billed as George Padmore, was none other than his childhood friend. They worked closely together from 1935, when Padmore first settled in London, to 1938, when James departed for the USA. Even during the war, with the Atlantic dividing them, they were in close contact.

The relationship with Nkrumah is instructive. James had got to know Nkrumah in Harlem. When in 1945 the latter decided to journey to London it was the most natural thing in the world for James, in effect, to pass him on to Padmore. Arriving on the boat-train at Euston station Padmore was waiting for him, initiating a political intimacy which survived many tests. In 1953, when in turn James returned to Britain, his friendship and political collaboration with Padmore picked up again. They were both with Nkrumah in Accra the night that Ghana was founded, on 6 March 1957, invited to witness the birth of the black nation.

These convergent trajectories tell us something about the unreconciled commitments of Caribbean radicalism, pulled both by socialism and by the imperatives of black emancipation. They tell us something too of the extraordinary journeys James and Padmore made, which could barely have been imagined in turn-of-the-century Tunapuna. After Padmore had died James planned to write the story of his life. As editor of Trinidad's People's National Movement paper, *The Nation*, he immediately contributed a long-running series entitled 'Notes on the life of George Padmore'.[1] Those close to James believe that by late in the 1960s the bulk of a biography had been drafted.[2] That it remained unfinished may have something to do with the fact that in telling Padmore's life, James would also have been narrating his own. In a lecture delivered in 1971 – in a strange, passing formulation – James alluded to this interweaving of their lives by declaring that if he were to work further on Padmore he might make it 'into an autobiography'.[3]

More particularly James's esteem for Padmore knew no bounds. When *The Nation* announced Padmore's death it not only described him, in words which undoubtedly were those of James, as 'a great gentleman' and 'a great citizen of the world', but also – 'with the exception of Marcus Garvey' – as 'the most famous West Indian of all time'.[4] Almost a decade later, in first naming the tradition of West Indian intellectuals whom he believed constituted the rightful heirs of John Jacob Thomas, James identified the following figures: Garvey, Césaire, Padmore and Fanon. Readers may know of Garvey, Césaire and Fanon. Padmore, on the contrary, barely registers in contemporary historical memory. James's tributes to those who moved him could be pardonably excessive. But what of Padmore? And what of Padmore's conception of the civilisation of the British?

In V. S. Naipaul's *Mimic Men* the father of the narrator walks out of his job at the Department of Education on the imagined locale of Isabella in order to become a millenarian street-preacher and agitator in the dock-strike of the late 1930s. His son, who narrates the story, was (we learn) deeply affected by this collapse in his family circumstances and thereafter proved to be duly sceptical of politics, especially a politics which purported to be anti-colonial. 'On the subject of empire', he claims, 'there is only the pamphleteering of churls.'[5] For Naipaul nothing could be more demeaning; for his compatriot, Padmore, the role of churlish pamphleteer, far from being an insult, signalled virtue and probity.

There are hints that whilst in Trinidad Padmore carried some formal commitments to black emancipation. In later life he talked much about the fact that his grandfather was a slave. He claimed, too, Henry Sylvester-Williams (the inspirational figure who inaugurated the first Pan-African Congress in London in 1900) to have been an uncle. His father converted to Islam searching, it seems, for a means to efface the inheritance of slavery. Certainly, we know that his father possessed an extraordinary library, which was used by both his son and by James. It is very likely that this contained classic writings of black intellectuals. James certainly recalls Padmore reading DuBois and Garvey whilst he was still in Trinidad. Padmore's insistence that his daughter be named after the early intellectual of black nationhood, Edward Blyden, is suggestive. But much of this is evidence cited retrospectively.

Padmore was inducted into politics in the USA and through Communism, though from the outset he was fired by the injustices of race and colonialism. In his early commitments no moment of equivocation is apparent. By 1928 he was prominent within the milieu of Harlem Communism, and when he travelled to Moscow he went as an expert on the colonial and racial question. His main task was to direct RILU's Negro Bureau. He lectured to classes of visiting colonials. He may have arranged Kenyatta's first visit to the Soviet Union in 1929;

certainly, he was Kenyatta's main contact on his second journey in 1932–33, his (Kenyatta's) biographer describing him as 'Padmore's protégé'.[6] Formal honours came his way: he was positioned on the central podium in Red Square one May Day, and (with Stalin) elected to the Moscow Soviet – his lack of Russian notwithstanding. He conducted many clandestine missions throughout Europe, and perhaps beyond, though he made the port-city and Communist stronghold of Hamburg his principal base, organising there in July 1930 the first international conference of Negro workers, a ramshackle affair but a landmark nonetheless. A year later, from Hamburg, he was editing for RILU the monthly *The Negro Worker* which, in the name of Communism, served as the organiser of the black masses throughout the Atlantic world. It was in Hamburg too that he was arrested, just at the moment when the Nazis acceded to power. He was fortunate to find himself deported to Britain, the Consul-General in Hamburg cabling the Foreign Office to inform them that Nurse (not Padmore) was on his way, and that 'Steps are being taken to safeguard his trunk which contains Communistic correspondence'.[7]

The seditious trunk is significant. Insurgent literature, coupled with sophisticated skills in organisation, represented Padmore's great strengths. Through his life he read everything he could find on the colonial situation. His speciality was to burn through official reports and statistics, turn them inside out, and reveal from the sources of the colonialists themselves the iniquities of colonialism. He wrote ferociously. Much was unsigned. After the break with Communism, he was in the habit of composing journalistic articles at great speed, making five or six carbon copies, and sending them to contacts throughout the world, in the hope that a portion of his output would be published – attaching to each article the request: 'Please pass on to other periodicals'.

Padmore's characteristic mode of writing is not easily accommodated to contemporary sensibilities. His relentless denunciations of colonial exploitation, and the frequently instrumental reasoning he enlisted in order to effect his critique, do not readily conform to current habits of thinking which emphasise the equivocal, the ambivalent and the contingent. This was a mode of writing which had been tutored in an exclusively Communist pedagogy, and which existed on the political extremities. But posterity can be condescending.

There is evidence, for example, that Padmore's contemporary readers could engage with his writings in ways which are not readily available to us today. Ras Makonnen provides some clues. Makonnen himself was a close collaborator of James and Padmore, an integral figure in the West Indian networks in Britain in the 1930s and 1940s, who migrated to Ghana at the time of independence and thence, following Nkrumah's downfall in 1966, to Kenya. Makonnen, born George Griffith in British Guiana at the turn of the century, was a West Indian of many talents, whose intellectual biography fits centrally into the themes addressed in this volume. Toward the end of his life he recounted his own vivid story. In so doing he recalled the moment when, in the United States in the early 1930s, he picked up and read Padmore's *The Life and Struggles of Negro Toilers.*

This was a book which arose from the Hamburg congress, written at the instigation of the RILU, and published in 1931. Its purpose was to reveal the exploitation of the world's two hundred and fifty million Negroes, *as Negroes.* Padmore argued that they were exploited as a class and as 'a nation', though locating the ultimate source of oppression in the systems of capital. This entailed his reviving the classic marxist interpretations of imperialism, though positioning race oppression at the analytical heart of his understanding of capitalism. These theoretical postulates are briefly laid out in a few opening pages. The greater part of the book delivers an empirical, synoptic view of the exploitation of black workers in Africa, the USA and the Caribbean. It concludes, as one might expect, that the revolutionary potentiality of the oppressed was in place. Thus, writing on South Africa, his confidence in the future remained characteristically undimmed: 'every act of Pirow, Hertzog, Smuts and Co merely increases the revolutionary mood of the masses'. Padmore warned his readers to be alert to the dangers of Garveyism (the struggle against which 'represents one of the major tasks of the Negro toilers in America and in the African and West Indian colonies'), which was to be equated to the dangers of Gandhism (representing the 'class interests of the black bourgeoisie and landlords').[8] These were views which were to be found in every page of *The Negro Worker*: the revolutionary capacities of the black masses were on the brink of realisation, held back only by the machinations of the false leaders – DuBois, Gandhi and, in Britain, Harold Moody.[9] Revolutionary optimism went hand in hand with sectarian denunciation, and both were driven by an unremitting class reductionism in which racial chauvinism was explained as the tool of a ruling class on the run.

But for Makonnen, and for those similarly minded, Padmore was 'a revelation'. Makonnen guessed from what he experienced as the vitality of the writing that the author of *The Life and Struggles of Negro Toilers* must have been his old friend Nurse (whom he had probably first encountered at Howard University). 'It was almost as if he had invented a new dictionary of terms with which he could burlesque the chiefs and yes-men of the various colonial regimes.' There was emphatically a 'magic' about Padmore.[10]

[ 136 ]

Five years after *The Life and Struggles of Negro Toilers* Padmore published, in 1936, *How Britain Rules Africa*. Interviewed in the 1970s Makonnen still felt the force of this latter book. It guided 'many of us' for years after; 'here was the anatomy of our misery laid bare'; it marked a kind of 'Magna Carta', leading those it spoke to from 'darkness'. 'I still feel the impact of that book upon us. It was part of our spiritual campaign.'[11]

Makonnen was not an uncritical thinker. His judgements on old friends could be harsh. On specifics he thought Padmore misguided, and – in one unexpected scenario – he took Padmore to task for vacillating on his commitments to the anti-colonial struggle.[12] His regard, in consequence, is the more convincing. Nor was Makonnen unique in his opinion of the quality of Padmore's insights. It's clear that the editors of journals to which Padmore contributed believed him to be an original thinker, of unusual intelligence and force.

Between the writing of *The Life and Struggles of Negro Toilers* and *How Britain Rules Africa* Padmore was expelled from the official Communist movement. After the Nazi party took power in Germany in January 1933 Moscow slowly began to lessen its vilification of the democratic nations of Western Europe, as a prelude to the later popular front strategy in which all enemies of fascism – socialist and non-socialist – would seek to unite in order to defeat the greater enemy. This reversal in the policy of the Communist International demanded also that hostility to the colonialism of the western European powers be suspended, winding back across the globe Moscow's support for anti-imperialist campaigns. In consequence, the Negro organisations which Padmore had animated were disbanded. On hearing this, in August 1933, he immediately resigned all his offices; his formal expulsion was set in motion in February 1934; and thereafter denunciations of him began to appear in the official Communist press.

From this time on, Padmore determined that the struggle for black emancipation could in the future never be subsumed to any other political force: blacks themselves needed to create their own autonomous organisations, free to operate as they saw fit. This shift in Padmore's thinking caused a more respectful position on Marcus Garvey to evolve – though both he and James were vociferous in condemning Garvey's conservatism during the outbreak of strikes and riots in the Caribbean in 1937 and 1938.[13] More importantly it took Padmore close to his erstwhile antagonist, W. E. B. DuBois. His had been a politics which had always been sympathetic to the ultimate aims of Pan-Africanism, even when sectarian denunciation had been in order. But from this time on, organisationally, he moved swiftly from Communism to Pan-Africanism.

Yet as Padmore crossed the threshold into the arena of Pan-Africanism he took with him many of the political categories of orthodox Bolshevism. He never expressed disillusionment with the basics of the marxism he had learned as a militant in the Communist movement. He continued to regard Lenin as the greatest political thinker of the century.[14] Though Padmore was not an intellectual given to abstraction, the classical marxist theories of imperialism, generated in the decade before the first world war, worked in his imagination as the logical starting point for an explanation of the global political realities of his own times. The underdeveloped and colonial world functioned, he believed, as the source of 'super-profits' for the metropolitan powers, and in the process created the conditions for buying off or for 'bribing' the labour leaders of the metropolitan working class – a conviction which remained with him long after he left the ranks of Communism.[15] But if the earlier emphasis of the classical theorists of imperialism had been on the global circuits of capital and on the various manifestations of financial capital, the emphasis Padmore offered was significantly different. His defining analytical and political category was the concept of exploitation. For Padmore, capitalism was a system predicated on exploitation; those most exploited inhabited the colonies; and of these, black Africans constituted 'the most oppressed of the Earth'.[16]

Padmore's journey from Communism to Pan-Africanism required continuous rethinking of political strategy, evident in his deepening commitments to the self-activity of the black masses. But the transition from one to the other did not bring with it dramatic conceptual renovation. From the start of his political life, colonial and racial issues had dominated his thinking. As the world crisis developed through the 1930s, while others were tempted to relegate colonial matters as secondary, or peripheral, Padmore reaffirmed their indispensable centrality. In so doing, he translated the categories of his Communist days into the idiom of Pan-Africanism.

Above all, he stretched the concept of fascism such that it would illuminate the historical realities of the super-exploited of the underdeveloped world.

His first sustained interpretation of fascism appeared in an unsigned editorial of *The Negro Worker* in April and May of 1933, in which he was at pains to draw out the centrality of race to the Nazi order:

> Most Negroes in Europe and America as well as in the colonies do not yet fully realize that fascism is the greatest danger which confronts not only the white workers, but it is the most hostile movement against the Negro race.
> The most glaring manifestation of this anti-Negro feeling is to be seen in the Hitler movement in Germany. Even before the fascists came into power in Germany, they carried on the most violent agitation against

Negroes, Jews, and all so-called non-Nordics. But since Hitler has become Chancellor, this Nazi agitation has taken on the form of open physical violence against all colored peoples ... the fascists in Germany are preaching race hatred and advocating lynch law.[17]

There is no evidence that either Padmore or *The Negro Worker* intended to offer theoretical reflection on the specific phenomenon of fascism. The term was invoked as a practical concept, fashioned on the run, to describe observable political realities and to signal the deepening authoritarianism of European politics – though having been jailed in Hamburg, Padmore had experienced the intensification of repression first-hand. Even so, his reading of the situation was striking, for he indicated that from the outset the decisive feature of the new regime in Germany was its dependence on the institutions of internal racial terror.

Like many blacks of his generation, Padmore was convinced that the Italian invasion of Abyssinia in October 1935 marked the critical watershed in the breakdown of the international situation. In May he contributed an article to *The Crisis*, the organ of the National Association for the Advancement of Colored People, warning of the dangers to come. Fascism, he declared, was already the dominant political force in Europe. However, its immediate fate, he believed, was to be decided in the underdeveloped world of Africa and Asia – in Abyssinia especially. If Abyssinia were to be defeated, the dominance of fascism in Europe would be consolidated. In this crisis, he wrote, the 'racial aspect looms large'. The destruction of Abyssinia would represent not only a regional victory for a fascist power but, more generally, the reassertion of the larger colonial authority of 'the white race' and the vindication of 'aggressive nationalism' and 'territorial expansion'.[18] These themes recurred in his writings in the next few years. He determined to show that the collapsing international order was inseparable from the colonial rivalries of the European powers.[19] But as the Abyssinian crisis unfolded there occurred an important shift in his thinking. The democratic powers, and their collective diplomatic representative the League of Nations, had failed to intervene to save Abyssinia. Padmore saw this as a betrayal – in much the same way as the European left saw the destruction of Czechoslovakia in 1938. Padmore concluded, however, that the European powers – fascist and non-fascist – were equally culpable in their disregard for colonial peoples.[20] This is what Abyssinia had demonstrated to him. In his final days at *The Negro Worker* he had identified fascism as 'the greatest danger', a danger located in the Nazi state. After Abyssinia fascism acquired a broader meaning for him, indicating not only the type of political regime evolving in Germany and Italy, but a racial politics linked to colonialism itself. This represented a radical reappraisal. From this shift in thought there emerged a sharper theoretical critique of the civilisation of imperial Britain; there also appeared, alongside it, a more rigorous scepticism toward the anti-fascism of the mainstream left, which in turn would take him, in 1939, to a principled refusal to support the Allied cause.

It was from these years that Padmore's peculiar pre-eminence as the arch-agent of African decolonisation became established. From 1935 he settled in London – first setting up in Guilford Street, which is where J. J. Thomas had lived at the end of the previous century, and then adopting a more permanent base at Cranleigh Street, just north of Euston station, handy, perhaps, for the boat-train from Harlem. In the summer of 1935 he joined the International Friends of Abyssinia, which had been launched by three West Indians (James, Amy Ashwood Garvey and Sam Manning) and two Africans, Kenyatta and Wallace Johnson. Padmore's authority on these matters quickly made itself felt to the others and when, in May 1937, the body broadened its ambit by renaming itself the International African Service Bureau (IASB), Padmore was the natural choice to chair it. Prominent Britons of left sympathies were invited to act as patrons: Sylvia Pankhurst, Nancy Cunard, Arthur Creech-Jones, D. N. Pritt and Victor Gollancz. Makonnen's business skills kept the organisation in funds. Padmore's activity comprised much the same as when he had been editing *The Negro Worker* – though he could no longer rely on the institutions of the Communist International. It was at this moment especially that he came into his own as a world-historical individual, the endless source of news, advice, addresses, contacts, such that countless of Africa's itinerant rebel intellectuals felt obliged to make the ritual journey to Cranleigh Street. Or as this was put in the unflattering prose of Jamaica's *Daily Gleaner*, he became 'some sort of master termite hidden in the recesses of a vast network of friendships', directing or encouraging 'a considerable revolution in the colonial world and more particularly in the British colonial world'.[21] In the process he became a mythic being.[22]

James commented on the oddity of the fact that three West Indians – himself, Padmore and Garvey – should fight out the distant battles of the Caribbean, during the upsurge of rioting, at Speakers' Corner in Hyde Park. Even more strange was the hubris of this tiny group of West Indians, in the IASB and its forerunners, in turning their attention to the entire stage of Africa, believing that they had it within their grasp to organise the emancipation of a continent. I'll come back to this.

In the mid 1930s both Padmore, after his break with Communism, and James moved into the orbit of the Independent Labour Party (ILP), which encouraged the expression of non-Communist variants of marxisant politics, and which was more ready than its rival organisations to concede the importance of 'the colonial question'. James first contributed to the ILP's *New Leader* in October 1935, just at the moment when Italian troops had crossed the Eritrean border and invaded Abyssinia. (Underneath the minuscule photo of James the editor, Fenner Brockway, explained that James was chairman of the Finchley branch of the ILP and that 'he writes fiercely'.) James confronted the veteran imperial ideologue, J. L. Garvin, and argued that the League of Nations itself had become a new tool of imperial aggression – a theme he was to develop over the weeks which followed.[23] At the start of 1936 he also alerted the readers to the duplicity of Stanley Baldwin, warning them that this 'perfect master of the sleight-of-hand' was nothing but a deep 'reactionary' encouraging the sub-editor to flag his article with the imperative: 'Look out for fascist developments!'[24] Padmore – despite lambasting Brockway in *How Britain Rules Africa* – started writing for the ILP's *Controversy* early in 1938, commenting on the government inquiries into the previous year's riots in Trinidad. Unlike James, Padmore never hinted that a domestic, British version of fascism might be just around the corner. But Padmore had no inhibitions in drawing on an expansive idea of fascism in order to demonstrate that contemporary colonialism – British colonialism included – was on the point of transmuting into a mode of fascism.

In Trinidad, for example, he believed that the government was 'inaugurating a policy which savours of Colonial Fascism'.[25] In *How Britain Rules Africa* he explained how in the settler colonies there existed the inescapable presence of 'stark imperial oppression and exploitation, allied with racial ignorance and arrogance, swaggering about without the least sign of shame'; they functioned as 'the breeding-ground for the type of fascist mentality which is being let loose in Europe to-day'.[26] In South Africa, where exploitation was more extreme, he declared that the 'unity of race as against class accounts for the widespread racial chauvinism which permeates all strata of the European population, and makes the Union *the world's classic* Fascist State'.[27] South Africa and Southern Rhodesia were totalitarian 'long before Hitler began to institute similar methods in Europe'.[28] From about the end of 1939 Padmore regularly equated the suffering of Jews in Germany with blacks in the British colonies, especially those in the white settler societies. In an article which carried the title 'The British empire is worst racket yet invented by man' he indicted the British for exercising in southern Africa the 'most blatant expression of racial superiority', which produced for the blacks a situation 'more tragic even than that of the Jews under the swastika'.[29] In the following year he asserted that there existed an 'indissoluble link' between the populations ruled by the Nazis and 'the right of coloured races to self-determination'. Those who had failed to appreciate this had, he claimed, 'objectively assisted the onward march of Fascism'.[30] Or as he concluded in 1941: 'Wherever Imperialism operates, Nazi methods are to be found'.[31]

For one prone to employ orthodox marxist categories, this interpretation of South Africa – and of fascism – is in fact strikingly heretical. Today, readers coming across such statements will be wary. (Though when Fanon arrives at much the same conclusion about the connections between colonialism and fascism, via more elaborately philosophical routes, it feels rather different.) Charges of fascism have been so common, and are often so reductive, that they rarely enlighten political thinking. As I've suggested, Padmore employed the term as a practical category, without much heeding the specificities of its European forms. But this shouldn't conceal the insights which his approach delivered. Fundamentally, fascism for Padmore represented state-directed racial supremacy, in which a dominant ethnic group enslaved a subordinate ethnic group (by employing extra-economic means, including terror, to compel it to labour) on the sole basis of its putative racial identity. From this perspective, South Africa could indeed be regarded as exemplifying a classic fascism, as could Germany, while elsewhere in the British colonies there occurred, in more restricted form, policies which 'savoured' of colonial fascism (Trinidad), or social mentalities which might in the future 'breed' colonial fascism (the white settler colonies). Within this reasoning, fascism was a term which had no direct application to the historical conditions of metropolitan Britain itself.[32]

The conviction that the will for racial purity lay at the core of fascism is powerful, conforming to certain currents of postwar European philosophy.[33] It worked to question the notion that fascism was a peculiarly German, or continental, phenomenon. Commensurately, it questioned the integrity of much of the anti-fascist folk-wisdom common in Britain from the mid 1930s to the mid 1940s, disclosing the repeated moments when Britain's vaunted democratic values buckled under the pressure of dangerous racial imperatives. In the closing pages of How Britain Rules Africa Padmore had expressed the hope that 'this book will serve to throw light into dark places'.[34] Makonnen echoed this when he claimed that Padmore possessed the ability to lay bare the 'darkness' of black subjugation. This, I think, explains Padmore's originality, and the source (for his contemporary readers) of his revelatory powers. His conjoining of Bolshevism and Pan-Africanism allowed him to become not merely the chronicler of the immiseration of the colonised, but – in a Gramscian sense, taking Padmore truly to be an intellectual organic to a larger, anti-colonial movement – the philosopher of the 'dark places' of empire in general, and of the British empire in particular. This was a philosophy which carried its appointed language, or as Makonnen put it, one which comprised a 'new dictionary of terms'. It strove to demonstrate that the darkest region of all resided deep in the imaginings of white civilisation.

Padmore had the knack for making speakable what previously had been unspeakable, and for shifting the terms of public debate. In relation to black Africa he sought to overturn the accepted wisdom on the polarity between civilisation and barbarism. And we can see something similar in his determination to portray the white settlers – in South Africa and Southern Rhodesia especially – not as the vanguard of English civilisation, exemplars of quiet fortitude and broad humanity, but as arrogant, swaggering racial chauvinists barely indistinguishable from Aryan thugs closer to home. To speak in these terms, in the 1930s and 1940s, constituted an astounding provocation.[35]

We don't have to share Padmore's judgements, nor do we need to endorse the political positions to which he journeyed. But we should recognise what he represents. There were before him, of course, many different currents of anti-imperial thought in Britain, the greater number of which derived from liberal or radical-liberal traditions. While these could be fierce on empire, on matters of race they often equivocated, attached at a profound level to a belief in the essential moral superiority of the civilisation of the English. In elaborating a political philosophy in Port of Spain, Harlem and Moscow Padmore brought into England systems of thought from outside, and although many ambiguities remain, the extremity of his views was supremely un-English. More particularly, this enabled him, and those won to his cause, to disengage from the presiding Westminster vision of the colonial world which, while deeply liberal in its precepts, insisted that independence for the colonies had to await the attainment of a requisite level of civilisation. Padmore, to the contrary, declared that independence should be immediate, 'regardless of their social and cultural development'.[36] Rather than assuming that emancipation was the gift of London he insisted that the black masses were the agents of their own liberation.[37] This determination to seek equal moral worth in the voice of the black masses of Africa was (and perhaps still is) the source, in part, of Padmore's 'magic'. It created the conditions in which 'the chiefs and yes-men' of the British empire could – in a nice West Indian turn – become the object not of reverence but of what they merited: 'burlesque'. 'Imagine', wrote Makonnen, 'what it meant to us to go to Hyde Park to speak to a race of people who were considered our masters, and tell them right out what we felt about their empire and about them.'[38]

Padmore's refusal to accept at face value the founding myths which gave life to colonial aspiration made new thought possible. An early witness to this was Stafford Cripps in 1937, momentarily espousing a role as outrider to the left sects. He contributed a foreword to *Africa and World Peace* in which he commended Padmore's 'courageous exposure of the great myth of the civilising mission of western democracies in Africa'.[39] Much later, in commenting on the success of the independence movement in Ghana, James picked up this notion of myth, and attempted to explain what it entailed and how it worked.

> One of the greatest modern myths has been the myth justifying and even ennobling 'colonialism' or, as it used to be called, 'the white man's burden'. At present it is a common belief that colonialism in the modern world is dead or dying.
>     Nothing could be further from the truth. Colonialism is alive and will continue to be alive until another *positive doctrine* takes its place.

The power of the myth of colonialism, James continued, derived from the fact that it worked beyond the reach of reason, or of rational critique. Those who propagated it were neither hypocrites nor liars: on the contrary, they lived within the 'unconscious premise' of the myth itself. 'It is not that the myth is not challenged. It is, but almost always on premises which it has itself created, premises which, as with all myths, rest on very deep foundations within the society which has created them.' The myth of colonialism, he argued specifically in relation to Britain, 'is now an organic part of the thought processes of the nation and to disgorge it requires a Herculean effort'. 'It must', he concluded, 'be routed, torn up by the roots, ridiculed.'[40] Both James and Padmore worked to make conscious the 'unconscious premise' of the myth of colonialism, and to step outside its givens: to effect, in other words, the intellectual labour of decolonisation.

In outline, with necessary brevity, I've described the main contours of Padmore's political thought from the days of *The Negro Worker* to the time of the Pan-African Congress in Manchester in October 1945. The Congress marks a turning point in Padmore's political life. Present were Nkrumah, Kenyatta and Hastings Banda – all poised to return to their home nations. DuBois and Amy Ashwood Garvey presided. The congress represented a direct continuation of the one organised by Padmore in Hamburg fifteen years earlier. (Though perhaps a little less ramshackle: the proceedings carefully record that £4-10-0 was spent on 'bunting and flags' and rather more – £4-15-0 – on the services of the local Red Cross band.)[41] It continued too the remarkable preponderance of West Indians in the Pan-African movement: of the fifty-eight accredited delegates, thirty-three were from the West Indies. But the following year Kenyatta returned to Kenya, and the year after that Nkrumah to the Gold Coast. Each became the principal actor in their respective national struggles for independence – 'moving out from London to declare war on the empire'.[42] Thereafter Padmore poured his energies into supporting Nkrumah in the Gold Coast, preoccupied with the internal demands of a political movement, but certain in his own mind that a lifetime's work was on the point of fruition. When success came in 1957 he could reasonably have thought that the emancipation he had dreamed of had become a historical reality – that they'd done it. Writing in *Présence africaine* in 1957 Padmore likened Nkrumah's autobiography to Tom Paine's *Common Sense*, the detonator which would set in train a continental revolution: 'L'indépendance du Ghana est justement le commencement de la liberté pan-africaine'.[43]

But for my purposes two interconnected questions remain outstanding. First, there is more to say about Padmore's conception of the British at home; second, is the matter of his West Indian provenance. Certain ambiguities arise.

We can return for a moment to the image of the young Malcolm Nurse on his wedding day, bedecked in tails in the Anglican church in Port of Spain. It offers a perfect snapshot of early twentieth-century colonial respectability. As we have seen, shortly after the wedding Malcolm Nurse transmuted into George Padmore, the Bolshevik agitator. But perhaps it is wrong to suppose that the identity of Malcolm Nurse, the respectable anglo-colonial, was entirely extinguished. The doubleness of Nurse–Padmore is important. James caught something of this in his eulogy, describing Padmore as simultaneously 'a great citizen of the world' and 'a great gentleman'. Padmore, James implied, embodied both a Jacobin spirit of insurgent, republican virtue and the lived forms of English gentlemanliness. To later generations this looks like a fusion of contraries, though it was clearly important to James, as it was to Padmore himself. All the reports of Padmore – firebrand politics notwithstanding – depict a man of deep courtesy, given entirely to English manners. 'A British West Indian of the old school', as James remarked later.[44] To Makonnen he appeared 'spick and span like a senator'.[45] Padmore never boasted, as James did, that he read *Vanity Fair* each year. Indeed, there was the suggestion that he affected a revolutionary disdain for the cultural artefacts of England. But James was never persuaded by this; and it is significant that in the brief obituary carried in *The Times* mention should have been made of Padmore's love for English literature.[46] In short, Padmore showed every sign that he had mastered the culture of the colonisers, having learned to inhabit Englishness at perfect pitch.

For Padmore as much as for James mastering the codes of England provided a way out from colonial Trinidad. Describing Padmore's situation in Trinidad, and his own, James noted that 'a proud and sensitive black man could feel a sense of intolerable restriction', which is about as near as he ever got in public to revealing his experiences of racial subordination.[47] For James coming to England, and coming to inhabit the civilisation of the English at its epicentre, were the means by which he fashioned himself as a modern being, in opposition to what he had experienced as colonial provincialism. There was something of this in Padmore too. We can catch a glimpse of it in the accounts of his relations with white English women – with Nancy Cunard (who faithfully typed out the entire manuscript of *How Britain Rules Africa*) and, most of all, with Dorothy Pizer, whom Padmore met in the late 1930s and later married. Pizer personified the attributes of the 'modern woman', 'a Londoner and sophisticated to the last degree'. She worked – on her own terms – as secretary to a 'big businessman'; she dressed with fashionable taste; she was an accomplished cook, learning how to prepare West Indian and Indian dishes; she had a facility for languages; after the war she persuaded Padmore to tour Italy. This talented woman of independent views chose 'to subordinate herself ... entirely to George and his work', earning the bulk of the money which kept them going. She contributed vast amounts of editorial work, did many if not all of the translations, and (once or twice) claimed sole or partial authorship. Although 'she didn't find it easy', she expended much labour cooking for their myriad of visitors, demanding only that George did the washing-up. On politics, she reserved the right to argue 'vigorously'.[48] This was essentially a modern, cosmopolitan, London relationship, far removed from the expectations of colonial Trinidad. In both the US and in the Soviet Union Padmore had experienced new freedoms: but in England too this 'British West Indian of the old school' was able to fashion his selfhood through his inhabitation of Englishness and to present himself as a fully modern – that is, a non-colonial – figure.

Except that this affiliation to modern selfhood was vitiated by race. Nurse–Padmore had a double existence, simultaneously located in and dislocated from his English way of life. Padmore – like James; like their shared foe Harold Moody; but unlike a later generation – did not easily find a voice in which this ambivalence could be spoken. On the one hand he could unleash his incessant indictment of the racism of empire, while on the other suggest that, in daily life, to complain about one's own experiences was to compromise one's integrity as a colonial whose colonial origins had been transcended. To rise above the pettiness of racial injustice was confirmation of one's having overcome colonial identity, testament to one's advanced viewpoint. On this Padmore was explicit. In 'A Negro looks at British imperialism', published in 1938, he remarked that 'it is impossible for any *progressively minded* Negro to isolate himself from the broader aspects of the subject and view the Colour Bar question from the purely personal standpoint'. To do this would be 'superficial'. He recognised that the 'British people, in their typically off-hand way', assumed that black colonials were a natural part of the empire 'in the same way that Mussolini now claims the Abyssinians'. Britons of all classes, he believed, accepted the myths of empire, just as they displayed a 'cultivated aloofness' to foreigners and 'an added aversion to peoples of darker skin'. But issues of racial prejudice were a political matter: 'we do not whine about them'.[49] James reflected on this, recounting the occasion in 1957 when he had bumped into Padmore on the Charing Cross Road (which James obviously frequented). Padmore burst out in anger: '"There are only two things in the world I cannot take ... One is race prejudice, the other is bureaucracy"' – and then went on to denounce the sins of bureaucracy, while remaining silent on racism. James, however, was surprised that he even mentioned race.

> George was a rare example of a certain type – he fought racialism as a social curse, he was ready to put in his place anyone who was personally offensive, but his preoccupation with large political issues left him little time or energy to 'carry a chip on his shoulder'.

In an uncharacteristically open manner, James discussed the self-discipline required to live in, and work politically in, a white society – revealing private instances of anguish and fury. ('English people in particular', he claimed without apparent irony, 'are very grateful when they see that you have had every justification for tearing the place apart but refuse to take it.') Throughout his life in England, James indicated, Padmore had been 'master of himself'. In 'the early days' he may have been angered by the 'dumb stupidity of English people on the race question'. 'But you get over it.'[50] 'Getting over it', however, resolved little, and left in place many difficulties – particularly for those colonials who had most successfully learned to embody the civilisation of the colonial power.

In Padmore's case this unease in confronting the home civilisation of the British bequeathed serious political and analytical problems. He never seemed able to decide what relations existed between Britons at home and Britons abroad, whose predispositions he was content to condemn as fascist. Nor was he able to determine whether racism in the metropolis was, in its fundamental forms, confined to 'the ruling class' or whether it was more general.[51]

Some of these difficulties also emerged in the relations between the

West Indians (Padmore, James, Makonnen) and the Africans (Kenyatta, Nkrumah). Much later, James conceded that, around 1935 in London, there was a 'definite cleavage' between the Africans and the West Indians. West Indians 'were very much more at home in London and with English people'. The West Indians, or the intellectuals amongst them, were sure that this was because they came from societies which were already modern: not as modern, perhaps, as the cities of the metropolis, but modern all the same. This confidence in knowing the colonial civilisation was the reason, according to James, that the Africans perceived the West Indians as 'black white men'.[52]

The contrast with Kenyatta is striking. From his first years in London, in 1929 and then again in 1932, Kenyatta adopted the role of colonial gentleman, aspiring to all things English.[53] By 1938, in a complex transformation, Kenyatta jettisoned this persona and refigured himself as Gikuyu native, repository of the collective memory of his people. This was most evident in the frontispiece to his anthropological study, *Facing Mt. Kenya*, in which he pictured himself wearing a Colobus monkey-skin and brandishing a spear. This invention of the traditional Gikuyu self was replete with ambiguity. It is clear, though, that for Kenyatta it represented an attempt to extricate himself from the symbolic and cognitive systems of those who colonised him. What James or Padmore made of this is not recorded. We do know, though, that James's opinion of Kenyatta (and in fact of Nkrumah too) was not without a sense of intellectual – West Indian – superiority. In telling of Padmore's skill in dealing with 'the more untutored Africans' in London in the 1930s, James admitted that he found Kenyatta 'very trying', believing him to be only 'the second African to have come out of Kenya'.[54] James, Padmore and the West Indians in general were conscious that they were products of a radically different history. But in their determination to assert the modernity of their colonial homelands they foreclosed for themselves anything akin to the reinvention of the self which Kenyatta undertook: which made it awkward for them to imagine a way of circumventing, in their lived relations, the codes of colonial England.

When the West Indians congregated in Ghana this situation was acted out in sharper form. In November 1957, on the eve of Padmore's departure for Accra, David Pitt hosted a farewell party at his Gower Street surgery in London. Friends clubbed together and presented to Padmore a briefcase – an appropriate accoutrement for the modern man, on his mission to become adviser to the president of a new nation. In Ghana, James wrote, 'the twentieth century and the future were battling with the middle ages and the past'.[55] The West Indians – principally Padmore, Arthur Lewis and Makonnen – were the cadres of

modernity, battling with the African past. Makonnen's restless entre-
preneurial spirit was ever-active, launching state bakeries one day,
hotels for tourism the next. Yet the larger his vision the greater his
sense of frustration, for each new project faced an array of difficulties.
He regretted the absence of the type of socialist intellectual whom he
remembered and admired from his days in Britain – 'the Oxford Greats
man', as he put it, 'going off to lose himself in miners' education in
Scotland'.[56] All the accounts of the early years of the Ghanian state
reveal how powerfully 'the past' reasserted itself, and how dreadful
were the dilemmas which confronted those who took it upon themselves to represent the future.

Padmore's dedication to the complexities of the local situation was
offset by his continuing hopes for the imminent continental revolution, in which Ghana would act as handmaiden for independence across
Africa. But this did little to diminish local hostility to the West
Indians.[57] Padmore himself was dogged by illness, and – toward the end
– by political frustration. He contemplated returning to the West
Indies.[58] In September 1959, mortally ill, he returned to London for
medical attention. He died the same month.

Padmore is now a forgotten figure. A handful of West Indians – George
Lamming, John La Rose amongst them – strive to pay him public
tribute. At the start of the twenty-first century we live in a political
world in which colonialism once again is justified by all manner of
sophistry. Padmore expressed – and lived – the elementary truth that
colonialism has neither moral nor intellectual justification.

## Notes

1 James's 'Notes on the life of George Padmore' were published in *The Nation* between October 1959 and January 1960, in eleven instalments; remaining copies – in London and Port of Spain – are difficult to track down. Excerpts were included, under the same title, in Anna Grimshaw (ed.), *The C. L. R. James Reader* (Oxford: Blackwell, 1992). In 1976 James lectured on Padmore in London, which is reproduced as 'George Padmore: black marxist revolutionary' in James's *At The Rendezvous of Victory* (London: Allison and Busby, 1984). I have also drawn from James Hooker, *Black Revolutionary. George Padmore's path from Communism to Pan-Africanism* (London: Pall Mall, 1967). I am grateful to all those who attended the symposium which accompanied the preparation of this volume for their responses to an early version of this chapter, and to Winston James; the resulting views are mine alone.
2 Conversation with George Lamming, Atlantis Hotel, Bathsheba, Barbados, 28 August 2001.
3 C. L. R. James, 'Lectures on *The Black Jacobins*', *Small Axe*, 8 (2000), p. 109.
4 'George Padmore dead', *Nation*, 25 September 1959.
5 V. S. Naipaul, *The Mimic Men* (Harmondsworth: Penguin, 1969), p. 32.
6 Jeremy Murray-Brown, *Kenyatta* (London: Allen and Unwin, 1979), p. 171.
7 Murray-Brown, *Kenyatta*, p. 166.

8   George Padmore, *The Life and Struggles of Negro Toilers* (London: Red International of Labour Unions, 1931), pp. 82, 125 and 126.

9   This began as *The Negro Workers' Review*, the organ of the International Trade Union Committee of Negro Workers, in January 1931. From March 1931 it became retitled *The Negro Worker*. Padmore served as editor from October 1931 to the issue dated August-September 1933.

10  Ras MaKonnen, *Pan-Africanism from Within* (Nairobi: Oxford University Press, 1973), pp. 102–3.

11  MaKonnen, *Pan-Africanism from Within*, p. 194.

12  MaKonnen, *Pan-Africanism from Within*, p. 181.

13  In August 1937 Padmore and James could be found in Hyde Park heckling Garvey; the deployed his own attack on them at the end of the month in the Trinidadian press. See Rupert Lewis, *Marcus Garvey. Anti-colonial champion* (London: Karia, 1987), p. 270.

14  George Padmore, *Africa and World Peace* (London: Secker and Warburg, 1937), p. 157.

15  Padmore, *Life and Struggles*, p. 6.

16  George Padmore, *How Britain Rules Africa* (London: Wishart, 1936), p. 396.

17  'Fascist terror against Negroes in Germany', *Negro Worker*, 3:4/5 (1933).

18  George Padmore, 'Ethiopia and world politics', *Crisis*, 42:5 (1935), pp. 138–9 and 156–7.

19  This was the thesis of *Africa and World Peace*.

20  George Padmore, 'Abyssinia, the last of free Africa'; 'Abyssinia betrayed by the League of Nations'; 'Hitler, Mussolini and Africa'; 'A new world order for colonies', *Crisis*, 44:5; 44:6; 44:9 and 44:10 (1937). See too Padmore's contribution on Abyssinia to Nancy Cunard's extraordinary *Negro Anthology* (London: Wishart, 1934) – a collection with which Padmore was closely involved.

21  Reported in the *Nation*, 23 October 1959. It wasn't only Africans, nor those who shared his views, who paid obeisance in this way. It's instructive that on his trip to London in autumn 1937 Grantley Adams, from Barbados, felt obliged to meet with Padmore: Adams was so impressed that he tried to persuade Padmore to return to the Caribbean. F. A. Hoyos, *Grantley Adams and the Social Revolution* (London: Macmillan, 1974), pp. 68–9.

22  This aspect of Padmore's life is manifest in Peter Abrahams's novel, *A Wreath for Udomo* (London: Faber, 1956). Reminiscences of this period can also be found in Abrahams's *The Coyaba Chronicles: reflections on the black experience in the twentieth century* (Kingston and Cape Town: Ian Randle and David Philip, 2000); and in Dudley Thompson, with Margaret Cezair Thompson, *From Kingston to Kenya: the making of a Pan-Africanist lawyer* (Dover, Mass: Majority Press, 1993).

23  C. L. R. James, 'Is this worth a war?', *New Leader*, 4 October 1935.

24  C. L. R. James, 'Baldwin's next move', *New Leader*, 3 January 1936.

25  George Padmore, 'Fascism in the colonies', *Controversy*, February 1938; and see too his 'The Trinidad Report', *Controversy*, March 1938.

26  Padmore, *How Britain Rules Africa*, pp. 3–4.

27  George Padmore, 'White workers and black', *Controversy*, May 1938; emphasis added. Versions of his contributions to *Controversy* also appeared in *New Leader* and *Crisis*.

28  George Padmore, 'Britain's black record' *New Leader*, 27 September 1941.

29  *New Leader*, 15 December 1939.

30  George Padmore, 'To defeat Nazism we must free the colonials', *New Leader*, 25 July 1940.

31  George Padmore, 'Not Nazism! Not Imperialism! But Socialism!', *New Leader*, 27 December 1941.

32  On the eve of Munich, Makonnen planned for James, Padmore, Kenyatta and himself to retreat to the relative security of Norway, where – he believed – they could witness the final collapse of the colonial powers: Murray-Brown, *Kenyatta*, p. 209.

33  I'm thinking especially of the traditions represented by those who followed Theodor

Adorno and Frankfurt critical theory. And, in different mode, the positions which emerged from Jean-Paul Sartre's fusion of existentialism and *négritude*, for which see especially his *Colonialism and Anti-Colonialism* (London: Routledge, 2001; first published 1964).

34  Padmore, *How Britain Rules Africa*, p. 395.

35  It is symptomatic that Padmore was very early on to the case of Earl Erroll, who was murdered in Kenya in 1941 – the so-called Happy Valley scandal. In *How Britain Rules Africa* he had described Erroll's arrival in Kenya in 1934 as a member of the British Union of Fascists (BUF), hoping to build a local branch. According to Padmore, however, Erroll discovered that the settlers for the most part were 'already full-blooded Fascists', and therefore not in need of outside organisation, leading Padmore to conclude that 'Kenya, together with South Africa, is the most Nazified section of the Empire', pp. 359–60. He returned to Erroll after his murder, designating him the 'fascist Don Juan', in 'The truth about the murdered fascist earl' *New Leader*, 14 June 1941. The first complete discussion of this episode concentrated on the Don Juan dimension rather than on his involvement with the BUF: James Fox, *White Mischief* (Harmondsworth: Penguin, 1984). More recently, while trying to show Erroll as morally upstanding, the latest account is much more up-front about the fascism, hinting that Erroll was assassinated by the British owing to his possession of dark secrets to do with very senior figures in the British state: Errol Trzebinski, *The Life and Death of Lord Erroll* (London: Fourth Estate, 2001).

36  Padmore, 'To defeat Nazism'.

37  Again, this proposition is difficult to see in its historical context. It came about as the result of hard political work. For example: when James reviewed *How Britain Rules Africa* – although he had been warmly acknowledged in the book itself – he announced that he was 'grievously disappointed' that Padmore, 'a man of African descent', had so underestimated the role of Africans in the making of their own emancipation: *New Leader*, 29 May 1936. James's own *Black Jacobins*, about Haiti but directed to the future revolution in Africa, comprised a further instalment in this debate.

38  MaKonnen, *Pan-Africanism from Within*, p. 123.

39  Padmore, *Africa and World Peace*, p. ix.

40  C. L. R. James, *Nkrumah and The Ghana Revolution* (London: Allison and Busby, 1982), pp. 29, 36 and 37. English readers might find the force of these comments tempered by James's addition of a footnote at this point, in which he cites the BBC's *Goon Show* as one moment of this Herculean struggle.

41  George Padmore (ed.), *Colonial and Coloured Unity: a programme of action. History of the Pan-African Congress* (Manchester: Pan-African Service, n.d., 1945?).

42  MaKonnen, *Pan-Africanism from Within*, p. 170.

43  George Padmore, 'L'autobiographie de Kwame Nkrumah', *Présence africaine*, 12 (1957), p. 31. Padmore was due to speak at the *Présence africaine* Congress of Negro Writers in Paris, but illness prevented him attending. Padmore's connection to the francophone intellectuals – and to Richard Wright – needs more research. His political impact in France in the 1930s is investigated in Philippe Dewitte, *Les Movements Nègres en France, 1919–1939* (Paris: Editions L'Harmattan, n.d., 1986?).

44  James, 'Notes on the life of Padmore', *Nation*, 4 December 1959.

45  MaKonnen, *Pan-Africanism from Within*, p. 120.

46  James, 'Notes on the life of Padmore', *Nation*, 15 January 1960; *The Times*, 25 September 1959.

47  James, 'Notes on the life of Padmore', in Grimshaw, *The James Reader*, p. 289.

48  James, 'Notes on the life of Padmore', *Nation*, 15 January 1960. Dorothy Pizer reviewed James's *Black Jacobins* (favourably) in *Controversy*, 28 (1939), and was named as the collaborator on Padmore's *How Russian Transformed Her Colonial Empire: a challenge to the imperial powers* (London: Dennis Dobson, 1946).

49  George Padmore, 'A Negro looks at British imperialism', *Crisis*, 45:12 (1938), pp. 396–7, emphasis added. For Moody's response to Padmore, see Harold Moody and W. B. Mumford, 'Reply to George Padmore', *Crisis*, 47:6 (1940), pp. 174 and 186.

50   James, 'Notes on the life of Padmore', *Nation*, 8 January 1960.

51   Padmore's views veered from a populist regard for the good sense of the British people, and exasperation. For the former, for example: George Padmore and Nancy Cunard, *The White Man's Duty* (London: W. H. Allen, 1943), especially p. 33; and James, 'Notes on the life of Padmore', *Nation*, 8 January 1960. And for the latter, for example: George Padmore, 'The second world war and the darker races', *Crisis*, 46:11 (1939), pp. 327–8.

52   James, 'Notes on the life of Padmore', *Nation*, 6 November 1959.

53   For a wonderful account, from which I have learned much, see Simon Gikandi, 'Pan-Africanism and cosmopolitanism: the case of Jomo Kenyatta', *English Studies in Africa*, 43:1 (2000), pp. 3–27.

54   James, 'Notes on the life of Padmore', *Nation*, 30 October 1959; and James, 'Padmore: black marxist revolutionary', pp. 257–8.

55   C. L. R. James, *Nkrumah and the Ghana Revolution* (London: Allison and Busby, 1977), p. 85. There is much rich material here both on the West Indian view of Ghana and (when James reflects on Dostoyevsky, Kierkergaard, Nietzsche and Sartre) on the role of intellectuals.

56   MaKonnen, *Pan-Africanism from Within*, p. 198. As this quote indicates, there was a generational divide. Kamau Brathwaite, of a distinctly younger generation, represents a very different (and very intriguing) West Indian experience of Ghana.

57   There are photographs of Padmore in West African dress, though they are nothing like those of Kenyatta – not least because of Padmore's refusal to relinquish his pipe. The image of the young Malcolm Nurse on his wedding day was not as distant as the African setting might seem to suggest. See Kwame Nkrumah, *Hands Off Africa!!! Some famous speeches* (Accra: Kwabena Owusu-Akyem, n.d., 1960?). This also carries a photo of Nkrumah receiving Padmore's ashes.

50   MaKonnen, *Pan-Africanism From Within*, p. 259.

# CHAPTER SEVEN

# C. L. R. James:
# visions of history, visions of Britain

Stephen Howe

C. L. R. James had intended in late 1938 to travel from his London base to the United States. His plan was to work with the Trotskyist movement there, but to return to England in time for the 1939 cricket season. We may well speculate that, in fact, his American sojourn would have extended for far longer than he envisaged, had world history not intervened. Neville Chamberlain's contemptuous rejection of the 'piece of paper' Hitler offered him at Munich plunged Britain into war in the autumn of 1938. James's Atlantic crossing had to be cancelled, and he spent most of the 1940s and 1950s as a British resident. For much of that period, he was a full-time political activist in tiny far-left groups. The mass of political material he wrote during these years, both alone and in collaboration, is of lasting interest only to those fascinated by the minutiae of ultra-left politics. Still, James's interests could not be confined in a single political mould: his later British years also produced a study of Robert Louis Stevenson's sea-stories, *Mariners, Renegades and Castaways* (1953), and above all the remarkable *British Civilisation*. The latter, never fully completed and only published in 1992 after James's death, was a pioneering work in many ways; not least in its analysis of 'popular culture' – cinema, comic books, radio serials, mass-market fiction – as a key to understanding British society.

These were also seminal, turbulent years in James's personal life. In 1939 in Manchester, he met and fell in love with the eighteen-year old Constance Duckfoot. It seemed a hopeless passion, for Constance did not initially return his love, was twenty years his junior and (still significant, even dangerous, in the Britain of the 1940s) she was white, he black. Despite all this, Nello's devotion was eventually reciprocated, and he and Constance were married in May 1946. Yet theirs remained an uneasy union, which finally broke down in 1950–51, to James's lasting sorrow. There is no doubt that the relationship with Constance was the most important of his life. His many, lengthy letters to her, posthumously published as *Special Delivery* (1996) are deeply touching as well as revelatory documents. They make clear not only how entranced James had become by the currents of almost Promethean, revolutionary modernity he discerned emerging in British life, but how those currents were, for him, embodied and crystallised in the image of the beloved.

Well, *some* of that happened – but most did not. James (born in Caroni, Trinidad, in 1901) did go to America, and stayed for fifteen years. His great love affair was with the young American Constance Webb, not her imaginary British near-namesake. Although most of his later life, from 1953 onwards, was spent in London, he never investigated Britain in anything like the way that, in the hugely ambitious, uncompleted *American Civilization*, he did the USA.[1] The suggestive but brief comments about Britishness in *Beyond a Boundary*, the seventieth and eightieth birthday lectures and elsewhere were never expanded upon by a man who, in his later British years, had neither energy nor inclination for new, large-scale projects.[2]

Speculation about what James *might* have written about Britain and Britishness may have its value. But in the absence of that imaginary seminal work *British Civilisation*, I shall try here to reconstruct the more fragmentary but important things James *did* say about Britain, Britishness and their relations to Caribbean histories and identities – and the influence those views have had, as well as the rather wider influence which, one might say, they *should* have had.

If the 'Jamesian hypothesis' around which this volume revolves – that in Bill Schwarz's words 'it was through the encounter with the formerly colonial peoples of the Caribbean that native white Britons were first able to see themselves in their true historical light' – can be sustained in relation to James's own work and influence, this must be done in somewhat *pointilliste* fashion.[3] Although he produced many commentaries on British writers and sportspeople, on the character of British socialism and, near the end of his life, on British race relations, and although his *Beyond a Boundary* includes substantial if oblique reflection on the nature of 'imperial Britishness', James's relevant writings are extremely scattered and mostly brief. This must have been because British society and culture were not strange to him as America's were: 'Britishness' was for James a largely pre-given cultural milieu more often than it was the object of active investigation. Yet James in the USA was intensely engaged in analysing *that* society throughout the years that, in retrospect, he regarded as his own most intellectually fertile. Moreover, James was committed, according to the political philosophy of his mature years, to stressing what Britain had in common with other industrial societies, rather than what was distinctive about it. In his Trotskyist writings and those for the 'Facing Reality' group, especially, he analysed British politics and industrial relations as instances of global trends which he saw working their way out also in France, the USA, Hungary and elsewhere. Yet it is not at all implausible to think that, given a different spin on the historical dice, we would have had a study of *Treasure Island* (or, perhaps more likely, of Conrad) rather than of *Moby-Dick*, one of British rather than of American culture as embodying the 'pursuit of happiness', astonishing love letters to an ideal of young British womanhood.

The nature of James's writings means also that discussion of their influence in Britain must explore not only a 'bilateral' British-Caribbean relationship, but a triangular one. That is, it must approach his stance towards and influence on Britain in part via his writings on the British *empire* and its aftermaths, shaping both 'Britishness' and 'West Indianness'.[4] As James several times hinted – and as numerous recent historians have sought to trace in more detail – the very idea of 'Britain' could not be thought historically without coming to terms with those imperial relations.

James's thought was not confined to any of these contexts: it is recognised that his intellectual importance stems largely from the sheer range of his interests and activities. He helped pioneer a Pan-Caribbean consciousness, and also came to be associated with visions of a truly global kind, involving 'Third World' and anticolonial solidarities. Much of the writing about James which has proliferated since his death, moreover, has tended to depict him as a somewhat abstracted and emblematic figure, representing a generalised exilic or diasporic world-view.[5] Yet he was a product of a very specific local milieu – indeed he often stressed not only the uniqueness, but the very smallness and intimacy, of that formative world. His family background, and what James once described as the 'Protestant and middle-class' values imbibed there,[6] have frequently been analysed as abjectly imitative of hegemonic British mores. So, still more, has the kind of education he received at Queen's Royal College. Certainly, aspirations to an idealised kind of middle-class Britishness, and to the ethos of the English public school, were strongly present in the West Indies of the early twentieth century. Those who could not attend a 'real' British-model elite school might still find themselves entranced and moulded by imaginary ones, as the young Edgar Mittelholzer was by Edwy Searle Brooks's fictional 'St. Frank's College'.[7] But, as we shall see, James was also concerned to explore how something more complex, and more ambivalent, than mere colonial mimicry was involved in his formative experiences.

There was nothing inevitable about the Englishness of James's education, or of Trinidad. Given its Spanish and French inheritance, the island could have remained a minimally anglicised hybrid, one where the formerly dominant languages remained the preferred, and prized, idioms of the elite, like French in Mauritius or Italian in Malta. Indeed a mainly French-derived creole was still the main popular language among poorer African-descended Trinidadians until shortly before James was born, while a section of the old white plantocracy remained francophone. Trinidad could have been, and nearly was, as polyglot as George Lamming's San Cristobel. It required conscious decisions, acts of will – on the part of both colonisers and colonised – for a British-model educational system and cultural ethos to take root there. The island's multilingual heritage obviously helped enable James's later historical researches;[8] but it meant that the 'English public school' education he received was part of a more complex cultural contestation than is usually recognised. Another aspect of that complexity, the presence of a large Indian-descended population, produced in Trinidad both unique forms of Afro-Asian-European cultural syncretism, but also elements of communalist politics and ethnic mobilisation which sometimes threatened to degenerate into the kind of violent polarisation which has marked Guyana. James's writings may be open to the charge of neglecting the Indian contribution to Caribbean culture; but he could not be indifferent to it.

Culturally complex this small society may have been, but for many critics that did not necessarily translate into cultural richness. 'I was moved by the fact that such a man came from something like my own background ... How, considering when he was born, had he become the man he was? How had he preserved his soul through all the discouragements of the colonial time?'[9] V. S. Naipaul poses these questions of his 'Lebrun', a fictional character who is largely modelled on James. Their point is that, in the light of Naipaul's conviction that the Caribbean was a cultural wasteland, there was something astonishing about someone from colonial Trinidad emerging as an erudite, scholarly cosmopolitan.[10]

James himself did not see it like that. He argued repeatedly that the West Indian milieu was, to the contrary, an especially propitious one for cultural, artistic, social or political innovation. 'The populations in the British West Indies', James averred in apparent concurrence with Naipaul, 'have no native civilisation at all. These populations are essentially Westernised and they have been Westernised for centuries.'[11] But it was precisely in this absence that their potential lay. For James, what made the West Indies distinctive was their thoroughgoing modernity – created by history in (as James insisted) a more complete way than any other people, they were consequently unable to delude themselves that they had been products of tradition, of the soil, of racial inheritance. This might seem to distinguish them sharply from the mythicised self-fashionings of the 'ancient English' and provide a basis for James's vantage point on the latter – except that, as we shall see, James insisted on the modernity of English life too.[12]

The distinctive modernity of Caribbean peoples, their formation through a very special kind of historical process, was for James just one of three crucial features, all of which together might account for the kind of impact which he – and West Indians in general – had on the world. They also, together, enabled the kind of perceptions about Britain which its Caribbean-originating minorities could bring to bear. The other two features James emphasised were internationalism and smallness of scale. West Indians, James believed, 'are essentially an international people ... therefore we are particularly open'.[13] The scale of the island societies was if anything more important: it contrasted sharply with Britain, and enabled West Indians' special perspective on the latter. In the West Indies, it was possible for the observer or intellectual to know the whole society, whereas 'the average English worker' knew only his own area and class. In that way, the Caribbean was in James's view 'more developed' than Britain. 'We brought that [to Britain] – at least I brought that with me, Padmore had it too – we kept on seeing the whole thing as a whole.'[14] Coming from a small-scale society, where it was possible to comprehend a society as a totality, produced also a particular kind of dynamism in both the arts and politics.[15] For the former, it enabled comparisons with the England of Shakespeare, in which, James insisted, the playwright's genius was crucially fired by the fact that his audience was composed of the whole society, of all classes.[16] It may also have helped shape something which Bill Schwarz, elsewhere in this volume, sees as a strong West Indian intellectual characteristic – a fluidity of movement between 'high' and 'low' culture, as with James's lifelong enthusiasm for calypso. Such fluidity was clearly *not* characteristic of British intellectual life when James first knew it in the 1930s. In both politics and the arts, it invited James's famous comparisons with ancient Greece: in a small-scale society, you could have a true *polis*, where 'every cook can govern'.[17]

Thus James turned the tables on those who argued that the smallness of Caribbean societies, with their supposed lack of any indigenous cultural tradition, doomed them to sterility, imitation, even absurdity – pessimists who included not only the scornful Naipaul, but the usually more affirmative Walcott:

> Tell me, what power, on these unknown rocks –
> A spray-plane Air Force, the Fire Brigade,
> The Red Cross, the Regiment, two, three police dogs
> that pass before you finish bawling 'Parade!'?[18]

A fourth feature, which James also often emphasised, was not specific to the Caribbean, or to its migrants in Britain. (It can of course be
argued that the other three were not so peculiarly West Indian as James
seemed to claim, either.) This was something which has, since his
death, become a truism: the notion of an especially acute vision to be
obtained from the margins of a society, from the position of being an
inside-outsider. James repeatedly made the point, and related it to
Caribbean peoples' distinctive 'openness' and internationalism. But he
also generalised it, suggesting that this was why, in his view, all important modern 'English' writers were outsiders to British society – even
enlisting Kipling as an 'Indian' in the argument.[19] By now, such claims
are indeed clichés, against which one wants to rebel and say that far
from always producing clarity of vision, the excentric may quite often
be the eccentric, the distorted or downright silly. But when James
advanced them, from the 1930s onwards – he wasn't quite the first, of
course – they had novelty and force. James, though, did not fetishise
marginality as some now seem to do. Nor did he write as if the distinctions between inside and outside, England and empire, were – or could
easily be – blurred or transgressed to the point of dissolution.[20] He
knew, for instance, that the capital of the West Indies was London, that
this was deeply damaging, and that it must cease to be so.[21]

James's stance towards the British influence on that unique West
Indian compound, and on his own upbringing, though complex, also
always remained mostly positive. Indeed the central message of much
of his writing, especially its autobiographical passages, is to stress how
far the ethos of Britishness in families, schools and sportsfields like his
was not merely *imposed*, but actively fashioned and worked for. It is
worth here recalling James's unbridled scorn for those who saw in the
unearthing of the colonial past 'a search for catharsis'. James did not
want to be liberated from, or by, his memories: 'They do not liberate
me in any sense except that once you have written down something
your mind is ready to go further ... I would consider liberation from
them a grievous loss, irreparable ... I do not wish to be liberated from
that past and, above all, I do not wish to be liberated from its future.'[22]
Those who wish to be liberated from the past – so he might have added
– are doomed to repeat it.

Much of this was class-specific: associated with Afro- (and to a
perhaps lesser extent Indo-) Caribbean elites, with ideas about respectability, correct, non-creole English, particular tastes in literature,
music, dress and so on. It has even, in James's case, been described in
terms of a Victorian public school ethos. This, though, is misleading
insofar as the educational system which formed James was a kind of
meritocracy. It was indeed – by comparison with anything in Britain at

the time – an exceptionally pure, though also exceptionally narrow meritocracy (as Oxaal says, the bridge of opportunity was a razor's edge[23]). And the cricketing manifestations of the pervading ethos were, as James always stressed, in significant and increasing part egalitarian. When, later in life, he could still call cricket 'the English game' whilst praising a great West Indian player, there is no sense of conflict or discomfort in the attribution.[24] James would, one suspects, have reacted with pretended puzzlement, thinly concealing sharp irritation, to arguments that his attachment to that ethos necessarily implied a debilitating 'divided consciousness'.[25] A great deal of recent writing about James, indeed, has revolved around such notions of divided or double consciousness, with an obvious debt to DuBois's famous ruminations.[26] But although occasionally James himself reflected on the idea of divisions of sensibility resulting from a colonial upbringing,[27] this was for him at least as much a source of intellectual strength as of psychic disturbance.

James came to Britain in the 1930s, then, from a social world which was profoundly shaped by Britishness – shaped in ways that should not glibly be reduced to colonial mimicry, to false or divided consciousness. But, as James insisted, this Britishness was part of a rich, complex, internationally open and distinctively modern cultural mix. Yet if his formation and experiences were in so many ways highly characteristic of the worlds from and to which he moved, they were not of course at all 'typical' or 'average'. Some themes which were widely significant for the generality of Caribbean migrants to Britain seem to have had little impact on him. One is very obvious. James was too well educated and worldly-wise to share the widely reported, naïve shock experienced by many migrants at certain features of British life, like the existence of a white working class, or the shabby dirtiness of buildings, streets and even people. James comments that although he 'was a strange compound of knowledge and ignorance' about Britain, he had at least read enough to know what he was ignorant about.[28]

His views on the character of racism in Britain, also, were distinctive. James makes almost no reference to personal encounters of discrimination, and even gently suggests that friends like Learie Constantine exaggerated their experience of it: 'He had a point of view which seemed to me unduly coloured by national and racial considerations.'[29] James insisted, writing in 1964, on the 'empiricism' of British racial attitudes. In Nelson in Lancashire in the 1930s, he and the Constantine family with whom he was living 'were very conscious that we were, so to speak, on exhibition' as representatives of the Caribbean. And of course they were admirable, and admired, exhibition pieces – so much so that, James recalls, one acquaintance who had visited the

Caribbean felt moved to 'warn' local people that not all West Indians were as distinguished and respectable as them! [30]

He does not seem anywhere to echo another widely noted theme of the Caribbean migrant experience. This was the contrast between West Indian societies with their complex, subtle hierarchy of skin-colours, modified or cross-cut by class distinctions, and Britain's stark counter-position of black and white. James was of course quite dark-skinned, and it may be that this difference between colony and metropole was most forcibly impressed on the lighter-coloured. He made no reference that I have found to the issue in Britain – although he had shown clear if seemingly unanguished awareness of it in Trinidad, as a much-cited passage from *Beyond a Boundary* on the social character of different cricket teams displays.[31]

He expected to find much that was familiar in Britain, and did so. More, he expected that familiarity to be recognised by others, by white Britons. Like many later Caribbean migrants, he anticipated being perceived not as an inferior alien, but as part of the national family, as someone who was also British – in some sense, and among other things. He was aware of the complexities involved. James's proclamation that when he first left Trinidad 'The British intellectual was going to Britain' is very often quoted.[32] But the ironic, self-aware edge to the statement is often missed. So is the extent to which for him and his contemporaries, being British and being colonial were not mutually exclusive, opposed identities. Nor was the relation of latter to former simply one of physical transplantation or imitation. Nor, finally, was it – as many recent post-structuralist critics have argued, often claiming inspiration from James – a matter of colonial experience exposing the instability of British identity-claims, of each being the other's constitutive outside, or of each being entirely dependent on the other for self-definition.[33] Something more complex than any of these was going on. In exploring this through James's ideas, two general preliminary remarks are necessary.

Both Britishness and Englishness have been intense, increasing objects of historians' attention in recent years. One strand of this investigation has focused on the formation – and dissolution – of an imperial or global Greater Britain. But analysis of Greater Britishness has been undertaken with almost exclusive reference to British-diasporic and settler-descended communities. Far less inquiry has addressed the ways in which non-white colonial peoples also grasped for, or sought to fashion, their own versions of Greater Britishness. Arguably, the peoples of the West Indies did so more wholeheartedly, and even in a sense successfully, than anyone else in the subject empire – though fainter echoes of the process can be found, for instance, among the

Bengali elites dissected by Tapan Raychaudhuri, or the West African ones discussed by Philip Zachernuk.[34] James both exemplified and commented on aspects of this, as did other subjects of the present collection like Harold Moody. Yet there has been a tendency to treat West Indians' affirmations of Britishness as a simple mistake, a dream from which there was, on exposure to attitudes in Britain itself, a rude awakening. It should, perhaps, be taken more seriously than that – and the career and ideas of James suggest some ways in which we might do so. Claims to Britishness could be and frequently were used by Afro-Caribbeans in both colony and metropole in pursuit of racial justice, political representation and social equality. Nor were they incompatible with local patriotism or even with some forms of political nationalism – though such a combination evidently became ever more difficult with time, in both colony and metropole. One could at least for a time – quite a long time – think of oneself as Trinidadian or Antiguan, *and* West Indian, *and* British. The erosion of such possibilities, in British-Caribbean contexts, clearly deserves more attention than I can give it here.

The second preliminary point is that these relationships of contested identity-formation were markedly asymmetrical. If Greater Britishness was crucial to but conflictual within Caribbean identities, the converse was far less the case. The West Indies – at least after emancipation, and after the region declined in its economic importance to Britain – played a very small role in British, Greater British and empire thought. Not only did most metropolitan imaginings of Greater Britishness focus overwhelmingly on the metropole's diasporic offspring, but enthusiasm for and argument about empire in general within Britain were differentiated and particularist. The white-settled dominions were the dominant objects of attention. India came second, Africa third (and a long way behind), while the Caribbean's place was still smaller.[35] James, like almost every other early Caribbean migrant or visitor to Britain, registered with force the sheer ignorance and indifference about their homelands which he encountered. He often found himself treated as an exotic curiosity. When he spoke in Edinburgh in 1938, the recollection of his host Willie Tait was naïve at best: 'the workers ... thought it was great that a Black man could talk to them about socialism'.[36] Acquaintances like Ethel Mannin, Fredric Warburg and Reginald Reynolds, in their frequently quoted but brief reminiscences of James, treated him in a rather similar if more urbanely expressed style.

Britain, indeed, largely ignored James until his very last years. His access to British audiences and readerships was extremely restricted. In the 1930s, his cricket writing appeared in mass-circulation newspapers,

[ 161 ]

but his other work was published almost exclusively in very small leftwing journals: those of Trotskyist groups or of the slightly larger Independent Labour Party. In the 1960s and 1970s, his only regular non-specialist outlet was as a book reviewer in *New Society*. He seems to have made just one radio broadcast – as a last-minute stand-in – in the 1930s, and a mere handful, on the BBC's Caribbean Service, in the 1960s. Only after Channel 4 took up multicultural programming (with friends and admirers of James, Darcus Howe and Farrukh Dhondy, in key positions), and near the end of his life, did he make TV appearances.

Neither the Labour left of the 1930s, nor the New Left of the 1960s, embraced James: his words were not to be found in the *New Statesman*, the *Daily Herald* or *Tribune*, nor (apart from one book review) in the *New Left Review*.[37] He was not closely associated with any of the more prominent figures of the British left. His French collaborators – Claude Lefort, Jean-François Lyotard, Cornelius Castoriadis – were more influential than his British ones. Even after his return to Britain in the 1950s, he remained more engaged with American than with British politics, writing constantly to his US supporters. Eventually, he was firing off reams of advice from London to an American 'party' of some twenty-five people; but this was apparently still a larger following than he could command in Britain. He had, it seems, some association with the International Socialists – before they became a more rigidly organised, sectarian formation as the Socialist Workers' Party. He attended a major conference on Workers' Control at Coventry in 1967, where his interventions were vividly remembered by participants, and where he clashed but then became friendly with the famed socialist historian E. P. Thompson.[38] None of this, however, amounted to the kind of sustained engagement or widespread attention which a figure of James's stature surely deserved.

When James did achieve rather greater British public exposure, in the 1980s – and in his own eighties – there were some uncomfortable edges and ironies. As Paul Buhle suggests, James found himself 'a living monument of sorts' not only in his very last years but for a good third of his political life.[39] Despite his continued enthusiasm for new ideas and experiences, both his admirers' expectations and aspects of his own self-presentation often trapped him into replaying memories of the 1930s rather than engaging with the 1970s and 1980s. Darcus Howe claimed that in James's final years British 'whites are pretty lost, drifting hither and thither ... suddenly they discovered that here is a man who knows them. He knows them more than they know themselves.' This, Howe felt, accounted for his late-found media popularity in Britain.[40] James himself echoed the sentiment, with a surely justified boast in old age that 'I astonished them because I knew more about English literature, and was more familiar with it, than most of them'.[41] Yet it all seemed again to reflect a kind of curiosity value, rather than a real appreciation of the range of James's ideas and interests. A yet more uncomfortable irony came when in 1985 the London borough of Hackney named its Dalston library after him: while almost simultaneously, this impoverished (and incompetent) local authority was closing many of its other libraries. Their derelict and municipally-vandalised interiors, piles of books mouldering in the dust, formed a miserable kind of tribute to the passionate bibliophile James.

The late-flowering cultural presence for C. L. R. James in Britain was not matched by a more strictly political influence. The exceptions were minor: Jamesian ideas were a presence in such 1960s libertarian marxist formations as Solidarity and Big Flame (both especially strong on Merseyside, though 'strong' is a very relative term when each group numbered its members in dozens rather than hundreds) as well as their rather larger groups of co-thinkers in France and Italy, *Socialisme ou Barbarie* and *Lotta Continua*. In the even smaller world of black British radical politics, a strong Jamesian influence was to be found among those who produced the journals *Race Today* (in whose pages James wrote frequently, and whose staff provided him with a home and daily care in his last years) and *The Black Liberator*.[42]

James's most important direct influence in Britain, then, is surely not to be found in any of these milieux, but rather in his involvement in anticolonialist politics, and his impact on circles of Caribbean and African émigrés, students and activists who were usually temporary residents in the imperial metropole between the 1930s and the 1960s. These activities, and James's ideas about colonialism and anticolonialism, are already the subjects of a substantial scholarly literature, and cannot be summarised here.[43] His own recollections rightly highlighted the crucial role of West Indians in campaigning not only for their own region's decolonisation, but Africa's too. The 1930s International African Service Bureau – or at least its core – was entirely West Indian at the start. Africans themselves only became involved later. James claimed (with a certain exaggeration) that nobody in British politics was talking about colonial questions before he began to do so – but (more accurately) stressed that George Padmore was more important than him in arousing concern with such issues.[44] He did not, he confessed, succeed in turning future African leaders into Trotskyists, but did succeed in warning them off Stalinism.[45] James and his colleagues may have played an unappreciated role in helping ensure that Communist support in most British ex-colonies was always meagre.

Yet James's political judgements on African affairs must be adjudged as erratic – and often seemed much at odds with his avowed theoretical principles or his enthusiasm for mass self-activation. He was capable of absurdly excessive praise for Kwame Nkrumah and his movement, and even for the pseudo-philosophy of 'Nkrumahism'.[46] Something like a 'cult of personality' seemed to creep into his African writings: Ghanaian developments are attributed almost entirely to the dynamism, but then the flaws, of Nkrumah, Tanzanian ones to the genius of Nyerere, and so on. James expressed strong agreement with those African politicians like Nkrumah, Nyerere and Chisiza who denounced the British constitutional model and multipartyism as unsuitable for Africa, and endorsed the chimera of 'single-party democracy' instead.[47] This seems to imply that James saw retention of a substantially British inheritance as desirable, if not inescapable, for the Caribbean and for himself, but not for Africa or the African leaders he admired. The reasons for the dichotomy were never spelled out.

During James's later periods of London residence, he became a mentor for many younger West Indian intellectuals, most of them students. Regular Friday night sessions at his north London home from 1962 onwards drew in such subsequently influential figures as Richard Small, Norman Girvan, Orlando Patterson and Walter Rodney.[48] Through them, through admirers like Tim Hector of Antigua, and of course through his writings, James had a renewed – and posthumous – political influence in the Caribbean.[49] It is striking, though again by no means uncharacteristic of the way ideas have circulated in the West Indies or even the wider postcolonial world, that this influence radiated from London, far more than it was generated during James's own years in Trinidad.[50]

On a broader, more theoretical plane, James's views of British colonialism were built around a stark contrast between imperial Britain and what he thought of as the truer, better values of Britishness 'at home'.[51] In his earliest major political writing, he argued that colonial despotism was a kind of self-betrayal by the libertarian English. 'Being an Englishman and accustomed to think well of himself' the colonial expatriate is convinced that only people of his own type can possibly rule – and this insistence is only made more strident by his encountering in the West Indies 'a thoroughly civilised community, wearing the same clothes that he does, speaking no other language but his own, with its best men as good as, and only too often, better than himself'.[52] James went on:

> It is not surprising that the famous English tolerance leaves him almost entirely. At home he was distinguished for the liberality and freedom of his views ... But in the colonies any man who speaks for his country, who tries to do for his own people what Englishmen are so proud that other Englishmen have done for theirs, immediately becomes in the eyes

of the colonial Englishman a dangerous person, a wild revolutionary ... What at home is the greatest virtue becomes in the colonies the greatest crime.[53]

It might have been thought that this was merely a tactical argument – that James, in echoing the classic British liberal claim that empire was incompatible with the spirit of liberty at home, was telling his prospective British readership what he felt they would want to hear. But he continued to advance similar contentions almost throughout his life, and to diverse audiences. As late as 1962 he could make the rather remarkable suggestion that if only Britain had had a truly socialist government at the time of the Kenyan Mau Mau revolt, that rebellion 'would have had socialist allies and would have been made under socialist slogans, representatives of the British government would have taken part in it and guided it'.[54] Sir Charles Arden-Clarke, the last British Governor of the Gold Coast, was praised for 'preserving the British government from the risk of adventures in which the character of the British people would have been indelibly besmirched'.[55] The officially promulgated version of colonial policy was 'an impudent fraud' perpetrated on the British people by their rulers.[56]

His usual acknowledgement of how much he had learned from and owed to Britain was, it is true, occasionally varied by a more harshly critical tone. Colonial leaders, he suggested, 'didn't learn about democracy in British schools, they learnt it in the jails into which the British had put them; and from those jails they taught the population and taught the Colonial Office what were the realities of independence'.[57] He recalled in one of his letters to Constance Webb that in his childhood history reading 'the English always won all the battles. I resented it fiercely. I used to read and re-read the few battles they had lost. I conceived a fanatical admiration for Napoleon ... Nobody ever discussed history or literature or writing with me. But I read that history and hated the British for always winning.'[58] Yet his central thrust always remained that of the extreme, indeed shameful, chasm between the British values he genuinely cherished and their betrayal in the colonies. He recalled his disturbance on discovering that the ideas he was learning about in school, values of parliamentary democracy 'and decent behaviour', were not being applied in Trinidad.[59] He emphasised several times that he found greater political freedom, and far more scope for anticolonial agitation, in Britain than in Trinidad.[60]

Britishness – in Britain itself – was, then, to be seen in a mainly positive light. More, it is striking how far, right to the end of his life, James emphasised egalitarian and modernising currents in Britishness. He could not without gross implausibility stress these *as* strongly as he did for American civilisation, and did not. But he always looked to forces of change rather than ones of 'tradition', and although of course he found these mainly in the proletariat, in socialist and later in black movements, they were not only there. James's view of the society as a whole was always surprisingly affirmative.

There was an intensely personal element in this, as there was in his decision to remain in Britain in his later years. People often, he said, pointed out the disadvantages of the climate. 'But the climate is outside. I am in here, in the warm ... In any case my education, the books I was brought up on, the sports, were all British. I feel at home here.'[61] Far more, though – and inevitably, for James's sensibility – the grounds were political. In the USA, he thought, 'they do not understand political democracy'. In Britain, by contrast, there was an almost instinctive respect for minority views: 'They have what I call the democratic temper which is not necessarily parliamentary.'[62] In his most strictly marxist writings he insisted, as one might expect, on a class element in this: the 'traditional virtues of the English nation' were to be found among struggling workers rather than in 'official society'.[63] In similar vein, he suggested that 'the conception of "good form" and "what is not done"' exercised a kind of tyranny of the majority in Britain. Here he was no doubt consciously echoing the complaints of John Stuart Mill a century earlier. Such attitudes, James protested, would have been considered barbaric by ancient Greek democrats.[64] Despite such constraints, he suggested a little later: 'The great mass of the British people have been the sanest in Europe for many years' – but Britain, he added, is ever more obviously just part of a western civilisation which is sinking into decay and rushing to self-destruction. The leaders of the underdeveloped world, he thought, show a way out from this.[65]

Yet James's marxism, no less than his transnationalism, predisposed him against mystifying or even emphasising such ideas as national character. Especially in the works of his Trotskyist years, he normally made claims about Britain only as examples of, or evidence for, what he believed to be general trends of capitalist society. Thus his most detailed discussion of British political developments was as part of his global surveys, in *World Revolution* (1937) and *Facing Reality* – one of modern publishing's less appropriate titles – in 1958. The former's discussion of Britain is written from an orthodox Trotskyist perspective, devoted mainly to denouncing the crimes, follies and betrayals of the CPGB.[66] In the latter and other writings of this era, James and his colleagues' passionate faith in grass-roots activism and spontaneous revolutionary consciousness led to some notably incautious claims. Thus James's analysis of the 1945 election indulged in what must be judged pure fantasy about the revolutionary socialist consciousness of the British working class – basing himself still at that stage on Trotsky's

1920s claims about British development, and on a highly orthodox gloss on Lenin's theory of imperialism.[67] There was indeed a repeated tendency in James's British writings – still evident long after he had ceased to be a Trotskyist – to praise the supposedly astonishing wisdom and prescience of Lenin's and Trotsky's writings about Britain.

*Facing Reality* referred confidently to 'The great Shop Stewards Movement, the most powerful social force in Great Britain' and attributed Labour's 1945 victory, peculiarly, to the shop stewards. The official British Labour movement was described as trapped in 'the Welfare State mentality' – but 'the British workers' knew better, and showed 'a widespread acceptance of the fact that the next stage for socialism is a Government of Workers Councils'. British social development was paving the way inexorably for this.[68] James was insistent that there was indeed a revolutionary tradition in Britain, with great relevance for the present; he alluded repeatedly to the seventeenth-century English revolution and to the Levellers.[69]

A little later Raymond Williams's *Long Revolution* evoked strong praise, but also sharp attack for not, in James's opinion, truly understanding either marxism or revolution. C. L. R. also assailed Williams's insularity – attributing this to the Welsh writer's supposed Englishness, and criticising not (as one might perhaps expect) his neglect of the post-colonial world, but his failure to consider Hungary or the USA.[70]

James's own intellectual formation and interests were far from insular: his literary, artistic and musical passions ranged wide. But the cast of his mind might still be judged very 'English', in more profound ways than the love of cricket or of Shakespeare. His lack of interest in economics; his 'naïve' coming to Hegel and other pre-marxist philosophers only when political pressures pushed him, Raya Dunayevskaya and other colleagues towards philosophical investigation (though thereafter his philosophical interests were broad and intense, if idiosyncratic); perhaps above all his lack of system, his failure or refusal to achieve a grand synthesis of ideas: all closely echoed dominant trends in the English intellectual life (including the marxist life) of his generation. His characteristic stress on individuals as shapers of the historical process – whether Toussaint, Nkrumah or Ahab – was not really very marxist, but it was very 'English'.[71] So too, it might even be said, was his attitude to monarchy. 'I have been a republican since I was eight years old. An Englishman, William Makepeace Thackeray, taught it to me. But the British people respect and some even love the Royal Family, and we revolutionists don't make a fuss about it.'[72] The importance of James's youthful reading of Thackeray is often noted, as a pre-marxist basis for his critique of bourgeois society – but he also himself marked the influence of Hilaire Belloc and G. K. Chesterton, right-wing

Catholic writers whose vision of English history offered a romantic, medievalist, conservative critique of modernity. That influence, and the romantic streak in James's anti-capitalism, deserve more attention. Certainly Leon Trotsky himself thought James's cast of mind all too typically English, finding in his book *World Revolution* 'a lack of dialectical approach, Anglo-Saxon empiricism, and formalism which is only the reverse of empiricism'.[73]

Thus although James argued that West Indians could bring a special kind of critical insight to bear on Britain and the British, the critique was essentially compatible – even identical – with the better elements in 'native' British society itself. Time and again he stressed those affinities: 'The British are very guilty on the question of slavery, you will find a lot of good will still and the West Indies, they feel, are nearest to them. You see, we haven't got a different language or religion from them, like Nigerians and Kenyans; the West Indians are westernised people. The ordinary British man can talk to West Indians and get on with them ... There is a tremendous lot of good will in Britain for us in the West Indies.'[74] Elsewhere he urged that 'there is far more in common between me and ninety-nine per cent of Englishmen than between the Englishman and the Italian, the Englishman and the German, the Englishman and the French ... We use the same books, we have similar social attitudes, the same basic ideas, even the same religion'.[75]

From all this flowed his insistence to British Afro-Caribbeans in his *80th Birthday Lectures* that 'you are not visitors here ... you belong here. You are living here, part of English society'.[76] Occasionally he could be more sweeping, almost apocalyptic, about the impact of West Indians in Britain: 'British capitalism went to the Caribbean and brought workers to Britain. Capitalism creates its own gravediggers. Now there are two or three million of them [sic] in Britain, and the recent upheaval in this country shows that they are a tremendous force in the struggles against this society ... the Black people here succeeded in posing the question of the revolution.' Yet he also insisted that in the 1981 riots (or 'uprisings' as they were often described in the overheated rhetoric of the day) 'the British workers did what they did because they were in Britain and they were trained in Britain ... a society that has trained them to act in the most advanced possible way'.[77]

Amidst all this James could be accused of having one significant blind spot. He never distinguished clearly between Britishness and Englishness – we have observed him using the terms interchangeably in several passages above – nor said anything much about Scotland, Wales or Ireland. '[B]y and large in Britain one part of the country is not so different from another part; you have Welsh and Scots but by and large the British working-class movement is pretty strong ...', he claimed in his *80th Birthday Lectures*. Later on that occasion James was challenged to comment on Ireland, and refused to do so.[78] On some levels this is surprising, for it was widely assumed that James, given his general political views, should have been sympathetic to Celtic nationalisms. He does seem to have believed there was a more natural empathy with his anticolonialism in Wales and Ireland than in England.[79] Moreover, it was already conventional in the colonial circumstances of James's youth, as it has been within Britain more recently, to use 'English' to refer to a native of the geographical entity England, and almost always to equate it with whiteness, while 'British' was a far more expansive, flexible and inclusive category. On the other hand, the composition and ethos of 'Greater Britain' – including its offshoots in the Trinidad of James's youth – were indeed mostly English. The great modern revival of Scottish and Welsh nationalism came only in James's last years, when his intellectual energies were much diminished. And the culturalist emphases of major strands in the Celtic national movements were potentially at odds with his insistence that West Indian claims to nationhood did *not* depend on possession of a distinct 'native' culture or language. On all these grounds, his seeming indifference to them is readily understandable.

In his most influential works, James set out to assail and demolish views of Britain's history – above all its imperial history – which he regarded as myths. The legend to be destroyed was the idea that the liberation of the enslaved, exploited or colonised could come from anything other than their own efforts – that it was or would be owed to benevolent, far-sighted metropolitan policy in relation to the colonies, or to a vanguard party in the case of the working class. The challenge gave rise to counter-myths or at least to errors of over-compensation: notably a near-messianic notion of spontaneous revolutionary consciousness. Still, his arguments retain an explosive force. The kind of Caribbean-British-imperial historical consciousness which he pioneered has perhaps dwindled since his time. Although the influence of the Caribbean on British society has been more intense and pervasive since the 1980s than it was when he first wrote, it has come far more through music, youth culture and (to a lesser degree) imaginative literature than through historical or political work. Indeed history has been the great missing element in the contemporary Caribbean impact on Britain. Rastafarianism, much reggae and rap orature, and the British offshoots of American afrocentrism have all espoused a mystical or eschatological rather than a genuinely historical consciousness. The dominant currents in cultural studies and postcolonial theory, as they have engaged with Caribbean materials, have done so in a largely ahistorical fashion, or else via a notably simplistic version of history. And the academic history of the anglophone Caribbean, in becoming professionalised and 'nationalised' since James's time, has also tended to become more inward-looking and parochial.[80]

James offered a breadth of historical vision which sorely needs renewal. He also, as I have sought to show, explored personal, and national, relationships to Britishness (perhaps, more truly, to Englishness) which were extraordinarily close, complex, many sided. James was, in his own phrase, 'of the West Indies West Indian' – but also of England, half English. He was an enemy of empire – but his was a peculiarly intimate enmity, shot through with love.[81]

## Notes

1 C. L. R. James, *American Civilization*, eds, Anna Grimshaw and Keith Hart (Oxford: Blackwell, 1992).

2 C. L. R. James, *Beyond a Boundary* (London: Hutchinson, 1969; first published 1963); James, 'The Old World and the New', in his *At the Rendezvous of Victory* (London: Allison and Busby, 1984); James, *80th Birthday Lectures* (London: Race Today, 1984).

3 The hypothesis is most explicitly advanced in James, 'The West Indian intellectual', introduction to J. J. Thomas, *Froudacity: West Indian fables by James Anthony Froude* (London and Port of Spain: New Beacon Books, 1969).

4 Ideally, one would be exploring a still more complex web of global interconnections, including also ideas from and images of Africa and the USA. After all, even between the 1950s and 1970s, more than twice as many West Indians migrated to the USA as to Britain.

5 Perhaps most influential here have been Edward W. Said's various allusions to James, in *Culture and Imperialism* (London: Chatto and Windus, 1993) and elsewhere. For a more sceptical view of these elements in James's thought and legacy, see Brett St Louis, 'The perilous "pleasures of exile": C. L. R. James, bad faith, and the diasporic life', *Interventions*, 1:3 (1999), pp. 345–60.

6 Stuart Hall, 'A conversation with C. L. R. James', in Grant Farred (ed.), *Rethinking C. L. R. James* (Oxford: Blackwell, 1996), p. 19.

7 Edgar Mittelholzer, *A Swarthy Boy: a childhood in British Guiana* (London: Putnam, 1963), pp. 91–2.

8 James could read and speak French when most around him in the British Trotskyist movement could not; and *The Black Jacobins* naturally relied mainly on sources in French.

9 V. S. Naipaul, *A Way in the World: a novel* (New York: Knopf, 1994), p. 117.

10 Conversely, on the strength and distinctiveness of a Trinidadian intellectual tradition lying behind James, see Selwyn Cudjoe, 'The audacity of it all: C. L. R. James's Trinidadian background', in Paget Henry and Paul Buhle (eds), *C. L. R. James's Caribbean* (London: Macmillan, 1992).

11 C. L. R. James, 'On Federation', in *Rendezvous*, p. 97.

12 His strongest statement on the unique potentials of Caribbean peoples, and their quintessential modernity, is in the 1966 lecture on 'The making of the Caribbean people', published for the first time in C. L. R. James, *Spheres of Existence* (London: Allison and Busby, 1980), p. 75.

13 C. L. R. James, 'A national purpose for Caribbean peoples', in *Rendezvous*, p. 143.

14 Hall, 'Conversation', p. 22; see also James, 'National purpose', p. 43.

15 See C. L. R. James, 'The artist in the Caribbean', in his *The Future in the Present* (London: Allison and Busby, 1977), pp. 186–7; and James, 'Discovering literature in Trinidad: the 1930s', in *Spheres*, pp. 239–40.

16   C. L. R. James, 'Popular art and the cultural tradition', in Anna Grimshaw (ed.), *The C. L. R. James Reader* (Oxford: Blackwell, 1992), pp. 249–50. Compare James, 'National purpose', pp. 148–50, where the development of Caribbean fiction as the expression of a new, dynamic society is likened to that of classic Russian literature. British society, by contrast, had not had enough ferment and upheaval to produce a great modern artist like Solzhenitsyn or Picasso: 'We haven't had a great writer in Britain since D. H. Lawrence': Hall, 'Conversation', p. 39. (Note the 'we'!)

17   C. L. R. James, 'Every cook can govern: a study of democracy in ancient Greece', in *Future in the Present*; see also James, *Modern Politics* (Port of Spain: PNM Publishing, 1960). Arguably, here the 'Rousseauian' James, stressing the advantages of smallness, was at odds with the marxist who saw such direct democracy as the fated future of all modern industrial societies.

18   Derek Walcott, 'The schooner *Flight*', in Walcott, *The Star-Apple Kingdom* (London: Jonathan Cape, 1980), p. 8. Naipaul's scorn is most famously vented in *The Middle Passage* (London: André Deutsch, 1962).

19   James, 'Discovering literature', pp. 243–4.

20   Perhaps the most sweeping claims that James's writing (specifically, *Beyond a Boundary*) achieves such a dissolution are in Ian Baucom's stimulating *Out of Place: Englishness, empire, and the locations of identity* (Princeton: Princeton University Press, 1999), especially chapter 4.

21   See for instance James, 'National purpose', p. 155; and the comments by Kenneth Surin in 'C. L. R. James's materialist aesthetic of cricket', in Hilary McD. Beckles and Brian Stoddart (eds), *Liberation Cricket: West Indies cricket culture* (Manchester: Manchester University Press, 1995), p. 317.

22   James, *Beyond a Boundary*, p. 65.

23   Ivar Oxaal, *Black Intellectuals Come to Power: the rise of creole nationalism in Trinidad and Tobago* (Cambridge, Mass: Shenkman, 1968), p. 61.

24   James, 'Garfield Sobers', in *Future*, p. 221.

25   Such claims are made, for instance, by Helen Tiffin in 'Cricket, literature and the politics of de-colonisation: the case of C. L. R. James', in Beckles and Stoddart, *Liberation Cricket*. Surprisingly, Tiffin believes that this supposed debility means that James's cricket writing 'fails to engage with the real issue of empire': p. 367.

26   In W. E. B. DuBois, *The Souls of Black Folk* (Chicago: McClurg, 1903). It has been argued to effect, however, that contemporary cultural criticism's stress on that point distorts and misunderstands DuBois himself, let alone such figures as James: Adolph L. Reed Jr, *W.E.B. DuBois and American Political Thought* (New York: Oxford University Press, 1997).

27   For instance, James, *Beyond a Boundary*, p. 30.

28   James, *Beyond a Boundary*, pp. 114–15.

29   James, *Beyond a Boundary*, p. 115.

30   C. L. R. James, 'Colour: another view', *New Society*, 10 December 1964.

31   James, *Beyond a Boundary*, pp. 55–65.

32   James, *Beyond a Boundary*, p. 114.

33   The notion of the 'constitutive outside' comes from the work of Ernesto Laclau and Chantal Mouffe – though close analogues can be found in a great deal of recent social theory. See especially Laclau, *New Reflections on the Revolution of Our Time* (London: Verso, 1990).

34   Tapan Raychaudhuri, *Europe Reconsidered: perceptions of the West in nineteenth century Bengal* (Delhi: Oxford University Press, 1988); Philip Zachernuk, *Colonial Subjects: an African intelligentsia and Atlantic ideas* (Charlottesville and London: University Press of Virginia, 2000).

35   Though even the relatively restricted range of contacts, ideas and images involved after the 1830s can still be investigated in ways that reveal a great deal about Victorian British life and thought, as Catherine Hall brilliantly shows in *Civilising Subjects: metropole and colony in the English imagination, 1830–1867* (Cambridge: Polity, 2002).

36   James D. Young, *The World of C. L. R. James: his unfragmented vision* (Glasgow:

Clydeside Press, 1999), p. 138. Young does, however, emphasise the broad range of James's contacts and interests in 1930s Britain, unearthing many pseudonymous or anonymous articles in British Trotskyist or ILP journals. One of the great merits of Young's generally disappointing book is his close attention to these.

37 On the vicissitudes and mainly narrow limits of James's reputation and audiences during his lifetime, mainly focused on the USA, see also Paul Buhle, 'From a biographer's notebook', in Selwyn Cudjoe and William E. Cain (eds), *C. L. R. James: his intellectual legacies* (Amherst: University of Massachusetts Press, 1995).

38 Young, *The World of C. L. R. James*, pp. 259–60 and 261–3; and personal communication from Bob Purdie.

39 Paul Buhle, *C. L. R. James: the artist as revolutionary* (London: Verso, 1988), pp. 133–4.

40 Darcus Howe and Ken Lawrence, 'Interview', in Paul Buhle (ed.), *C. L. R. James: his life and work* (London: Allison and Busby, 1986), pp. 149–50.

41 Televised discussion with Linton Kwesi Johnson and Michael Smith, BBC *Arena* 'Michael Smith: Upon Westminster Bridge', 1982, prod. Alan Yentob (repeated 25 September 1983: exact date of first transmission not traced). 'Preface to criticism', in Grimshaw, *James Reader*, pp. 255–60, shows how closely James continued to follow the British cultural scene, both literary criticism and aspects of the popular arts, at that time.

42 Among the few attempts to present an overview of such groups' political and theoretical perspectives, see especially Stuart Hall *et al.*, *Policing the Crisis: mugging, the state, and law and order* (London: Macmillan, 1978), pp. 345–97. The main theoretician of *The Black Liberator*, A. X. Cambridge, later – and in more academic vein – produced important essays on James's philosophy. An explicitly Jamesian praise of spontaneity and distrust of organised politics also pervades Paul Gilroy's early work; see especially *There Ain't No Black in the Union Jack* (London: Hutchinson, 1987).

43 My own interpretation of them may be found in *Anticolonialism in British Politics: the left and the end of empire 1918–1964* (Oxford: Oxford University Press, 1993). The character of James's anti-imperialism is debated in many of the works cited in other notes here, and in Anthony Bogues, *Caliban's Freedom: the early political thought of C. L. R. James* (London: Pluto, 1997) and John Gaffar La Guerre, *The Social and Political Thought of the Colonial Intelligentsia* (Mona: Institute of Social and Economic Research, 1982).

44 *C. L. R. James and British Trotskyism: an interview* (London: Socialist Platform pamphlet, 1987), pp. 5–6.

45 *James and British Trotskyism*, Social Platform pamphlet, pp. 6–7.

46 James, 'Government and party', in his *Nkrumah and the Ghana Revolution* (London: Allison and Busby, 1977), especially pp. 163–4.

47 For instance James, 'Slippery descent', in *Nkrumah*, p. 187.

48 Rodney spoke extensively of his debts to James. On the relationship, see Rupert Charles Lewis, *Walter Rodney's Intellectual and Political Thought* (Kingston: University of the West Indies Press, 1998) especially pp. 34–40, 171–3 and 241–3.

49 On the travails of the anglophone Caribbean left since the 1950s, including the influence of Jamesian ideas, see Perry Mars, *Ideology and Change: the transformation of the Caribbean Left* (Mona: University of the West Indies Press, 1998). James's impact on these currents is also discussed in several contributions to Henry and Buhle, *James's Caribbean*, especially those of George Lamming, Paget Henry and Walton Look Lai.

50 Analogous phenomena among West Indian creative writers were noted already by Lamming in the 1950s, and are discussed elsewhere in this volume. One might compare the way in which someone like Thomas Mapfumo came to be seen as the emblematic national figure of Zimbabwean music only after, and because of, his international popularity.

51 As noted above, much secondary literature on James credits him with challenging or subverting this very distinction. I am suggesting that this interpretation is hard

to sustain: in politics, if not necessarily in cricket, James drew the boundaries quite sharply.

52  James, 'The case for West Indian self-government,' in Grimshaw, *James Reader*, p. 52.
53  James, 'Case for self-government', p. 53.
54  James, *Nkrumah*, p. 69.
55  James, *Nkrumah*, pp. 155–6.
56  James, *Nkrumah*, p. 35.
57  James, 'Making of the Caribbean people', p. 182.
58  Anna Grimshaw (ed. and intro.), *Special Delivery: the letters of C. L. R. James to Constance Webb, 1939–1948* (Oxford: Blackwell, 1996), pp. 173–4. Letter dated July 1944.
59  Hall, 'Conversation', p. 20. With a typical Jamesian twist, he added that on arriving in Britain he discovered that, worse, they weren't applied there either!
60  Hall, 'Conversation', p. 21. In another mischievous tweak of the argument, he noted the additional advantage that in Britain he could get involved in politics without bringing disgrace on his family.
61  1986 *Trinidad Guardian* interview with Clive Davis; quoted in Kent Worcester, *C. L. R. James: a political biography* (Albany: State University of New York Press, 1996), p. 208. See also his passionate affirmation of pleasure at being back in Britain, in 1953 in the *Manchester Guardian*: James, *Cricket*, ed. Anna Grimshaw (London: Allison and Busby, 1986), pp. 71–3.
62  James, 'The battle for survival', in *Rendezvous*, p. 138.
63  James, with Grace Lee and Pierre Chaulieu, *Facing Reality* (Chicago: Correspondence Publishing, 1958), p. 73.
64  James, 'Every cook can govern', p. 168.
65  James, 'Lenin and the problem', in Grimshaw, *James Reader*, pp. 332–3. James several times proposed sweeping indictments of the whole idea of western civilisation, as having given birth to Hitler and Stalin from its very heart, but did so frustratingly briefly, and perhaps inconsistently with many of his other ideas including his love for European, especially English, culture. This is a major theme in C. L. R. James, *Mariners, Renegades and Castaways* (London: Allison and Busby, 1985). In 'Wilson Harris and the existentialist doctrine' the idea is floated that the old European order and its conceptions of civilisation had irrevocably broken down – but that the Caribbean, or even the New World as a whole, had never shared that conception of a fixed order anyway: in *Spheres*, especially p. 168. The influences of Spengler – by whom James confessed to having been much affected in his youth – and of Heidegger are evident in all this.
66  C. L. R. James, *World Revolution 1917–1936: the rise and fall of the Communist International* (London: Secker and Warburg, 1937).
67  James, 'The British vote for socialism', in *Future*.
68  James, *Facing Reality*, pp. 112 and 157.
69  For instance James, in 'Dialectical materialism and the fate of humanity', in *Spheres*, pp. 91–2; 'Marxism and the intellectuals', in *Spheres*, pp. 115–16; 'Peasants and workers', in Spheres, pp. 206–7; and *Facing Reality*, p. 138. James's allusions to this history were not always accurate (he seems to have thought that the Levellers were not represented at the Putney debates), but they were invariably enthusiastic.
70  Indeed the second half of James's review is entirely devoted to reiterating his ideas about the American working class: 'Marxism and the intellectuals'.
71  On this trait, especially in relation to *The Black Jacobins*, see Brian Meeks, 'Rereading *The Black Jacobins*: James, the dialectic and the revolutionary conjuncture', *Social and Economic Studies*, 43:3 (1994), pp. 75–103.
72  James, 'The mighty sparrow', in *Future*, pp. 195–6.
73  James, 'Discussions with Trotsky,' in *Rendezvous*, p. 60.
74  James, 'A national purpose', p. 157.
75  James, 'The old world and the new', in *Rendezvous*, p. 202.
76  James, *80th Birthday Lectures*, p. 48.

77 'C. L. R. James' (interviewed by Paul Gilroy) in MARHO, *Visions of History* (New York: Pantheon, 1984), pp. 271, 273 and 272. The interview was conducted in 1982, and the 'recent upheaval' was the British urban disturbances of the previous summer.

78 James, *80ᵗʰ Birthday Lectures*, pp. 33 and 37–8.

79 *James and British Trotskyism*, Socialist Platform pamphlets, p. 3.

80 As is noted by several contributors to B. W. Higman (ed.), *General History of the Caribbean, vol.VI: Methodology and historiography* (London and Oxford: UNESCO, 1999).

81 The allusions are, in order, to the last lines of James's 'Appendix: from Toussaint L'Ouverture to Fidel Castro' to the 1963 edition of *The Black Jacobins*; to Colin MacInnes, *England, Half English* (London: MacGibbon and Kee, 1961); and to Ashis Nandy, *The Intimate Enemy: loss and recovery of self under colonialism* (Delhi: Oxford University Press, 1983).

# CHAPTER EIGHT

# George Lamming

## Mary Chamberlain

It was a chance encounter, the Trinidadian, Sam Selvon and the Barbadian, George Lamming, on the boat from Trinidad to Britain. Two young, unknown writers, indistinguishable (as George Lamming recalled) from all the other 'ordinary' young men and women immigrating to Britain at that time, all coming 'to look for a better break ... in search of an expectation'.[1] When they came, in 1950, West Indian immigration to Britain was approaching its zenith. Selvon and Lamming, sharing Selvon's *Imperial* typewriter, charted this immigration, a middle passage in reverse, explored its historical origins and cultural dynamics – and noted its subversiveness and challenges. For as West Indians 'creolised' the cities, and indigenised (in Susan Craig James's memorable phrase) where there were no original indigenes,[2] they changed irrevocably the social vocabulary of the metropole.

The role of culture as a means of subverting the dominant order is, arguably, at its most refined in the Caribbean.[3] The long centuries of slavery provided a fitting apprenticeship where the ground rules of alternative, creolised, cultural forms and social practices were laid and where the conditions for its evolution were most refined. While full emancipation in 1838 introduced the legal framework for freedom, in practice the plantation economy maintained its stranglehold over the material conditions of Caribbean society and the planters an indifference to the practices of freedom. For the former slaves, however, the struggle for, and meaning of, freedom remained a – perhaps *the* – dominant concern throughout the nineteenth and twentieth centuries, including the struggles for (and after) independence. As Lamming observed in 1966,

> in spite of the constitutional arrangements for political independence, West Indian society is still in the era of emancipation. The phase we call emancipation is not yet over, and the values which inform the most progressive political sentiment do not indicate that the paradox has been grasped.[4]

[ 175 ]

The lack of opportunity to engage in meaningful citizenship for the former slaves, and the failure of the colonial authorities to understand, recognise and acknowledge creole cultural forms, social practices and gender responses, generated a crucial space in which these became signifiers of resistance and identity. At the same time, the poverty of the nineteenth- and twentieth-century Caribbean resulted in large migrations away from the plantations and the islands. There was (is) scarcely a family in Barbados which has not been touched by migration, a point poignantly brought out by G. in Lamming's autobiographical novel, *In the Castle of My Skin*:

> My birth began with an almost total absence of family relations. My parents on almost all sides had been deposited in the bad or uncertain accounts of all my future relationships, and loneliness from which had subsequently grown the consolation of freedom was the legacy with which my first year opened.[5]

Absence and exile were built deep into the cultural psyche from the beginning. Families were created around them, accommodated to them, and survived on them. But migrants returned: with money, *and* with experience of organised labour, and of the power of ideas, particularly of race, which could explain the meaning – and failure – of freedom in the post-emancipation Caribbean. This was a key insight which Trumper, returning from America, in *In the Castle of My Skin*, shared with G.:

> 'You know the voice?' Trumper asked. He was very serious now.
> I tried to recall whether I might have heard it. I couldn't.
> 'Paul Robeson,' he said. 'One o' the greatest o' my people.'
> 'What people?' I asked. I was a bit puzzled.
> 'My people,' said Trumper ... 'The Negro race'.[6]

While the Caribbean may have invented colour and linked it, before and after emancipation, with every nuance of rank, status and class, the idea that race existed as an autonomous organising political agent was for the most part a concept alien to the British West Indies. The experience of being defined by race was one which West Indians encountered in their migrations abroad, either working for an American company (as in Panama in the early years of the twentieth century) or in the United States itself. The experience left an indelible impression, not lost on the generation of migrants who returned in the 1930s and who played an active part in the disturbances of that decade.

The riots of the 1930s which racked the Caribbean surfaced in Barbados in 1937. They were the culmination of a century of frustration, and a watershed marking the transition from the struggle for emancipation to one for independence. The symbols of independence, at this stage in its political history, lay in the structures of subversion, in domestic organisation and village life, in Tuk Bands[7] and Landship,[8] in Banja songs and banter,[9] in the grammar and lexicography of creole, in faith practices and workplace negotiations, in the entire cultural topography of black Caribbean life misunderstood, denigrated and vilified by the colonial authority. The importance of the riots as a catalyst for cultural renovation and nationalism is central to understanding not only Lamming but also the subsequent explosion of literary creativity through which the struggle for freedom could be imagined. As Lamming recently argued,

> It is not often recognized that the major thrust of Caribbean literature in English rose from the soil of labor resistance in the 1930s. The expansion of social justice initiated by the labor struggle had a direct effect on liberating the imagination and restoring the confidence of men and women in the essential humanity of their simple lives. In the cultural history of the region, there is a direct connection between labor and literature.[10]

George Lamming was ten years old when the riots broke out. His village – Carrington's Village – was close to their epicentre, and to the Governor's residence. He had grown up in a landscape in which difference, privilege and class, and the histories that produced them, were enshrined in every contour, hill and valley. Every grand plantation house was visible from its neighbour, while the police (formerly militia) stations guarded the landscape from the hilltops. Surveillance was part of the topography, demanding ingenuity to evade its scrutiny. For children, what must have entered into their imagination, walking past the governor's mansion, surrounded by its forbidding walls, protected by the sentinels in their colonial liveries? Or wandering in the adjoining neighbourhoods of Belmont and Bellevue – solid, white and wealthy – past the mansions of the moneyed, cleaned, manicured and pampered by the men and women from the village? Carrington's Village was also close enough to Queen's Park for him to be aware of (but forbidden to attend) the speeches by Clement Payne and other popular leaders. By the time he wrote *In the Castle of My Skin* he was able to translate the fear, misery and violence he had witnessed into a sophisticated literary analysis of the complexities of poverty and powerlessness.

Lamming won a scholarship to Combermere School, one of the few secondary schools in Barbados. In 1930, of a population of approximately 180,000, only 704 boys and 331 girls were educated to secondary level.[11] Frank Collymore, a white Barbadian with an unrivalled passion for Caribbean literary form, was his teacher, and was to be the founding editor of *Bim*,[12] which emerged in the 1940s as a decisive regional cultural journal. Collymore also had a personal library to which he allowed pupils access. It was through Collymore that Lamming was introduced to the writings of, among others, Thomas Hardy and Joseph Conrad, and the poetry of Wilfred Owen. At a very young age Lamming could begin to imagine the cultural conditions of a new nationalism and the consequent 'revisioning' of the history of the colonisers,[13] which itself anticipated the emergence of a full citizenship for the people coming out from the shadows.

Migration was also lurking in those shadows. For Lamming's generation the destination was Britain. Lamming, having moved from Barbados to Trinidad when he was eighteen re-migrated to Britain in 1950. The migrants who came, like him, in the aftermath of the second world war came with insights which had been informed by an altogether different *gestalt,* what DuBois or Gilroy might term a 'double consciousness',[14] an awareness which provided them with one vision rooted in the colonies, one in the metropole.

Lamming's arrival in Britain coincided with, and was part of, an explosion of Caribbean literature and poetry. In common with other aspiring writers, he gravitated towards the BBC from where Henry Swanzy broadcast the weekly *Caribbean Voices.* As Glyne Griffith demonstrates, the impact of the programme was immense bringing together, via the airwaves, aspiring writers from the entire Caribbean, introducing them to each other and to their different island vernaculars. That all of this came from the metropolitan heartland was an irony not lost on the writers: as Lamming points out, 'It was not only the politics of sugar which was organised from London. It was language, too.'[15]

In the 1940s and 1950s writers in the West Indies – despite the success of *Caribbean Voices* – were barely regarded as artists. There was no Caribbean-based publishing house which provided them with the means for establishing a shared voice. Recognition, publication, and performance resided not in the West Indies, but in London. For many, their debut was on radio. This, too, had an impact for writers had to think about the orality of their work, 'I still write very much, first of all, with the ear'.[16] They were aware of the contributions each was making to the joint endeavour of West Indian literature, and aware that they were part of a far wider philosophical, cultural and political world in the West Indies, supplementing the work of cultural journals such as *Bim* in Barbados, or *Kyk-over-al* in British Guiana, or *Focus* in Jamaica, or London where, for instance, Derek Walcott's play *Henri Christophe,* with an all West Indian cast, opened to critical acclaim in 1952 (with a prologue written by Lamming).[17]

In London, Lamming mixed with the poets Dylan Thomas, Louis McNeice, and George Barker, and with fellow West Indians, through whom he entered into a European network of exiled, black intellectuals. His friend C. L. R. James was in contact with Richard Wright in Paris. Wright wrote the introduction to the first (American) edition of *In the Castle of My Skin,* and was close to Jean-Paul Sartre. Simone de Beauvoir introduced *In the Castle of My Skin* to Sartre, who chose to publish it in his series *Les Temps Modernes* in 1958. Lamming's networks also included African, Indian and Asian dissidents through whom he became 'increasingly conscious of the political continuities between the Caribbean and the kind of discussion taking place among Ghanaians and Nigerians at the West African Students' Union',[18] where nationalism and the struggles for independence in Africa ran in parallel with the increasing talk about, and preparations for, Federation in the West Indies.

At the time London and Paris were at the heart of the colonial world – and at the centre of radical anticolonialism, whose protagonists were engaging not only with political struggles for independence but also with the psychologies and psychoses of dependence. In this, artists, writers and intellectuals played a leading role, where the milestones towards independence were marked as much by cultural and intellectual achievement as by direct political confrontation. Much of this intellectual activity was engaged in radical philosophical questioning which ran along the lee-line between the nature of self, at one end, and the nature of the collective, at the other, in which subjectivity, race and colonisation were reimagined as the conditions for culture, nation and freedom.

In France *Présence africaine (Revue Culturelle du Monde Noir),* founded in 1947, was dedicated to revitalising, illustrating and creating 'values that belong to the black world'. Building on the intellectual precedents established by an earlier generation of black intellectuals, including Leopold Senghor from Senegal and Aimé Césaire of Martinique, *Présence africaine* became not only 'a publishing enterprise but an intellectual group and a cultural movement'.[19] 'Culture', as Senghor argued, 'is at once the basis and the ultimate aim of politics.'[20] 'What we're trying to do is multidisciplinary', was how Lamming saw it:

> My contribution has been to bring this kind of discussion into political organizations, to address political party conferences raising this theme. Bringing them onto the terrain of how do you conceive of sovereignty, how does your party conceive of cultural policy.[21]

Lamming published at a key moment in the anticolonial struggle. *In the Castle of My Skin,* published in 1953, resonated not only in the Caribbean – Kamau Brathwaite felt 'everything was transformed'[22] – but far wider afield. The Kenyan novelist, Ngugi wa Thiong'o, claimed

Lamming as his mentor. Richard Wright believed that Lamming articulated his own North American experience. *In the Castle of My Skin* was followed by *The Emigrants* (1954), *Of Age and Innocence* (1958), *Season of Adventure* (1960), and his collection of essays *The Pleasures of Exile* (1960), all of which were written in London, and all of which were inspired by the predicament of colonial subjugation.

His writing – 'analogous imagery, metaphor ... the method par excellence of Negro-African speech'[23] – has to be seen as part of this larger collective moment. Jean-Paul Sartre's 1948 essay, '*Orphée Noir*', argued that *négritude* was the antithesis to the white colonial thesis; the synthesis would be 'the realisation of the human in a society without races'.[24] *Négritude* was, in this reading, a passing moment in the dialectic of progress. While Sartre's conclusions on the transitory nature of *négritude* were contested (not least by Frantz Fanon and Alioune Diop, who saw 'African reaffirmation as an end point rather than an antithesis in a dialectical movement'),[25] the notion that the colonised and coloniser stood not simply in opposition, but in a dialectical *relationship* emerged also in Lamming. This was so most noticeably in his insights on the language shared, and synthesised, by both Caliban and Prospero.[26] For the language which Prospero gave to Caliban created new possibilities for thought itself:

> Prospero has given Caliban Language; and with it an unstated history of consequences, an unknown history of future intentions. This gift of Language meant not English, in particular, but speech and concept in a way, a method, a necessary avenue towards areas of the self which could not be reached in any other way. It is this way, entirely Prospero's enterprise, which makes Caliban aware of possibilities. Therefore, all of Caliban's future – for future is the very name for possibilities – must derive from Prospero's experiment which is also his risk.[27]

George Lamming was invited to speak at the First Congress of Negro Writers and Artists organised by *Présence africaine* in September 1956, held in the Descartes Lecture Theatre at the Sorbonne in Paris. Alioune Diop, in his opening speech, and Senghor, in his, likened the congress to a 'second Bandung'. The Bandung Conference in 1955, convened by the newly independent Asian states and attended by delegates from elsewhere in Asia and Africa asserted their opposition to any form of colonialism and imperialism. The Paris Congress of Negro Writers not only declared its opposition to colonialism and oppression, but linked cultural determination to political autonomy. Its final resolution declared:

> We maintain that the growth of culture is dependent upon the termination of such shameful practices in this twentieth century as colonialism, the oppression of weaker peoples and racialism.

We affirm that all peoples should be placed in a position where they can learn their own national cultural values (history, language, leterature (sic) etc.) and enjoy the benefits of education within the framework of their own culture.[28]

Lamming was one of twenty-seven invited speakers who included Frantz Fanon, Aimé Césaire from Martinique, Leopold Senghor from Senegal, Richard Wright, Alioune Diop also from Senegal, and the novelist Jean Alexis from Haiti.[29] Other participants among the 600 crammed into the smoky lecture hall included James Baldwin and Langston Hughes. The majority were acutely aware of being linked through the shared experience of being black in a white, colonial world. This experience rode roughshod over the divisions of the world generated by colonialism, and of nation states which relied on notions of difference for their national identities, and oppression for their racial identities. It articulated a new vision of world power fused, and fissured, by race. This vision required a politics of a different order.

But if the Congress was preoccupied with decolonisation, it was as much a decolonisation of the mind, an affirmation of pride and identity, as a manifesto for political autonomy. It was making links with a common black encounter that could unite this experience in the Caribbean, America, Europe and Africa. The papers ranged in style and content, from scientific treatises on 'The tonal structure of Yoruba poetry', to representations of ethnography, from theological discourses on Christianity and Africa to critiques of colonialism.[30] Nothing was permitted to be overtly political (Algeria, for instance, was not publicly on the agenda), yet the Congress was charged with sublimation, and silences.[31] It was charged also with fierce debate over the meaning and crisis of culture, of Africa, of colonialism, of racial identity, and also with passions and dangers – of the anticolonial wars in progress or in waiting, of delegates refused permission to travel, or of fearing imprisonment on return – all of this against the predatory, possibly annihilatory, backdrop of the Cold War. But while the common experience of being black could provide a degree of unity, it also illuminated the sharp divide between colonial life in Africa and the situation in the New World.

Lamming spoke on the third day, 'raw-boned, untidy and intense', as James Baldwin described him.[32] He addressed the issue of subjectivity, arguing that for blacks subjective life was predicated on internalising the destructive gaze of the Other. As a consequence, he believed, blacks experienced a 'lack' or a 'gap' from which arose a driving 'desire for totality':

a desire to deal effectively with that gap, that distance which separates one man from another, and also in the case of an acute reflective

self-consciousness, separates a man from himself. In the isolated case of
the Negro it is the desire, not merely to rebel against the consequences of
a certain social classification, but also a fundamental need to redefine
himself for the comprehension of the Other ...[33]

His insights into the 'Other' echo Fanon's concerns. 'Ontology ... does
not permit us to understand the being of the black man. For not only
must the black man be black; he must be black in relation to the white
man.'[34] Like Fanon and Sartre, we can see in Lamming's work a home-
grown existentialism which offered a route into an understanding of
the self and a way through the states of non-being induced by the colonial context. '[The Negro Writer] does not emerge as an existence which
must be confronted as an unknown dimension; for he is not simply
*there* ...'.[35] It was an idea that found echoes in Richard Wright, too, in
his descriptions of the black American experience,

> 'Frog Perspectives.' This is the phrase that I've borrowed from Nietzsche
> to describe someone looking from below upward, a sense of someone who
> feels himself lower than others ... A certain degree of hate combined with
> love (ambivalence) is always involved in this looking from below upward
> and the object against which the subject is measuring himself undergoes
> constant change. He loves the object because he would like to resemble
> it; he hates the object because his chances of resembling it are remote,
> slight.[36]

Being-there, existing in-and for-yourself were not possible at the best
of times, as Sartre pointed out, but as Lamming insisted, for the black
West Indian it was not even possible to imagine what these might mean
in constructing the self. The ability to define and defend the self by
making an existential choice were inhibited and distorted by racism and
colonialism. Freedom was, therefore, essential if the individual was to
become fully human and the ego whole rather than incomplete.
Freedom was both a personal and a public choice, and neither could be
achieved while colonialism corrupted the psyche *and* the polis. The category of non-existence was a collective category. It involved 'my people'
as Trumper argued. As Stuart Hall pointed out as early as 1955, it
required for Lamming a representation of the self as 'the social self, the
consciousness, a national consciousness ... [a] refusal to localise the
centre of interest in a single character or a limited set of characters ...'.[37]
It involved engaging in 'the creative power of mass ... [as] ... the central
character',[38] a position which Lamming acknowledged owed its influence to C. L. R. James.[39] It involved, above all, a consistent reworking of
the colonial relationship, and of the state of exile as a complex metaphor
of both 'absence' and 'freedom'. Yet, as Richard Wright could also argue,
the experience of being black (in his case, from Mississippi) offered par-

ticular insights and perspectives on the West, on oppression, race and identity. For the search for what Lamming called 'totality' had echoes in DuBois's 'double consciousness', in Wright's 'double vision' as well as in Fanon and in Baldwin, all of whom, as Paget Henry points out, have 'focused on the deformation (double consciousness) that accompanied the racialisation of African identities and their subjugation to the onto-logical needs of white ego genesis'.[40] To this one could add that the black experience of slavery in the plantation system was, as the anthropolo-gist Sidney Mintz observed, the first experience of modernity. No wonder, therefore, that the dislocation and alienation identified with the modern condition were first and most acutely experienced in the plantation regimes of the New World, and that the search for reconcili-ation between what DuBois termed the 'two warring souls within one black body'[41] would be first perceived by those intellectuals who had emerged from that history. Indeed, as Paul Gilroy argues of Wright:

> He was not straining to validate the African-American experience in European terms but rather demonstrating how the everyday experience of blacks in the United States enabled them to see with a special clarity of vision – a dreadful objectivity – the same constellation of problems which these existential authors had identified in more exalted settings.[42]

This point could be extended beyond Wright.

The 'problems' related to the phenomenological world: for the exis-tentialists, the certainties, once mediated through religion, were no longer sufficient to explain the world, let alone the self within it. The self, they believed, had become bifurcated, identity doubtful, and res-olution sought in the search for authenticity. These philosophical ideas, adumbrated in their exalted Parisian settings, served to illumi-nate the black experience. In this lies the significance of the Paris Congress of 1956: and of Frantz Fanon, Richard Wright ... and George Lamming.

For Lamming, in common with Fanon and Wright, the search for authenticity necessitated a profound reworking of the colonial relation-ship. Insofar as this turned not only on phenomenological but also his-torical issues, it questioned decisively the relations between past, present and future. It is, on a grand scale, the Ceremony of Souls with which Lamming opens *The Pleasures of Exile* and which featured so acutely in *A Season of Adventure*. The Ceremony of Souls, observed by Lamming in Haiti, involved (via a medium) the trial of the dead by the living, who then judged whether forgiveness was appropriate or pos-sible before the dead could rest in peace, and the living move forward. It was a process essential to the pursuit of truth, self-discovery and authenticity. But, as Lamming demonstrates, for Caliban and Prospero,

[ 183 ]

the living metaphor of colonialism, everyone was implicated in the shared history of colonialism, whether as spectator or accessory. There were no extenuating circumstances:

> The confession of unawareness is a confession of guilt. This corpse, dead as he may be, cannot be allowed to go free; for unawareness is the basic characteristic of the slave. Awareness is a minimum condition for attaining freedom.[43]

In the same year as the Paris Congress Lamming visited the Gold Coast. He also won a Guggenheim scholarship to travel through the Caribbean and North America, where Langston Hughes was his guide. Those travels, in the Caribbean and in Africa, deepened his intellectual understanding of the practicalities of anticolonial struggle. They connected him, a West Indian, with Africa. And his journeys through the Caribbean opened for him an appreciation of the importance of a regional Caribbean identity. These experiences of Paris, of Africa and of the Caribbean, all the ambivalences of colonial self-hood notwithstanding, also provided him the means to comprehend the civilisation of the English with a sharper eye, unambiguously recognising the need for the English to return to 'the original condition of a man among men'.[44]

There was another chance encounter, this time on the Charing Cross Road in London, shortly after the publication of *In the Castle of My Skin*, where Lamming was accosted by a tall, middle-aged Trinidadian – C. L. R. James.[45] It was an important encounter, between two exemplary West Indian intellectuals and writers of their respective generations. 'I did not hold him in awe', Lamming recalled of that encounter, 'Having hardly heard of him … But as I got to know him I became very aware of a special quality [which influenced my writing]'.[46] They met, not in the Caribbean, but in exile. The meeting inspired *The Pleasures of Exile*, a dialogue between the Caribbean and England, between Caliban and Prospero, between the colonies and the metropole, between Lamming and James, anticipating the theoretical insights of postcolonial theory, and a critical and revolutionary reading of the literary canon. 'My subject', says Lamming, 'is the migration of the West Indian writer, as colonial and exile, from his native Kingdom, once inhabited by Caliban, to the tempestuous island of Prospero's and his language.'[47] Exile, for Lamming, was not solely about absence. It was about identification:

> No Barbadian, no Trinidadian, no St. Lucian, no islander from the West Indies sees himself as a West Indian until he encounters another islander in foreign territory … The category West Indian, formerly understood as a geographic term, now assumes a cultural significance.[48]

And about indigenisation:

> There is a Caribbean in Amsterdam, Paris, London, and Birmingham; in New York and in other parts of North America ... wherever you are, outside of the Caribbean, it should give you not only comfort, but a sense of cultural obligation, to feel that you are an important part of the Caribbean as external frontier.[49]

It was about creating West Indianness, the cultural struggle for nationalism – or, more correctly, regionalism and federalism. It involved a dialogue between the metropolitan centres and the Caribbean. This dialogue was already premised on a very Caribbean conversation, for 'Here Africa and India shake hands with China, and Europe wrinkles like a brow begging every face to promise love ...'.[50] Migrants, he believed, could hold a privileged relationship with the territories they had left and those they had settled, redefining the boundaries of the nation-state, and extending the Caribbean frontier beyond geography into culture.

All of Lamming's fiction is concerned with migrants, leaving or returning to the Caribbean. Lamming's tour through the Caribbean and North America consolidated his sense of the Caribbean as a whole, unified by a common historical experience.[51] Similarly, his travels in Africa provided vital insights into the peculiarity of the Caribbean experience, for Ghana 'owed Prospero no debt of vocabulary'. Ghana was free, independent, 'And the implication of that silence was an acute awareness that the West Indies were not ...'.[52]

It is in *The Pleasures of Exile* that the role of Caliban as a metaphor for the colonial equation is first introduced. Although Caliban was a slave, his history, as Lamming points out, belongs to the future.[53] The legacy of slavery and of colonialism was a legacy of power relations where the victor can only maintain his position through destroying the other. The result was an inheritance of inferiority and superiority which ate into the essence of existence, corrupting both. But the ironies are manifest. Prospero both needs and fears Caliban – as the primitive and primitivised Other. Caliban's encounter with Prospero has caught them both in a joint enterprise of exile and colonialism. Yet as a slave Caliban has lost the innocence of the primitive. A slave is not 'in a State of Nature. A slave is a project, a source of energy, organised in order to exploit Nature'.[54] At the same time, Caliban's descendants, literally and metaphorically, are descended not only from Caliban, but also from Prospero,

> using the legacy of his language – not to curse our meeting – but to push it further, reminding the descendants of both sides that what's done is done, and can only be seen as a soil from which other gifts, or the same gift endowed with different meanings, may grow towards a future which

is colonised by our acts in this moment, but which must always remain open.[55]

Appropriately Lamming highlights C. L. R. James's *The Black Jacobins*. In a chapter entitled, tellingly, 'Caliban orders history', Lamming assesses the significance of Toussaint L'Ouverture, endorsing James's confidence that 'the narrative will prove that between 1789 and 1825, with the single exception of Bonaparte himself no single figure appeared on the historical stage more greatly gifted than this Negro, a slave till he was forty-five'.[56] In reinstating and endorsing Toussaint as hero, James himself, as Lamming argues, breathes the spirit of Toussaint. For his work of historical excavation and interpretation needs to be read, not solely as history, but history as action, as praxis. It also needs to be read as literature, as the product of an artist. James, in rendering Toussaint's account, gave Toussaint, and all that he represented in terms of freedom, an acknowledged place in the modern world, alongside and equal to Bonaparte. Toussaint, in other words, is not only inscribed in history, but the course of history – of Europe and the modern world Europe inaugurated – cannot be read without reference to him. In giving voice to Toussaint, James gave voice (language) to Caliban, thereby challenging the authority of Prospero. As Edward Said argued, 'The main thing [for Lamming] is to be able to see that Caliban has a history capable of development, as part of the process of work, growth and maturity to which only Europeans had seemed entitled'.[57]

It is, of course, significant that Lamming focused on James, Toussaint, *The Tempest*, and that his essays were entitled *The Pleasures of Exile*, for both Caliban *and* Prospero were exiles. It was Caliban who reminded Prospero that his ambitions were temporal, that his actions were limited by what was humanly possible, and that Caliban himself embodied those parts of Prospero's past which he disavowed.

> Caliban is his convert, colonised by language, and excluded by language. It is precisely this gift of language, this attempt at transformation which has brought about the pleasure and paradox of Caliban's exile. Exiled from his gods, exiled from his nature, exiled from his own name! Yet Prospero is afraid of Caliban. He is afraid because he knows that his encounter with Caliban is, largely, his encounter with himself.
>
> The gift is a contract from which neither participant is allowed to withdraw ...[58]

Arguably, the role of the colonial writer, was (is), to make colony *and* metropole strange. West Indians were strangers in the nation which called itself the mother country and, as residents abroad, strangers equally to their country of birth. Colonised and excluded: the pleasure and paradox of exile. Lamming opened a pathway through which what

Fanon described as the 'existential deviation',[59] could be directed. Creativity was the route back into a sense of Caribbean self-hood, redirecting the ego by relating West Indian experience 'from the inside'[60] into a reconciliation with its internalised imago. But this could not be done without a corresponding challenge (political, philosophical, historical) to the authority of the metropole. The very presence of West Indians in London necessarily changed the chemistry and the circumstances of the colonial relationship. The first of the crises induced by this encounter came with the 1958 Notting Hill riots, which ripped open the veneer of politeness, tolerance and civilisation which had cloaked England's self-perception.

In his essay, 'A way of seeing', Lamming writes:

> it is my right, while things remain as they are – to speak; and it is my responsibility as a writer who is also a colonial to report honestly my feelings about matters which deeply concern us both. I could not accept any uniqueness of privilege in an atmosphere capable of gratuitous murder.[61]

The murder referred to was that of a young West Indian in Notting Hill. It occurred some months after the white riots of September in Notting Hill and Nottingham. The police had been reluctant to defend the West Indians, and the Home Secretary slow to intervene. For many West Indians, the riots marked the turning point in their relations with the police and the white community. Henceforth, trust was replaced by suspicion, a mindset for which the West Indian had, at that time, been unprepared. For the white community, 'Caliban' was 'now seen not only for who he is, but for what he has always been'.[62] Yet, as always, these positions, for Lamming, were not simple polarisations, but complicated by a relationship of mutual dependence. 'The history of the Other', as Lamming observes, 'has never been far from the history of ourselves.'[63] The implications for the metropole were clear: the Caribbean – Caliban – is 'here to stay'.[64] His – their – presence in the metropole must change not only the relationship between the colonies and the metropole, but the nature of the metropole itself. Whereas in the past it was the colonials who had to adapt to the change forced upon them, an adaptation which had brought them into history, now 'it is Prospero's turn to submit to the remorseless logic of his own past'.[65] In this, Prospero has no choice. 'He must act; and he must act with Caliban; or he must die ... To change or not to change? That is the question which has already set up an atmosphere of change in Prospero ... Prospero's role is now completely reversed ... And he is terrified.'[66]

Lamming was and remains a committed West Indian. His first and his last reference points are the Caribbean, and the Caribbean in the widest sense.

I always make the point that the first time I heard of the Cuban poet, Nicolás Guillén and the French poet, Aimé Césaire, was through [Eric] Williams who was telling me that if you are going to be a writer of and for the region, you've got to make this contact ... So that by the time I got to England, this seed was very firmly planted and then it blossomed there in a way because it was one of the ironies of history that here we were separated by imperialism – Jamaica from Barbados, Barbados from Trinidad and so on, but it was really at the metropole at London that we came together, so I first got to know Jamaica and Guyana and other territories at London and then that was really an extension of that learning to be a Caribbean person.[67]

His island, San Cristobel, the geographic heartland of all his novels, is everywhere and nowhere in the Caribbean. It is simultaneously Haiti and Guyana, Barbados and St Lucia, Trinidad and Cuba, Jamaica and Martinique. It is a metaphor for a shared Pan-Caribbean history and experience, and a tool for incorporating (and corporealising) a shared Caribbean reality, already federated by blood[68] and by history. Lamming is a political writer.[69] It is not a role to be taken lightly. 'Every word you use', argues one of the (anonymised) characters in *The Emigrants*,

> can be a weapon turned against the enemy or inward on yourself, and to live comfortably with the enemy within you is the most criminal of all betrayals ... you are articulate not only for yourself, but thousands who will never see you in person, but will know you because the printed page is public property. And if you betray yourself, you can betray thousands too. To be trivial, dishonest or irresponsible is to be criminal.[70]

Thus the writer must bear the weight of, and be the protagonist in, a process of historical reinvestiture, sustaining a dialogue with the past, and integrating it with the present. The Caribbean people, as C. L. R. James argued, 'are a people, more than any other people, constructed by history',[71] and, as Lamming put it, 'every Caribbean writer carries with him the weight of history'.[72] To be a West Indian writer is to be 'one of the more serious social historians by bringing to attention the interior lives of men and women who were never thought to be sufficiently important for their thoughts and feelings to be registered'.[73] Every line of Lamming, as James points out, 'is permeated with a sense of the origins, alignments and movements of the classes in the Caribbean'.[74] For Lamming, history centred on creolity, on the ways in which West Indian civilisation was fashioned by the will of its peoples. It was a culture born of defiance and out of survival: as resistance, as nation.

Lamming's history is not a narrative of history. Indeed, with the exception of *Natives of My Person*, he charts a very contemporary presence: childhood (*In the Castle of My Skin*), emigration (*The Emigrants, Water with Berries*), independence (*Age of Innocence*) and post-independence (*Season of Adventure*). *Natives of My Person* exploits an historical moment, but it is a past, with neither date nor chronology. Like San Cristobel, it is a generic past and what Lamming explores is historical meaning, derived from the relationship between colonised and coloniser. For if migration and exile link the novels so, too, does the colonial relationship, at various stages of its development.[75] If there is no obvious mention of 'history' by name or theme, how is a conversation with history sustained?

In a metaphor which has become a byword for postcolonial literature, Caliban has taken the language of Prospero and inverted it, or reinvented it, for his own purposes. 'We shall never explode Prospero's old myth', Lamming argues in *The Pleasures of Exile*, 'until we christen Language afresh'.[76] To command the master's language, for the slave, was to complain in it, to satirise and ridicule it.[77] It exasperated the Jamaican planter and historian Bryan Edwards,[78] who noted the loquaciousness of the 'Negro slave' but who realised also that when she or he chose, the same slave could speak with brevity and clarity. To command the master's language was to convey his orders – or to resist. And resistance, as Paget Henry argues,

> can be viewed as the media in which an oral population formulates its answer to a social problem. Such actions [strikes, insurrections and revolutions] become the books in which they write and therefore should be read as carefully as the written texts of Labat, Long or Saco.[79]

Language is, therefore, a double-edged sword: delight in linguistic subversion had a powerful history.[80] Lamming christened language afresh by (among other means) introducing the dialect of the vernacular, by switching between creole dialogue and standard prose, a form which at once highlighted how subversion takes place. In juxtaposing two versions of English, he deployed an interlinguality which, in Kamau Brathwaite's words, symbolises an interculturality 'which is our island inheritance'.[81] He textualised the language of *the peasant*, gave voice to the underdog which hitherto had been silenced, and gave voice, by implication, to the bedrock of West Indian society at that time. But for Lamming, the peasant had a particular relationship to the production of culture, for without food there can be no culture.[82] The *popular* voice of the peasant had always been the voice of resistance, and as Carolyn Cooper points out:

> Lamming, in emphasising the role of folklore, singing and banter in the discovery of West Indianness in Britain, provides yet another example of the transformative movement of parody beyond mere mockery ... The Caribbean intellectual and the Caribbean folk, sharing equally in that moment of discovery of the ridiculousness of their mutual displacement in the Mother Country, become one ...[83]

[ 189 ]

It is these peasant voices which convey the narrative, acting at times like a Greek chorus which carries the story to its inexorable fate,[84] at other times assuming the shadowy masks of the protagonists moving in and out of centre stage, sometimes emerging with a name, sometimes disguised by a nickname, or obscured by a generic title. It is a form particularly pronounced in *Natives of My Person*, the most overtly historical of Lamming's novels, but present in all, from Ma and Pa in *In the Castle of My Skin*, to the anonymised voices in *Age of Innocence*, and the revolutionary plotters in *Water with Berries*. Anonymised, genericised, disenfranchised, these interior voices from the countryside drift in and out, operating on the margins of colonial society, unheard by the master.

The master's language sets the context. Lamming's prose is musical and rhythmic, conscious of the melody of orality, and how that translates into the poetry of prose. He is aware too that the melody was absorbed not only through *listening* but through his readings of the literature of the colonisers and, above all, through the 'music of the King James version of the Bible'.[85] Lamming is conscious that he had a fascination 'with the word as sound, with the word as component of rhythm, removed now from actual meaning'.[86] The master's language is his own, and his own language, that of the educated West Indian, became distanced by that very education from the voices of the village. It is an ironic alienation, but one also that stands as a metaphor for the larger colonial relationship.[87]

Yet the afterword that lingers when reading Lamming is that of the peasant, for they are the agents who make his stories move. The form of his fiction conveys its content. As Stuart Hall perceptively argued, 'The technique – by which I mean both the language and the structure – is itself part of what the novel *means*'.[88] The anonymised voice is the collective voice of the West Indies. It is a social, not an individual, voice.[89] As Lamming himself reflected, some thirty years after the publication of *In the Castle of my Skin*, 'It is the collective human substance of the Village, you might say, which is the central character ... community, and not person'.[90] In this voice the ego has been submerged, or transcended, and resides therefore not in a state of existential anxiety, but in a condition of harmony with the fates,[91] and with his own imago. In Lamming's writings, this collectivity interrogates the past, through the juxtaposition of creole and standard Englishes, a continuing, linguistic Ceremony of Souls.

Meaning is built into the structure of the novels. The relationship of the village to the plantation, the black villagers to the white plantation owner, mirror the historical relationship of the Caribbean to Britain, and point to the essential precariousness of that colonial relationship.

An estate where fields of sugar cane had once crept like an open secret across the land had been converted into a village that absorbed some three thousand people. An English landowner, Mr. Creighton, had died, and the estate fell to his son through whom it passed to another son who in his turn died, surrendering it to yet another. Generations had lived and died in this remote corner of a small British colony ... From any point on the land one could see on a clear day the large brick house hoisted on the hill ... The landlord, accompanied by his friends, indicated in all directions the limits of the land ... The villagers ... looked on, unseen, open-mouthed.[92]

Similarly, the ambivalence of the migrants to Britain is reflected in *The Emigrants*, as they metamorphose from confident young men and women, chancing their luck, like Anansi, to diffident, confused, shadowy figures operating at the margins of British society. At the same time, the complex relationship of attraction and repulsion between the migrants and their mother country, the 'pull' of return and the 'pleasure' of exile, are equally built into the fabric of *Water with Berries* and of *Age of Innocence*.

Lamming's voice is also the voice of action. Language has been reinvented as praxis, requiring new interpretative forms to read the semiotics of movement. In his writing we witness the embodiment of language. It derives from an old language, indigenous to the Caribbean, embodied in every insolent look of the slave, in every act of feigned stupidity, in every act of suicide, in every way by which the regime of slavery was resisted. After Haiti, Lamming suggests,

Language changed its name. A new word had been spoken. Action and intention became part of the same plan ... the miracle had happened. The ploughs had spoken. The human spirit had been redeemed, inscribed in fire by one act of freedom.[93]

As Hall in 1955,[94] and most recently Dabydeen in 1999,[95] have pointed out, there is little characterisation in Lamming's novels, or linear narrative or plot. What emerge are episodes and encounters, themes and impressions. Of course, throughout the history of colonialism and of slavery in particular, the alleged inability of the African to reason, to think logically and to progress intellectually in an ordered, linear manner was recruited as a powerful justification for colonial domination. Lamming's prose follows the laws of composition, the logic of grammar, only to break down in the dialogue, as that in turn breaks up the narrative formation. His narratives are interrupted narratives, modelled not on the compulsion of reason but on the convergences of history. The history of the Caribbean is a story of disjointed arrivals, and departures, of layering and synthesis. As Edouard Glissant has argued, the implosion of Caribbean history (of the converging histories of our peoples) relieves us of the linear, hierarchical vision of a single History that would run its unique course. It is not this History that has roared around the edge of the Caribbean, but actually a question of the subterranean convergence of our histories.[96]

It is this history, this narrative structure, that shapes the Caribbean imagination which Lamming offers us: it is cast in his dialogue with the past, in his dialogue with the self, and above all with his dialogue with England.

For much of his career, Lamming has been as involved in politics as in literature and for over a decade (between 1960 and 1972) published no novels, focusing instead on critical, editorial and political work. He is not an easy novelist: his work is too complex to be absorbed in a single sitting. But what he did and does was to keep alive the memory of a long colonial relationship, whose history lies deep in the civilisation of colonisers and colonised alike. This memory was shaped by the unresolved questions of freedom which dominated post-emancipation Barbados and by the riots of 1937, by cultures of resistance and the dogged autonomy of the peasant. His aesthetics led him, like many of his generation, to reflect on authenticity and oppression, to translate those philosophical musings into political action and critical reflection on the lingering impact of colonialism. In this, his dialogue with England has been decisive.

## Notes

1  'George Lamming talks to Caryl Phillips', *Wasafiri*, 26 (1997), pp. 10–17.
2  Susan Craig James, 'Intertwining roots', *Journal of Caribbean History*, 26:2 (1992), pp. 216–28.
3  For a fascinating discussion of the use of Jamaican in popular culture see Carolyn Cooper, *Noises in the Blood: orality, gender and the 'vulgar' body of Jamaican popular culture* (London: Macmillan, 1993). For the Barbadian context, see Curwen Best, 'Popular/folk/creative arts and the nation', in Glenford D. Howe and Don D. Marshall (eds), *The Empowering Impulse: the nationalist tradition of Barbados* (Barbados: Canoe Press, 2001).
4  George Lamming, 'Caribbean literature: the black rock of Africa', in Richard Drayton and Andaiye (eds), *Conversations: George Lamming. Essays, addresses and interviews, 1953–1990* (London: Karia Press, 1992).
5  George Lamming, *In the Castle of My Skin* (Harlow: Longman, 1986), p. 4.
6  Lamming, *In the Castle*, p. 286.
7  Tuk band music is played on outings and public holidays, accompanied by a group of players in masquerade. It dates to at least the mid-nineteenth century and 'has been an important means of expression for the black masses in Barbados': Trevor Marshall, Peggy McGeary and Grace Thompson, *Folksongs of Barbados* (Bridgetown: Macmarson, 1981), p. 29.
8  The Landship movement – first noted c. 1860 – is part parody of British naval tradition, performing often to Tuk music, but also part a savings and loan club.
9  Banja and banter are forms of popular song. See Marshall *et al.*, *Folksongs of Barbados*. Banter is also a form of repartee.

10    Lamming, cited in Glyne Griffith, 'Deconstructing nationalisms: Henry Swanzy, Caribbean voices and the development of West Indian literature', *Small Axe*, 10 (2001).

11    Leonard Shorey and Gerald St Rose, 'Education and development', in Trevor Carmichael (ed.), *Barbados: thirty years of independence* (Kingston: Ian Randle, 1996).

12    *Bim*, along with *Focus* in Jamaica, and *Kyk-over-al* in British Guiana, all emerged in the 1940s as influential cultural journals.

13    See Supriya Nair, *Caliban's Curse: George Lamming and the revisioning of history* (Ann Arbor: University of Michigan, 1996). Lamming's position, Nair argues, is that 'literature itself contributes to the ambitious enterprise of the making of history'. Lamming 'sees literature as a kind of imaginative record that paradoxically substantiates and challenges historical narratives', p. 2.

14    Paul Gilroy, *The Black Atlantic: modernity and double consciousness* (London: Verso, 1993), p. 146.

15    George Lamming, *The Pleasures of Exile* (London: Allison and Busby, 1984; first published 1960) p. 67.

16    'Lamming talks to Phillips', p. 14.

17    To date, I have not found this prologue.

18    'Lamming talks to Philips', p. 14.

19    Bennetta Jules-Rosette, 'Conjugating cultural realities: *Présence Africaine*', in V. Y. Mudimbe (ed.), *The Surreptitious Speech: Présence africaine and the politics of otherness, 1947–1987* (Chicago: University of Chicago Press, 1992).

20    Leopold Senghor, 'Nationhood: report on the doctrine and program of the Party of African Federation', in his *On African Socialism* (New York: Praeger, 1964), p. 49.

21    'C. L. R. James: West Indian. George Lamming interviewed by Paul Buhle', in Paget Henry and Paul Buhle (eds), *C. L. R. James's Caribbean* (Durham: Duke University Press, 1992), p. 36.

22    Quoted in Louis James, *Caribbean Literature in English* (London: Longman, 1999), p. 34.

23    Leopold Senghor, 'The African road to socialism', in his *On African Socialism*, p. 74.

24    Quoted in Rosette, 'Conjugating cultural realities', pp. 27–8.

25    Rosette, 'Conjugating cultural realities', p. 28.

26    Lamming was the first within the English language to re-read *The Tempest* as a colonial metaphor. Cognate developments occurred in French (Aimé Césaire) and in Spanish (Roberto Fernandez Reamer). See Peter Hulme and William H. Sherman (eds), *'The Tempest' and its Travels* (London: Reaktion, 2000).

27    Lamming, *Pleasures*, p. 109.

28    *Présence africaine*, 8–10 (1956), p. 364.

29    Barbados and Jamaica were the only two British West Indian islands who sent delegates (four in all). Guadeloupe sent three, Martinique four, Cuba one and Haiti eight.

30    *Présence africaine*, 8–10 (1956). See also James Baldwin, 'Princes and powers', in his *Nobody Knows My Name: more notes of a native son* (London: Michael Joseph, 1964).

31    See David Macey, *Frantz Fanon* (London: Granta, 2000), pp. 278–91.

32    Baldwin, 'Princes and powers', p. 44.

33    George Lamming, 'The Negro writer and his world'. Address delivered to the First International Congress of Black Writers and Artists in Paris, 21 September 1956, in Drayton and Andaiye, *Conversations*.

34    Frantz Fanon, *Black Skin, White Masks* (London: Paladin, 1970), p. 77.

35    Lamming, 'The Negro writer and his world', p. 37.

36    Richard Wright, *White Man Listen!*, as cited in Gilroy, *The Black Atlantic*, p. 161.

37    Stuart Hall, 'Lamming, Selvon and some trends in the West Indian novel', *Bim*, 23 (1955), p. 175.

38    'Lamming interviewed by Buhle', p. 29.

39    'The creative power of the mass, in *Season of Adventure*, that the drums bring out

is not too far away from what James sees as spontaneous confrontation', in 'Lamming interviewed by Buhle', p. 29.

40  Paget Henry, *Caliban's Reason: introducing Afro-Caribbean philosophy* (New York: Routledge, 2000), p. 156.

41  Cited in Gilroy, *Black Atlantic*, p. 161.

42  Gilroy, *Black Atlantic*, p. 171.

43  Lamming, *Pleasures*, p. 12.

44  Lamming, *Pleasures*, p. 178.

45  I am grateful to Bill Schwarz for this story.

46  'Lamming interviewed by Buhle', p. 29.

47  Lamming, *Pleasures*, p. 13.

48  Lamming, *Pleasures*, p. 214.

49  George Lamming, 'Concepts of the Caribbean', in Frank Birbalsingh (ed.), *Frontiers of Caribbean Literature in English* (London: Macmillan, 1996), p. 9.

50  George Lamming, *Of Age and Innocence* (London: Michael Joseph, 1958), p. 58.

51  See, for instance, Lamming, 'Concepts of the Caribbean'.

52  Lamming, *Pleasures*, pp. 162–3.

53  Lamming, *Pleasures*, p. 107.

54  Lamming, *Pleasures*, p. 15.

55  Lamming, *Pleasures*, p. 15.

56  Lamming, *Pleasures*, p. 120.

57  Edward Said, *Culture and Imperialism* (London: Chatto and Windus, 1993), p. 257.

58  Lamming, *Pleasures*, p. 15.

59  Fanon, *Black Skin, White Masks*. See also Henry, *Caliban's Reason*, p. 93.

60  Lamming, *Pleasures*, p. 38.

61  Lamming, *Pleasures*, p. 83.

62  Lamming, *Pleasures*, p. 83.

63  'Damming Lamming', an interview with George Lamming (2000), www.panmedia. com.jm/features/lamming.htm

64  Lamming, *Pleasures*, p. 63.

65  Lamming, *Pleasures*, p. 85.

66  Lamming, *Pleasures*, p. 85.

67  Interview with George Lamming (1989), *Banyan*, www.pancaribbean.com/banyan/ lamming.htm

68  Cited in 'Renewed interest in an open market': www.cweek.com/fpl.html, 22 October 2001.

69  'I would say that from about the beginning of the sixties, I entered into the region not just as witness and observer, but in a sense as a certain kind of activist ...', 'Interview with Lamming', *Banyan*.

70  George Lamming, *The Emigrants* (Ann Arbor: University of Michigan Press, 1994), p. 101.

71  C. L. R. James, 'The West Indian intellectual', in J. J. Thomas *Froudacity: West Indian fables by James Anthony Froude* (London and Port of Spain: New Beacon Books, 1969), p. 46.

72  'Damming Lamming'.

73  Lamming, 'Concepts of the Caribbean', p. 5.

74  James, 'The West Indian intellectual', p. 46.

75  See Nair, *Caliban's Curse*.

76  Lamming, *Pleasures*, p. 119.

77  Orlando Patterson, *The Sociology of Slavery* (London: MacGibbon and Kee, 1968).

78  Bryan Edwards, *The History, Civil and Commercial of the British Colonies in the West Indies* (Dublin: Luke White, 1793).

79  Henry, *Caliban's Reason*, p. 73. Jean-Baptiste Sabat was a seventeenth-century French missionary and chronicler of the Antilles. Edward Long was an eighteenth-century Jamaican planter who published, in 1774, his three volumes on *The History of Jamaica*.

80  For contemporary examples see, for instance, Gordon Rohlehr, *Calypso and Society*

*in Pre-Independence Trinidad* (Port of Spain: Gordon Rohlehr, 1990), and Louis Regis, *The Political Calypso: true opposition in Trinidad and Tobago, 1962–1987* (Kingston: The Press, The University of the West Indies, 1999).

81  Edward Kamau Brathwaite, introduction to Roger Mais, *Brother Man* (London: Heinemann, 1974), p. xiv.

82  Lamming, 'Concepts of the Caribbean', pp. 4–5. Belinda Edmondson argues that the focus on peasants is part of the European romantic inheritance: *Making Men: gender, literary authority and women's writing in Caribbean narrative* (Durham: Duke University Press, 1999), pp. 61–5.

83  Cooper, *Noises in the Blood*, p. 184.

84  There are, perhaps, parallels here with the use of a female chorus to carry the historical narrative in C. L. R. James's play, *Toussaint L'Ouverture*. See Cora Kaplan, 'Black heroes/white writers: Toussaint L'Ouverture and the literary imagination', *History Workshop Journal*, 46 (1998), pp. 32–62.

85  'Music of language: an interview with George Lamming', in Erika J. Waters, *Caribbean Writers On Line*, www.thecaribbeanwriter.com/volume13/v13p190.html

86  'Lamming talks to Phillips'.

87  Relatedly, Peter Hulme points out that Lamming (in his re-readings of *The Tempest*), argues that 'post-colonial intellectuals, whilst having to recognise themselves in Caliban, should at the same time refuse any full identification and find another ground on which to stand. Part of that ground might be as readers and interpreters of *The Tempest*, ground which Prospero had long thought of as rightfully his. He will expect a nail in the head and take precautions, as the play shows; but he will not expect to be displaced as a literary commentator. Always take the enemy by surprise.' Peter Hulme, 'Reading from elsewhere: George Lamming and the paradox of exile', in Hulme and Sherman, *'The Tempest'*.

88  Hall, 'Lamming, Selvon and the West Indian novel'.

89  Hall, 'Lamming, Selvon and the West Indian novel'. Nair also points out how Lamming often begins with a first person narrative which eventually dissolves into a third person account, thus 'combining the individual and the collective to indicate a representative situation: all of them in the same boat, figuratively and literally speaking': Nair, *Caliban's Curse*, p. 59.

90  Lamming, *'In the Castle of My Skin'*, in Drayton and Andaiye, *Conversations*, p. 47.

91  See Henry, *Caliban's Reason*, pp. 84–5.

92  Lamming, *In the Castle of My Skin*, p. 18.

93  Lamming, *Pleasures*, p. 125.

94  Hall, 'Lamming, Selvon and the West Indian novel'.

95  David Dabydeen, 'West Indian writers in Britain', from *The Second 'Sea Change' Seminar*, The British Council, Hamburg, 22 February 1999, www.britcoun.de/e/education/studies/seach994.htm

96  Edouard Glissant, *Caribbean Discourse*, cited in Nana Wilson-Tagoe, *Historical Thought and Literary Representation in West Indian Literature* (Gainesville: University Press of Florida, 1998), p. 79.

# CHAPTER NINE

# 'This is London calling the West Indies': the BBC's *Caribbean Voices*

## Glyne Griffith

On 27 November 1953 Henry Swanzy, the producer of the BBC's literary radio programme, *Caribbean Voices*, wrote from his Oxford Street office in London to the programme's West Indian contact, Gladys Lindo, in Kingston, Jamaica. His letter sought advice on editorial comments which he intended to make in a future programme.

> I am thinking of referring in the next summary to the death of Seepersad Naipaul, and to the illness of Sam Selvon, and the failure to send [Derek] Walcott to Europe. The last two would be critical remarks, and perhaps you think they would not be suitable in a thing like a summary. It does seem to me that the powers-that-be ought to be made aware of the value of literary work, from the prestige point of view, and the neglect of West Indian writers is really shocking ... I might also refer ... to the arrest of Martin Carter in Guyana, one poet who was never a contributor [to *Caribbean Voices*].[1]

Neglect of the literary talent of a new generation of Caribbean writers was, in Swanzy's mind, not only an aesthetic matter: it was economic too. The following year he learned that Oxford University had received an endowment for colonial studies from the Carnegie Foundation. He wrote to Margery Perham of Nuffield College in an attempt to procure funding for his programme:

> The reason for my writing is that I learned yesterday from Arthur Creech Jones who was doing a broadcast that the latest gift to Oxford has been £30,000 from Carnegie for Colonial Studies. He also told me that you said that the authorities did not quite know what they were going to do with it. I wonder therefore, if you would be prepared to consider doing something to help creative writers in the West Indies particularly, but to some extent in Africa as well?[2]

He pointed out that the BBC's allowance for *Caribbean Voices* of £1,500 per year was inadequate, for (he went on) he needed to support promising writers, such as Sam Selvon who was trying to get a London flat for himself, his wife and their child, all recently recovered from prolonged illness; Derek Walcott, who was looking to travel to England; Eric Roach and Wilson Harris, who were facing hardships in their respective home-nations of Trinidad and Guyana; and even Vidia Naipaul who was then a young student at Oxford University.

It was not usual practice for BBC producers to seek charity in this way. It illustrates not only the colonial hierarchies reproduced inside the institutions of the BBC, but also – more positively – the degree to which Swanzy appreciated the existence of an emergent cultural formation in the Caribbean which needed support from the centre.[3] This was a new culture which depended, in part, on the migration from periphery to centre – discussed in other chapters in this volume. But the story does not follow any easy symmetry. What might be called a West Indian perspective also complicated Britishness and, conversely, a sense of British rectitude could complicate West Indian affiliations. Movement of personnel was only part of the issue. The story of *Caribbean Voices* demonstrates that conservative colonial attitudes could be as prevalent at the periphery as at the imperial centre, and conversely, that hostility toward the myopic authority of colonial culture could be active among those of privilege and influence within the imperial centre.

The programme that evolved into *Caribbean Voices* was initially conceived by the Jamaican journalist and poet, Una Marson.[4] In March 1943 Marson had organised a feature programme for the BBC overseas service entitled *Calling the West Indies*. Through this medium Caribbean servicemen based in Britain during the second world war were able to maintain contact with relatives and friends back home. After a while, as a result of Una Marson's initiative, the programme began to include literary and cultural features from the Caribbean.

Marson's own reputation as a journalist had been formed in the heat of the Jamaican riots of May 1938, when she reported for the *Jamaica Standard*. Her editor, William Makin, prevailed upon her to travel to London in order that she could report on the Moyne Commission, which had been established by the imperial government to inquire into the causes of the Caribbean insurrections. While in London, Marson met with the 1939 winner of the Miss Jamaica competition, Winnie Casserley, who was visiting the mother country as part of her prize. When Winnie Casserley was interviewed by the BBC Marson, who had accompanied her as a journalist for the *Standard,* joined her. BBC staff were impressed by Marson's performance and offered her freelance work on *Picture Page*, where she worked closely with the producer Cecil Madden.[5] As Delia Jarrett-Macauley indicates:

Marson kept in frequent contact with Cecil Madden, occasionally suggesting programme alterations for West Indian broadcasts ... Grateful and impressed, Madden took up a number of her suggestions, forwarding them to his colleagues. Whenever possible he aimed to increase and improve the West Indian service ... BBC broadcasts to the Caribbean region were abysmally few. A detailed BBC memorandum written in 1929 had exposed the lack of facilities in the West Indies and colonial Africa and the discrepancy between this and the service to other parts of the empire. No attempt was made to serve the West Indies except on special occasions such as test matches, and therefore no in-house expertise existed. With the outbreak of war, therefore, the quandary troubling senior staff at the Empire Division responsible for West Indian programming was twofold. One issue was the delicate handling of British policy towards colonies where nationalist activism had been in ascendancy during the late 1930s – a political challenge also for the Ministry of Information under whose general influence the BBC now operated. The second, lesser consideration was the staffing of this section, bearing in mind financial and other managerial constraints, such as supervision.[6]

Thus the impetus for the programme derived in part from British concerns about the escalation of nationalist sentiment in the Caribbean, particularly in the aftermath of the crisis of the 1930s. Yet with no in-house expertise the BBC was obliged to call upon intellectuals from the West Indies.

As Marson's career at the BBC suggests, however, there could never be any firm distinction between the Corporation's wish for boosting the morale of the colonies for the war-effort, on the one hand, and on the other, the formulation of a wider cultural strategy which carried with it the prospect of emancipation from colonialism. As Jarrett-Macauley states:

> She was invited to broadcast morale-boosting talks on West Indians and the war effort: 'The empire at war and the colonies' went out on 1 April 1940 and 'West Indians' part in war' later that month. She ended one broadcast: 'I am trying to keep the flag flying for dear old Jamaica in my own way here and I am always in a rush as I used to be over there. Special love for you, my sisters.'[7]

Marson's pioneering work with the BBC spanned a five-year period, from April 1940 to December 1945. Her early participation in the West Indian Service had led to an invitation to contribute to the poetry magazine series, *Voice*, edited by George Orwell for the Indian Service. She read poetry over the airwaves alongside T. S. Eliot, William Empson and other notable literary figures. It was as a result of this experience that she devised a specifically Caribbean version of the same sort of programme.

*Caribbean Voices*, twenty-five minutes long, was first broadcast on BBC's West Indian service on 11 March 1943, with June Grimble as announcer and Cameron Tudor reading a short story by R. L. C. Aarons, 'Mrs. Arroway's Joe.' The following week the late-night broadcast displayed a wider range of Caribbean authors, including Neville Guiseppe of Trinidad, John Wickham, Barbadian short-story writer and later editor of the influential literary magazine *Bim*, and Ruth Horner, a Jamaican poet. The Jamaican literary journals, Edna Manley's *Focus* and the Poetry League of Jamaica's yearbook for 1940 were used as sources. Constance Hollar, the Jamaican poet and an acquaintance of Una's, who had died earlier that year, was the subject of the third programme.[8]

Marson had to operate in difficult conditions, not only confronting senior figures in the BBC whose commitments to the Caribbean were, to say the least, unreliable, but in addition a range of sceptical opinion in the West Indies itself. The very centrality of *Caribbean Voices* – the fact that it was the only such programme broadcast from London – inevitably meant it became a hostage to fortune, each enthusiastic listener convinced of its partiality. It was faulted for its narrowness. For example, one Mr Minshall, the government's Information Officer for Trinidad and Tobago, complained to Madden that it was unpopular in Trinidad because (he insisted) there was too much attention on Jamaica. West Indian critics blamed Marson for what they saw as the many shortcomings of the programme, which they always seemed ready to adumbrate.[9] Despite these challenges Marson pressed on, sure in her own convictions, and in this she was ardently supported by John Grenfell-Williams, who as Director of the African Service also had responsibility for broadcasting to the English-speaking Caribbean.

The personal costs were high. Marson herself experienced a sense of isolation within the BBC, which was aggravated by an increasing feeling of distance from the Caribbean, whose world she was responsible for representing. She knew too that she needed to widen her knowledge of the Caribbean beyond the culture of her own native Jamaica. After the war had ended she obtained permission from the BBC to make an extended five-month trip to the Caribbean.

> I felt that somehow I must leave London and come to the West Indies. I wanted to get away from the cold and the atmosphere of war, but more than anything else I wanted to come to the West Indies to meet as many people as possible to whom I had been speaking for nearly five years. I asked for permission to come, feeling very definitely that I could not go on broadcasting to you without learning about life in other islands of the West Indies I had not visited before.[10]

Soon after her return to London, however, she found herself overwhelmed by the pressure of her travels and debilitated by her continuing sense of isolation at the BBC. She became increasingly despondent suc-cumbing to the clinical depression which had haunted her for years. After a brief period in a nursing home in the English countryside, she returned home with her friend, the Jamaican poet Clare McFarlane, in April 1946. This departure brought an end to her official relationship with the BBC, and with the programme that she had been instrumental in establishing.

When it became clear that Marson could no longer carry on, John Grenfell-Williams invited the English writer, and close friend of Marson's, Mary Treadgold to organise the *Caribbean Voices* broadcasts until a more permanent appointment could be found. After three months Henry Swanzy, who was already employed as a producer in the Overseas Service, was asked to serve as producer and editor of *Caribbean Voices*.

Alongside the new appointment Grenfell-Williams understood that, in Marson's absence, the BBC needed someone 'on the ground', based in the Caribbean. He arranged that a regional office be set up in Kingston, and appointed a local man and friend of Marson's, Cedric Lindo, to act as Caribbean representative. In an unexpected develop-ment, however, Lindo didn't want to be seen to compromise his public standing, so proposed that his wife, Gladys, should take his place. (Cedric Lindo worked for the Jamaica Fruit and Shipping Company: it is revealing that he should think that working for the BBC as a literary agent might be considered a conflict of interests.)[11]

Swanzy, clearly, needed this regional support. He was an Irishman, trained as a historian, and – alongside his professional work at the BBC – an aspiring poet in his own right. Much later in life he reflected on the commitments which animated him:

> An odd passage through life which might explain something to the alert. The key, I think, has been my sympathy with the different peoples brought into contact by an imperial structure, perhaps too much linked by politics and economics, and not enough by art and culture.[12]

Grenfell-Williams had first become aware of Swanzy's literary interests when in 1941 the latter had submitted a long poem on the Battle of Britain to the BBC. The poem, in fact, received only rather measured praise from the influential writer, Cecil Day Lewis. In Swanzy's later recollections, this rebuff was connected to his subsequent champion-ing of Caribbean writers.

> Cecil Day Lewis said things about the poem which were justified, I think, but still he might have been a little less lukewarm. Thereafter, I never had sufficient confidence as I didn't get much encouragement, really, and I thought, perhaps out of a sort of empathy, that it would be nice to assist

some of these writers from the West Indies if I could, because they didn't get much help either, really.[13]

Swanzy came to *Caribbean Voices*, therefore, with literary interests, with experience in broadcasting, and with some empathy for aspiring writers who, like himself, had lacked encouragement and guidance. What, though, of the Caribbean? When late in his life I asked him about this, he answered in the following way:

I mean, one had the idea of *Glory Dead* which one had read, and one also had the sort of 'left-wing' view of encouraging people who had had a raw deal, really ... And my problem of course is that I come from Ireland, you see. I'm Irish, and although I left Ireland when I was five and never went back, or seldom did, one did have the feeling that what one wrote and was interested in was not the kind of thing that somebody like a Philip Larkin or a Gavin Ewart would write, really.[14]

This answer fuses together a number of issues. It conveys the mild though nonetheless significant democratic or egalitarian spirit common to many creative artists in Britain during the mid 1940s, when Swanzy first took over *Caribbean Voices*. It expresses a continuing allegiance to Ireland which set him apart from the conventions of the English literary establishment – a commitment which remained with him, judging by the names he cites, who were poets famous at the time he was speaking (in 1992) rather than in the time of *Caribbean Voices*. And it alludes to a book, *Glory Dead*, written by Arthur Calder-Marshall. It was through this book that Swanzy's imagination had been touched by the Caribbean.

Given the salience of this book for Swanzy, and given too the fact that he persuaded Calder-Marshall to become involved in *Caribbean Voices*, it is worth indicating something of the context. In 1938, the year following the height of the social unrest in Trinidad, Calder-Marshall spent three months in Trinidad and Tobago. His background was that of a conventionally English man of letters – private school, Oxford, and a string of novels by the time he was in his early thirties, when he embarked on his trip to the Caribbean. *Glory Dead* recounts this experience. It is, partially, a predictable piece of travel-writing, bringing together a range of vignettes of the social life of the islands. But the radical tempo of literary life in Britain in these years, combined with the political volatility of the Caribbean, gave the book a sharper subversive edge. Calder-Marshall wanted his account to confront the problem of 'white domination', and one of its themes is the 'shame' he experienced as a 'white man'.[15] He became involved, initially, with the cultural circles which existed on the edge of the labour movement, lecturing on aesthetic matters at L'Ouverture Club, speaking again to the

Oilfield Workers' Union, and eventually attempting to put on a production of that classic play of the anglophone Popular Front, *Waiting for Lefty*. (On his death the *Daily Telegraph* quaintly observed that in the 1930s he had 'experimented' with marxism.)[16] Gradually, it seems, he was pulled into social and political agitation. He attended various demonstrations (including one which was addressed by Clement Payne, who had recently become the hero of the disaffected masses of Barbados), spoke at some, and before long became the object of police attention. *Glory Dead* represents perhaps the only sympathetic recounting of the labour unrest in the Enlish-speaking Caribbean, written from a colonial perspective, though it is now almost completely forgotten. His conclusions were forthright:

> The struggle of the coloured worker will not be peaceful, because force will be used to suppress each effort towards greater responsibility, in the same way that force was used in Trinidad and Barbados in 1937 and in Jamaica and British Guiana in 1938. Commissions will be appointed as they have been in the past. They will make recommendations, most of which will be ignored. But each time certain advances will be made ... A new spirit has arisen among the workers. They have tasted freedom; they begin to know their power. And they intend to use that power, not as whites fear and perhaps like to think, for the stupid display of violence, but for the attainment of better education, better conditions of work and a higher standard of life.[17]

There are in the book, it is true, more conventional accounts of the lives of the subordinated in the Caribbean, which repeat the common prejudices of colonial mentalities of the period. But these are offset by an appreciation of the complexity of social interaction in everyday situations, and by an astute sense of the power of collective memory. Here, for example, Calder-Marshall tries to enter the imagination of an 'ordinary' Trinidadian working woman, in order to reveal the psychological workings of racial subordination:

> Mrs. Tournevant's great-grandmother was freed from slavery when she bore her master's bastard. As she talks to Mrs. Wilson, she is torn in two directions. Being seen talking to a white woman raises her prestige among neighbours and that gives her pleasure. But she knows that behind Mrs. Wilson's affability is contempt and maybe hatred. The pretence of equality is a mask for white superiority: it is like a millionaire wearing dungarees. She is being patronised and she is submitting to being patronised to gain caste with neighbours. So Mrs. Tournevant, laughing and smiling, hates Mrs. Wilson from West Kensington, and hates herself for talking to her.[18]

Such reflections on the masquerades of white supremacy were not usual in colonial discussion of the Caribbean in the 1930s.

*Glory Dead* also demonstrated a knowledge of Caribbean literature. As much as in the sphere of politics, Calder-Marshall had definite – and judged again by the colonial conventions of the time – unorthodox views on aesthetics. Here he comments on a lecture he delivered on art and society at the L'Ouverture Hall in Port of Spain:

> I tried to describe the way literature springs from the relation of the author, with his gifts, to the society of his time, and the variations thus entailed between literatures of different countries and ages. I pointed to Alfred Mendes as a Trinidadian novelist who represented native qualities of the island. I deplored the local verse as derivative from the Victorian and Edwardian traditions of English literature and having no relation to the life of the island ... I tried to explain ... [t]hat universality is only achieved by particular definition of character. I tried to make plain that a great work of art could be enjoyed by a wide audience, but that it would only be a great work of art if it had its roots in the life and thought of a particular time and place.[19]

This championing of a popular, locally rooted aesthetic, shaped by the social relations of its own colonised locations, marked the cultural dimensions of Calder-Marshall's commitments to a broader progressive politics. It also anticipated the intellectual affiliations of *Caribbean Voices*.

It's not certain how Swanzy came across *Glory Dead*, nor if this represented his sole means of access to the literary culture of the Caribbean. It is clear, though, that some fifty years after the event he could talk of the book as if it were a common cultural landmark for those who were serious in knowing about the Caribbean. Calder-Marshall and Swanzy shared the hope of bettering the lives of those 'who had had a raw deal', and shared too a scepticism about the spurious claims of a – metropolitan-driven – universal aesthetic. Calder-Marshall argued in terms of the need for a literature rooted in 'the life and thought of a particular time and place', while Swanzy made the same point by invoking the need for 'local colour'. In 1946, during his first year as editor of the programme, Swanzy explained his reasons for rejecting various manuscripts which had been forwarded to him:

> I am gradually working my way into the stockpile of *Caribbean Voices*, and now return various manuscripts which I do not think we should like to use. As you will see, they include several classes: patriotic poems, sweetly pretty poems ... and finally, the occasional exiles writing about conditions which have nothing to do with the Caribbean. On the whole, I think they all have something in common, and that is a complete absence of local colour. That seems to me to be the greatest crime in this series, unless of course the writer is a genius with a universal message.[20]

[ 203 ]

In a strange paradox, this determination to support what Swanzy called the 'local' undermined what many aspiring – 'local' – writers in the Caribbean considered to be a proper mode of writing. As the piles of rejected manuscripts attest, many of those West Indians who submitted work to Swanzy believed that art should reproduce the literary conventions of the metropolis – or at least, those with which they had been able to become acquainted. Swanzy's conception of the local, however, was set dead against the 'patriotic' and 'sweetly pretty'.

If this strategy discriminated against tradition it did so in favour of encouraging a wider plurality of authorship. As the Jamaican academic and poet, John Figueroa, has observed:

> [O]ne of the great contributions of *Caribbean Voices* was that it offered an outlet to all and sundry, as any full list of its contributors shows. And in doing this it executed an odd twist and inversion of what would then have been considered the proper metropole/periphery relationship.[21]

Critical in this respect was the question of language. Swanzy's espousal of regional forms embraced a vernacular manner of writing that transgressed the cultural norms which, in other arenas, were propagated fiercely by the BBC. Figueroa, who as a reader on the programme was caught in the crossfire of these controversies, goes on to say:

> One is not dealing just with a general tendency of critics, but with special complicated Caribbean 'colonial' attitudes. Nothing better illustrates this than the fact that many people in the Caribbean felt that poetry on the BBC, even Caribbean poetry, should be read by English voices ... Often critics appear to be criticizing individual readers, almost to be carrying out a vendetta, but when one looks more carefully, and observes who are strongly praised as readers, one cannot help noticing that they are either English or have very 'Oxford English' voices ... The very existence of *Caribbean Voices*, and particularly its mode of operation, raised the whole question of the meaning and actuality of the metropole/periphery relationship: the relationship between London and the Caribbean.[22]

Swanzy was quick to employ readers on the programme such as Sam Selvon from Trinidad, Pauline Henriques from Jamaica, George Lamming from Barbados, and other London-based, Caribbean writers and artists. Indeed, his critical sense of the uniqueness of an emergent Caribbean literature necessarily turned on the question of language, and more especially on the particularities of idiomatic expression. Interviewed in later years he put it like this: 'It is certainly true that the dialect, the accent and the turn-of-phrase, the spoken language was extremely rich; I always remembered phrases such as, "Their eyes made four"'.[23] The more West Indians came to London, the more he was able to employ West Indians as readers. In retrospect, this may seem an obvious thing to have happened, an elementary requirement that the West Indian imagination be represented – spoken – by West Indians. But this is to underestimate the reflexes of social authority underwriting language itself, such that the attainment of culture excluded those who (in the colonial situation) could not, or would not, master the correct forms. Many listeners assumed that, on this question above all, the BBC would hold the line. When, under Swanzy's direction, *Caribbean Voices* made evident its conviction that commitment to the local meant also commitment to local vernacular idioms, a certain disarray could be discerned in the ranks of the programme's West Indian audience. In response to one broadcast, for example, Gladys Lindo complained that:

> Incidentally, there were some very caustic remarks from my friends on the programme of the 2nd November. There was quite a large group listening – fourteen in all – and the opinion of the majority was that it was not only poor, but very poor.
>
> I was unable to identify the story, as I missed the name and did not recognise it as one passed through this office ... The reader also was not good. I think it was Mr. [Gordon] Bell of Barbados. I appreciate that it is better to have West Indians reading in the programme, but suggest that if it is not possible to get a good West Indian reader, a good English one would be preferable.[24]

The complaints from Lindo's office regarding Barbadian reader, Gordon Bell, as well as the Jamaican reader, John Figueroa, were prominent themes of several of Lindo's letters to Swanzy during the early period of his direction. By June 1948 it was clear that Swanzy had had enough.

> Dear Mrs. Lindo,
> Far from 'sitting in a corner and weeping', he [Michael G. Smith, whose poetry John Figueroa had read on a previous broadcast] said that Figueroa read better than he could himself, and although he thought he was a little bit histrionic, he thought it was a very good performance. In this, I must say that we all agree over here, including Mr. Grenfell-Williams ... don't you think that the campaign of criticism in Jamaica may not be unconnected with the founding of a local poetry programme by the local poetry 'ring'? ... The long and the short of it is that we shall continue to regard Figueroa as our main poetic exponent, but we shall try to get more variation in readers, perhaps from some of the West Indian actors and others who are living in London. I still think it would be a pity if we went back to the BBC Repertory Company.[25]

Swanzy's determination to privilege the local also had unexpected consequences. He soon received many more submissions in the local vernacular. This brought with it the discovery, though, that there were many 'locals'. Listeners in each island believed that the particular rhythms of their speech were necessary to communicate the intricacies of their own particular forms of writing. To have a Jamaican read a Bajan poem could seem like another sort of external authority impos-ing itself, even if it were in the name of a larger nationalism. In a radio programme dedicated to the integrity of the spoken word, controversies such as these were both inevitable and decisive.

It's difficult to judge the effect that the medium of radio – pre-emi-nently through *Caribbean Voices* – had on encouraging an entire gen-eration of writers to think in new ways about representing the tone of the spoken voice on the page. There can be no doubt, however, of the more general significance of *Caribbean Voices* in creating a new West Indian literature. George Lamming recalled it in these terms:

> Our sole fortune now was that it was Henry Swanzy who produced *Caribbean Voices*. At one time or another, in one way or another, all West Indian novelists have benefited from his work and his generosity of feeling. For Swanzy was very down to earth. If you looked a little thin in the face, he would assume that there might have been a minor famine on, and without in any way offending your pride, he would make some arrange-ment for you to earn. Since he would not promise to 'use' anything you had written, he would arrange for you to earn by employing you to read. No comprehensive account of writing in the British Caribbean during the last decade [the 1950s] could be written without considering his whole achievement and his role in the emergence of the West Indian novel.[26]

But at the same time, the flux of new readers and writers passing through Swanzy's office ensured that different aspects of Caribbean culture came to life, new viewpoints were opened and, inevitably, that the authority of the likes of Calder-Marshall began to diminish. One little bit of the BBC not only serviced the Caribbean: in so doing it quietly became creolised.

Notwithstanding competing claims on local idioms, Swanzy's insis-tence on submissions that spoke in a voice that was peculiarly West Indian led many writers from the region to cast what Kamau Brathwaite would later call 'nation-language'. Respecting local forms while attempting to imagine into existence a larger Caribbean reality was not easily achieved – though *Caribbean Voices* clearly contributed to the possibility of imagining a federation of the English-speaking West Indies as a unified cultural region.

Laurence Breiner believes that the privileging of the spoken voice, which radio demanded, proved vital in this respect.

> It was a great piece of luck for the development of West Indian poetry that the cachet of metropolitan approval came first of all not in the form of publication by a British anthology or magazine (venues which would con-

sciously or not have tended to encourage more exotic subject matter and less exotic language), but in the form of a radio program that made poets think about how their work would sound to a diverse West Indian audience listening at home.[27]

John Figueroa makes a similar point, though emphasising the specifics of wireless technologies:

The other great source of influence which *Caribbean Voices* possessed is very easy to overlook or underestimate in this age of TV and satellites: it was a radio programme, a short-wave radio programme. That would have been important anywhere, but it was pre-eminent in the Caribbean, where 1200 miles of sea separated Trinidad and Jamaica, and where communication was by infrequent ocean liners from North to East and South, or by regular schooner in the South. Short-wave radio really eradicated time and space. And *Caribbean Voices* brought together those who were interested from St. Lucia and Tortola and Guiana and Trinidad and Barbados and Jamaica in a way that nothing else, except cricket broadcasting, ever has. Furthermore, in a society not too well known for reading, the spoken word, by way of radio, even when it was producing literature, had an impact that books would have lacked, except among the very few.[28]

For a critical period *Caribbean Voices*, organised from the metropole, became the medium for a new Caribbean literature. Swanzy, and the programme he nurtured, allowed many West Indians both in Britain and in the Caribbean, *to become* intellectuals and artists. And in so doing, they created the means for imagining a new homecoming, not only for themselves, but for the multitudes they represented.

## Notes

1  Henry Swanzy, letter to Gladys Lindo, 27 November 1953, Henry Swanzy Archive, Birmingham University Library, UK.
2  Henry Swanzy, letter to Margery Perham, 14 July 1954, Swanzy Archive.
3  For a slightly later reflection on the colonial relations inside the BBC, see George Lamming's angry comments in *The Pleasures of Exile* (London: Allison and Busby, 1984; first published 1960), p. 51.
4  Rhonda Cobham, 'The *Caribbean Voices* programme and the development of West Indian short fiction, 1945–1958', in Peter Stummer (ed.), *The Story Must Be Told: short narrative prose in the new English literatures* (Bayreuth: Konigshanson and Newmann, 1986), pp. 146–60.
5  Delia Jarrett-Macauley, *The Life of Una Marson, 1905–65* (Manchester: Manchester University Press, 1998), p. 144. Madden went on to become a pioneer of TV light entertainment, renowned for his discoveries of Petula Clark, the Beverley Sisters and Jimmy Edwards.
6  Jarrett-Macauley, *Marson*, p. 146.
7  Jarrett-Macauley, *Marson*, p. 147.
8  Jarrett-Macauley, *Marson*, p. 158.
9  Jarrett-Macauley, *Marson*, p. 152.
10 Jarrett-Macauley, *Marson*, p. 167.

11  Wycliffe Bennett (former secretary of the Jamaica Poetry League), personal interview, 30 March 2001.
12  Henry Swanzy, letter to the author, 2 November 1993.
13  Henry Swanzy, personal interview, 24 October 1992.
14  Swanzy, interview, 24 October 1992.
15  Arthur Calder-Marshall, *Glory Dead* (London: Michael Joseph, 1939), pp. 12 and 100. The title comes from an old local song. It re-emerges later in V. S. Naipaul: 'The history I carried with me, together with the self-awareness that had come with my education and ambition, had sent me into the world with a sense of glory dead; and in England had given me the rawest stranger's nerves', *The Enigma of Arrival: a novel* (Harmondsworth: Penguin, 1987), p. 52.
16  Obituary of Arthur Calder-Marshall, *Daily Telegraph*, 20 April 1992. For an interesting (and positive) review of *Glory Dead*, see *New Leader*, 19 May 1938. George Lamming can also be found recommending *Glory Dead* in 'Music of language. An interview with Erika Waters', *The Caribbean Writer*, 13 (1999). He tells of Calder-Marshall's role in helping get *In The Castle of My Skin* published in Ian Munro and Reinhard Sander (eds), *Kas Kas. Interviews with three Caribbean writers in Texas. George Lamming, C. L. R. James and Wilson Harris* (Austin, Texas: African and Afro-American Research Institute, University of Texas at Austin, 1972).
17  Calder-Marshall, *Glory Dead*, p. 239.
18  Calder-Marshall, *Glory Dead*, p. 43.
19  Calder-Marshall, *Glory Dead*, pp. 148–9.
20  Henry Swanzy, letter to Gladys Lindo, 13 August 1946, Swanzy Archive.
21  John Figueroa, 'The flaming faith of these first years: *Caribbean Voices*', in Maggie Butcher (ed.), *Tibisiri: Caribbean writers and critics* (Aarhus: Dangaroo Press, 1989), p. 72.
22  Figueroa, 'Flaming faith', pp. 61–3.
23  Henry Swanzy, personal interview, 22 October 1992.
24  Gladys Lindo, letter to Henry Swanzy, 10 November 1947, Swanzy Archive.
25  Henry Swanzy, letter to Gladys Lindo, 23 June 1948, Swanzy Archive.
26  Lamming, *Pleasures of Exile*, p. 67.
27  Laurence Breiner, *Black Yeats: Eric Roach and the politics of poetry* (unpublished ms, Boston University, 2000), p. 7.
28  Figueroa, 'Flaming faith', pp. 72–3. Figueroa has also emphasised the importance of *Caribbean Voices* in bringing the larger world into the enclosed culture of the Caribbean, which he discusses in his contribution to the BBC Radio 4 documentary, *What does Mr Swanzy want?* (first transmitted 27 November 1998; presented by Philip Nanton). Although no recordings remain, this commemoration provides a rich portrayal of the defining themes, and shows too the degree to which Swanzy's paradoxical espousal of the local – from his BBC redoubt in London – was the cause of deep resentments.

# CHAPTER TEN

# The Caribbean Artists Movement

## Louis James

At a Conference of the Caribbean Artists Movement (CAM) held at the University of Kent in 1969, C. L. R. James spoke with typical energy of his experience of growing up in Trinidad.

> I didn't get literature from the mango-tree, or bathing on the shore and getting the sun of the colonial countries; I set out to master the literature, philosophy and ideas of Western civilization. This is where I have come from, and I would not pretend to be anything else. And I am able to speak of the underdeveloped countries infinitely better than I would otherwise have been able to do.[1]

On the same occasion Edward (now Kamau) Brathwaite, as a founder member of CAM, spoke in a very different way about his attitude to growing up in a society dominated by Western culture.

> The point I am making here is that my education and background, though nominally middle class, is, on examination, not of this nature at all. I had spent most of my boyhood on the beach and in the sea with 'beach-boys', or in the country, at my grandfather's with country boys and girls. I was not therefore in a position to make any serious intellectual investment in West Indian middle class values.[2]

The two statements are not necessarily in opposition. C. L. R. James was speaking of his fiercely independent reading in 'the literature, philosophy and ideas of Western civilization'. Brathwaite was reacting against the European tradition, as it emerged in his experience of 'West Indian middle class values'. Nevertheless, placed side by side, they point to the variety of attitudes and positions that fed into what became known, at its second meeting, as 'the Caribbean Artists Movement', or CAM.

CAM grew out of a small informal meeting held in a basement flat in Mecklenberg Square, London, on the evening of 19 December 1966. Six years later, when CAM as an organisation ended, it had made a major impact on the emergence of a Caribbean cultural identity, particularly in Britain, where it also had changed attitudes within the host community. Anne Walmsley has written the indispensable history of CAM's activities, personalities and achievements.[3] Other accounts wait to be written by the Caribbean members of CAM. This essay, emphatically, will not be a substitute for either. My perspective is that of a 'white' English academic who had the good fortune to be involved in CAM's activities from the beginning, but by upbringing and profession, inevitably remained outside the grass-roots elements in the movement.

The origins of CAM can be traced back some years before 1966, to the University of the West Indies (UWI) at Mona, Jamaica, where Edward Brathwaite had become a lecturer in the History Department in 1962. The University had opened its doors to students in 1949, and was already a creative force in the region. It was attracting young local talent that would previously have gone on to universities in Britain and the United States. The History Department, led by a group of outstanding West Indians, including Elsa Goveia, Douglas Hall and Roy Augier, was pioneering a new phase in Caribbean Studies. Members of the Departments of Sociology and Education were conducting research into the lives of the Jamaican underprivileged classes that later was to feed into Caribbean literature.[4] The Departments of French and Spanish were mapping a Caribbean that went beyond the English-speaking West Indies.

The Department of English Literature stood out on the campus in keeping to a colonial academic framework. It kept strictly to the London University syllabus. The research of Robert le Page and Frederick C. Cassidy into Jamaican speech[5] was kept separate in linguistics. English literature educated West Indians to read and write in the British tradition. (In fairness, it must be said that the same could be said of most Jamaican schools and many middle-class families at that time.) The Department radical was W. I. (Bill) Carr, an explosive, complex figure who wrote fiery anti-establishment articles for the opposition weekly, *Public Opinion*. He read and discussed Caribbean literature, particularly admiring the Jamaican novelist Roger Mais. But in teaching he was a follower of F. R. Leavis, committed to the 'great tradition' of English writers.[6]

I became a lecturer in English at Mona in September 1963. It was my second university post. I had been drawn to the new writing emerging from Africa and the Caribbean by a missionary childhood in what was then Northern Rhodesia. Entering the University of Hull Extramural Department in 1958, I taught my adult classes Chinua Achebe's *Things Fall Apart* in rural Lincolnshire soon after its appearance, and used South African literature to discuss apartheid. I had also developed an interest in Jamaica, which became independent in 1962.

When I arrived on the Mona campus in 1963, what George Lamming in *The Pleasures of Exile* had called the 'phenomenon' of postwar Caribbean literature in English[7] was well under way. Samuel Selvon's *A Brighter Sun* (1952), George Lamming's *In the Castle of My Skin* (1953), Wilson Harris's *Palace of the Peacock* (1960), V. S. Naipaul's *A House for Mr Biswas* (1960) and Derek Walcott's *In a Green Night* (1962) were all in print. There was promise in the air. Several of my students, including Gordon Rohlehr, Victor Chang, Wayne Brown, Maureen Warner Lewis and Victor Ramraj, were to become leading Caribbean writers and academics. Derek Walcott had taken a degree in English, French and Latin at Mona in 1953, and by then was in Trinidad. But his younger compatriot, Wayne Brown, brought to my class for comment a draft of 'Noah', a remarkable poem later published in *On the Coast* (1972). There were other such excitements.

During my second year Norman Jeffares called the first Conference on Commonwealth Literature at the University of Leeds. It brought together an international group of academics (the UWI sent John Figueroa from the Department of Education, but no one from English), writers, broadcasters, publishers, as well as London representatives from the British Council and Arts Council. The Conference set up the Association for the Study of Commonwealth Literatures and Language (ACLALS), marking the institutional beginnings of Commonwealth and postcolonial studies. In 1965, I reviewed the published proceedings in *Caribbean Quarterly*, the academic journal of the Extramural Department, making a plea that the UWI English literature syllabus be widened to include Caribbean literature: 'there are certain things that University of the West Indies, in particular, should be doing'.[8] Later, in 1970, the UWI at Mona was to host the second triennial Conference of ACLALS. But in 1965 my review went unnoticed. Pressure to bring the English syllabus into line with other developments in Caribbean culture came from elsewhere. Working in the early morning cool in my office, the rattle of my typewriter echoed that of Brathwaite working in the History Department above, and we became friends. He was working on poems he was to build into his longer work, *Rights of Passage* (1967), and researching into Jamaican popular culture.[9] When I was asked to edit the first published book of essays on West Indian writing, I recommended that Brathwaite should be a contributor. But his enthusiasm for Caribbean folk culture had made his name anathema in the English Department. A Jamaican colleague protested against the idea so vehemently that I dropped the proposal, a decision I was bitterly to regret. The seed ideas of what was to become CAM were germinating in Brathwaite's activities at Mona in the previous decade.

In the summer of 1966 I returned to England to take up a teaching post at the University of Kent. Kent had been established in 1965, one of the innovating 'plate-glass' universities founded in the 1960s. It emphasised interdisciplinary studies, and had a particular interest in 'Third World' societies. First year students were offered a course in 'Colonial Cultures', which combined literature and history from India, Africa and the Caribbean. Its popularity led, in 1967, to a course entirely devoted to African and Caribbean literatures. All this made it a natural seedbed for the ideas of CAM.

The year I came to Kent, Brathwaite followed, coming with his wife Doris to work on a D.Phil. under Donald Wood at the University of Sussex. Sussex, like Kent, had an interest in African and Caribbean studies, and the staff included Gerald Moore, who had joined the University from Nigeria, and was also to become a CAM supporter. Brathwaite had come to Britain with great hopes. West Indian artistic activity in London led him to expect a Caribbean community in hot debate about their regional culture. But nothing was happening. John La Rose, a Trinidadian who had come to London in 1961, was also anxious to bring together the West Indian 'novelists, poets, literary critics, painters and sculptors'.[10] When the two met, drawn together by interest in each other's poetry, they decided to include the Jamaican writer and broadcaster Andrew Salkey, who 'knew everybody'. In December the three called the inaugural meeting in the Brathwaites' flat.

This was followed by a series of informal discussions which many of those who participated remember as providing their most valuable experience of CAM. Writers, painters, critics, teachers and theatre people met to discuss how their work related to a sense of a Caribbean culture. Those who had been separated by a fragmented Caribbean in London began to discover a common culture. The meetings included some from outside the Caribbean, drawn by shared interests. One of these was the young Leeds postgraduate, James Ngugi (later Ngugi wa Thiong'o), who applied the discussions to his own search for an African identity.

As the year progressed, an organisation began to take shape. The Movement appointed officers, set a small subscription (one pound), and produced a cyclostyled *Newsletter*, which printed CAM talks and interviews, correspondence, bibliographies, and publicised cultural events in England and the Caribbean. CAM used the West Indian Student Centre, Earl's Court, for public discussions. In September 1967, its committee organised a residential conference at the University of Kent which consolidated CAM's expanding interests in literature, painting and the performing arts. Its success led to a second at the University in 1968. But there was a growing opposition from black radicals against a grass-roots Caribbean movement becoming associated with what was seen as an elitist white establishment, and a third conference, in

1969, was non-residential and held at the West Indian Student's Centre in London.

Brathwaite had returned to the UWI at Mona the year before, in 1968. But in trying to organise CAM activities there he found that Jamaica was working out its own cultural agenda, and was in social and political turmoil. In 1969 CAM joined with the New World Group on the campus to run Sunday morning seminars on 'The arts in the Caribbean today'. However, CAM's major activity there became the publication of the periodical, *Savacou*, from 1970 to 1979, edited mainly by Brathwaite, Salkey and Kenneth Ramchand. The second number was retrospective, reprinting papers from CAM conferences and meetings. But the double issue *Savacou* 3–4 (1970/71) comprised a substantial anthology of contemporary Caribbean writing that aroused a storm of controversy because it included writing in the Rastafarian idiom by Bongo Jerry and Ras Dizzy. This in turn provoked a brilliant defence from the CAM member Gordon Rohlehr, of the use of the vernacular idiom in Caribbean verse.[11]

In Britain, CAM played a significant role in the emergence of a new Caribbean strand in black British culture. Stuart Hall opened up the issues in his opening address to the second CAM conference. Here he defined black Caribbean culture as distinctively shaped by its slave past as being both in opposition to, and intimately involved with, Europe: an 'enemy within'. The crisis of identity that now faced a generation of British-born West Indians, also living within but apart from English culture, was CAM's concern. This proved true, and the special double issue of *Savacou*, 'Writing away from home' (published in 1974 but three years in the editing) is now recognised as the first anthology of black British literature.[12] In early 1971 the Commonwealth Institute rewarded CAM's encouragement of young painters by mounting a major exhibition, 'Caribbean artists in Britain'. In 1972 the opening of the Keskedee Centre in Islington offered an ideal venue for extending CAM activities to include a new generation of young West Indian talent. But the pioneering work had been done, and there was no committee intact able to take advantage of the new initiative.

CAM as a movement was too diverse to be easily defined. Brathwaite was its driving spirit, providing ideas and enthusiasm, insisting the movement include all the arts, drawing in and encouraging younger members, and open to new concepts. He had grown up on the most conservative of British West Indian islands, Barbados. His family had roots in the rural community but had become largely middle class, and Brathwaite was sent to the island's best school, Harrison College, where he received a rigorous education modelled on that of an English public school.[13] Early, however, he showed independent tastes. He formed a passion for jazz, music that the island 'culture censors' considered low and unsuited to a Harrison College boy. When, in the sixth form, he persuaded the Barbados Rediffusion radio station to let him broadcast programmes of blues and jazz music, there were scandalised protests, and the series was closed down after only two sessions.[14] Nevertheless, in 1950 he won an island scholarship to Cambridge. It was a good place for a budding poet. Brathwaite's contemporaries included Thom Gunn, Peter Redgrove and Ted Hughes, with whom he remembers spending his last day in Cambridge. But in 1953 he read *In the Castle of My Skin* by his fellow Barbadian George Lamming, whom he also met when Lamming visited Cambridge friends. Brathwaite wrote later that he felt 'everything was transformed. Here breathing to me from every pore of line and page, was the Barbados I had lived. The words, the rhythms, the cadences, the scenes, the people, their predicament. They all came back'.[15] He knew now he could not be an 'Afro-Saxon'. After graduation he took a certificate in education, and instead of returning home to join the Barbadian establishment, went to Africa, to what was then the Gold Coast to work from 1955 to 1962 in the Ministry of Education.

Brathwaite faced the frustrations of accommodating to African ways of life. But in retrospect these became forgotten. They were heady years. The country was progressing towards independence, and became Ghana under President Nkrumah in 1957. Brathwaite helped administer the education system of a new nation. As he worked in the Ghanaian villages, he became aware how much African traditional life had survived the Middle Passage into the Caribbean. He was touched by the welcome he received in the rural communities, experiencing warmth lacking in the formal Barbados society of his childhood. He felt 'welcomed back' to Africa, 'a stranger/after three hundred years'.[16] His happiness there was deepened when, in 1960, he revisited Barbados and met Doris, born in Guyana, who had studied home economics in England. They fell immediately in love, were married within a month, and returned to share Brathwaite's last years in Ghana.[17]

In verse, Brathwaite was to write of this 'key period of my what I call my *de/education*' as being

> like
> when I first saw through the eye of the navel/heard the drum speak God
> and cd talk of drum belly drum centred earth sounding culture
> like
> when I began to recognise the importance and meaning of ceremony ...
> ritual ... tradition ...[18]

The Ghana years changed Brathwaite's outlook on Caribbean history and culture. As he declared in the CAM talk already quoted, he now saw his education in Barbados as playing with village boys on the beach, for it was they who had preserved their African roots.[19] He was drawn to the sense of spiritual forces immanent in African ways of life, and wrote of them as connected by 'submarine'[20] links to the rituals and religious ceremonies of the Caribbean. In 1971 in a religious ceremony he was to change his name 'Edward' to 'Kamau'. He received the name, however, not in Ghana, but in Limuru, Kenya, from Ngugi wa Thiongo's grand-mother,[21] indicating his widening, Pan-African sense of identity.

Africa also changed Brathwaite's views of music and poetry. The rhythms of its rituals and song showed him the charismatic effect of the human voice in verse speaking. He heard the sounds that United States slave culture had preserved in the music of blues and jazz. He was later to read Marshall Stearns's *The Story of Jazz* (1956), and *Blues People* (1963) by LeRoy Jones (now Amiri Baraka), studies that related jazz to the history of black American peoples. The formation of CAM offered a public platform for these ideas. In February 1967, two months after its inaugural meeting, Brathwaite read a paper on 'Jazz and the West Indian novel'.[22] In this he outlined 'a possible alternative to the European cultural tradition which has been imposed upon us and which we have more or less accepted and absorbed, for obvious histor-ical reasons, as the only way of going about our business'.[23] Jazz was 'a spontaneous, open, improvisatory' form, centred in the 'belly', not the intellect. It related to the idiom that he saw emerging in the Caribbean novel. 'There is no West Indian jazz', he stated,[24] claiming, controver-sially, that Caribbean popular music had not evolved out of protest and spiritual chaos in the way that the American form had done. But the West Indian jazz aesthetic had emerged in the fiction now being written by such writers as George Lamming and Roger Mais.

Whatever the limitations of Brathwaite's thesis as an assessment of the West Indian novel, it brilliantly illuminated his own intentions as a poet. For his long poem *Rights of Passage,* which he charismatically performed at the Jeanetta Cochrane Theatre, London, the following month, did indeed embody the qualities he saw in jazz – its questing, open-ended form, the melding of diverse cultural idioms and rhythms, a voice of hurt and yearning held within a celebration of a cultural iden-tity. 'The "personal urge for words" [is] the West Indian writer's trumpet', he had written,[25] and as he declaimed, the rich tones of his voice, with its Barbadian lilt, soared like a trombone solo:

> Drum skin whip
> lash, master sun's
> cutting edge of
> heat, taut
> surfaces of things

I sing
I shout
I groan
I dream
about [26]

In his performance, Brathwaite also assumed for the poet the role of a shaman. *Rights of Passage* took the form of a visionary quest, moving across time and space to create a tapestry of the lives of the common people within the black diaspora – plantation Uncle Tom, Jamaican Rastafarian, a shop full of Barbadian village women – each identity mediated through characteristic rhythms of speech or music. Weaving through it all was the poet's quest for cultural identity. In *Masks*, which followed in 1968, the seer returns, as Brathwaite had once done, to find roots in Africa; in *Islands* (in 1969), he went back to the Caribbean to revisit the scenes of *Rights*. The trilogy, collected as *The Arrivants* (1973), was to become a central document for CAM. The *négritude* movement had its Caribbean origins in Aimé Césaire's poetic *Cahier d'un retour au pays natal* (1939). In a similar way, Brathwaite's work grounded CAM not in a set of precepts, but in a creative work that opened up new dimensions of form and imaginative perception.

Brathwaite throughout his CAM activities was closely supported by his wife Doris. Her quiet good sense and radiant personality made a positive contribution to its meetings. In a similar way, John La Rose's work in CAM was indebted to the encouragement and organising skills of Sarah White. La Rose was, with Brathwaite and Salkey, a key figure in CAM. His quiet voice and unobtrusive manner were deceptive. He had been active in black radical movements both in the Caribbean and Britain.[27] He had grown up in an atmosphere of political debate absent in contemporary Jamaica or Barbados. He considered himself a marxist by the age of eighteen, and later rose to become General Secretary of the Trinidad West Indian Independence Party, and executive member of the island's Federated Workers Trade Union. In 1961 he came to England, bringing organisational experience and a network of contacts that would prove invaluable to CAM.

Where Brathwaite and Salkey had felt alienated from their middle-class upbringing, La Rose had grown up happily in Arima in rural Trinidad, part of a vibrant culture whose customs and festivals had readily assimilated influences from Caribs, Africans and cosmopolitan Europe. His enthusiasm for carnival and steel band music led him to see Trinidad popular culture as a key resource for the subversion of the colonial order. From 1956 to 1958 he worked closely with Raymond Quevedo (the calypsonian 'Attila the Hun') to write a ground-breaking study of the social significance of 'Kaiso', the forerunner of calypso.[28]

But La Rose was never exclusively interested in popular culture. In Trinidad he also worked to encourage local theatre, writing and reading circles, and discussion groups. He enjoyed classical and modern music, and Wilson Harris remembers giving La Rose and Sarah spare tickets to Wigmore Hall concerts when they met in London in the early 1960s. Earlier, while working in Venezuela, La Rose had studied French and Spanish literature. This gave him a window on the creative literature emerging from the postwar cultural ferment of Cuba, Martinique, Haiti and Venezuela. Reading the work of Rafael Cadenas, Nicolás Guillén, Jacques Roumain and Aimé Césaire, he was able to place the English-speaking Caribbean in a wider scene, one in which British debates about race and identity appeared parochial. A sense of the region's complexity steered La Rose away from conceiving of CAM as a movement with a tightly specified programme. His greatest pleasure was in sessions that the Guyanese painter Aubrey Williams called 'warishi nights', using the Amerindian term for 'unburdening'. When it had created a Caribbean community in which hopes and ideas could truly be shared, CAM's purpose would have been achieved.

Such a community would need ready access to relevant books. His experience organising radical discussion groups in Trinidad had taught La Rose that the publication of Caribbean literature served the interests of London publishers and their British readers. CAM needed to gain control of book publishing and communications. In 1966 he had started his own independent West Indian publishing imprint, New Beacon Books, taking the name of the literary journal *The Beacon* (1931–33) with which C. L. R. James, Alfred Mendes and Albert Gomez had blazed new cultural trails in Trinidad in the 1930s. His first title was a slim volume of his own poetry, significantly titled *Foundations* (1966). For other founding texts he turned to John Jacob Thomas. As early as 1869, Thomas had laid a foundation from which to oppose the colonial Standard English by writing *Creole Grammar*, a study of Trinidad speech considered as an authentic and independent language. He later turned to British colonial attitudes writing his exemplary rebuttal of Froude, *Froudacity*. In Trinidad La Rose had to use Thomas's works in typescript. For La Rose in the late 1960s these had become obvious texts for New Beacon to promote.

New Beacon Books and CAM were to develop hand in hand. By republishing Thomas's pioneering studies alongside contemporary writings, La Rose and Sarah White provided an invaluable service to CAM; it was an intervention which did much to heighten CAM's recognition that it was the inheritor of an existent tradition of West Indian thought. La Rose and White began a book service for CAM members, and listed relevant publications in the CAM *Newsletter*. The New

Beacon bookstall became an important feature of CAM meetings. After particularly large sales at the 1967 CAM Conference, they opened a bookstore in their house in Stroud Green Road, in North London, to cater for an ever-growing demand for Caribbean and African titles.

The third founder member of CAM was Andrew Salkey. Salkey was a Panamanian-born Jamaican who had come to study English at the University of London in 1952, and had stayed. His marxist sympathies gave him a burning interest in the exploitation of West Indian immigrants. But his bent was literature, not politics, and he joined no party. Two finely crafted novels, *A Quality of Violence* (1959) and *Escape to an Autumn Pavement* (1960), had given him a place in the first phase of postwar West Indian literature, and he became deeply involved in the evolution of Caribbean writing in London. He made it his business to know of new writers, and he and his wife Pat gave a warm welcome at their Moscow Road flat to any West Indian author living in or passing through London. Salkey used contacts made as a freelance broadcaster and editor to promote Caribbean writing on the BBC, and to encourage London publishers like Faber and Faber and André Deutsch to publish their work. Several authors, who might otherwise have remained unknown – including Wilson Harris – owe their first appearance in print to Salkey. He used his sharp eye for emerging talent to edit anthologies of West Indian short stories and verse,[29] volumes that marked out, with remarkable accuracy, the future shape of the field. He brought to CAM an encyclopaedic knowledge of Caribbean writers, and an interest in the wider region, particularly Cuba, whose fate after Fidel's revolution was always a matter of passionate debate in CAM discussions.

I was also invited to the evening of discussion that created CAM. My place in the movement was chiefly in organisation. For a while I was editor of the *Newsletter*, and CAM's liaison with the University of Kent for the two conferences held there. If I say something about myself, it is not because I was an important figure in the movement, but because my experience was representative of the issues CAM presented to the white, British academic community in general. Why did I commit myself to CAM so completely? Work as a young lecturer in a new university left me little spare time. Meetings could last deep into the night in London, leaving me to drink coffee with the newspaper reporters at the all night Black and White Restaurant in Fleet Street before driving back through the dawn to teach, bleary-eyed, my morning classes. My wife and four small children suffered even more.

I was also involved in a movement associated with black rights movements at a time of mounting racial tension. While the 1962 Commonwealth Immigration Act reduced black immigrants to second-class citizens, violent attacks on black people increased. There was much racial anger. While Enoch Powell inflamed white reactionaries, black radicals were roused by the speeches of Malcolm X and the Black Power Movement in the United States. In the summer of 1967 the charismatic Stokely Carmichael (Kwame Ture) visited England. John La Rose organised a meeting for black London activists to meet him, and Brathwaite was among the CAM members impressed when at a speech at the Round House, Carmichael called for worldwide black solidarity.[30] A strong presence at CAM meetings was Franz Fanon's *The Wretched of the Earth* which, backed by Fanon's experience of the bloody Algerian war of liberation, asserted that only violence could shake off the psychic legacy of colonialism. At black activist centres like the West Indian Students Union, I was treated with an extraordinary courtesy that my black counterpart would certainly not have met with on the other side of the racial divide. Nevertheless, as a lone white Englishman with a university accent, I could not find them comfortable places. Most of my white colleagues kept well back from the battle lines.

I remained there, convinced that the lines of dialogue needed to be kept open, and passionately believing in the importance of CAM's work. But how far in fact could I truly identify with a Caribbean movement? My interest in West Indian literature, I realise now, was heightened by my own sense of cultural displacement. This originated partly in a South African childhood where, shuttled between boarding school and mission station, I was alternately bullied by my white and black peers. Michael Gilkes has identified the angst that featured often in the first wave of West Indian writing in English as a 'cultural schizophrenia'[31] created by competing racial and cultural identities in the Caribbean. When I read of Guyana's Edgar Mittelholzer, suicidal at being born a 'swarthy' boy in a light-skinned family, or the conflicting African and European identities of Lionel/Lobo Froad in Denis Williams's *Other Leopards* (1963), I thought I felt a twinge of recognition. But this was misleading. Brathwaite's thinking in CAM was not concerned with 'cultural schizophrenia'. He believed that the Caribbean peoples should go beyond the divisions of history in order to see clearly the situation that existed in the present, to open the way to a creative culture that was, paradoxically, both 'torn and new'.[32]

There was, too, the continuing CAM preoccupation with finding a true Caribbean idiom, whether in art, music or language. Even after my three years in Jamaica, armed with a glossary, I still had difficulties with Kingston patois. But comprehension was not the main problem. As John Figueroa once demonstrated with tape recordings, Caribbean speech was a local affair in which Barbadian speech could be unintelligible to a Trinidadian.[33] Moreover, Samuel Selvon in his short stories had brilliantly demonstrated that it was possible to write speech that was both Caribbean and universally comprehensible, even to English readers. But the difficulty was that I had not been brought up with Caribbean language in my bones.

This landed me in controversy when the book of critical essays *The Islands in Between* finally appeared, a year after Brathwaite's *Rights of Passage* had changed the literary landscape in which they had been written. In my introduction I had stressed the importance of Caribbean language, and made it obvious, as I thought, that West Indian writers had to use their own idiom. I added, rather clumsily, that 'for all its flexibility, its unique rightness for certain experiences, dialect is not precise or subtle enough to express all the complex fate of being a West Indian'.[34] In using the term 'dialect' there I had in mind particularly Louise Bennett's performance poetry, spoken in the persona of an ebullient Jamaican village woman, 'Miss Lou'. Bennett herself spoke of using 'dialect', and when her collection *Jamaican Labrish* (1966) was published, it was subtitled 'Jamaica Dialect Poems'.[35] Bennett's brilliant verse was instrumental in helping popular West Indian speech become accepted in Jamaican literary circles. I knew this. But I also had an eye on the work of writers like Wilson Harris and Derek Walcott who had a fine ear for Caribbean speech, but had incorporated the popular into other literary forms. Good as it was, I was saying, not all West Indian writing had to be like Louise Bennett's. But Brathwaite was furious. He saw that I wrote out of my English education, believing I could have little conception of a society where for generations of school children 'dialect' had been scorned as 'nigger speech', forbidden under threat of the cane. For Brathwaite, 'dialect' was a colonial term that had been used to break the culture of a subjugated people – hence, in part, his determination to create new concepts and think in terms of the people's 'nation-language'. By referring to Caribbean speech as 'dialect' I showed that I remained an English academic who could not see the profound resources of the vernacular speech of the Caribbean.

*The Islands in Between* was a slim volume, but it was the first book of criticism on West Indian writing in English, and appeared at the moment when radical Caribbean critics were looking for a crusty piece of colonial writing to get their teeth into. The Jamaican writer Sylvia Wynter was not directly involved with CAM, but her scathing critique of my introduction to *Islands* in the *Jamaica Journal* became anthologised as marking a new phase in Caribbean criticism, and became part of CAM debates.[36] I had written of the need for a sympathetic understanding of the many cultural elements in the complex Caribbean region. This in itself was I thought obvious. But for Wynter, I was an English critic and, in appearing to strike a balance between different cultures from a 'reasonable' point of view, I was attempting to 'sketch the history of the Caribbean from an Archimedian point outside the historical process'. My analysis, 'mediated to [my] bones by the colonial system, by the colonial myth', was irrelevant to the actual Caribbean.[37] Reading Wynter's critique, I was still left believing what I had written was broadly right, but looking back at the political context in which I had written, I can now understand her hostility.

For Brathwaite, too, my position presented problems of cultural ontology.[38] My search for a reasonable balance between the forces of history assumed a hidden centre, not so much outside the cultural framework, but within my European background. Western civilisation had been imposed on the Caribbean a eurocentric perspective in which Africa, its history and culture, was passive and subordinate. But Africa and its civilisations were neither passive nor subordinate. Moreover, the great majority of Caribbean peoples had originated there. For them, the centre was Africa, not Europe. Once the African centre had been recognised, the significance of Caribbean culture, its customs, rituals, art, music, folklore, language and above all, its religion, took on their true meaning.[39]

Brathwaite's concern with the continuation of colonised attitudes in the Caribbean was incisively reinforced in the paper, 'The socio-cultural framework of the Caribbean', that Elsa Goveia, Professor of History at the University of Jamaica in Mona, read at the 1967 CAM Conference. Reprinted in the CAM *Newsletter*, and later in *Savacou*,[40] it stood with Brathwaite's *Rights of Passage* as a beacon for the movement. Ranging from language to religion and other aspects of Caribbean society, Goveia described a region sharply divided between a minority hegemony, imposed from Europe and North America, and the subordinate majority of its peoples. Democracy with 'one man one vote' had given the black peoples the opportunity to take over responsible power. But the deeply ingrained colonial mentality had preserved a system in which a wealthy and usually light-skinned minority still governed the predominantly poor and dark-skinned masses. Moreover, the integration and stability of the region was based on this mutual acceptance of a social inequality based on wealth and colour. Goveia continued:

> Now this is the framework within which Caribbean artists have to operate, and it seems to me that they have a vested interest in ensuring that the system of race and of wealth classification in the West Indies should be abandoned at the earliest possible time. I am not suggesting that the writers need to be politicians though I believe that some of them are. But the fact is that unless the writer throws his weight on the side of the democratisation of West Indian society he is unlikely ever to be able to find a way of living in his own society.[41]

[ 221 ]

Writers and artists in the Caribbean and the Guyanas between the 1930s and 1960s had already played a part in emancipating their societies from old rankings of inferiority and superiority. They had written without prejudice about the deprived peoples of the region, destroying myths of race, and validating the language of the people. 'The artist cannot afford to isolate himself from the question of how the future is to be formed and what its content is to be.'[42]

CAM members found Goveia's address, like Brathwaite's privileging of folk culture, hugely liberating. The colonial system had marginalised the Caribbean popular arts as the inferior entertainment of the ignorant: now they took centre stage as having preserved the cultural identity that slavery and its aftermath had tried to suppress. The question of language was central. When I gave a dismal paper to the first CAM Conference, looking at West Indian poetry through the eye of an English academic, it met with short shrift from an audience that included C. L. R. James, Brathwaite and Gordon Rohlehr.[43] In comments which were later expanded in an address printed in *Savacou*,[44] Rohlehr identified a natural poetic idiom belonging to Trinidad speech within the songs of the Trinidad calypsonian Mighty Sparrow.

> There is a definite speaking voice behind the lyrics. One doesn't feel that language is being coerced into the rigidity of form, but the language is alive and fluid as it plays against the necessary strictness of the music … It seems to me that there is in the spoken language of Trinidad a potential for rhythmic organisation, which our poets have not yet discovered or if they have, have not yet exploited … I feel that just as the calypsonian is able to use speech rhythms in his songs, the poet, working from the opposite direction, may be able to use calypso rhythms in his verse, *and still preserve the* sense of being true to the speaking voice.[45]

If Trinidadians focused on carnival and calypso, Aubrey Williams, from Guyana, was concerned with the aesthetic potential contained within his country's heartland. Williams was a hugely talented painter never given his due by the British art establishment. His art recognised the limitations of high realism. Yet in an address reprinted in *Savacou*, Williams strenuously rejected the idea that his non-figurative painting was in any way 'abstract', declaring 'I am not very sure that I understand the meaning of the word'.[46] If his art appeared non-representational, it was because certain mental preconceptions blinded Western viewers. What Williams painted was a reality, located in native Guyanese traditions, shared by artists and the Guyanese villagers, who journeyed by dray cart to Georgetown to see his paintings.

> Ours is a beautiful landscape; unbelievably beautiful in some cases; but, as compared with the ordered landscape in the countries that have been

over-lived in, bizarre, unreal, incongruous. It is a very strong landscape, and the primitive art that came out of this landscape remains unique. We should be proud of our non-configuration. We should be proud of the essences of human existence that the people from that neck of the woods have produced.[47]

Aubrey Williams was an enthusiastic and effective supporter of CAM. Yet he believed that Brathwaite's search for an African cultural perspective could be as exclusive as a European one. Rather than deny any strand in the region's historical heritage Williams looked for ways to accept and transcend it. This approach had been developed by Wilson Harris, who also came from Guyana. Harris's revolutionary views were circulated before the inception of CAM in a 1965 pamphlet, *Tradition and the West Indian Novel.* Harris's essay, republished by La Rose as one of the first New Beacon titles, formed an important background to CAM's discussions and was reinforced by his impressive address to the second CAM conference.[48] Harris saw that its history gave the Caribbean region a unique complexity. Yet, paradoxically, as a cultural area it was extraordinarily open, for its fragmentation and natural environment had kept it free from the monolithic constraints of the Old World. Where traditional societies were imprisoned in predictive structures of identity and values, the Caribbean offered unique possibilities for imaginative transcendence.

> What in my view is remarkable about the West Indian in depth is a sense of subtle links, the series of subtle and nebulous links, which are latent within him, the latent ground of old and new personalities. This is a very difficult view to hold, I grant, because it is not a view which consolidates, which invests in any way in the consolidation of popular character. Rather it seeks to visualise the *fulfilment* of character. Something which is more extraordinary than one can easily imagine.[49]

If Brathwaite provided the driving force of CAM, Harris expressed its unifying concerns, aspirations defined in the introduction James wrote to Harris's 1965 essay:

> [West Indian] identity conceals rather or rather constricts an enormous potentiality. We have a history, we don't know it, and we will never know it until we respect ourselves, and relate our present, our past and out future. On this interrelation, Harris is very strong and very clear.[50]

As a Caribbean movement, CAM's discussions revealed the region's diversity as much they did as its coherence. As we have seen, Jamaicans tended to focus on folk language and culture, Trinidadians on carnival and calypso, while Guyanese like Harris and Williams contemplated the psychic spaces of the South American interior. There were also omissions. There was little about the East Indians of the Caribbean, although it was a personal refusal to be part of a Caribbean 'movement', rather than Indian ethnicity, that kept V. S. Naipaul and Sam Selvon out of CAM. Similarly those representing the light-skinned Caribbean creoles, including John Hearne,[51] and – as is discussed elsewhere in this volume, Jean Rhys[52] – tended to be excluded. The earlier CAM discussions reflected a male dominance until in 1970 Merle Hodge's *Crick-Crack Monkey* opened a flood of women's writing. CAM responded in 1977 with a special women's issue of *Savacou*, which began by acknowledging the pioneering achievement of Una Marson.[53]

Kenneth Ramchand once protested[54] that CAM was a contradiction, a movement devoted to Caribbean roots, but located in London. For CAM's formative years, in the late 1960s, this was largely true. Until CAM in effect moved with Brathwaite to Jamaica, and published original Caribbean writing in *Savacou*, writers and artists based in the West Indies including Derek Walcott, Mervyn Morris, Eric Roach, Denis Scott and Martin Carter, featured little in CAM's debates. Nevertheless CAM's discussions in London were moving in parallel with cultural developments in the Caribbean. Carifesta, the first Pan-Caribbean Festival of the Arts, was conceived independently of CAM. Yet Brathwaite and other CAM members took an active part in the triumphant Festival when it was held in Guyana in 1972. As a celebration of the region's cultural creativity, Carifesta can be seen as CAM's fragmented vision coming together in the Caribbean. This was followed by the following cultural festivals, whose importance went largely unnoticed in Britain, held in Jamaica (1976), Cuba (1979), Barbados (1981) and Trinidad (1992). CAM members, and Brathwaite in particular, also became associated with the highly influential activities of the Casa de las Américas in Cuba.

In Britain CAM has had a lasting impact. The New Beacon Books enterprise of John La Rose and Sarah White, closely linked to CAM, marked the beginning of independent Caribbean publishing and bookselling in Britain, and its success prompted Bogle L'Ouverture, Race Today Publications, and other ventures in community publishing. Besides reprinting important texts that otherwise would have remained in obscurity, New Beacon went on to publish works specifically for Caribbean readers such as Erna Brodber's *Jane and Louisa will Soon Come Home* (1980). From 1982, New Beacon organised the annual International Book Fair of Radical and Third World Books in London with its lectures and public readings. CAM's activities alerted British publishers to the growing market for Third World texts. James Currey, who was editing Heinemann's African Writers Series, attended the first CAM Conference, and his experience there encouraged him to found a Caribbean Writers Series. Anne Walmsley of Longmans, who became a keen supporter and the chronicler of CAM, in 1968 brought out her fine anthology of Caribbean verse for schools, *The Sun's Eye*.

CAM drew in interested teachers and educational publishers, becoming a pervasive influence on schools and universities. Its work encouraged the teaching of Caribbean literature at the universities of Sussex and at Kent; at Kent in 1975 the Faculty of Humanities launched the world's first honours degree in English with African and Caribbean Studies. This included a course entirely devoted to Caribbean writing. At a subsequent conference at Kent in 1978, past CAM members founded the Association of Teachers in Caribbean and African Literatures (soon extended to include Asian material). ATCAL published booklets on Third World literatures for schoolteachers, lobbied for such texts to be accepted by British Schools Examination Boards, and published the journal *Wasafiri*, which still continues. In the Caribbean, Kenneth Ramchand and Gordon Rohlehr, both CAM activists, introduced Caribbean literature into the UWI syllabuses at Mona and St Augustine, Trinidad, and encouraged its teaching in local secondary schools. In Kenya, Ngugi's experience of CAM was translated into the indigenisation of literature teaching at the University of Nairobi.

CAM's influence was also felt in the visual arts. Urged on by Brathwaite, it promoted exhibitions of Caribbean visual arts. The first was of 'New art and sculpture', hung in June 1967 with the blessing of Joan Littlewood at the Theatre Royal, Stratford East. CAM promoted some eleven exhibitions, culminating in shows at the House of Commons and at the Commonwealth Institute.[55] Besides presenting work by recognised artists like Aubrey Williams and Ronald Moody, these included relative newcomers like Errol Lloyd, Karl Craig and Althea McNeish. CAM engagement with theatre involved Evan Jones, a founder member, Marina Maxwell, Lloyd Reckord, Pearl Connor, Marina Maxwell and Ram John Holder in its discussions. But its most pervasive influence will remain hidden, the encouragement it gave to young artists, writers, performers and teachers. CAM meetings offered opportunities to meet Caribbean personalities. John La Rose at New Beacon Books gave advice and opened fresh fields of reading. In different ways, CAM touched the lives of a whole generation of young talent, including James Berry, Faustin Charles, Sebastian Clarke (Amon Saba Sekaana) and, most importantly, Linton Kwesi Johnson.

What did CAM have to offer a white English academic? Speaking for myself, to some CAM members I was always to be in some ways an outsider, separated by history, race, language and my Oxford education. Yet also, and often to the same people, I was also an 'insider', sharing common humanistic concerns, imaginative insights, and a belief in the central importance of the creative arts. I learnt much about Caribbean culture, and perhaps even more about European civilisation and my place within it – an uncomfortable knowledge. In the end, however, I gained something other than simple understanding of either the Caribbean or Britain. This essay began with a quotation from C. L. R. James's CAM address. Let another from the same paper close it.

It is when you are outside, but can take part as a member, that you see differently from the ways that they see, and you are able to write independently.[56]

## Notes

1  C. L. R. James, 'Discovering literature in Trinidad: the nineteen-thirties', *Savacou*, 2 (1970), pp. 54–5.
2  Edward Brathwaite, 'Timehri', *Savacou*, 2 (1970), p. 37.
3  Anne Walmsley, *The Caribbean Artists Movement 1966–1972* (London and Port of Spain: New Beacon Books, 1992).
4  See Erna Brodber, 'Fiction in the scientific procedure', in Selwyn R. Cudjoe (ed.), *Caribbean Women Writers* (Wellesley, Mass: Calaloux Publications, 1990), pp. 164–8. Brodber used her sociological research to write her innovative novels, *Jane and Louisa Will Soon come Home* (1980) and *Myal* (1988).
5  See Frederic G. Cassidy, *Jamaica Talk* (London: Macmillan, 1961).
6  On Bill Carr, see Matthew Carr, *My Father's House* (London: Hamish Hamilton, 1998).
7  George Lamming, *The Pleasures of Exile* (London: Michael Joseph, 1960), p. 19.
8  Louis James, 'Commonwealth literature studies, where do we stand?', *Caribbean Quarterly*, 11:3 & 4 (1965), p. 72. In 1970 the ACLALS triennial Conference was held at Mona; on this occasion, Brathwaite challenged the concept of Caribbean writing as part of Commonwealth studies.
9  The basis of Brathwaite's thesis, later published as *The Development of Creole Society in Jamaica* (Oxford: Clarendon University Press, 1971).
10  John La Rose, 'Kamau Brathwaite: a heartfelt memoir', in Timothy J. Reiss (ed.), *For the Geography of a Soul* (Trenton, NJ and Asmara, Eritrea: Africa World Press, 2001), p. 88.
11  See Walmsley, *Caribbean Artists Movement*, pp. 261–6.
12  *Savacou*, 9/10 (1974). My thanks to Ian Diefenthaller for this point.
13  Major sources of information on Kamau Brathwaite's life and work include: Stewart Brown (ed.), *The Art of Kamau Brathwaite* (Bridgend: Seren Books, 1955); Djelal Kadir (ed.), *World Literature Today*, 68.4, special issue on Brathwaite (1994); Kamau Brathwaite, *Barabajan Poems* (New York and Mona: Savacou North, 1994); Reiss, *Geography of a Soul*, contains a full bibliography.
14  Gordon Rohlehr, *Pathfinder* (Tunapuna, Trinidad: privately published, 1981), p. 5; Brathwaite, *Barabajan Poems*, pp. 35–7.
15  Brathwaite, 'Timehri', p. 37.
16  Brathwaite, 'Timehri', p. 71.
17  Kamau Brathwaite, *The Zea Mexican Diary* (Madison: University of Wisconsin Press, 1993), p. 191.
18  Brathwaite, *Barabajan Poems*, pp. 69–70.
19  Brathwaite, 'Timehri', p. 37.
20  See Bridget Jones, '"The unity is submarine": aspects of a Pan-Caribbean consciousness in the work of Kamau Brathwaite', in Brown, *Brathwaite*, pp. 86–100.
21  Brathwaite, *Barabajan Poems*, pp. 236–40.
22  Brathwaite's lecture 'Jazz and West Indian Novel' was from the essays published in *Bim*, 11:44 (1967); 12:45 (1967); 12:46 (1968); and republished in Kamau Brathwaite,

    *Roots* (Havana: Ediciones Casa de las Américas, 1993; and reprinted Ann Arbor: University of Michigan Press, 1993). I quote from the Ann Arbor edition.

23  Brathwaite, *Roots*, p. 72.

24  Brathwaite, *Roots*, p. 58.

25  Brathwaite, *Roots*, p. 65.

26  Kamau Brathwaite, *Rights of Passage* (London: Oxford University Press, 1967), p. 3.

27  Roxy Harris and Sarah White (eds), *Foundations of a Movement. A Tribute to John La Rose* (London: John La Rose Tribute Committee, 1991) assembles an impressive range of contributors witnessing to the many aspects of La Rose's life and work.

28  See Raymondo Quevedo, *Atilla's Kaiso: a short history of Trinidad calypso* (St Augustine, Trinidad: University of the West Indies, 1983).

29  Andrew Salkey (ed.), *West Indian Stories* (London: Faber, 1960); Salkey, *Stories from the Caribbean* (London: Elek, 1965); Salkey, *Breaklight* (London: Hamish Hamilton, 1971).

30  Walmsley, *Caribbean Artists Movement*, pp. 91–3.

31  Michael Gilkes, *Wilson Harris and the Caribbean Novel* (London: Longman Caribbean, 1975).

32  Edward Brathwaite, *Islands* (London: Oxford University Press, 1979), p. 113. For Brathwaite's rejection of 'cultural schizophrenia' see Glyne A. Griffith, 'Kamau Brathwaite as cultural critic', in Brown, *Brathwaite*, pp. 75–85.

33  A paper given to the ACALAS Conference in Jamaica, 1970. It was not, I think, ever published.

34  Louis James, *The Islands in Between* (London: Oxford University Press, 1968), p. 23.

35  'Yoh gwine kill dialect!' – see Louise Bennett, 'Ban's o' Killing', in her *Jamaica Labrish* (Kingston: Sangster's Book Stores, 1966), pp. 218–19.

36  Sylvia Wynter, 'Reflections on West Indian criticism', *Jamaica Journal* (1968), pp. 23–32, reprinted in John Hearne (ed.), *Carifesta Forum* (Jamaica: Carifesta 76, 1976), pp. 129–38; and Edward Baugh (ed.), *Critics on Caribbean Literature* (London: Allen and Unwin, 1978), pp. 19–23.

37  Wynter, 'Reflections', in *Carifesta Forum*, pp. 134–5.

38  Edward Brathwaite, 'Caribbean critics', *New World Quarterly*, 5:1 & 2 (1969), pp. 264–72.

39  See Brathwaite, 'The African presence in Caribbean literature', in *Roots*, pp. 190–258.

40  Elsa Goveia, 'The social framework', *Savacou*, 2 (1970), pp. 7–15.

41  Goveia, 'Social framework', p. 13.

42  Goveia, 'Social framework', p. 14.

43  My talk was later printed, heavily revised, as 'Caribbean poetry in English: some problems', in *Savacou*, 2 (1970), pp. 78–86.

44  See CAM *Newsletter*, nos 2–4; Gordon Rohlehr, 'Sparrow and the language of Calypso', *Savacou*, 2 (1970), p. 99; and Rohlehr, *Calypso and Society in Pre-Independence Trinidad* (Tunapuna: privately printed, 1990).

45  Rohlehr, 'Sparrow', p. 99.

46  Aubrey Williams, 'The artist in the Caribbean', *Savacou*, 2 (1970), pp. 16–18.

47  Williams, 'The artist', p. 17.

48  Wilson Harris, with an introduction by C. L. R. James, *Tradition and the West Indian Novel* (London: West Indian Students Union, 1965); and Harris, *Tradition, the Writer and Society* (London and Port of Spain: New Beacon Books, 1967).

49  Harris, *Tradition and the West Indian Novel*, p. 7.

50  Harris, *Tradition and the West Indian Novel*, p. 5.

51  Hearne was involved in one stormy CAM meeting. See Walmsley, *Caribbean Artists Movement*, pp. 78–9.

52  See Helen Carr's chapter in this volume.

53  Special women's issue: *Savacou*, 13 (1977).

54  Walmsley, *Caribbean Artists Movement*, pp. 53–4.

55  These are listed in Walmsley, *Caribbean Artists Movement*, pp. 326–7.

56  James, 'Discovering literature', p. 60.

# CHAPTER ELEVEN

# V. S. Naipaul

## Sue Thomas

Vidiadhur Surajprasad Naipaul's narratives of arrival in England return repeatedly to his father Seepersad's nurturing of his artistic ambition in Trinidad, and his early prescience that the 'idea of the writing vocation' given him by a colonial acculturation could be realised and practised in England.[1] In making himself a writer,[2] he has abjured being categorised as West Indian, most famously in withdrawing the manuscript of *Guerillas* (1975) from publisher Secker and Warburg after being described in a catalogue as 'the West Indian novelist'.[3] His career as a determinedly 'extraregional' writer of fiction, travel books and memoir[4] has been both stellar and controversial. In 1990 he was awarded Trinidad's Trinity Cross and knighted by British monarch Elizabeth II. The biographical note in his latest novel *Half a Life* (2001) rather acerbically states that '[h]e has won every major literary award bar the Nobel'.[5] Cited by the Swedish Academy as a 'British writer, born in Trinidad', he finally did win the Nobel Prize for Literature in 2001 'for having united perceptive narrative and incorruptible scrutiny in works that compel us to see the presence of suppressed histories ... Naipaul is Conrad's heir as the annalist of the destinies of empires in the moral sense: what they do to human beings. His authority as a narrator is grounded in the memory of what others have forgotten, the history of the vanquished'.[6] Naipaul's work is praised here as being faithful to history and a historical constituency of the oppressed, his interpretation of them being motivated by moral rigour and truth, rather than by cultural and artistic values which have ideological and political groundings. Given the controversies generated by his writing and his public persona the claim is extraordinary. His stances on and representations of the politics of decolonisation are frequently denounced as reactionary. Edward Said, for instance, has decried Naipaul as 'immoral', a pedlar of 'the tritest, the cheapest and the easiest of colonial mythologies about wogs and darkies' and comforting imperialist theses concerning the 'self-inflicted wounds' of the colonised.[7] The relation of Naipaul and his work to the post-imperial encounter in Britain is, however, more complicated than such denunciations suggest. Exacting anxieties have haunted his witness of his journey from the 'exotic' periphery to the centre of English culture through the practice of a vocation he idealises and conceptualises with such rigid conservatism.

## Negotiating the periphery

In 1958, on the eve of the Notting Hill riots, Naipaul saw himself as an 'exotic writer', 'liv[ing] in England and depend[ing] on an English audience'.[8] Born in Chaguanas in 1932, Naipaul had arrived in England in 1950 to study English at Oxford University, after a long period in Port of Spain 'spent in a blind, driven kind of colonial studying' to win his scholarship.[9] Explaining his decision not to return to Trinidad to his mother Droapati in 1954, he writes: 'The place is too small, the values are all wrong, and the people are petty ... This country [England] is hot with racial prejudices, and I certainly don't wish to stay here.'[10] He was then in the process of identifying his early subject matter: social comedies set in Trinidad, focusing on local 'characters', 'easy material for the writer'.[11] This would be the metier of his first four books of fiction, including his highly acclaimed *A House for Mr Biswas* (1961), the protagonist of which is based loosely on his beloved father. Coming from the 'enclosed life' of an extended rural Indo-Trinidadian family, 'the disintegrating world of a remembered India', Naipaul 'never ceased to feel a stranger' in Port of Spain after his family's move there. His sense of living on the periphery of a dominant black colonial culture in Port of Spain and later of a dominant white English culture is figured as inhabiting a 'kind of limbo', as an existential homelessness in relation to elusive community.[12] In this English 'limbo' 'he suffered periods of deep depression and anxiety, even once attempting to gas himself'.[13] 'I saw people of other groups from the outside; school friendships were left behind at school or in the street. I had no proper understanding of where I was, and really never had the time to find out', he writes of Port of Spain.[14] Black characters, for instance, Man-man or B. Wordsworth in *Miguel Street* (1959), are part of the theatricality of communal street life.[15]

To achieve mass appeal with an English audience as a regional West Indian writer, Naipaul suggests in 1958, he would need to supplement writing skill with a few thematic and structural 'devices': 'Sex'; writing a narrative around 'an English or American character' in a Caribbean setting; and 'Race'. His horror at being categorised as the 'West Indian' author of *Guerillas* might be related to the fact that it does have these stock narrative motors of the popular fiction he so despises, including a 'quick-to-strip' female protagonist. While anathematising all of these mechanisms, Naipaul deals with 'Race' in most detail. He finds 'the race issue is too complicated to be dealt with at best-seller, black-and-white level', especially after his time in England. He worries that such 'stories of oppression and humiliation' with their mandatory 'clear oppressors and clear oppressed' may pander to an audience's 'sadistic pleasure', its 'vicarious sense of power'. He usefully raises the question whether a British tabloid audience of the 1950s would necessarily identify with the victim rather than the perpetrator of racial discrimination. His own point of identification is problematic, he states, because of his Indian heritage, his origins in 'an easy-going multi-racial society', and his awareness that racialised conflict can also take the form of black-on-black violence as in the persecution of Tamil people in the then Ceylon.[16]

In *The Enigma of Arrival* (1987), the narrator of which Naipaul acknowledges to be an autobiographical figure,[17] he points to a more primal character formation which has shaped his handling of conflict: 'The fear of extinction which I had developed as a child had partly to do with this: the fear of being swallowed up or extinguished by the simplicity of one side or the other, my side or the side that wasn't mine'.[18] Naipaul's use of evolutionary discourse, here, is telling: it implies a belief that he can make himself fitter in relation to this threat by transcending clear-cut loyalties and causes. Naipaul's unwillingness to hone his sense of imperialism as an analytic category is related, he suggests in 1998, to his resistance to simplifications: he 'grew up with this idea that it was important to look inwards and not always define an external enemy … We must examine ourselves, examine our own weaknesses'.[19]

'Tell me who to kill' in *In a Free State* (1971) might be read as a story *à thèse* about Naipaul's sense of the complicatedness of the 'race issue' in England of the 1950s and 1960s. The unnamed first-person narrator of the story, a Hindu from a West Indian island, attends the wedding of his brother Dayo and a white woman. He has lived in England for eight years. Three years before the wedding he has apparently had a breakdown and responded to racist bullying by 'young English louts' in his roti-and-curry shop,[20] possibly killing one or some of them. He attends the wedding with a white friend Frank, a protector figure. Frank wants always to draw the narrator out about the racial discrimination he has experienced from white people, reducing his experience of England to a series of insults culminating in the breakdown, and his humanity to the fact of racialised difference, 'darkness'.[21] For Frank the narrator's life before his arrival in England is a *tabula rasa*; the narrator's enemy is external. The narrator, reflecting on his life, realises that Frank's positioning of him as a 'weak' victim[22] allows him the pleasure and strength of the homoerotically charged protector role. For Frank the role is the site of his spiritual war against English racism.

The narrator's description of himself as having 'work[ed] like a man in blinkers' in England to support his brother and draw strength from his savings has a wider application to his experience. He has character-istically repressed his anger and humiliation at discrimination, because to focus on this would be 'opening up manholes for' him 'to fall in'.[23] The metaphor implies castration anxiety. His breakdown has also been scripted by a series of humiliations dating back to the extended family dynamics of his childhood in the West Indies, the protector role he has assumed in relation to his brother (and his brother's abuse of it), a fet-ishisation of the prospect of Dayo's move via education into a profes-sional class, growing out of touch with his own human needs while, 'donkey'-like, working two jobs,[24] a poor business decision in opening the shop, and anxieties around changed financial status. It illustrates in part Naipaul's more general proposition that 'the colonial setting ... reduces people to work machines, encourages them to compete as such, strips them of personality'.[25] England becomes for the narrator a space of decay and death, and he can only read Dayo's marriage to a white woman as a social death. Hollywood B-movies consumed while growing up in the West Indies are a crucial reference point for the narrator. In *The Middle Passage* Naipaul associates this kind of 'second-rate' cine-matic influence with 'minds' that 'are rigidly closed'; this is, for him, a critical sign of 'modernity' in Trinidad.[26] A template drawn from a scene in Alfred Hitchcock's film *Rope* (1948) continues to function for the nar-rator as a screen memory for the scene of his violence in his shop.

Naipaul's authorial voice in 'Tell me who to kill' is compassionate towards the narrator and his dilemma that he cannot identify a clear-cut enemy responsible for his despair; the sympathy is also grounded in a protective rescue of the narrator from Frank's kind of simplicities. The narrator's stylised patois enriches his humanity; elsewhere, as in *The Middle Passage* and *Guerillas*, Naipaul's citation of ungrammati-cal English and patois serves a mocking function.

In the early stages of his career Naipaul is resistant to his sense of how the 'West Indian writer' is recognised in Britain and restrictive expectations of his or her work and approaches to sex, the exotic, and race relations. He refuses to commodify his writing to meet these expectations, grounded as they are in porno-tropic fantasies of the colo-nial and ex-colonial world as a site on which 'forbidden sexual desires and fears' might be projected,[27] and, as he strives to demonstrate, in reductive understandings of the complexity of race relations and of the humanity of the victims of racism.

[ 231 ]

## Extraregional English subjects

In *Reading & Writing* (2000) Naipaul acknowledges that in his early years he had not found the 'imaginative key', what he calls elsewhere the 'human experience, the literary experience'[28] to comprehend fully 'English and European fiction'.[29] In 'London' he writes that he knew 'little about England', the intricacies of life there being kept 'behind closed doors'. 'I have met many people but I know them only in official attitudes – the drink, the interview, the meal. I have a few friends. But this gives me only a superficial knowledge of the country and in order to write fiction it is necessary to know so much: we are not all brothers under the skin.' The public/private dichotomy in English culture, and in London specifically, operates as a barrier to 'communal pleasures' and interaction, a 'barrier of self-consciousness'. This threatens 'sterility' for him.[30] His sense of vulnerability is perhaps heightened by his growing sense that he could not 'make a living' as a writer 'by being regional'.[31] In *The Enigma of Arrival* the narrator notes with some chagrin that he had in the 1950s passed up an important theme, the 'flotsam of Europe' in London boarding houses after the war, 'the beginning of that great movement of peoples that was to take place in the second half of the twentieth century ... These people's principal possessions were their stories, and their stories spilled easily out of them. But I noted nothing down. I asked no questions. I took them all for granted, looked beyond them'.[32]

'Fiction works best in a confined moral and cultural area, where the rules are generally known; and in that confined area it deals best with things – emotions, impulses, moral anxieties – that would be unseizable or incomplete in other literary forms', Naipaul insists.[33] He would return in his fiction set in England or containing sojourns in England on the parts of his protagonists to such confined areas: the communal intimacies and shifting loyalties of boarding houses; England in the late 1940s and 1950s; little Englandism; the making of the black prophet in the 1960s and 1970s; the constrained lives of male immigrants whose search for community, acceptance and masculine reassurance resolves itself illusively and elusively into sex; the country manor and cottage; and the vocation of writing.

The first of Naipaul's novels with an English setting and English characters is *Mr Stone and the Knights Companion* (1964), usually regarded as his 'attempt to escape from being regarded as a regional writer'.[34] Naipaul develops a searching critique of little Englandism. The librarian protagonist Mr Stone is the epitome of a little Englandism nearing the end of its working life, and reflecting anxiously on its achievements. His anxieties are shaped by pressures on his everyday white masculinity. Alison Light argues that inter-war little Englandism was a 'conservative modernity', characterised by 'a move away from formerly heroic and officially masculine public rhetorics of national destiny and from a dynamic and missionary view of the Victorian and Edwardian middle classes in "Great Britain" to an Englishness at once less imperial and more inward-looking, more domestic and more private'. It valued 'the quiet life', the 'known and the familiar', the 'nice, decent'.[35] At the opening of the novel Mr Stone's domestic territorialism, and his familiar comfort with 'slow decay' and 'bulky nineteen-thirty furniture', is affronted by the presence of a black tomcat in his garden and home. Mr Stone is fixated on traces of its 'obscene scuttlings and dredgings and buryings'.[36] Business involving the cat, associated with newcomers to the neighbourhood, may be read as a sign of bachelor Mr Stone's sexual anxiety as he approaches retirement age. It might also, however, be read as a sign of his anxiety about the permissive encroachment of the foreign in his corner of England.

He seeks to manage his sexual anxiety through a prospect of white regeneration, which is, however, short-lived. He marries Margaret Springer, when, symbolically, a tree in view of his back window has 'swollen' buds and 'in sunshine were like points of white'. Margaret introduces a 'new and alien mustiness' into his home and a tigerskin, seemingly a family heirloom, which exacerbate his sense of masculine inadequacy.[37] 'The "odor di femina" becomes odious, nauseous', Michèle Montrelay argues, 'because it threatens to undo the achievements of repression and sublimation, threatens to return the subject to the powerlessness, intensity and anxiety of an immediate, unmediated connection with the body of the mother.'[38] The tigerskin is a trophy of imperial masculinity, signalled in the photograph of an 'English cavalry officer', with 'one hand caressing a rifle laid neatly across his thighs', and a 'highly polished boot' on the chest of a dead tiger. In the background are 'three sorrowful, top-heavily turbanned Indians, beaters or bearers or whatever they were'.[39]

On a belated honeymoon in Cornwall Mr Stone experiences a shattering and emasculating moment of 'white void',[40] 'enveloped' in smoke which robbed him and Margaret 'of earth and reality', him of 'judgment, of the will to act'.[41] The experience prompts him to develop a welfare scheme for retired employees of his company Excal which will rescue them from an effeminising passivity in retirement and the unremitting 'confinement of family relationships', that is, by women.[42] While in the days of the Knights Companion scheme he does accommodate himself to the cat's presence in the neighbourhood and its symbolic promise of spring, it is as observer, a distance which comes to signify to him 'his emptiness and the darkness to come'.[43]

[ 233 ]

Stone's foil is the younger Mr Whymper, the Public Relations Officer at Excal, who represents the more aggressive and dynamic masculinity of late 1950s and early 1960s British consumer capitalism. The medieval trappings Whymper gives Stone's welfare scheme mask its efficacy as a contemporary vehicle for marketing and for the enmeshing of Whymper's masculine individualism with consumer capitalism.[44] Whymper is more overtly and casually xenophobic, racist and misogynistic than Stone. In general non-white people in England register in Stone's consciousness as faces in crowds in localised parts of London (Earl's Court, the streets around the city office, Brixton) and as objects of racist address, for example, by street campaigners for the British National Party. Whymper's sexual adventurousness marks him as a member of a newer permissive generation. His name implies, through allusion to T. S. Eliot's 'The hollow men', that his values will be 'the way the world ends'.[45]

Stone's illumination at the end of the novel that all is flesh, 'man's own frailty and corruptibility', and that triumph over this mocking, feminised nature lies in 'destruction' – the imposition of masculinised will on it – is undercut by his reaction to a young black cat. After exhilaratingly re-energising his sense of masculinity with this 'possibility' of triumph, he realises when his response to the presence of the cat in his home shifts from 'fear' through 'guilt into love' that he was 'no destroyer'.[46] 'Between the idea/And the reality', 'Between the potency/and the existence' falls the shadow of his desire for the 'calm' of little Englandism's 'sexual and social economies'.[47] Appeasing this desire has become habitual.

Becoming 'extraregional' for Naipaul has entailed not just a broadening of his range of literary subjects as in *Mr Stone and the Knights Companion*; it has also involved a more active dissociation of himself from West Indian communities in England and social and political developments within them. Winston James has highlighted the ways in which racial categorisation in Britain after 1945 operated on a black/white binary, and non-white West Indian immigrants from cultures with a more elaborate and graduated 'pigmentocracy' or shade hierarchy would find themselves interpellated as black.[48] Indo-Caribbeans would also be called black.[49] James argues that this epistemic violence has had a productive political effect in developing a pan-black consciousness that might be mobilised against the racism of the dominant culture. He draws attention, too, to a process of Pan-Caribbeanisation: the development of a sense of a regional rather than island or national identity. He attributes this, in part, to British indifference to diversity of colonial or national origins (West Indians generally being homogenised as Jamaican) and island chauvinism, as well as to community-building abroad. Naipaul is scathing about a pigmentocracy among black people which he reads as a sign of internalised racial inferiority that keeps whiteness as a desired norm: 'Pursuing the Christian-Hellenic tradition, the West Indian accepted his blackness as his guilt, and divided people into the white, fusty, musty, dusty, tea, coffee, cocoa, light black, black, dark black'.[50] Naipaul has resisted the process of Pan-Caribbeanisation. 'I have nothing in common with people from Jamaica', he comments in 1968. 'Or the other islands for that matter.'[51] More pointedly he has abjured being interpellated as black (preferring the terms Indian or Asiatic).[52] This move has two historical dimensions. First, he is refusing the black/white binary of British racism that will not accommodate his West Indian Indian heritage. Kobena Mercer explains, too, that especially in the 1980s, the derogatory sign black 'was dis-articulated out of its natural-ised [racist] meaning and reference, and re-articulated into an alternative chain of signification in which it became a sign of solidarity among Asian, African and Caribbean peoples. As a sign of political rather than genetic identity, blackness was reappropriated out of one discursive system and rearticulated into another.'[53] In distancing himself from this emerging solidarity, Naipaul reclaims a genetic identity.

Naipaul also points out in 1968 that he was not part of a community of West Indian writers in London: 'We don't have anything in common, you see'. 'I used to read a lot of West Indian novels until 1956. Since then I have stopped really. This is because they have stopped feeding me. It is really hard to read books that don't feed me.'[54] This, of course, feeds his fantasy of being a self-made writer; again, as in double-edged comments like 'I have grown out of Trinidad',[55] his acerbic relation to the West Indies is represented as a sign of maturity. Naipaul tends to praise in West Indian novels what confirms his world-view and to inter-pret them through it. For instance, his assessment of Jean Rhys in 1971, important for placing her as West Indian, emphasises the senses of exile and the psychological shipwreck of 'dependence and defeat', the 'woman's half-world' of her protagonists. He commends Rhys for being 'above causes'.[56]

He responds appreciatively in her work to what is a major thematic in his own writing – the displaced colonial subject in England – handled by him in both deeply empathetic and satirical ways. The fear of ship-wreck and a sense of being adrift had been leitmotifs of *The Mimic Men* (1967). Ralph Singh's journeys from the fictive West Indian island of Isabella to London, energised at first by colonial myths of place, are jour-neys to two-dimensionality – the parts of 'the dandy, the extravagant colonial, indifferent to scholarship' and of the sexualised child to Lady Stella – which like his sexual adventures with 'anonymous flesh' take him 'deeper into emptiness'. In England he finds himself injured into feeling 'spectral, disintegrating, pointless, fluid'. [57] Naipaul reinflects aspects of this topos in *Half a Life*. Willie Chandran's journey from India to London to an unnamed African colony (recognisably Mozambique) is also a progressive movement to dependence and defeat. His anxieties centre on emasculation and inauthenticity. His 'half' life is one characterised by hiding. For example, as a child he revises European stories movingly, yet obliquely, to accuse his parents of emotional neglect and violence. Pursuing a writing career in England he manufactures fiction from European sources, and because of his skin colour and Indian name, his work is assumed to be authentically Indian.

Naipaul's decision in the 1960s to embrace an extraregional identity as a writer was produced by economic considerations, a determination in the face of interpretative difficulties to broaden his range to include stringent treatments of England and the English, and a pointed disssociation of himself from forms of racist address and racial and Pan-Caribbean solidarity. As a writer of fiction and criticism he is, though, appreciative of the personal and psychological costs of displacement and exile from community for colonial subjects in England.

## The political fray of the 1960s

Naipaul observes of himself in 1958: 'after eight years here I find I have, without effort, achieved the Buddhist ideal of non-attachment. I am never disturbed by national or international issues. I do not sign petitions. I do not vote. I do not march. And I never cease to feel that this lack of interest is all wrong. I want to be involved, to be touched even by some of the prevailing anger.'[58] In *An Area of Darkness* (1964) he attributes this to an Indian 'philosophy of despair, leading to passivity, detachment, acceptance' which had allowed him to 'withdraw completely from nationality and loyalties except to persons; it had made me content to be myself alone, my work, my name (the last two so very different from the first); it had convinced me that every man was an island, and taught me to shield all that I knew to be good and pure within myself from the corruption of causes'.[59] By the mid-1960s, however, Naipaul is 'touched' by his 'anger' at social change.

Naipaul's metaphor for social change in Trinidad and England becomes the proletariat; his well-known attack in 2000 on Tony Blair's Labour government and what he perceives to be its anti-elitist programme uses a similar metaphor of the plebeian, which perhaps carries more connotations of vulgarity.[60] He insists to Derek Walcott in 1964 that a 'sinister' process of proletarianisation has eroded structures of 'aspiration' and the animation of culture by the spirit. In Trinidad 'aspiration has been dropped ... the manners of the proletariat have infil-

trated the rest of society'. In England the rise of popular racism mani-
fested in Conservative Peter Griffiths's electoral win in Smethwick in
1964 is a key sign of proletarianisation.[61] Stuart Hall argues that
Griffiths's victory was 'a turning point in the history of British racism':
'the first moment when racism is appropriated into the official policy
and programme of a major political party and legitimated as the basis of
an electoral appeal, specifically addressed to the popular white classes.
Here is the beginning of racism as an element in the official politics of
British populism – racism in a structured and "legitimate" form'.[62]
Institutionalised popular racism, Naipaul insists, 'is how a civilisation
dies'. Anti-Nazism and anti-apartheid, he declares, are 'good causes',
even if organised political activism is anathema to him personally.[63]
Ethnocentrism as a practice of pervasive racism is not targetted by
Naipaul in the same vein.

In his essay 'What's wrong with being a snob?' (1967) Naipaul links
the degrading proletarianisation of England – emblematically the 'mini-
man in his mini-car' – with a crisis of liberalism.[64] Naipaul attacks under
the umbrella of proletarianisation the discourse of classlessness, the rise
of the welfare state, changing men's fashions, pop musicians as a 'cause
for national pride', capitalist consumerism, popular racism, failure of
political leadership on the issue of racism, and in the field of the novel
'pretentious pornography and sadism'. 'In the hysteria of self-congratu-
lation, the new greed [of "a booming capitalist society"] expressed itself
most hideously', he angrily laments, 'in the persecution of immigrants
from the former Empire. Yesterday's slogan on the wall – SEND
NIGGERS HOME – was embodied in today's White Paper on limiting
immigration.' This is a pointed attack on the repatriation provisions of
the August 1965 White Paper issued by the Labour Government; it
might also extend to the proposed cut in work-vouchers and stricter con-
trols on dependent relatives.[65] In depicting Naipaul as an anglophile
'patriotic' racist Rob Nixon overlooks his critiques of the institutional-
isation of racism both in this essay and elsewhere.[66] Naipaul urges that
the 'romance of the "classless" new society is' being 'ceaselessly offered
as compensation' for 'social' and 'economic' 'decay'. He advocates a
snobbish 'recognition' of personal and cultural 'difference' from the
'low' as a basis for a renovated civilising mission. As liberalism is
brought into 'disrepute' through an unthinking endorsement of a universal humanity, he worries that, 'in the confusion, the liberal principle
itself might be totally submerged in weakness, defeat. And fear'.[67]

There is incoherence in Naipaul's panic over the decay he attributes
to the proletarianisation that is at its most visible in the metropolis. It is
perhaps for him an unmanageably diffuse area for fictional scrutiny. His
most compelling meditation on decay is *The Enigma of Arrival*, a novel

which Frank Kermode notes 'is set in a part of rural England that doesn't count racism or colonialism among its most pressing problems'.[68]

As well as proletarianisation, the rise of black consciousness and Black Power movements during the 1960s disturbed Naipaul. Implicitly assigning himself rationality and authentic knowledge, he interprets both as symptoms of racial hysteria and inauthenticity. For Naipaul Black Power is an 'infection' carried from the United States,[69] characterised by catchcries and '[b]orrowed words'. The critiques of the materiality of the lives of black people made by 'the spokesmen for Black Power' offer 'sharp analysis of black degradation'; Naipaul is more scathing about 'Black Power as rage, drama and style', his perception of its 'undermining' of multi-racial politics, and its appeal to popular 'apocalyptic' expectations.[70] In 'Michael X and the Black Power killings in Trinidad' Naipaul asserts that Michael de Freitas, also known as Michael X and Michael Abdul Malik, 'passed' as 'a Negro' in London.[71] Naipaul draws on 'local knowledge' to fix Malik as a 'red', a person of mixed African and Portuguese ancestry, and hence a commodified fraud: 'Malik's Negro was, in fact, a grotesque: not American, not West Indian, but an American caricatured by a red man from Trinidad for a British audience'.[72] Naipaul seems to take a grim pleasure in repeating sexist insults relating to miscegenation reportedly levelled at Malik's mother. Malik would become the basis for Jimmy Ahmed in *Guerillas*; aspects of Percy Cato's career in *Half a Life* also replicate an early phase of de Freitas's life in England.

Naipaul is harshly critical in *Guerillas* of the sectors of English society responsible for the making of Jimmy Ahmed: liberals for whom the demonstration and the political meeting are a diversion before tea; those on 'Right and Left' for whom 'race' is a 'topic of entertainment';[73] women who use a black man as a 'plaything', a 'playboy'; the sexually permissive woman, 'adrift, enervated, her dissatisfactions vague'. Jimmy's writing of his desire for Englishwoman Jane, the type of the permissive woman, in the idiom of romance fiction demonstrates his psychic dependency on the presumption of the middle-class white woman's fetishisation of his Hakwai (black and Chinese) masculinity. Naipaul, though, is at his most punitive in his representation of Jane, 'white rat', 'rotten meat', and implicitly a succubus.[74] Authorial horror at her is also expressed in her crossing sexually into masculine postures, Jimmy's anal rape of her and her murder.

Naipaul's comment about West Indian books no longer feeding him resonates in the context of his representation of C. L. R. James as flawed prodigy Lebrun in 'On the run', part of his sequence *A Way in the World* (1994), '"a settling of accounts" ... for what he regards as errors of artistic judgment'.[75] In a 1963 review he had praised James's *Beyond a*

*Boundary* as 'one of the finest and most finished books to come out of the West Indies, important to England, important to the West Indies'. He concedes there that 'Mr James's career is of particular interest' to him as much for the dissimilarity of their 'backgrounds', as for them both 'speaking the same language' and having 'charmed' themselves 'away from Trinidad'.[76] The fictive Lebrun, after writing a book that is recognisably *The Black Jacobins*, has spent a life as a marxist 'revolutionary ... on the run'. He is 'discovered' in 'extreme old age' in England 'as one of the prophets of black revolution, a man whose name didn't appear in the history books, but who for years had worked patiently, had been behind the liberation movements of Africa and the Caribbean'. This 'idea of himself ... had anchored him, had been a kind of livelihood',[77] which eventually 'began to feed on itself'.[78] Naipaul's story feeds on his earlier work – most pointedly his travel narrative 'The crocodiles of Yamoussoukro'[79] – in ways which caution against any easy identification of the narrator as an autobiographical Naipaul figure.

The narrator of the story, a writer by profession, thinks Lebrun is a 'prodigy' of 'rhetoric' and erudition, and is seemingly haunted by the question, 'How, considering where he was born, had he become the man he was?'[80] The narrator comes to appreciate that Lebrun's marxism, his 'political resolution', is an effort 'to submerge his racial feelings in the universality of his political beliefs', to 'shed one smarting skin' to be 'reborn in another', and that his role as 'black prophet' works to undermine some of his equanimity.[81] His developing double consciousness of himself as black and British is politically but not personally empowering; instead it returns him to the 'rawness of sensibility' which Naipaul associates with the colonial stranger.[82] Lebrun becomes more susceptible to the shame of a family heritage that includes an Uncle Tom figure, to anger about cross-racial sex on the part of black women, and to the 'hysteria' of the West Indies, 'expressed most usually in self-satire, jokeyness, fantasy, religious excess, sudden spasms of cruelty'.[83] Lebrun's patronym (which means dark man or boy in French) essentialises the anxieties that structure his career in his racial ancestry.

The narrator's refusal of assumptions of political community, his resistance to being seen as 'part of Lebrun's revolution', 'an expression of Lebrun's will',[84] is realised in his inability to eat the food served to him among Lebrun's admirers. The narrator's ultimate emblem of Lebrun's disillusioning failure to denounce 'a black racial regime'[85] becomes the 'black diet' – imprisonment without sustenance until death – that the president of Guinea imposes on political enemies identified by Lebrun. As a symbol of savagery it is linked with another alleged local atrocity: human sacrifice to perform a foot-washing ceremony. The narrator asserts that as 'a revolutionary without a base'

Lebrun is 'always a failure in one way, in another way fortunate, never having to live with the consequences of his action'.[86]

During the 1960s two major strands of Naipaul's response to institutionalised racism and to the rise of black consciousness, as a form of resistance to racial subordination, begin to emerge. Both are historical signs of processes of decolonisation and the diasporic manifestations of it. Naipaul interprets institutionalised racism in England and its former settler colonies as a sign of degenerate proletarianisation and failure of moral leadership, although his comments on this are sparse. In essays and fiction he excoriates aspects of the black consciousness and Black Power movements and the political and social forces in England that abetted their rise there. Naipaul's fictive representation of C. L. R. James as Lebrun in 'On the run' emphasises what he perceives to be the deleterious psychological consequences of racial self-consciousness and the manner in which political investment in pan-black nationalism may undermine the universality of the application of moral standards.

## Mythologising a 'universal civilization'

Naipaul's charge that Lebrun/James was able fortunately to escape measures of responsibility for his acts might in turn be levelled at himself, an eloquent conservative who embraces a sense of existential national homelessness, travelling with or able to purchase a return ticket home to England. He never has to live fully with the everyday consequences or implications of his acts of representation. The negativity of his commentary on travel destinations and cultures outside what is often termed the First World can feed the prejudices of and recirculate stereotypes for his readers. In a 1979 interview with Elizabeth Hardwick Naipaul says, for instance: 'I do not write for Indians ... who in any case do not read. My work is only possible in a liberal, civilized Western country. It is not possible in primitive societies.'[87] To Tarun J. Tejpal in 1998 he speaks casually of 'writing from India or other retarded or former colonies'.[88] One thinks here, too, of his famous dismissal of the West Indies in The Middle Passage – 'History is built around achievement and creation; and nothing was created in the West Indies'.[89] As with Black Power, Naipaul represents multiculturalism as a neocolonising import from the United States to Britain. Yet, too, in terms of the clash of civilisations theory through which Naipaul currently interprets world history, it is a policy 'fostered by Islamic groups'. In 2001 he mocks the policy as 'multi-culti', mobilising again, as with his denunciation of Black Power politics, a belittling discourse of redemptive desire and unreason, and treats it as a contributing factor to England's current 'cultural mess'. For him the key sign of the deficiency of the policy is the 'cover[ed]' up Islamic woman. She represents 'oppressive regimes', an 'oppressive faith' which 'hates humanity', 'old customs' which have 'kept' her community 'down'. Her veil becomes a site of cross-generational contagion: her children are bearers of religious fundamentalism. Some, Naipaul insists, despite being British nationals, 'become terrorists in foreign lands' – Yemen, Bosnia, Kashmir, 'places like that'. The stubborn spectacle of the veiled woman in Britain is a symbol of missionary inertia on the part of the more enlightened.[90] The tone of such judgements amply exhibits the 'authorial absolutism' which Homi Bhabha discerns in Naipaul's 'large-scale civilizational arguments' of the variety 'Certain societies are quite limited. It is difficult anyhow to be profound about them.'[91] It is more often in the imaginative reaches afforded by fiction that Naipaul is able to transcend the simplicities of his side.

Naipaul might define his more recent work as an elaboration of the value of a 'universal civilization', a concept that he begins to articulate explicitly around 1980: 'the idea of the individual, responsibility, choice, the life of the intellect, the idea of vocation and perfectibility and achievement'. 'It is the civilization, first of all, which gave me the idea of the writing vocation', he explains. 'It is the civilization in which I have been able to practice my vocation as a writer ... [M]y movement within this civilization has been from the periphery to the centre.' This civilisation is not synonymous with the colonialism of his upbringing, but rather, he insists in 1991, a liberal, evolutionary development of it, which is in the process of transcending 'racialism' and working 'to accommodate the rest of the world, and all the currents of that world's thought'.[92] This accommodation involves in Britain a respect for 'human rights and human needs'.[93] As Jan Pettman points out, 'Human rights have long been associated with a western, liberal and individualistic approach to rights'.[94] Naipaul consciously represents his ideal of the individual as being grounded in 'metropolitan assumptions about society: the availability of a wider learning, an idea of history, a concern with self-knowledge'.[95]

Naipaul writes of Conrad that rather than 'discover' himself and his 'world' through writing, his 'character had been formed' before he 'settled down to write'. He implicitly associates this with Conrad's propensity to cite 'portable truths, as it were, that can sometimes be rendered as aphorisms – and work through to their demonstration'. Giving Conrad's story 'The return' as an example of the method, he notes that 'the people remain abstractions'.[96] Naipaul's discourse of civilisation is replete with 'portable truths', a vocabulary of the '"barbarous", "primitive", "tribal", "static", and "simple" societies, "world civilization", "bush", "philistine", the "colonial", the "whole man", "security", "sentimentality", "parasitic", "borrowed culture", and "mimicry". Reiteratively, and in combination', as Nixon notes, 'these terms of reference become a compressed expression of Naipaul's *Weltanschauung*'.[97] These 'truths' profoundly reduce the humanity of the people and characters about whom Naipaul writes, producing them as abstractions, bearers of cultural and often racialised essences. The method is one that justifies Akeel Bilgrami's observation that Naipaul's 'cultural commentary' on the non-West 'typically combined an effortless contempt with a cultivated ignorance of the historical and the institutional sources of a culture's surface presentation'.[98] The meticulousness of Naipaul's detailing of that presentation – 'the sketches of fellow travellers, of the daily routines, the vessels, living quarters and facilities, food, drink, recreations, chance and deliberate encounters, conversations engaged in or, just as often, overheard' – nonetheless, as Mustafa suggests, 'establishes an aura of verisimilitude'.[99] The specificity of local detail belies the grounding of his broader cultural observations in formulaic, portable truths.

Naipaul's travel writing, advocacy of the standards of a universal civilisation, and casual cultural commentary in interviews illustrate amply the reactionary conservatism of his politics of decolonisation. His view of historical progress is more pessimistic than that of C. L. R. James, whose position is outlined by Bill Schwarz and Catherine Hall in this volume. Naipaul's attitude to a lived British liberalism is markedly ambivalent. He is fierce both in his denunciations of liberal support for Black Power during the 1960s and 1970s and for multiculturalism as a policy of national belonging since the 1980s, and in his defence of the liberal principles integral to his ideal of a universal civilisation.

## '[S]hed[ding] the nerves of being a stranger'

After a year spent in India in the early 1960s, Naipaul found himself again in London alienated by the prospective domestication of his difference – home in a 'separate warm' cell – which abandoned him to 'emptiness', a 'feeling of being physically lost',[100] a return to a being in which he became his 'flat', his 'desk', his 'name'. The dream of the metropolis, a 'mythical' land, was unravelling.[101] This demystification is a central theme of *The Mimic Men* in which Ralph Singh, the first-person narrator, reconstructs his first sojourn in London, 'this dying mechanized city'.[102] In moving from London to the cottage on the manor, the autobiographical narrator of *The Enigma of Arrival* had desired 'to strip' his 'life down' through a 'spirit of withdrawal', to accommodate himself to the style of the cottage, altering 'as little as possible' there.[103]

*The Enigma of Arrival* is structured around a thematic of looking and being looked at, and a contrast between two writer figures, the narrator and his fictive landlord, who both suffer from nervous illness. The narrator mentions repeatedly his raw nerves of the stranger, of the colonial in England. His experience of rural England – solitude, the steady measure of walking, isolation, 'surrender' to his 'way of looking', and indulgence of his 'linguistic or historical fantasies' – enables him 'to shed the nerves of being a stranger'.[104] The nerves are metonymic of his epidermalised racial difference, the 'smarting skin' he observes of Lebrun. In *An Area of Darkness* Naipaul acknowledges that 'recognition' of his Indian 'difference was necessary to' him.[105] The narrator of *The Enigma of Arrival*, however, desires not to be seen by his landlord; the landlord recognises him as fellow artist by sending gifts of his work through an intermediary. The landlord's representations of racial difference are grounded, the narrator insists, in 'sensual' romances of empire from 'the days of imperial glory',[106] and a 'joke knowledge of the world ... fed by the manor and the grounds',[107] emblems of 'England, wealth, empire, the idea of glory, material satiety, a very great security'.[108] In them the narrator discerns a nostalgic fascination with decadence and homoerotic fantasies of foreign men. The illness of the landlord, accidia, resonates with 1920s literary representations of English degeneracy. The landlord's relation to his place in England after the second world war is compressed in his claustration, a possession of the manor through panoramic vision from the country house that is his sign of ownership, the 'physical helplessness' which Sara Suleri reads 'as a synecdoche for imperial devolution',[109] and the parasitic destructiveness of the ivy he orders should not be cut. Here Naipaul inverts the trope of parasitism that often figures the postwar immigrant's relation to the British state in racist discourse. The narrator's desire for invisibility in relation to the landlord marks a desire not to be fixed by or to have recognition as an artist tainted by a stereotyping and potentially homoerotic gaze.

Through familiarity and minute analysis of the disruption of simple myths of rural Englishness by more elemental complexities of decay and renewal, the narrator's gaze in the novel assumes renovated features of what Mary Louise Pratt terms 'Victorian discovery rhetoric' attached to a 'monarch-of-all-I-survey scene'. Pratt characterises Victorian discovery rhetoric as aestheticising the landscape, often ordering through the genre of painting – 'large and small, back and front'; conferring '*density of meaning*' through 'adjectival modifiers'; and developing a relation of mastery 'between the seer and the seen'.[110] A formative English literary and artistic tradition, a remembered Trinidad, and his vocation are the homes which act as the narrator's reference points in his self-consciously precise dramatisation of ways of seeing and their relation to being. His meditations secure an increasing analytic and philosophical mastery over a feminised nature that threatens man's achievements with ruin and decay.

Naipaul has modelled himself as writer in a conservative mould: dedicated to mastery over craft, close moral examination, ambition and nature; affecting political disinterest in creative prose; and wilfully transcending the vulgarities of popular cultures (including their perceived racisms), and the anxieties that have beset his journey to the centre of English culture. Arguably, and I pointedly echo here Naipaul's representation of Lebrun in 'On the run', his artistic resolution is an effort to submerge his racial feelings in the perceived universality of his transcendent and scrupulous vision of the Olympian writer. Naipaul's accounts of being formatively placed on peripheries of community in Port of Spain and England are permeated by a sense of loss: loss of material as a writer; and, more faintly, of a sense of civic identity that might confer substance outside vocation. The sense of civic displacement that has haunted his journey movingly informs an important and finely nuanced thread in his fiction: the sense of unease and exile the colonial subject may experience in England. This is a pervasive preoccupation of West Indian writers who treat Caribbean immigrant and expatriate experience in Britain. Naipaul has pointedly dissociated himself from West Indian social and political communities and their late modern histories both in the Caribbean and in Europe, preferring instead to claim an extraregional identity and scope and more recently to champion the ideals of a prized 'universal civilization'. His reputation as a reactionary in relation to the politics of decolonisation and race is certainly merited, but Said's and Nixon's condemnations of that politics, which are typical of those of his detractors, are too sweeping. Naipaul's representations of England and the English do not uniformly indulge a patriotic racism and imperial nostalgia or play to persistent racial stereotypes of non-white peoples in England. His conservatism, too, is characterised by deeply conflicted attitudes to liberal principles with respect to racial issues and histories.

## Notes

1   V. S. Naipaul, 'Our universal civilization', *New York Review of Books*, 31 January 1991, p. 22.
2   Naipaul speaks of having 'made' himself a writer by the age of twenty-five in *Reading & Writing: a personal account* (New York: New York Review of Books, 2000), p. 19.
3   Diana Athill, *Stet: a memoir* (London: Granta, 2000), p. 232.
4   Mel Gussow, 'V. S. Naipaul: "It is out of this violence I've always written"', *New York Times*, 16 September 1984.
5   V. S. Naipaul, *Half a Life: a novel* (London: Picador, 2001).

6   'Nobel Prize for Literature 2001 – Press Release'.
7   Edward Said, 'Intellectuals in the post-colonial world', *Salmagundi*, 70:1 (1986), p. 53.
8   V. S. Naipaul, 'London' (1958), in his *The Overcrowded Barracoon and Other Articles* (Harmondsworth: Penguin, 1976; first published 1972), p. 9.
9   Naipaul, *Reading & Writing*, p. 15.
10  V. S. Naipaul, *Letters Between a Father and Son* (London: Abacus, 2000; first published 1999), p. 313.
11  Naipaul, 'London', p. 10.
12  Naipaul, *Reading & Writing*, p. 13; 'Without a place: V. S. Naipaul in conversation with Ian Hamilton', *Times Literary Supplement*, 30 July 1971, in Feroza Jussawalla (ed.), *Conversations with V. S. Naipaul* (Jackson: University Press of Mississippi, 1997), p. 15.
13  Stephanie Bunbury, 'An audience with Sir Vidia', *Age* (Melbourne), 18 August 2001, p. 4.
14  Naipaul, *Reading & Writing*, pp. 13–15.
15  V. S. Naipaul, *Miguel Street* (London: André Deutsch, 1959).
16  Naipaul, 'London', pp. 11–12.
17  'The writer, the observer, that is scrupulously myself. The minute other people are in the picture, that is where the fictive element comes in', Naipaul comments in an interview with Mel Gussow, 'The enigma of V. S. Naipaul's search for himself in writing', *New York Times*, 25 April 1987.
18  Naipaul, *The Enigma of Arrival: a novel in five sections* (London: Penguin, 1987), p. 140.
19  Tarun J. Tejpal, 'Arrivals and other enigmas: V. S. Naipaul's way in the world', *at random magazine*, (1998), www.stanford.edu.au/~amitm/naipaul/tejpal.html, p. 3 (accessed August 2001).
20  V. S. Naipaul, 'Tell me who to kill', in his *In a Free State* (London: André Deutsch, 1971), p. 94.
21  Naipaul, 'Tell me who to kill', p. 91.
22  Naipaul, 'Tell me who to kill', p. 91.
23  Naipaul, 'Tell me who to kill', p. 91.
24  Naipaul, 'Tell me who to kill', p. 107.
25  V. S. Naipaul, 'A plea for rationality', in I. J. Bahadur Singh (ed.), *Indians in the Caribbean* (New Delhi: Sterling, 1987), p. 21.
26  V. S. Naipaul, *The Middle Passage: impressions of five societies – British, French and Dutch – in the West Indies and South America* (London: André Deutsch, 1963), p. 61.
27  Anne McClintock, *Imperial Leather: race, gender and sexuality in the colonial contest* (New York: Routledge, 1995), p. 22.
28  V. S. Naipaul, *Finding the Centre: two narratives* (Harmondsworth: Penguin, 1985; first published 1984), p. 10.
29  Naipaul, *Reading & Writing*, pp. 16 and 19.
30  Naipaul, 'London', pp. 14–17.
31  'Naipaul: an interview with Ewart Rouse', *Trinidad Guardian* (1968), in Jussawalla, *Conversations*, p. 10.
32  Naipaul, *The Enigma of Arrival*, p. 130.
33  Naipaul, *Reading & Writing*, pp. 49–50.
34  John Thieme, *The Web of Tradition: uses of allusion in V. S. Naipaul's fiction* (Hertford: Dangaroo Press/Hansib Publications, 1987), p. 93.
35  Alison Light, *Forever England: femininity, literature and conservatism between the wars* (London: Routledge, 1991), pp. 8 and 11–12.
36  V. S. Naipaul, *Mr Stone and the Knights Companion* (London: André Deutsch, 1963), pp. 22, 42 and 6.
37  Naipaul, *Mr Stone*, pp. 34 and 41.
38  Summarised by Jane Gallop, *The Daughter's Seduction: feminism and psychoanalysis* (Ithaca, NY: Cornell University Press, 1982), p. 27.

39  Naipaul, *Mr Stone*, p. 44.
40  Naipaul, *Mr Stone*, p. 71.
41  Naipaul, *Mr Stone*, p. 64.
42  Naipaul, *Mr Stone*, p. 84.
43  Naipaul, *Mr Stone*, p. 134.
44  Graham Dawson associates medieval knights with pre-capitalist adventure in *Soldier Heroes: British adventure, empire and the imagining of masculinities* (London: Routledge, 1994), p. 59.
45  T. S. Eliot, 'The hollow men', *Selected Poems* (London: Faber, 1961), p. 80.
46  Naipaul, *Mr Stone*, p. 160.
47  Eliot, 'The hollow men', p. 80; Naipaul, *Mr Stone*, p. 160; Light, *Forever England*, p. 13.
48  Winston James, 'Migration, racism and identity formation: the Caribbean experience in Britain', in Winston James and Clive Harris (eds), *Inside Babylon: the Caribbean diaspora in Britain* (London: Verso, 1993), p. 239.
49  James, 'Migration, racism and identity formation', p. 276.
50  Naipaul, *The Middle Passage*, pp. 67–8.
51  'Naipaul: an interview with Ewart Rouse', in Jussawalla, *Conversations*, p. 10.
52  Jussawalla, 'Introduction', *Conversations*, p. iv.
53  Kobena Mercer, 'Back to my routes: a postscript to the 1980s (1990)', in James Procter (ed.), *Writing Black Britain 1948–1998: an interdisciplinary anthology* (Manchester: Manchester University Press, 2000), p. 288.
54  'Naipaul: an interview with Ewart Rouse', in Jussawalla, *Conversations*, pp. 10–11.
55  Derek Walcott, 'Interview with V. S. Naipaul', *Sunday Guardian* (Trinidad), 7 March 1965, in Jussawalla, *Conversations*, p. 7.
56  V. S. Naipaul, 'Without a dog's chance', review of *After Leaving Mr Mackenzie*, by Jean Rhys, *New York Review of Books*, 18 May 1972, pp. 30–1.
57  V. S. Naipaul, *The Mimic Men* (London: André Deutsch, 1967), pp. 24, 34 and 61.
58  Naipaul, 'London', p. 16.
59  V. S. Naipaul, *An Area of Darkness* (Harmondsworth: Penguin, 1968; first published 1964), p. 188.
60  He traces the origins of the decay of cultural elitism which 'has destroyed the idea of civilisation in this country' to the 1945–51 Labour governments of Clement Attlee: Fiachra Gibbons, 'It is terrible, this plebeian culture that celebrates itself', *Guardian*, 11 July 2000.
61  Walcott, 'Interview', pp. 6–7.
62  Stuart Hall, 'Racism and reaction', in *Five Views of Multi-Racial Britain: talks on race relations broadcast by BBC TV* (London: Commission for Racial Equality, 1978), p. 29.
63  Walcott, 'Interview', p. 8.
64  V. S. Naipaul, 'What's wrong with being a snob?' (1967), in Robert D. Hamner (ed.), *Critical Perspectives on V. S. Naipaul* (London: Heinemann, 1977), p. 36.
65  See Ann Dummett and Andrew Nicol, *Subjects, Citizens, Aliens and Others: nationality and immigration law* (London: Weidenfeld and Nicolson, 1990), pp. 194–5.
66  Rob Nixon, *London Calling: V. S. Naipaul, postcolonial mandarin* (Oxford: Oxford University Press, 1992), p. 47.
67  Naipaul, 'What's wrong with being a snob?', pp. 35–7.
68  Frank Kermode, 'In the garden of the oppressor', review of *The Enigma of Arrival*, *New York Times*, 22 March 1987.
69  Naipaul, *Overcrowded Barracoon*, p. 270.
70  V. S. Naipaul, 'Power?', *New York Review of Books* (1970), in *Overcrowded Barracoon*, pp. 269–70.
71  V. S. Naipaul, *The Return of Eva Perón* with *The Killings in Trinidad* (Harmondsworth: Penguin, 1981; first published 1980), p. 52.
72  Naipaul, *The Return of Eva Perón*, p. 37.
73  Naipaul, *The Return of Eva Perón*, pp. 25 and 29.

74  Naipaul, *Guerillas*, pp. 26, 48, 90, 60 and 239.
75  Mel Gussow, 'V. S. Naipaul in search of himself: a conversation', *New York Times*, 24 April 1994.
76  V. S. Naipaul, 'Cricket' (1963), in *Overcrowded Barracoon*, p. 23.
77  V. S. Naipaul, *A Way in the World: a novel* (New York: Alfred A. Knopf, 1994), pp. 109–10. The novel was subtitled *A sequence* in the British edition.
78  Naipaul, *A Way in the World*, p. 135.
79  The essay is the second of the narratives in Naipaul's *Finding the Centre*.
80  Naipaul, *A Way in the World*, p. 117.
81  Naipaul, *A Way in the World*, pp. 119, 133, 128 and 135.
82  Naipaul, *A Way in the World*, p. 161.
83  Naipaul, *A Way in the World*, p. 134.
84  Naipaul, *A Way in the World*, p. 127.
85  Naipaul, *A Way in the World*, p. 135.
86  Naipaul, *A Way in the World*, p. 161.
87  Elizabeth Hardwick, 'Meeting V. S. Naipaul', *New York Times Book Review* (1979), in Jussawalla, *Conversations*, p. 45.
88  Tejpal, 'Arrival and other enigmas'.
89  Naipaul, *The Middle Passage*, p. 29.
90  Rachael Kohn, 'India through V. S. Naipaul's eyes', *The Spirit of Things*, Radio National (Australia), 9 September 2001.
91  Homi Bhabha, 'Naipaul's vernacular cosmopolitans', *Chronicle of Higher Education*, 26 October 2001.
92  Naipaul, 'Our universal civilization', pp. 22 and 25.
93  Charles Wheeler, '"It's every man for himself" – V. S. Naipaul on India', *Listener* (1977), in Jussawalla, *Conversations*, p. 44.
94  Jan Jindy Pettman, *Worlding Women: a feminist international politics* (Sydney: Allen and Unwin, 1996), p. 210.
95  Naipaul, *Reading & Writing*, pp. 50–1.
96  V. S. Naipaul, 'Conrad's darkness', *New York Review of Books* (1974), in Hamner, *Critical Perspectives on Naipaul*, pp. 61, 63 and 64.
97  Nixon, *London Calling*, p. 109.
98  Quoted in Chinua Achebe, *Home and Exile* (Oxford: Oxford University Press, 2000), p. 86.
99  Fawzia Mustafa, *V. S. Naipaul* (Cambridge: Cambridge University Press, 1995), pp. 77–8.
100  Naipaul, *An Area of Darkness*, p. 266.
101  Naipaul, *An Area of Darkness*, p. 42.
102  Naipaul, *Mimic Men*, p. 97.
103  Naipaul, *The Enigma of Arrival*, p. 174.
104  Naipaul, *The Enigma of Arrival*, p. 23.
105  Naipaul, *An Area of Darkness*, p. 43.
106  Naipaul, *The Enigma of Arrival*, pp. 192–3.
107  Naipaul, *The Enigma of Arrival*, p. 253.
108  Naipaul, *The Enigma of Arrival*, p. 193.
109  Sara Suleri, 'Naipaul's arrival', *Yale Journal of Criticism*, 2:1 (Fall 1988), p. 46.
100  Mary Louise Pratt, *Imperial Eyes: travel writing and transculturation* (London: Routledge, 1992), pp. 204–5.

# AFTERWORD

# The predicament of history

Bill Schwarz

The moment in 1968 when C. L. R. James explicitly named a tradition of West Indian intellectuals symbolised an ending rather than a beginning. Essentially, the West Indian intellectual, so named, was a colonial phenomenon. As Catherine Hall demonstrates in the opening chapter, the term 'West Indian' always represented a complex of competing ideas, a resource for both colonial and anticolonial politics. Its meanings in any particular historical situation derived from the overall balance of forces between colony and metropolis. By the time independence was in sight 'West Indian' had principally come to signify the aspiration of the anglophone peoples of the Caribbean for a future free from colonial rule, in which the deepest instincts of the formerly-colonised would find unimpeded expression. That this transformation in meaning had occurred was due to the determination of Caribbean intellectuals, broadly conceived, to devise an identity which was *theirs*, and which belonged to those whom they represented. Once independence had been achieved, however, and once new political circumstances obtained (the impact of the Cuban Revolution; the coming of Black Power), inherited traditions found themselves facing radical interrogation on every front. Historical time itself seemed to accelerate. Thought previously championed as West Indian was recast in new forms, as Caribbean, or Black. 'West Indian' spoke too easily of earlier – colonial – times.

In the urban landscapes of contemporary Britain there are few visible traces of the social history of West Indian intellectual activity, despite the magnitude of the great migration from the Caribbean. No cafés or book or record shops or dance halls carry commemorative plaques, or retain a place in the larger collective memory.[1] Even educated opinion can still profess a certain puzzlement that there *could* be such a thing as an intellectual tradition deriving from the experience of the Caribbean, testament to the continuing power of colonial mentalities.

If this tradition is recalled at all it is so as something local, only of concern to the West Indians themselves and disconnected from all that was significant in British life.

Of those whom we discuss, only Naipaul now lives in the old metropole, and he has chosen to do so as literary grandee, the Tartuffe of West Indian literary endeavour: elevated, isolated, eccentric, only ever appearing in order to send a pot-shot or two towards those whom he perceives to be instigators of an ever-gathering, demotic barbarism. Some of Naipaul's generation found themselves remaining in the UK; others re-crossed the seas once more to North America; and a minority discovered ways in which they could reinhabit their own homelands in the Caribbean. For younger generations of Caribbean thinkers and artists the allure of Britain and its capital has long since faded. Long before the exodus to Britain in the middle of the last century Caribbean peoples had been accustomed to migration, either within the region itself or further afield. Britain was only ever 'one stop in a sequence': distinct, of course, in very many ways, but nonetheless only part of a larger, more varied collective memory.[2]

Why, then, should we return to this colonial moment? Why should we be concerned with a tradition of social thought which, it might seem, even in its own nations came to be superseded the very moment it claimed its existence? And why should we be so exercised about the British dimensions of this story when all the evidence suggests that the British themselves regard it as something which barely pertains to them at all?

If nothing else, we hope to have shown how wrong it is to assume that the West Indian presence was somehow disconnected from the British and their civilisation. If this argument has been won, as perhaps it has within the historiography, there might then be any number of reasons to encourage us to return to this past. But the most pressing may be the one which historians are usually most reluctant to confront: the idea that in recovering these traditions of West Indian thought we ourselves, in Britain, might be able *to think* more creatively about our own historical situation. Or in other words, the overriding reason may be an intellectual one, drawing into question our own analytical procedures.

In the middle decades of the twentieth century mass emigration from the Caribbean coincided with the final phase of decolonisation. This represented a particular conjunction of events, with significant consequences, for to an uncommon degree much of the intellectual work of Caribbean decolonisation was conducted in the metropolis. The metropolitan locations of, say, *Caribbean Voices*, or of the Caribbean Artists Movement, let alone of the preoccupations of particular individuals, are themselves historical facts of importance. Exile constituted the

[ 249 ]

*mise-en-scène* for Caribbean decolonisation. This has been recognised well enough within the Caribbean, if not in Britain. The fact that substantial elements of Caribbean thought were produced in the metropolis is neither contingent nor merely the occasion for fleeting curiosity. Location mattered, shaping the intellectual life which emerged. As we have argued, the West Indians were colonial Britons who experienced the civilisation of the British, in Britain, from a very particular vantage. It is the resultant perspectives on British civilisation that we've attempted to retrieve in the preceding chapters. Here were generations of West Indians encountering the civilisation of the empire in its very heartlands, who determined to work through for themselves an idea of life after colonialism. If for the domestic British decolonisation was something which occurred 'elsewhere' – overseas and out of sight – then the Caribbean experience may provide a partial exception: it happened, had those in the metropole only been able to see, before their very eyes.

In recovering these traditions of intellectual thought we might more easily be able to imagine what, for us in Britain, becoming postcolonial entails. To say this is to recognise that the work of becoming postcolonial has yet to be completed. In turn, to argue in these terms is to argue for the intellectual power of history. It suggests that unseen in the past are experiences which can valuably be brought to bear on the present. *That* past, we suggest, can be revealed in such a way that it can speak to the situation of *our* present.

The chapters in this volume provide many clues which indicate how, from our chosen perspective, we might isolate the specifics of the intellectual contribution of West Indians in Britain. To conclude, in summary form, I'll indicate just three overlapping and interconnected areas of thought: race and ethnicity; the project of decolonisation; and the historical imagination itself.

On race and ethnicity I'll say only a little. There is no doubt that of those non-white West Indians we discuss, born before the cataclysm of the 1930s, the majority strove hard in their personal lives to rise above race. In this, the political ultras, James and Padmore, were little different from self-styled moderates, such as Moody. (McKay, as so often, represents the exception; Marson is perhaps the most intriguing.) To transcend one's colonial status and become a fully modern subject required, they believed, relegating the subjective travails of racial subordination to the status of the interpersonal, which they couldn't regard as properly political. James's imaginings of race were certainly complex, leading him on occasion to positions which from a contemporary perspective look very odd. But even so, the various silences enveloping the lived experiences of racial subjugation did not prevent the emergence of analyses of Britain in which race was accorded a centring, systemic conceptual role. Padmore's theorisation of the empire as a system of racialised exploitation was of huge importance in this regard; but so too, in a different manner, was Moody's growing conviction of the power of racism deep in the heart of the metropolis. Positions such as these represented a provocation to the official upholders of nation and empire, to a degree which is difficult for us who live in different historical times to comprehend. But out of the confrontations which followed, there slowly evolved the possibilities for a politics of race to become speakable in the public domain, and for new thought to flourish.

The force of much of this thinking was negative, highlighting the hidden or not-so-hidden racial codes of imperial imaginings. Implicitly, it interrogated the imperatives of whiteness. But it simultaneously created the conditions for reconceptualising black, and the impetus for elaborating a philosophy of human life able fully to incorporate the formerly-enslaved and colonised. There were many strands to this intellectual movement, which shouldn't be conflated. For our purposes, though, we might point to the personal and intellectual connections established between the West Indian migrants in Britain and, to put this loosely, non-British cultures of thought. The controversial estimations of Jean Rhys's commitments to a heterodox *négritude* are significant in this respect. So too, as Mary Chamberlain establishes, was George Lamming's entry in the middle 1950s into the Parisian intellectual milieu which brought together Sartrean phenomenology and *négritude* – from which so much contemporary thinking on 'the fact of blackness' has subsequently derived. Insofar as French philosophy touched the intellectual culture of the British in the 1950s and early 1960s, the preoccupation with the question of black subjectivity barely registered at all, despite its centrality. Its presence in the West Indian diaspora half a century ago anticipated much contemporary conceptual inquiry.

So too, in a later transformation, West Indians in Britain in the 1960s were in the forefront of introducing into the metropolis the various political philosophies deriving from Civil Rights and Black Power.[3]

Maybe this is only to state what readers might expect: that out of the lived experience of Britain's non-white populations emerged the means to conceptualise and to counter the logics of racial thought. But if this seems self-evident, the detailed, situated, historical story remains far from clear – as do the resulting ambiguities. For the reasons we describe, the West Indian dimension has been an influential component of this larger story. So much so that its very obviousness can inhibit, rather than encourage, critical reflection.

Second, raising some of the same issues, is the problem of decolonisation. Decolonisation can be thought from a narrow purview, in which the transfer of political sovereignty marks the final end of colonial domination. This literal rendition is obviously necessary, but it remains partial. The extraordinarily creative assertion of West Indian thought in the middle of the twentieth century, which effectively encompassed – amongst other things – the making of the West Indian novel, presaged a more expansive conception of decolonisation, in which the end of colonial rule would signal not merely a transfer of political power, but the renovation of the entire colonial civilisation, from top to bottom. In the decade or so from the middle 1950s to the middle 1960s this dedication to the decolonisation of *the culture* of the Caribbean moved to the centre of what it was to declare oneself a West Indian. In the writings of the time of C. L. R. James, George Lamming or Claudia Jones, for example, one can plot the crystallisation of this mode of thought. Rather than conceiving of decolonisation as a passive affair, orchestrated by the political leaders from above, the more radical of the West Indian intellectuals came to imagine a more fully popular transformation, in which the people themselves would take active charge of commanding their own historical destinies.

To think of decolonisation in this expansive manner opened an entire new domain of thought. One of the forces driving the emergence of the West Indian novel had been the need felt by a new generation of writers, in the wake of the labour riots of the 1930s, to devise a form in which the indigenous popular voices of the Caribbean could be articulated. That this was only ever partially achieved can be seen from the debates generated within the Caribbean Artists Movement in the later 1960s, where the question of creating appropriate popular forms was incessantly addressed, and where it became the cause, it seems, of incessant disputation. The issue of the popular brought the cultural activists of CAM hard up against the question of British civilisation: how, in politics, in the aesthetic imagination, in the everyday organisation of civic life, and perhaps most of all in language itself, were the legacies of the colonial epoch to be overcome? Moreover: if popular life in the Caribbean represented the stratum of the cultural order least touched by European norms – blacker, say, or more non-white; where Africa or Asia were more proximate; more heterogeneous and hybrid, *more Caribbean* – then where did this leave those who had been most deeply formed, in intellect and bearing, in the schools and colleges of the British system? How could they, their learning notwithstanding, represent the universal aspirations of the Caribbean peoples?

There were as many resolutions to these dilemmas as there were people asking the questions. In the biography and intellectual career of Kamau Brathwaite, for example, we can see one particularly dramatic working through of these issues, a process punctuated by many refashionings and inventions of the self, but where overall the movement from a Britain to an Africa of the mind prevails. For all his singularities, Brathwaite is nonetheless representative. Other Caribbean intellectuals of his generation have not made his choices, or not made them with his commitments. But each has felt compelled to discover a strategy for divesting themselves of *something* of what the mother country had bestowed upon them.

To be confronted by the question of British civilisation in this way, not only as a matter of the formal exterior culture but as a matter of the self, was to understand the intricacy of the interrelations between a civilisation and political power. Or more radically, it marked the recognition that civilisation, the symbolic ordering of human life, *is* power. Today, with the insights of Gramsci and Foucault part of the common currency of at least some domains of the academic intellectual culture, such notions trip easily from the tongue. A generation ago this was not so. In the British case – yet more if we were to think of the dominating position of English culture – there barely existed a conceptual vocabulary in which such a critique could be expressed. Imagine suggesting that the ineffable refinement of the English, or the cultivated sensibility of their greatest men of letters, encoded a system of active, continuing authority. How preposterous! How vulgar! Yet we can discern a group of texts – most notably George Lamming's *The Pleasures of Exile*, C. L. R. James's *Beyond a Boundary*, and Claudia Jones's *West Indian Gazette* – which, in their different idioms, attempted to create a language in which just such insights could be deployed.

This, however, is where location intervenes most sharply. Those writers from the West Indies who had crossed the seas were not only confronting a colonial Britishness, organised island by island, but the Britishness of the mother country itself. From their situation, the interconnections between colony and metropolis were vividly present. In order to achieve decolonisation in their home nations, they had to engage the source of colonial authority, in the culture of the metropolis. But that is also where they *were*, working and living as migrants. The social and cultural hierarchies in metropolis and colony were not *the same*: but they demonstrably derived from the same principles which articulated what a civilisation was, and how it should operate. The West Indian migrant could experience herself or himself to be colonised as much in the metropolis as in their island colony: in fact, after independence, the experience of colonisation could be felt *more* keenly in the metropolis. From this could derive the following paradoxical idea: that in the realm of culture, the metropolis too needed to be decolonised.

We can see something of this happening. At the start of 1962 George Lamming contributed an article to the *West Indian Gazette*. He told of

[ 253 ]

a visit to a working-class neighbour in Chiswick early on in his time in England, and contrasted that experience to dinner at high table at a Cambridge University college. Dinner at high table brought home to him the intractable complexity of the unspoken rituals of upper-class England. His hosts at Cambridge represented, he believed, a culture which was entirely centred, conscious only of the fact that those whose lives fell outside its boundaries were somehow aberrant, lacking in refinement, reason and cultivation. Lamming's friend in Chiswick inhabited a different mental universe. He told Lamming that when he listened to the wireless he only tuned into the Light Programme, 'knowing' that the other programmes – devoted to Shakespeare (as he put it) – were not for him. 'I realised', wrote Lamming, 'that almost two-thirds of the population of this country were in a colonial relation to the culture and traditions which were called England. And it was at this point that my own process of decolonisation began.'[4]

This brief reflection raises many points of great interest. It suggests, amongst other things, that the work of decolonisation in its expansive register requires popular self-activity, not only on the part of the colon-ised but on the part too of the native citizens of the metropolis. Implicitly, Lamming was insisting that there exists an inextricable con-nection between the postcolonial and the creation of new vernacular forms: that to become fully postcolonial depends on the maximal expansion of popular life.

I don't mean to privilege the West Indians at the cost of ignoring other intellectual innovators of the period. It was not only West Indians of the diaspora who were opening up the issue of race, or expanding the notion of decolonisation, or theorising the centrality of the popular in new ways. All I would propose is that the historical situation of the migrants from the Caribbean gave their rendering of these issues a peculiar urgency, or immediacy, which more easily enabled them to connect what otherwise appeared to exist in isolation.

To listen to Lamming talking of the contrasts between working-class Chiswick and the high tables of Cambridge is to be reminded of a differ-ent, if contemporaneous, intellectual formation. The determination to elaborate an anthropological and democratic conception of culture of the British undertaken by Raymond Williams, Edward Thompson and Richard Hoggart in the 1950s and early 1960s reproduced a critical stance paralleling that which that can be found in the work of the West Indians. Williams and Hoggart (Thompson less so) made *their* journeys from the provinces to the centred redoubts of English civilisation. They too found themselves compelled to compile their ethnographic accounts and polit-ical audits of the 'traditions which were called England', fully aware that in so doing they were exploring the mechanisms by which a civilisation simultaneously organised structures of inclusion and exclusion. They too imagined a new popular will, capable of dismantling inherited social hierarchies. But their theoretical tone remained distinct. Their readiness to fall back on a radical nationalism, to ignore or downplay issues of race and racism, and their failures to think through the constitutive interaction between metropole and colony have for long been a source of controversy.[5] One cannot easily imagine them, or those who shared their vision, thinking through these issues, in these years, in terms of the decolonisation of the British.

Close to Williams, Thompson and Hoggart, though, was one who did: Stuart Hall, who moved easily between the distinct perspectives of these two intellectual formations. By any reckoning, Hall was in his making a West Indian intellectual. The journey from Kingston, Jamaica, to Oxford University in 1951 conformed exactly to that generic crossing of seas which we have described throughout these pages. Yet the degree to which this formative experience is excised from accounts of his intellectual life, or given merely a gestural place, can be startling. Conventional wisdom in Britain presents him as a figure who entered intellectual life in the middle 1950s, as one of the inspirations for the emergent New Left, and who thence moved seamlessly into becoming the effective progenitor of what has subsequently become known as British cultural studies. This is a reading which entirely ignores his earliest publications and his active involvement in the network of West Indian cultural institutions in London in the 1950s; it ignores his continuing involvement with Caribbean organisations in Britain through the 1960s; and it ignores too the complicated but significant role he has played in Caribbean intellectual life in the Caribbean, in his home-nation of Jamaica and beyond. What I've indicated here as constituting the defining preoccupations of mid-twentieth-century West Indian intellectual life in Britain – the developing critique of racial systems; the concern with the displacement of political authority in symbolic or cultural forms; the implacable commitments to maximise and cherish the power of innovative vernacular forms; the expansive conception of what comprised the civilisation of the British; and the consequent understanding that future emancipation required cultural work on the broadest front – all these are not merely close to the heart of Hall: he gave them voice in Britain, addressing a British as much a West Indian audience. In these terms one can see how Hall has worked to *translate* elements of West Indian traditions of thought into a broader philosophy or theory of culture, which has served as the basis for a series of conjunctural analyses of the civilisation of the British. From early on, he worked as a kind of relay by which the debates and discussions of the West Indians could acquire a wider influence in the national cultures of

[ 255 ]

Britain, and by which they could reach out to and connect with other traditions of intellectual inquiry. In so doing they became something else. They ceased to be identifiably West Indian. They acquired a larger, more universal dynamic. It is in this movement, especially, that we can locate significant links in the chain between older traditions of West Indian thought and contemporary theoretical concern with the complex imperatives embedded in the processes of becoming postcolonial.

To see these connections is to remind ourselves that the crossing of seas has not been an experience enclosed by its past, of finite duration: it truly remains unfinished, an experience whose outcomes still retain the power to reverberate in the present.

This touches on my final point, which turns on the nature of the historical imagination. A dominating theme of Caribbean thought concerns the problem of the proximity of past and present. In the introduction I quoted James's remark that West Indians are 'more historical' than other peoples. There are many possible ways of interpreting a comment like this. But James, we know, had in mind the proximity of the past violence of slavery in the memories of the living. In different registers, consciousness of this unappeased past runs through every dimension of the Caribbean imagination. This may be experienced as a continuing burden, the present but a continuation of a longer duration of a state of unfreedom. Yet it can carry too a privileged sense of historical knowledge. After all, as Lamming observed, it was the migrants – not the hosts – who carried within them the knowledge that 'we have met before'.

Impressive in contemporary Caribbean cultures is the manner in which a vast range of narrative strategies has been employed in order to explore the interactions between past and present. All serve to shed light on how different moments of the historical past are organised or articulated in the present. This is apparent in popular forms, where long traditions of eschatological thought persist. It is apparent too in the more formally orchestrated narratives of imaginative writings, where highly varied resources are employed as inspiration: cosmological (in the work of Brathwaite), geological (in Wilson Harris), classical or mythological (in Derek Walcott), and so on. Whatever the distinctive personal idiom, and whatever the shared interactions between writers of different temperaments, a common theme is evident: the felt need to reimagine the very basis of historical inquiry, such that it can adequately represent the complexities of competing, simultaneous historical times.

Implicit in such endeavours lies a critique of the contemporary conventions of mainstream historiography. This is a literature which assumes that only by devising narratives which can fully encompass the past in the present can the burden of the past be appeased. Yet we – the British we – are coming to understand that this Caribbean past is also ours. The Middle Passage and the plantation are not only Caribbean matters. They impinge on our – British – present too. We have indeed met before. This is a past which breaks also into our present, and which needs to be identified, known and acknowledged. In ways we might not yet completely comprehend our – British – lives lie deep *inside* the Caribbean and colonial past.

Maybe in the future the most profound impact of Caribbean thought will be on our capacity to imagine the past, and to strive to bring it into consciousness.

## Notes

1 Stephen Howe notes that the London Borough of Hackney has laid claim to James in the naming of one its libraries – as it has done for its municipal housing. One can't help but agree with him that, rather than being evidence of commemorative justice, this signals more the scale of lost hopes. In the same part of north London there exists the Claudia Jones Organization of Afro-Caribbean Women and (atop the long-standing New Beacon bookstore), the George Padmore Institute.
2 Mary Chamberlain, *Narratives of Exile and Return* (London: Macmillan, 1997), p. 86.
3 It would be important to track the degree to which the various traditions of West Indian thought we outline here were continued, appropriated or recast in the energetic retheorising of the relations between blackness and Britishness in the 1970s and 1980s. There is a huge literature here, as well as a veritable renaissance of black aesthetic practice. *Race and Class* and *Race Today* would signal appropriate starting points for such a genealogical investigation; and for the point when these issues began significantly to turn academic thinking, Centre for Contemporary Cultural Studies, *The Empire Strikes Back: race and racism in seventies Britain* (London: Hutchinson, 1982); and Paul Gilroy, *'There Ain't No Black in the Union Jack': the cultural politics of race and nation* (London: Hutchinson, 1987).
4 *West Indian Gazette*, February 1962.
5 See especially Gilroy, *'There Ain't No Black'*.

# INDEX